Commentaries on John
By
Albert Barnes

THE GOSPEL ACCORDING TO JOHN

THE GOSPEL ACCORDING TO JOHN-Chapter 1

PREFACE

TO THE GOSPEL ACCORDING TO JOHN.

John, the writer of this Gospel, was the son of Zebedee and Salome; compare Mt 27:56 with Mr 15:40,41. His father was a fisherman of Galilee, though it would appear that he was not destitute of property, and was not in the lowest condition of life. He had hired men in his employ, Mr 1:20. *Salome* is described as one who attended our Saviour in his travels, and ministered to his wants, Mt 27:55; Mr 15:41. Jesus commended his own mother Mary, on the cross, to John, and he took her to his own home (Joh 19:26,27), with whom, history informs us, she lived until her death, about fifteen years after the crucifixion of Christ; and John was known to Caiaphas, the high-priest, Joh 18:15. From all this it would seem not improbable that John had some property, and was better known than any of the other apostles.

He was the youngest of the apostles when called, and lived to the greatest age, and is the only one who is supposed to have died a peaceful death. He was called to be a follower of Jesus while engaged with his father and his elder brother James mending their nets at the Sea of Tiberias, Mt 4:21; Mr 1:19; Lu 5:10.

John was admitted by our Saviour to peculiar favour and friendship. One of the ancient fathers (Theophylact) says that he was related to him.

"Joseph," he says, "had seven children by a former

wife, four sons and three daughters, Martha, Esther,

and *Salome*, whose son John was; therefore Salome was

reckoned our Lord's sister, and John was his nephew."

If this was the case it may explain the reason why James and John sought and expected the first places in his kingdom, Mt 20:20,21. These may also possibly be the persons who were called our Lord's "brethren" and "sisters," Mt 13:55,56. This may also explain the reason why our Saviour committed his mother to the care of John on the cross, Joh 19:27. The two brothers, James and John, with Peter, were several times admitted to peculiar favours by our Lord. They were the only disciples that were permitted to be present at the raising of the daughter of Jairus, Mr 5:37; Lu 8:51; they only were permitted to attend the Saviour to the mount where he was transfigured, Mt 17:1; Mr 9:2. The same three were permitted to be present at his sufferings in the garden of Gethsemane, Mt 26:36-45; Mr 14:32-42. And it was to *these* disciples, together with Andrew, to whom the Saviour specially addressed himself when he made known the desolations that were coming upon Jerusalem and Judea; compare Mt 24:12; Mr 13:3,4.

John was also admitted to *peculiar* friendship with the Lord Jesus. Hence he is mentioned as "that disciple whom Jesus loved" (Joh 19:26), and he is represented (Joh 13:23) as leaning on his bosom at the institution of the Lord's Supper-an evidence of peculiar friendship. See Barnes "Joh 13:23".

Though the Redeemer was attached to *all* his disciples, yet there is no improbability in supposing that *his* disposition was congenial with that of the meek and amiable John—thus authorizing and setting the example of special friendships among Christians.

To John was committed the care of Mary, the mother of Jesus. After the ascension of Christ he remained some time at Jerusalem, Ac 1:14; 3:1; 4:13.

John is also mentioned as having been sent down to Samaria to preach the gospel there with Peter (Ac 8:14-25); and from Acts chapter 15 it appears that he was present at the council at Jerusalem, A.D. 49 or 50. All this agrees with what is said by Eusebius, that he lived at Jerusalem till the death of Mary, fifteen years after the crucifixion of Christ. Till this time it is probable that he had not been engaged in preaching the gospel among the Gentiles.

At what time he went first among the Gentiles to preach the gospel is not certainly known. It has commonly been supposed that he resided in Judea and the neighbourhood until the war broke out with the Romans, and that he came into Asia Minor about the year 69 or 70. It is clear that he was not at Ephesus at the time that Paul visited those regions, as in all the travels of Paul and Luke there is no mention made of John.

Ecclesiastical history informs us that he spent the latter part of his life in Asia Minor, and that he resided chiefly at Ephesus, the chief city of that country. Of his residence there little is certainly known. In the latter part of his life he was banished to Patmos, a small desolate island in the AEgean Sea, about twenty miles in circumference. This is commonly supposed to have been during the persecution of Domitian, i.n the latter part of his reign. Domitian died A.D. 96. It is probable that he returned soon after that, in the reign of the Emperor Trajan. In that island he wrote the book of Revelation. See Barnes "Re 1:9".

After his return from Patmos he lived peaceably at Ephesus until his death, which is supposed to have occurred not long after. He was buried at Ephesus; and it has been commonly thought that he was the only one of the apostles who did not suffer martyrdom. It is evident that he lived to a very advanced period of life. We know not his age, indeed, when Christ called him to follow him, but we cannot suppose it was less than twenty-five or thirty. If so, he must have been not far from one hundred years old when he died.

Many anecdotes are related of him while he remained at Ephesus, but there is no sufficient evidence of their truth. Some have said that he was taken to Rome in a time of persecution and thrown into a caldron of boiling oil, and came out uninjured. It has been said also that, going into a bath one day at Ephesus, he perceived *Cerinthus*, who denied the divinity of the Saviour, and that he fled from him hastily, to express his disapprobation of his doctrine. It is also said, and of this there can be no doubt, that during his latter years he was not able to make a long discourse. He was carried to the church, and was accustomed to say nothing but this, "Little children, love one another." At length his disciples asked him why he always dwelt upon the same thing. He replied, "Because it is the Lord's command; and if this be done, it is sufficient."

Learned men have been much divided about the *time* when this Gospel was written. Wetstein supposed it was written just after our Saviour's ascension; Mill and Le Clerc, that it was written in 97; Dr. Lardner, that it was about the year 68, just before the destruction of Jerusalem. The common opinion is that it was written at Ephesus after his return from Patmos, and of course as late as the year 97 or 98. Nothing can be determined with certainty on the subject, and it is a matter of very little consequence.

There is no doubt that it was written by John. This is abundantly confirmed by the ancient fathers, and was not questioned by Celsus, Porphyry, or Julian, the acutest enemies of revelation in the early ages. It has never been extensively questioned to have been the work of John, and is one of the books of the New Testament whose canonical authority was never disputed. See Lardner, or Paley's *Evidences*.

The design of writing it John himself states, Joh 20:31. It was to show that Jesus was the Christ, the Son of God, and that those who believed might have life through his name. *This design is kept in view through the whole Gospel, and should be remembered in our attempts to explain it.* Various attempts have been made to show that he wrote it to confute the followers of Cerinthus and the Gnostics, but no satisfactory evidence of such a design has been furnished.

As he wrote after the other evangelists, he has recorded many things which they omitted. He dwells much more fully than they do on the *divine character* of Jesus; relates many things pertaining to the early part of his ministry which they had omitted; records many more of his discourses than they have done, and particularly the interesting discourse at the institution of the Supper. See chapters 14-17.

It has been remarked that there are evidences in this Gospel that it was not written for the Jews. The author explains words and customs which to a Jew would have needed no explanation. See Joh 1:38,41 Joh 5:1,2; 7:2; 4:9.

The style in the Greek indicates that he was an unlearned man. It is simple, plain, unpolished, such as we should *suppose* would be used by one in his circumstances. At the same time it is dignified, containing pure and profound sentiments, and is on many accounts the most difficult of all the books of the New Testament to interpret. It contains more about Christ, his person, design, and work, than any of the other Gospels. The other evangelists were employed more in recording the *miracles*, and giving *external* evidence of the divine mission of Jesus. John is employed chiefly in telling us what he was, and what was his peculiar doctrine. His aim was to show,

1st. That Jesus was the Messiah.

2nd. To show, *from the words of Jesus himself*, what the Messiah was. The other evangelists record his parables, his miracles, his debates with the Scribes and Pharisees; John records chiefly his discourses about *himself*. If anyone wishes to learn the true doctrine respecting the *Messiah, the Son of God*, expressed in simple language, but with most sublime conceptions; to learn the true nature and character of God, and the way of approach to his mercy-seat; to see the true nature of Christian piety, or the source and character of religious consolation; to have perpetually before him the purest model of character the world has seen, and to contemplate the purest precepts that have ever been delivered to man, he cannot better do it than by a prayerful study of the Gospel by John. It may be added that this Gospel is of itself proof that cannot be overthrown of the truth of revelation. John was a fisherman, unhonoured and unlearned, Ac 4:13. What man in that rank of life now could compose a book like this? Can it be conceived that any man of that rank, unless under the influence of inspiration, could conceive so sublime notions of God, could present so pure views of morals, and could draw a character so inimitably lovely and pure as that of Jesus Christ? To ask these questions is to answer them. And this Gospel will stand to the end of time as an unanswerable demonstration that the fisherman who wrote it was under a more than human guidance, and was, according to the promise that he has recorded (Joh 16:13 comp. Joh 14:26), *guided into all truth.* It will also remain as an unanswerable proof that the character which he has described—the character of the Lord Jesus—was real. It is a perfect character. It has not a flaw. How has this happened? The attempt has often been made to draw a perfect character—and as often, in every other instance, failed. How is it, when Homer and Virgil, and the ancient historians, have all failed to describe a perfect character, with the purest models before them, and with all the aid of imagination, that in every instance they have failed? How is it that this has at last been accomplished only by a Jewish fisherman? The difficulty is vastly increased if another idea is borne in mind. John describes one who he believed had a divine nature, Joh 1:1. It is an attempt to describe *God in human nature*, or to show how the Divine Being acts when united with man, or when appearing in human form. And the description is complete. There is not a word expressed by the Lord Jesus, or an emotion ascribed to him, inconsistent with such a supposition. But this same attempt was often made, and as often failed. Homer and Virgil, and all the ancient poets, have undertaken to show what the gods would be if they came down and conversed with man. And what were they? What were Jupiter, and Juno, and Venus, and Mars, and Vulcan? Beings of lust, and envy, and contention, and blood. How has it happened that the only successful account which has been given of the divine nature united with the human, and of living and acting as became such a union, has been given by a Jewish fisherman? How, unless the character was real, and the writer under a guidance far superior to the genius of Homer and the imagination of Virgil—the guidance of the Holy Spirit?

THE
GOSPEL ACCORDING TO JOHN.

Verse 1. *In the beginning.* This expression is used also in Ge 1:1. To that place John evidently has allusion here, and means to apply to "the Word" an expression which is there applied *to God.* In both places it clearly means "before creation," "before the world was made," "when as yet there was nothing." The meaning is, that the *Word* had an existence before the world was created. This is not spoken of the *man* Jesus, but of that which *became* a man, or was incarnate, Joh 1:14. The Hebrews, by expressions like this, commonly denoted eternity. Thus the eternity of God is described (Ps 90:2): *Before the mountains were brought forth,* &c.; and eternity is commonly expressed by the phrase, *before the foundation of the world.* Whatever is meant by the term "Word," it is clear that it had an existence before *creations.* It is not, then, a *creature* or created being, and must be, therefore, uncreated and eternal. There is but *one* Being that is uncreated, and Jesus must be therefore divine. Compare the Saviour's own declarations respecting himself in the following places: Joh 8:58; 17:5;6:62; 3:13; 6:46; 8:14; 16:28.

Was the Word. Greek, "was the *Logos.*" This name is given to him who afterward became *flesh,* or was incarnate (Joh 1:14)—that is, to the Messiah. Whatever is meant by it, therefore, is applicable to the Lord Jesus Christ. There have been many opinions about the reason why this name was given to the Son of God. Those opinions it is unnecessary to repeat. The opinion which seems most plausible may be expressed as follows:

1st. A *word* is that by which we communicate our will; by which we convey our thoughts;

2nd. The Son of God may be called "the Word," because he is the medium by which God promulgates his will and issues his commandments. See Heb 1:1-3.

3rd. This term was in use before the time of John.

(a) It was used in the Chaldee translation of the Old Testament, as, e.g., Is 45:12: "I have made the earth, and created man upon it." In the Chaldee it is, "I, *by my word,* have made," &c. Isa 48:13: "Mine hand also hath laid the foundation of the earth." In the Chaldee, *"By my word* I have founded the earth." And so in many other places.

(b) This term was used by the Jews as applicable to the Messiah. In their writings he was commonly known by the term "Mimra "—that is, "Word;" and no small part of the interpositions of God in defence of the Jewish nation were declared to be by "the Word of God." Thus, in their Targum on De 26:17,18, it is said, "Ye have appointed THE WORD OF GOD a king over you this day, that he may be your God."

(c) The term was used by the Jews who were scattered among the Gentiles, and especially those who were conversant with the Greek philosophy.

(d) The term was used by the followers of Plato among the Greeks, to denote the second person of the *Trinity.* The term *nous,* or *mind,* was commonly given to this second person, but it was said that this *nous* was *the word* or *reason* of the first person. The term was therefore extensively in use among the Jews and Gentiles before John wrote his Gospel, and it was certain that it would be applied to the second person of the Trinity by Christians, whether converted from Judaism or Paganism. It was important, therefore, that the *meaning* of the term should be settled by an inspired man, and accordingly John, in the commencement of his Gospel, is at much pains to state clearly what is the true doctrine respecting the Logos, or Word. It is *possible*, also, that the doctrines of the Gnostics had begun to spread in the time of John. They were an Oriental sect, and held that the *Logos* or *Word* was one of the *AEons*that had been created, and that this one had been united to the man Jesus. If that doctrine had begun then to prevail, it was of the more importance for John to settle the truth in regard to the rank of the Logos or Word. This he has done in such a way that there need be no doubt about its meaning.

Was with God. This expression denotes friendship or intimacy. Comp. Mr 9:19. John affirms that he was *with God* in the beginning— that is, before the world was made. It implies, therefore, that he was partaker of the divine glory; that he was blessed and happy with God. It proves that he was intimately united with the Father, so as to partake of his glory and to be appropriately called by the name God. He has himself explained it. See Joh 17:5: *And now, O Father, glorify thou me with thine own self, with the glory which I had with thee before the world was.* See also Joh 1:18: *No man hath seen God at any time, the only-begotten Son, which IS IN THE BOSOM OF THE FATHER, he hath declared him.* See also Joh 3:13: *The Son of man, which is in heaven.* Comp. Php 2:6,7.

Was God. In the previous phrase John had said that the Word was *with God.* Lest it should be supposed that he was a different and *inferior* being, he here states that *he was God.* There is no more unequivocal declaration in the Bible than this, and there *could* be no stronger proof that the sacred writer meant to affirm that the Son of God was equal with the Father; for,

1st. There is no doubt that by the *Logos* is meant Jesus Christ.

2nd. This is not an *attribute* or quality of God, but is a real subsistence, for it is said that the Logos was made *flesh*—that is, became a man.

3rd. There is no variation here in the manuscripts, and critics have observed that the Greek will bear no other construction than what is expressed in our translation-that the Word*was God.*

4th. There is no evidence that John intended to use the word *God* in an *inferior* sense. It is not "the Word was *a god,*" or "the Word was *like God,*" but the Word *was God.* He had just used the word *God* as evidently applicable to Jehovah, the true God; and it is absurd to suppose that the would *in the same verse,* and without any indication that he was using the word in an inferior sense, employ it to denote a being altogether inferior to the true God.

5th. The name *God* is elsewhere given to him, showing that he is the supreme God. See Ro 9:5; Heb 1:8,9,10-12; 1 Jo 5:20; Joh 20:28.

The meaning of this important verse may then be thus summed up:

1st. The name Logos, or Word, is given to Christ in reference to his becoming the Teacher or Instructor of mankind; the medium of communication between God and man.

2nd. The name was in use at the time of John, and it was his design to state the correct doctrine respecting the Logos.

3rd. The *Word*, or Logos, existed *before creation*—of course was not a *creature*, and must have been, therefore, from eternity.

4th. He was *with God*—that is, he was united to him in a most intimate and close union *before* the creation; and, as it could not be said that God was *with himself*, it follows that the Logos was in some sense *distinct* from God, or that there was a *distinction* between the Father and the Son. When we say that one is *with another*, we imply that there is some sort of distinction between them.

5th. Yet, lest it should be supposed that he was a different and inferior being—a creature—he affirms that he was God—that is, was equal with the Father. This is the foundation of the doctrine of the Trinity:

1. That the second person is in some sense distinct from the first.

2. That he is intimately united with the first person in essence, so that there are not two or more Gods.

3. That the second person may be called by the same name; has the same attributes; performs the same works; and is entitled to the same honours with the first, and that therefore he is "the same in substance, and equal in power and glory," with God.

{a} "In the beginning" Pr 8:22-31; Col 1:16,17; 1 Jo 1:1

{b} "the Word" Re 19:13 {c} "with God" Joh 17:5 {d} "was God" Php 2:6; Heb 1:8-13; 1 Jo 5:7

THE GOSPEL ACCORDING TO JOHN-Chapter 1-Verse 2

Verse 2. *The same*. The Word, or the Logos,

Was in the beginning with God. This seems to be a repetition of what was said in the first verse; but it is stated over again *to guard the doctrine*, and to prevent the possibility of a mistake. John had said that he existed before the creation, and that he was *with God*; but he had not said in the first verse *that the union with God existed in the beginning*. He now expresses that idea, and assures us that that union was not one which was commenced *in time*, and which might be, therefore, a mere union of *feeling*, or a *compact*, like that between any other beings, but was one which existed in *eternity*, and which was therefore a union of *nature or essence*.

THE GOSPEL ACCORDING TO JOHN-Chapter 1-Verse 3

Verse 3. *All things*. The universe. The expression cannot be limited to any part of the universe. It appropriately expresses everything which exists—all the vast masses of material worlds, and all the animals and things, great or small, that compose those worlds. See Re 4:11; Heb 1:2; Col 1:16.

Were made. The original word is from the verb *to be*, and signifies "were" by him; but it expresses the idea of creation here. It does not alter the sense whether it is said "*were* by him," or "were *created* by him." The word is often used in the sense of *creating*, or forming from nothing.

See Jas 3:9; Ge 2:4 Isa 48:7, in the Septuagint.

By him. In this place it is affirmed that creation was effected by the *Word*, or the Son of God. In Ge 1:1, it is said that the Being who created the heavens and the earth was God. InPs 102:25-28, this work is ascribed to Jehovah. The Word, or the Son of God, is therefore appropriately called *God*. The work of creation is uniformly ascribed in the Scriptures to the second person of the Trinity. See Col 1:16; Heb 1:2,10.

By this is meant, evidently, that he was the agent, or the efficient cause, by which the universe was made. There is no higher proof of *omnipotence* than the work of *creation*; and hence God often appeals to that work to prove that he is the *true* God, in opposition to idols. See Isa 40:18-28 Jer 10:3-16; Ps 24:2; 39:11; Pr 3:19.

It is absurd to say that God can invest a creature with *omnipotence*. If he can make a creature omnipotent, he can make him *omniscient*, and can in the same way make him omnipresent, and infinitely wise and good; that is, he can invest a creature with all his own attributes, or make another being like himself, or, which is the same thing, there could be two Gods, or as many Gods as he should choose to make. But this is absurd. The Being, therefore, that *created* all things must be divine; and as this work is ascribed to Jesus Christ, and as it is uniformly in the Scriptures declared to be the work of God, Jesus Christ is therefore *equal* with the Father.

Without him. Without his agency; his notice; the exertion of his power. Comp. Mt 10:29. This is a strong way of speaking, designed to confirm, beyond the possibility of doubt, what he had just said. He says, therefore, in general, that all things were made by Christ. In this part of the verse he shuts out all doubt, and affirms that there was *no exceptions*; that there was not a single thing, however minute or unimportant, which was not made by him. In this way he confirms what he said in the first verse. Christ was not merely *called* God, but he did the *works* of God, and therefore the name is used in its proper sense as implying supreme divinity. To this same test Jesus himself appealed as proving that he was divine. Joh 10:37: *If I do not THE WORKS of my Father, believe me not.* Joh 5:17: *MY FATHER worketh hitherto, and I work.*

{e} "All things" Ps 33:6; Eph 3:9

THE GOSPEL ACCORDING TO JOHN-Chapter 1-Verse 4

Verse 4. *In him was life.* The evangelist had just affirmed Joh 1:3 that by the *Logos* or *Word* the world was originally created. One part of that creation consisted in *breathing into man the breath of life*, Ge 2:7. God is declared to be *life*, or the *living* God, because he is the source or fountain of life. This attribute is here ascribed to Jesus Christ. He not merely made the *material* worlds, but he also gave *life*. He was the agent by which the *vegetable* world became animated; by which *brutes* live; and by which *man* became a living soul, or was endowed with immortality. This was a *higher* proof that the "Word was God," than the creation of the material worlds; but there is another sense in which he was *life*. The *new creation*, or the renovation of man and his restoration from a state of sin, is often compared with the *first creation*; and as the Logos was the source of *life* then, so, in a similar but higher sense, he is the source of life to the soul dead in trespasses and sins, Eph 2:1. And it is probably in reference to this that he is so often called *life* in the writings of John. "For as the Father hath life in himself, so hath he given to the Son to have life in himself," Joh 5:26; "He giveth life unto the world," Joh 6:33; "I am the resurrection and the life," Joh 11:25; "This is the true God and eternal life," 1 Jo 5:20. See also 1 Jo 1:1,2; 5:11; Ac 3:15; Col 3:4.

The meaning is, that he is the source or the fountain of both natural and spiritual life. Of course he has the attributes of God.

The life was the light of men. Light is that by which we see objects distinctly. The light of the sun enables us to discern the form, the distance, the magnitude, and the relation of objects, and prevents the perplexities and dangers which result from a state of darkness. Light is in all languages, therefore, put for *knowledge* —for whatever enables us to discern our duty, and that saves us from the evils of ignorance and error. "Whatsoever doth make manifest is light," Eph 5:13. See Isa 8:20; 9:2. The Messiah was predicted as the *light* of the world, Isa 9:2, compared with Mt 4:15,16; Isa 60:1. See Joh 8:12, "I am the light of the world;" Joh 12:35,36,46

"I am come a light into the world." The meaning is, that the Logos or Word of God is the *instructor* or *teacher* of man-kind. This was done before his advent by his direct agency in giving man reason or understanding, and in giving his law, for the "law was ordained by angels *in the hand of a mediator*" (Ga 3:19); after his advent by his personal ministry when on earth, by his Spirit (Joh 14:16,26), and by his ministers since, Eph 4:11; 1 Co 12:28.

{f} "In him was life" Joh 5:26; 1 Jo 5:11 {g} "the light of men" Joh 8:12

THE GOSPEL ACCORDING TO JOHN-Chapter 1-Verse 5

Verse 5. *The light shineth in darkness.* Darkness, in the Bible, commonly denotes ignorance, guilt, or misery. See Is 9:1,2, Mt 4:16; Ac 26:18; Eph 5:8,11; Re 13:12.

It refers here to a wicked and ignorant people. When it is said that "the light shineth in darkness," it is meant that the Lord Jesus came to teach an ignorant, benighted, and wicked world: This has always been the case. It was so when he sent his prophets; so during his own ministry; and so in every age since. His efforts to enlighten and save men have been like light struggling to penetrate a thick, dense cloud; and though a few rays may pierce the gloom, yet the great mass is still an impenetrable shade.

Comprehended it not. This word means *admitted* it not, or *received* it not. The word *comprehend*, with us, means to *understand*. This is not the meaning of the original. The darkness did not *receive* or *admit* the rays of light; the shades were so thick that the light could not penetrate them; or, to drop the figure, men were so ignorant, so guilty, so debased, that they did not appreciate the value of his instructions; they despised and rejected him. And so it is still. The great mass of men, sunk in sin, will not receive his teachings, and be enlightened and saved by him. Sin always blinds the mind to the beauty and excellency of the character of the Lord Jesus. It indisposes the mind to receive his instructions, just as *darkness* has no affinity for *light*; and if the one exists, the other must be displaced.

{light shineth in darkness} Joh 3:19 {comprehendeth it not} 1 Co 2:14

THE GOSPEL ACCORDING TO JOHN-Chapter 1-Verse 6

Verse 6. *A man sent from God.* See Matthew, Chapter 3. The evangelist proceeds now to show that John the Baptist was not the Messiah, and to state the true nature of his office. Many had supposed that he was the Christ, but this opinion he corrects; yet he admits that he was *sent from God*—that he was divinely commissioned. Though he denied that he was the *Messiah*, yet he did not deny that he was sent from or by heaven on an important errand to men. Some have supposed that the sole design of this gospel was to show that John the Baptist was not the Messiah. Though there is no foundation for this opinion, yet there is no doubt that *one* object was to show this. The *main* design was to show that *Jesus was the Christ*, Joh 20:31. To do this, it was proper, in the beginning, to prove that John was not the Messiah; and this might have been at that time an important object. John made many disciples, Mt 3:5. Many persons supposed that he might be the Messiah, Lu 3:15; Joh 1:19. *Many of these disciples of John remained AT EPHESUS, the very place where John is supposed to have written this gospel, long after the ascension of Jesus,* Ac 19:1-3. It is not improbable that there might have been many others who adhered to John, and perhaps many who supposed that he was the Messiah. On these accounts it was important for the evangelist to show that John *was not the Christ*, and to show, also, that he, who was extensively admitted to be a prophet, was an important witness to prove that Jesus of Nazareth was the Christ. The evangelist in the first four verses stated that "the Word" was divine; he now proceeds to state the proof that he was *a man*, and was the Messiah. The *first* evidence adduced is the testimony of John the Baptist.

{k} "man sent from God" Lu 3:2,3

THE GOSPEL ACCORDING TO JOHN-Chapter 1-Verse 7

Verses 7, 8. *For a witness.* To give testimony. He came to prepare the minds of the people to receive him (Mt. 3; Lu. 3.); to lead them by repentance to God; and to point out the Messiah to Israel when he came, Joh 1:31.

Of the Light. That is, of the Messiah. Comp. Isa 60:1.

That all men, &c. It was the object of John's testimony that all men might believe. He designed to prepare them for it; to announce that the Messiah was about to come, to direct the minds of men to him, and thus to fit them to believe on him when he came. Thus he baptized them, saying "That they should believe on him who should come after him" (Ac 19:4), and thus he produced a very general expectation that the Messiah was about to come. The testimony of John was peculiarly valuable on the following accounts:

1st. It was made when he had no *personal* acquaintance with Jesus of Nazareth, and of course there could have been no *collusion* or agreement to deceive them, Joh 1:31.

2nd. It was sufficiently long before he came to excite general attention, and to fix the mind on it.

3rd. It was that of a man acknowledged by all to be a prophet of God—"for all men held John to be a prophet," Mt 21:26.

4th. It was *for the express purpose* of declaring beforehand that he was about to appear.

5th. It was *disinterested*. He was himself extremely popular. Many were disposed to receive him as the Messiah. It was evidently in his *power* to form a large party, and to be regarded extensively as the Christ. This was the highest honour to which a Jew could aspire; and it shows the value of John's testimony, that he was willing to lay all his honours at the feet of Jesus, and to acknowledge that he was unworthy to perform for him the office of the humblest servant, Mt 3:11.

Through him. Through John, or by means of his testimony.

Was not that Light. Was not *the Messiah*. This is an explicit declaration designed to satisfy the disciples of John. The evidence that he was not the Messiah he states in the following verses.

From the conduct of John here we may learn,

1st. The duty of laying all our honours at the feet of Jesus.

2nd. As John came that all might believe, so it is no less true of the ministry of Jesus himself. He came for a similar purpose, and we may ALL, therefore, trust in him for salvation.

3rd. We should not rely too much on ministers of the gospel. They cannot save us any more than John could; and *their* office, as *his* was, is simply to direct men *to the Lamb of God that taketh away the sin of the world*.

THE GOSPEL ACCORDING TO JOHN-Chapter 1-Verse 8

Verse 8. No Barnes text on this verse.

{1} "He was not" Ac 19:4

THE GOSPEL ACCORDING TO JOHN-Chapter 1-Verse 9

Verse 9. That *was the true Light*. Not John, but the Messiah. He was not a false, uncertain, dangerous guide, but was one that was true, real, steady, and worthy of confidence. A false light is one that leads to danger or error, as a false beacon on the shores of the ocean may lead ships to quicksands or rocks; or an *ignis fatuus* to fens, and precipices, and death. A true light is one that does not deceive us, as the true beacon may guide us into port or warn us of danger. Christ does not lead astray. All false teachers do.

That lighteth. That enlightens. He removes darkness, error, ignorance, from the mind.

Every man. This is an expression denoting, in general, the whole human race—Jews and Gentiles. John preached to the Jews. Jesus came *to be a light to lighten the Gentiles, as well as to be the glory of the people of Israel*, Lu 2:32.

That cometh into the world. The phrase in the original is ambiguous. The word translated "that cometh" may either refer to the *light*, or to the word *man*; so that it may mean either "this true *light that cometh* into the world enlightens all," or "it enlightens every *man that cometh* into the world." Many critics, and, among the fathers, Cyril and Augustine, have preferred the former, and translated, "The true light was he who, coming into the world, enlightened every man." The principal reasons for this are,

1st. That the Messiah is often spoken of as he that cometh into the world. See Joh 6:14; 18:37.

2nd. He is often distinguished as "*the light that cometh into the world.*" Joh 3:19: "This is the condemnation, that *light* is come into the world." Joh 12:46: "I am come *a light* into the world." Christ may be said to do what is accomplished by his command or appointment. This passage means, therefore, that by his own personal ministry, and by his Spirit and apostles, light or teaching is afforded to all. It does not mean that every individual of the human family is enlightened with the knowledge *of the gospel*, for this never yet has been; but it means,

1st. That this light is not confined to the Jews, but is extended to *all*—Jews and Gentiles.

2nd. That it is provided for all and offered to all.

3rd. It is not affirmed that at the time that John wrote all *were actually enlightened*, but the word "lighteth" has the form of the *future*. *This is that light so long expected and predicted, which, as the result its coming into the world, will ultimately enlighten all nations.*

{m} "true light" Isa 49:6

THE GOSPEL ACCORDING TO JOHN-Chapter 1-Verse 10

Verse 10. *He was in the world.* This refers, probably, not to his pre-existence, but to the fact that he became incarnate; that he dwelt among men.

And the world was made by him. This is a repetition of what is said in Joh 1:3. Not only *men*, but all material things, were made by him. These facts are mentioned here to make what is said immediately after more striking, to wit, that men did not receive him. The proofs which he furnished that they *ought* to receive him were,

1st. Those given while he was *in the world*—the miracles that he wrought and his instructions; and,

2nd. The fact that the *world was made by him*, It was remarkable that the world did not know or approve its own maker.

The world knew him not. The word knew is sometimes used in the sense of *approving* or *loving*, Ps 1:6; Mt 7:23. In this sense it may be used here. The world did not love or approve him, but rejected him and put him to death. Or it may mean that they did not understand or know that he was the Messiah; for had the Jews *known and believed* that he was the Messiah, they would not have put him to death, 1 Co 2:8: "Had they known it, they would not have crucified the Lord of glory." Yet they *might* have known it, and therefore they were not the less to blame.

{m} "and the world knew him not" Joh 1:3

Verse 11. *He came unto his own.* His own *land* or *country*. It was called *his* land because it was the place of his birth, and also because it was the chosen land where God delighted to dwell and to manifest his favour. See Isa 5:1-7. Over that land the laws of God had been extended, and that land had been regarded as peculiarly his, Ps 147:19,20.

His own. His own *people.* There is a distinction here in the original words which is not preserved in the translation. It may be thus expressed: "He came to his own *land* and his own people received him not." They were \@his\ @people, *because God had chosen them to be his above all other nations; had given to them his laws; and had signally protected and favoured them,* De 7:6; 14:2.

Received him not. Did not acknowledge him to be the Messiah. They rejected him and put him to death, agreeably to the prophecy, Isa 53:3,4.

From this we learn,

1st. That it is reasonable to expect that those who have been peculiarly favoured should welcome the message of God. God had a right to expect, after all that had been done for the Jews, that they would receive the message of eternal life. So he has a right to expect that we should embrace him and be saved. Yet

2nd. It is not the abundance of mercies that incline men to seek God. The Jews had been signally favoured, but they rejected him. So, many in Christian lands live and die rejecting the Lord Jesus.

3rd. Men are alike in every age. All would reject the Saviour if left to themselves. All men are by nature wicked. There is no more certain and universal proof of this than the universal rejection of the Lord Jesus.

{o} "He came unto his own" Ac 3:26; 13:46

Verse 12. *To as many as received him.* The great mass; the people; the scribes and Pharisees rejected him. A few in his lifetime received him, and many more after his death. To *receive him,* here, means to believe on him. This is expressed at the end of the verse.

Gave he power. This is more appropriately rendered in the margin by the word right *or* privilege. *Comp.* Ac 1:7; 5:4; Ro 9:21; 1 Co 7:37; 8:9; 9:4,5.

Sons of God. Children of God by adoption. See Barnes "Mt 1:1".

Christians are called sons of God—

1st. Because they are adopted by him, 1 Jo 3:1.

2nd. Because they are

like him

; they resemble him and have his spirit.

3rd. They are united to the Lord Jesus, the Son of God—are regarded by

him *as his brethren* (Mt 25:40), and are therefore regarded as the children of the Most High.

On his name. *This is another way of saying believeth in* him. *The name of a person is often put for the person himself,* Joh 2:23

Joh 2:18; 1 Jo 5:13. From this verse we learn,

1st. That to be a child of God is a privilege-far more so than to be the child of any man, though in the highest degree rich, or learned, or honoured. Christians are therefore more honoured than any other men.

2nd. God

gave *them this privilege. It is not by their own works or deserts; it is because God chose to impart this blessing to them,* Eph 2:8; Joh 15:16.

3rd. This favour is given only to those who believe on him. All others are the children of the wicked one, and no one who has not

confidence in God *can be regarded as his child. No parent would acknowledge one for his child, or approve of him, who had no* confidence *in him, who* doubted

or denied all he said, and who despised his character. Yet this the sinner constantly does toward God, and he cannot, therefore, be called his son.

{p} "as many as received him" Isa 56:4,5; Ro 8:15; 1 Jo 3:1

{1} "power to become" or, "*the right* or *privilege*

Verse 13.

Which were born. *This doubtless refers to the* new birth, *or to the great change in the sinner's mind called regeneration or conversion. It means that they did not become the children of God in virtue of their natural birth, or because they were the children of Jews, or because they were descended from pious parents. The term "to be born" is often used to denote this change. Comp.* Joh 3:3-8

1 Jo 2:29. It illustrates clearly and beautifully this great change. The natural birth introduces us to life. The new birth is the beginning of spiritual life. Before, the sinner is dead in sins (Eph 2:1); now he begins truly to live. And as the natural birth is the beginning of life, so to be born of God is to be introduced to real life, to light, to happiness, and to the favour of God. The term expresses at once the

greatness *and the* nature

of the change.

Not of blood. *The Greek word is plural; not of bloods—that is, not of man. Comp.* Mt 27:4.

The Jews prided themselves on being the descendants of Abraham, Mt 3:9. They supposed that it was proof of the favour of God to be descended from such an illustrious ancestry. In this passage this notion is corrected. It is not because men are descended from an illustrious or pious parentage that they are entitled to the favour of God; or perhaps the meaning may be, not because there is a

union *of illustrious lines of ancestry or bloods in them. The law of Christ's kingdom is different from what the Jews supposed. Comp.* 1 Pe 1:23.

It was necessary to be

born of God *by regeneration. Possibly, however, it may mean that they did not become children of God by the bloody rite of* circumcision, *as many of the Jews supposed they did. This is agreeable to the declaration of Paul in* Ro 2:28,29.

Nor of the will of the flesh
. Not by natural generation.

Nor of the will of man. *This* may *refer, perhaps, to the will of man in* adopting *a child, as the former phrases do to the natural birth; and the design of using these three phrases may have been to say that they became the children of God neither in virtue of their descent from illustrious parents like Abraham, nor by their natural birth, nor by being* adopted *by a pious man. None of the ways by which we become entitled to the privileges of* children

among men can give us a title to be called the sons of God. It is not by human power or agency that men become children of the Most High.

But of God. *That is, God produces the change, and confers the privilege of being called his children. The heart is changed by his power. No unaided effort of man, no works of ours, can produce this change. At the same time, it is true that no man is renewed who does not himself* desire *and* will *to be a believer; for the effect of the change is on his* will *(*Ps 110:3), and no one is changed who does not strive to enter in at the strait gate, Php 2:12. This important verse, therefore, teaches us,

1st. That if men are saved they must be born again.

2nd. That their salvation is not the result of their birth, or of any honourable or pious parentage.

3rd. That the children of the rich and the noble, as well as of the poor, must be born of God if they will be saved.

4th. That the children of pious parents must be born again, or they cannot be saved. None will go to heaven simply because their parents

are Christians.

5th. That this work is the work of God, and no man can do it for us.

6th. That we should forsake all human dependence, cast off all confidence in the flesh, and go at once to the throne of-grace, and beseech of God to adopt us into his family and save our souls from death.

{r} "born, not of blood" Jas 1:18

Verse 14.

And the Word was made flesh. *The word* flesh, *here, is evidently used to denote* human nature *or* man. *See* Mt 16:17; 19:5; 24:22; Lu 3:6; Ro 1:3; 9:5.

The "Word" was made

man. *This is commonly expressed by saying that he became* incarnate. *When we say that a being becomes incarnate, we mean that one of a higher order than man, and of a different nature, assumes the appearance of man or becomes a man. Here it is meant that "the Word," or the second person of the Trinity, whom John had just proved to be equal with God, became a man, or was united with the man Jesus of Nazareth, so that it might be said that he* was made flesh

.

Was made. *This is the same word that is used in* Joh 1:3.

"All things were made by him." It is not simply affirmed that he

was *flesh, but that he was* made *flesh, implying that he had pre-existence, agreeably to* Joh 1:1.

This is in accordance with the doctrine of the Scriptures elsewhere. Heb 10:5: "A

body *hast thou prepared me."* Heb 2:14

: "As the children are partakers of flesh and blood, he also himself likewise took part of the same." 1 Jo 4:2. "Jesus Christ is come in the flesh." See also 1 Ti 3:16; Php 2:6; 2 Co 8:9

Lu 1:35. The expression, then, means that he became a man, and that he became such by the power of God providing for him a body. It cannot mean that the divine nature was changed into the human, for that could not be; but it means that the Logos, or "Word," became so intimately united to Jesus that it might be said that the Logos, or "Word" became or was a man, as the

soul *becomes so* united *to the body that we may say that it is* one person *or a* man

.

And dwelt among us. *The word in the original denotes "dwelt as in a tabernacle or tent;" and some have supposed that John means to say that the human body was a tabernacle or tent for the Logos to abide in, in allusion to the tabernacle among the Jews, in which the Shechinah, or visible symbol of God, dwelt; but it is not necessary to suppose this. The object of John was to prove that "the Word" became* incarnate. *To do this he appeals to various evidences. One was that he* dwelt *among them; sojourned with them; ate, drank, slept, and was with them for years, so that they saw him with their eyes, they looked upon him, and their hands handled him,* 1 Jo 1:1.

To

dwell *in a tent with one is the same as to be in his family; and when John says he* tabernacled *with them, he means that he was with them as a friend and as one of a family, so that they had full opportunity of becoming familiarly acquainted with him, and could not be mistaken in supposing that* he was really a man

.

We beheld his glory. *This is a new proof of what he was affirming*-that THE WORD OF GOD became man. *The first was, that they had seen him as* a man. *He now adds that they had seen him in his proper glory* as God and man united in one person, *constituting him the unequalled Son of the Father. There is no doubt that there is reference here to the transfiguration on the holy mount. See* Mt 18:1-9.

To this same evidence Peter also appeals, 2 Pe 1:16-18. John was one of the witnesses of that scene, and hence he says, "WE beheld his glory," Mr 9:2. The word

glory

here means majesty, dignity, splendour.

The glory as of the only-begotten of the Father

. The dignity which was appropriate to the only-begotten Son of God; such glory or splendour as could belong to no other, and as properly expressed his rank and character. This glory was seen eminently on the mount of transfiguration. It was also seen in his miracles, his doctrine, his resurrection, his ascension; all of which were such as to illustrate the perfections, and manifest the glory that belongs only to the Son of God.

Only-begotten. *This term is never applied by John to any but Jesus Christ. It is applied by him five times to the Saviour,* Joh 1:14,18; 3:16,18; 1 Jo 4:9.

It means literally an only child. Then, as an only child is peculiarly dear to a parent, it means one that is especially beloved. Comp. Ge 22:2,12,16; Jer 6:26; Zec 12:10.

On

both

these accounts it is bestowed on the Saviour.

1st. As he was eminently the Son of God, sustaining a peculiar relation to him in his divine nature, exalted above all men and angels, and thus worthy to be called, by way of eminence, his only Son. Saints are called his sons or children, because they are born of his Spirit, or are like him; but the Lord Jesus is exalted far above all, and deserves eminently to be called his only-begotten Son.

2nd. He was peculiarly dear to God, and therefore this appellation, implying tender affection, is bestowed on him.

Full of grace and truth. *The word* full *here refers to the Word made flesh, which is declared to be full of grace and truth. The word* grace *means favours, gifts, acts of beneficence. He was kind, merciful, gracious, doing good to all, and seeking man's welfare by great sacrifices and love; so much so, that it might be said to be characteristic of him, or he* abounded *in favours to* mankind. He was also full of truth. He declared the truth. In him was no falsehood. He was not *like the false prophets and false Messiahs, who were wholly impostors; nor was he like the emblems and shadows of the old dispensation, which were only types of the true; but he was truth itself. He* represented things as they are, *and thus became the* truth *as well as* the way and the life

.

{s} "Word" Lu 1:35; 1 Ti 3:16 {t} "and we beheld" 2 Pe 1:17; 1 Jo 1:1,2
{u} "full of grace and truth" Ps 45:2; Col 2:3,9

Verse 15.

John bare witness of him

. The evangelist now returns to the testimony of John the Baptist. He had stated that the Word became incarnate, and he now appeals to the testimony of John to show that, thus incarnate, he was the Messiah.

He that cometh after me. *He of whom I am the forerunner, or whose way I am come to prepare.* See Barnes "Mt 3:3".

Is preferred before me. *Is superior to me. Most critics have supposed that the words translated "is preferred" relate to* time, *and not to* dignity; *meaning that though he came* after him publicly, being six months younger than John, as well as entering on his work after John, yet that he had existed long before him. Most, however, have understood it more correctly, as our translators seem to have done, as meaning, He was worthy of more honour than I am.

He was before me. *This can refer to nothing but his preexistence, and can be explained only on the supposition that he* existed *before John, or, as the evangelist had before shown, from the*

xxii

beginning. He came after *John in his public ministry and in his human nature, but in his divine nature he had existed long before John had a being—from eternity. We may learn here that it is one mark of the true spirit of a minister of Christ to desire and feel that Christ is always to be preferred to ourselves. We should keep ourselves out of view. The great object is to hold up the Saviour; and however much ministers may be honoured or blessed, yet they should lay all at the feet of Jesus, and direct all men to him as the undivided object of affection and honour. It is the business of every Christian, as well as of every Christian minister, to be a* witness

for Christ, and to endeavour to convince the world that he is worthy of confidence and love.

{v} "John bare witness of him" Mt 3:13

Verse 16.

Of his fullness. *In* Joh 1:14

the evangelist has said that Christ was

full of grace and truth. *Of that* fulness *he now says that all the disciples had received; that is, they derived from his abundant truth and mercy grace to understand the plan of salvation, to preach the gospel, to live lives of holiness; they* partook *of the numerous blessings which he came to impart by his instructions and his death. These are undoubtedly not the words of John the Baptist, but of the evangelist John, the writer of this gospel. They are a continuation of what he was saying in the 14th verse, the 15th verse being evidently thrown in as a parenthesis. The declaration had not exclusive reference, probably, to the apostles, but it is extended to all Christians, for all believers have received of the* fulness of grace and truth*that is in Christ.* Comp. Eph 1:23; 3:19; Col 1:19; 2:9.

In all these places our Saviour is represented as the fulness of God—as abounding

in mercy, as exhibiting the divine attributes, and as possessing in himself all that is necessary to fill his people with truth, and grace, and love.

Grace for grace

. Many interpretations of this phrase have been proposed. The chief are briefly the following:

1st. "We have received, under the gospel, grace or favour, instead

of those granted under the law; and God has added by the gospel important favours to those which he gave under the law." This was first proposed by Chrysostom.

2nd. "We, Christians, have received grace

answering to, *or corresponding to that which is in Jesus Christ. We are* like him in meekness, humility," &c.

xxiii

3rd. "We have received grace

as grace—*that is, freely. We have not purchased it nor deserved it, but God has conferred it on us* freely

" (Grotius).

4th. The meaning is, probably, simply that we have received through him

abundance *of grace or favour. The Hebrews, in expressing the him. He knew him intima superlative degree of comparison, used simply to repeat the word—thus, "pits, pits," meaning many pits (Hebrew in* Ge 14:10). So here grace for grace may mean

much

grace; superlative favours bestowed on man; favours superior to all that had been under the law —superior to all other things that God can confer on men. These favours consist in pardon, redemption, protection, sanctification, peace here, and heaven hereafter.

{w} "fulness" Joh 3:34

Verse 17.

The law was given

. The Old Testament economy. The institutions under which the Jews lived.

By Moses. *By Moses, as the servant of God. He was the great legislator of the Jews, by whom, under God, their polity was formed. The* law *worketh wrath (*Ro 4:15); it was attended with many burdensome rites and ceremonies (Ac 15:10); it was preparatory to another state of things. The gospel succeeded that and took its place, and thus showed the

greatness

of the gospel economy, as well as its grace and truth.

Grace and truth came by Jesus Christ. *A system of religion full of favours, and the* true *system, was revealed by him. The old system was one of* law, *and* shadows, *and* burdensome rites; this

was full of mercy to mankind, and was true in all things. We may learn from these verses—

1st. That all our mercies come from Jesus Christ.

2nd. "All true believers receive from Christ's fulness the best and greatest saints cannot live without him, the meanest and weakest may live by him. This excludes proud boasting that we have nothing but

we have received it, *and silenceth perplexing fears that we want nothing but* we may receive it

."

{x} "grace and truth" Ps 85:10; Ro 5:21

Verse 18.

No man hath seen God at any time. *This declaration is probably made to show the superiority of the revelation of Jesus above that of any previous dispensation. It is said, therefore, that Jesus* had an intimate knowledge of God, *which neither Moses nor any of the ancient prophets had possessed. God is invisible; no human eyes have seen him; but Christ had a knowledge of God which might be expressed to our apprehension by saying that he* saw *him intimately and completely, and was therefore fitted to make a fuller manifestation of him. See* Joh 5:37; 6:46; 1 Jo 4:12; Ex 33:20; Joh 14:9.

This passage is not meant to deny that men had witnessed

manifestations *of God, as when he appeared to Moses and the prophets (comp.* Nu 12:8; Is 6:1-13); but it is meant that no one has seen the essence of God, or has

fully known *God. The prophets delivered what they* heard *God speak; Jesus what he* knew of God as his equal

, and as understanding fully his nature.

The only-begotten Son. See Barnes "Joh 1:14".

This verse shows John's sense of the meaning of that phrase, as denoting an intimate and full knowledge of God.

In the bosom of the Father. *This expression is taken from the custom among the Orientals of reclining at their meals.* See Barnes "Mt 23:6".

It denotes intimacy, friendship, affection. Here it means that Jesus had a knowledge of God such as one friend has of another— knowledge of his character, designs, and nature which no other one possesses, and which renders him, therefore, qualified above all others to make him known.

Hath declared him. *Hath fully revealed him or made him known. Comp.* Heb 1:1,4.

This verse proves that, Jesus had a knowledge of God above that which any of the ancient prophets had, and that the fullest revelations of his character are to be expected in the gospel. By his Word and Spirit he can enlighten and guide us, and lead us to the true knowledge of God; and there is no true and full knowledge of God which is not obtained through his Son. Comp. Joh 14:6; 1 Jo 2:22,23.

{y} "No man hath seen" Ex 33:20; 1 Ti 6:16 {z} "The only-begotten" 1 Jo 4:9

Verse 19.

This is the record. *The word* record *here means* testimony, *in whatever way given. The word* record *now commonly refers to* written

evidence. This is not its meaning here. John's testimony was given without writing.

When the Jews sent. *John's fame was great. See* Mt 3:5.

It spread from the region of Galilee to Jerusalem, and the nation seemed to suppose, from the character of his preaching, that he was the Messiah, Lu 3:15. The great council of the nation, or the Sanhedrim, had, among other things, the charge of religion. They felt it to be their duty, therefore, to inquire into the character and claims of John, and to learn whether he was the Messiah. It is not improbable that they

wished

that he might be the long-expected Christ, and were prepared to regard him as such.

When the Jews sent priests and Levites. See Barnes "Lu 10:31,32".

These were probably members of the Sanhedrim.

{a} "the record of John" Lu 3:15

Verse 20.

I am not the Christ. *This confession proves that John was not an impostor. He had a wide reputation. The nation was expecting that the Messiah was about to come, and multitudes were ready to believe that John was he,* Lu 3:15.

If John had been an impostor he would have taken advantage of this excited state of public feeling, proclaimed himself to be the Messiah, and formed a large party in his favour. The fact that he did not do it is full proof that he did not intend to impose on men, but came only as the forerunner of Christ; and his example shows that all Christians, and especially all Christian ministers, however much they may be honoured and blessed, should be willing to lay all their honours at the feet of Jesus; to keep themselves back and to hold up before the world only the Son of God. To do this is one eminent mark of the true spirit of a minister of the gospel.

Verse 21.

Art thou Elias? *This is the Greek way of writing Elijah. The Jews expected that Elijah would appear before the Messiah came.* See Barnes "Mt 11:14".

They supposed that it would be the real Elijah returned from heaven. In this sense John denied that he was Elijah; but he did not deny that he was the Elias or Elijah which the prophet intended (Mt 3:3), for he immediately proceeds to state (Joh 1:23) that he was sent, as it was predicted that Elijah would be, to prepare the way of the Lord; so that, while he corrected their false notions about Elijah, he so clearly stated to them his true character that they might understand that he was really the one predicted as Elijah.

That prophet. *It is possible that the Jews supposed that not only Elijah would reappear before the coming of the Messiah, but also* Jeremiah. See Barnes "Mt 16:14".

Some have supposed, however, that this question has reference to the prediction of Moses in De 18:15.

{2} "that prophet" or, "a prophet"

THE GOSPEL ACCORDING TO JOHN-Chapter 1-Verse 22
Verse 22. No Barnes text on this verse.

THE GOSPEL ACCORDING TO JOHN-Chapter 1-Verse 23
Verse 23.
I am the voice, *&c.* See Barnes "Mt 3:3"

{b} "He said" Mt 3:3; Mr 1:3; Lu 3:4; Joh 3:28
{c} "prophet Esias" Isa 40:3

THE GOSPEL ACCORDING TO JOHN-Chapter 1-Verse 24
Verse 24.
Were of the Pharisees. *For an account of this sect,* See Barnes "Mt 3:7".
Why

they *are particularly mentioned is not certainly known. Many of the* Sadducees *came to his baptism* (Mt 3:7), but it seems that they did not join in sending to him to know what was the design of John. This circumstance is one of those incidental and delicate allusions which would occur to no impostor in forging a book, and which show that the writers of the New Testament were honest men and knew what they affirmed. For,

1st. The Pharisees composed a great part of the Sanhedrim, Ac 23:6. It is probable that a deputation from the Sanhedrim would be of that party.

2nd. The Pharisees were very tenacious of rites and customs, of traditions and ceremonies. They observed many. They believed that they were lawful, Mr 7:3,4. Of course, they believed that those rites might be increased, but they did not suppose that it could be done except by the authority of a prophet or of the Messiah. When, therefore, John came

baptizing—*adding a rite to be observed by his followers— baptizing not only* Gentiles, *but also* Jews—*the question was whether he had* authority

to institute a new rite; whether it was to be received among the ceremonies of religion. In this question the Sadducees felt no interest, for they rejected all such rites at once; but the Pharisees thought it was worth inquiry, and it was a question on which they felt themselves specially called on to act as the guardians of the ceremonies of religion.

xxvii

Verse 25.

Why baptizest thou then, &c. *Baptism on receiving a proselyte from* heathenism *was common before the time of John, but it was not customary to baptize a Jew. John had changed the custom. He baptized* all, *and they were desirous of knowing by what authority he made such a change in the religious customs of the nation. They presumed, from the fact that he*introduced *that change, that he claimed to be a prophet or the Christ. They supposed that no one would attempt it without* pretending

, at least, authority from heaven. As he disclaimed the character of Christ and of the prophet Elijah, they asked whence he derived his authority. As he had just before applied to himself a prediction that they all considered as belonging to the forerunner of Christ, they might have understood why he did it; but they were blind, and manifested, as all sinners do, a remarkable slowness in understanding the plainest truths in religion.

Verse 26.

I baptize. *He did not deny it; nor did he condescend to state his authority.* That *he had given.* He admitted *that he had introduced an important* change *in the rites of religion, and he goes on to tell them that* this *was not all. Greater and more important changes would soon take place without* their *authority. The Messiah was about to come, and the* power

was about to depart from their hands.

There standeth one. *There* is
one.

Among you. *In the midst of you. He is undistinguished among the multitude. The Messiah had already come, and was about to be manifested to the people. It was not until the next day* (Joh 1:29) that Jesus was manifested or proclaimed as the Messiah; but it is not improbable that he was then among the people that were assembled near the Jordan, and mingled with them, though he was undistinguished. He had gone there, probably, with the multitudes that had been drawn thither by the fame of John, and had gone without attracting attention, though his real object was to receive baptism in this public manner, and to be exhibited and proclaimed as the Messiah.

Whom ye know not
. Jesus was not yet declared publicly to be the Christ. Though it is probable that he was then among the multitude, yet he was not known as the Messiah. We may hence learn,

1st. That there is often great excellency in the world that is obscure, undistinguished, and unknown. Jesus was

near

to all that people, but they were not conscious of his presence, for he was retired and obscure. Though the greatest person-age ever in the world, yet he was not externally distinguished from others.

2nd. Jesus may be near to men of the world, and yet they know him not. He is everywhere by his Spirit, yet few know it, and few are desirous of knowing it.

{d} "there standeth" Mal 3:1

Verse 27.

Whose shoe's latchet. See Barnes "Mt 3:11".

The

latchet

of sandals was the string or thong by which they were fastened to the feet. To unloose them was the office of a servant, and John means, therefore, that he was unworthy to perform the lowest office for the Messiah. This was remarkable humility. John was well known; he was highly honoured; thousands came to hear him. Jesus was at that time unknown; but John says that he was unworthy to perform the humblest office for Jesus. So we all should be willing to lay all that we have at the feet of Christ, and feel that we are unworthy to be his lowest servants.

Verse 28.

In Bethabara. *Almost all the ancient manuscripts and versions, instead of* Bethabara *here, have* Bethany, *and this is doubtless the true reading. There was a Bethany about 2 miles east of Jerusalem, but there is said also to have been another in the tribe of Reuben, on the east side of the river Jordan, and in this place, probably, John was baptizing. It is about 12 miles above Jericho. The word* Bethabara *means* house or place of a ford. *The reading* Bethabara, *instead of* Bethany, *seems to have arisen from the conjecture of Origen, who found in his day no such place as Bethany, but saw a town called Bethabara, where John was said to have baptized, and therefore took the liberty of changing the former reading.—Rob., Lex*

.

Beyond Jordan

. On the east side of the river Jordan.

{e} "in Bethabara" Jud 7:24

Verse 29.

The next day
. The day after the Jews made inquiry whether he was the Christ.

Behold the Lamb of God. *A lamb, among the Jews, was killed and eaten at the Passover to commemorate their deliverance from Egypt,* Ex 12:3-11.

A lamb was offered in the tabernacle, and afterward in the temple, every morning and evening, as a part of the daily worship, Ex 29:38,39. The Messiah was predicted as a lamb led to the slaughter, to show his patience in his sufferings, and readiness to die for man, Isa 53:7. A lamb, among the Jews, was also an emblem of patience, meekness, gentleness. On

all *these accounts, rather than on any one of them alone, Jesus was called the Lamb. He was innocent* (1 Pe 2:23-25); he was a sacrifice for sin—the substance represented by the daily offering of the lamb, and slain at the usual time of the evening sacrifice (Lu 23:44-46); and he was what was represented by the Passover, turning away the anger of God, and saving sinners by his blood from vengeance and eternal death, 1 Co 5:7.

Of God. *Appointed by God, approved by God, and most dear to him; the sacrifice which he chose*
, and which he approves to save men from death.

Which taketh away. *This denotes his bearing the sins of the world, or the sufferings which made an atonement for sin. Comp.* Isa 53:4; 1 Jo 3:5; 1 Pe 2:24.

He takes away sin by
bearing *in his own body the sufferings which God appointed to show his sense of the evil of sin, thus magnifying the law, and rendering it consistent for him to pardon.* See Barnes "Ro 3:24, See Barnes "Ro 3:25".

Of the world. *Of all mankind, Jew and Gentile. His work was not to be confined to the Jew, but was also to benefit the Gentile' it was not confined to any one part of the world, but was designed to open the way of pardon to all men. He was the propitiation for the sins of the whole world,* 1 Jo 2:2.
See Barnes "2 Co 5:15".

{f} "Lamb of God" Ex 12:3; Isa 53:7,11; Re 5:6
{g} "which" Ac 13:39; 1 Pe 2:24; Re 1:5
{3} "taketh" or, "beareth" Heb 9:28

Verse 30. No Barnes text on this verse.

Verse 31.

I knew him not. *John was not* personally *acquainted with Jesus. Though they were remotely related to each other, yet it seems that they had had heretofore no personal acquaintance. John had lived chiefly in the hill country of Judea. Jesus had been employed with Joseph at Nazareth. Until Jesus came to be baptized (*Mt 3:13,14), it seems that John had no acquaintance with him. He understood that he was to announce that the Messiah was about to appear. He was sent to proclaim his coming, but he did not personally know Jesus, or that

he *was to be the Messiah. This proves that there could have been no* collusion *or* agreement between them to impose on the people.

Should be made manifest

. That the Messiah should be exhibited, or made known. He came to prepare the way for the Messiah, and it now appeared that the Messiah was Jesus of Nazareth.

To Israel
. To the Jews.

Verse 32.
Bare record
. Gave testimony.

I saw the Spirit, *&c.* See Barnes "Mt 3:16,17"

Verses 33, 34.

The same said, *&c. This was the sign by which he was to know the Messiah. He was to see the Spirit descending like a dove and abiding on him. It does not follow, however, that he had no* intimation *before this that Jesus was the Christ, but it means that by this he should* infallibly know it. *From* Mt 3:13,14, it seems that John supposed, before the baptism of Jesus, that he

claimed *to be the Messiah, and that he believed it; but the* infallible, certain
, testimony in the case was the descent of the Holy Spirit on him at his baptism.

That this is the Son of God. *This was distinctly declared by a voice from heaven at his baptism,* Mt 3:17.

This John heard, and he testified that he had heard it.
{h} "descending and remaining" Joh 3:34 {i} "baptizeth" Ac 1:5; 2:4

Verse 34. No Barnes text on this verse.

Verse 35.

The next day

. The day after his remarkable testimony that Jesus was the Son of God. This testimony of John is reported because it was the main design of this evangelist to show that Jesus was the Messiah. See the Introduction. To do this, he adduces the decided and repeated testimony of John the Baptist. This was impartial evidence in the case, and hence he so particularly dwells upon it.

John stood

. Or was standing. This was probably apart from the multitude.

Two of his disciples. *One of these was Andrew* (Joh 1:40), and it is not improbable that the other was the writer of this gospel.

Verse 36.

Looking upon Jesus

, &c. Fixing his eyes intently upon him. Singling him out and regarding him with special attention. Contemplating him as the long-expected Messiah and Deliverer of the world. In this way should all ministers fix the eye on the Son of God, and direct all others to him.

As he walked

. While Jesus was walking.

Verse 37.

They followed Jesus. *They had been the disciples of John. His office was to point out the Messiah. When that was done, they left at once their master and teacher, John, and followed the long-expected Messiah. This shows that John was sincere; that he was not desirous of forming a party or of building up a sect; that he was willing that all those whom he had attracted to himself by his ministry should become followers of Christ. The object of ministers should not be to build up their own interests or to extend their own fame. It is to point men to the Saviour. Ministers, however popular or successful, should be willing that their disciples should look to Christ rather than to them; nay, should forget them and look away from them, to tread in the footsteps of the Son of God; and the conduct of these disciples shows us that we should forsake all and follow Jesus when he is pointed out to us as the Messiah. We should not delay nor debate the matter, but leave at once all our old teachers, guides and companions, and follow the Lamb of God. And* we should do that, too, though to the world *the Lord Jesus may appear, as he did to the multitude of the Jews, as poor, unknown, and despised. Reader, have you*

left all and followed him? Have you forsaken the guides of false philosophy and deceit, of sin and infidelity, and committed yourself to the Lord Jesus Christ.

THE GOSPEL ACCORDING TO JOHN-Chapter 1-Verse 38

Verse 38.

What seek ye? This was not asked to obtain information. Comp. Joh 1:48.

It was not a harsh reproof, forbidding them to follow him. Comp. Mt 11:28-30. It was a kind inquiry respecting their desires; an invitation to lay open their minds, to state their wishes, and to express all their feelings respecting the Messiah and their own salvation. We may learn,

1st. That Jesus regards the first inclinations of the soul to follow him. He
turned
toward these disciples, and he will incline his ear to all who begin to approach him for salvation.

2nd. Jesus is ready to hear their requests and to answer them.

3rd. Ministers of the gospel, and all other Christians, should be accessible, kind, and tender toward all who are inquiring the way to life. In conformity with their Master, they should be willing to aid all those who look to them for guidance and help in the great work of their salvation.

Rabbi. This was a Jewish title conferred somewhat as literary degrees now are, and meaning literally a great one, *and was applied to a teacher or master in the Jewish schools. It corresponded with the title* Doctor. *Our Saviour solemnly forbade his disciples to wear that title.* See Barnes "Mt 23:8".

The fact that John
interpreted
this word shows that he wrote his gospel not for the Jews only, but for those who did not understand the Hebrew language. It is supposed to have been written at Ephesus.

Where dwellest thou? This question they probably asked him in order to signify their wish to be with him and to be instructed by him. They desired more fully to listen to him than they could now by the wayside. They were unwilling to interrupt him in his travelling. Religion teaches men true politeness, or a disposition to consult the convenience of others, and not improperly to molest them, or to break in upon them when engaged. It also teaches us to desire to be with Christ; to seek every opportunity of coremration with him, and chiefly to desire to be with him where he is when we leave this world. Comp. Php 1:23.

{5} "tenth hour" or,
that was two hours before night

.

Verse 39.

Come and see

. This was a kind and gracious answer. He did not put them off to some future period. Then, as now, he was willing that they should come at once and enjoy the full opportunity which they desired of his conversation. Jesus is ever ready to admit those who seek him to his presence and favour.

Abode with him

. Remained with him. This was probably the dwelling of some friend of Jesus. His usual home was at Nazareth.

The tenth hour

. The Jews divided their day into twelve equal parts, beginning at sun-rise. If John used their mode of computation, this was about four o'clock P.M. The Romans divided time as we do, beginning at midnight. If John used their mode, it was about ten o'clock in the forenoon. It is not certain which he used.

{5} "tenth hour" or, "That was about two hours before night"

Verse 40. No Barnes text on this verse.

Verse 41.

He first findeth *He found him* and told him about Jesus
before he brought him to Jesus.

We have found the Messias. *They had learned from the testimony of John, and now had been more fully convinced from conversation with Jesus, that he was the Messiah. The word Messiah, or Messias, is Hebrew, and means the same as the Greek word Christ,* anointed. See Barnes "Mt 1:1".

From the conduct of Andrew we may learn that it is the nature of religion to desire that others may possess it. It does not lead us to monopolize it or to hide it under a bushel, but it seeks that others also may be brought to the Saviour. It does not
wait *for them to come, but it goes* for *them; it seeks them out, and tells them that a Saviour*

is found. Young converts should seek

their friends and neighbours, and tell them of a Saviour; and not only their relatives, but all others as far as possible, that all may come to Jesus and be saved.

{6} "the Christ" or, "

the anointed

.

Verse 42.

Cephas. *This is a Syriac word, meaning the same as the Greek word Peter, a stone.* See Peter "Mt 16:17".

The stone, or rock, is a symbol of firmness and steadiness of character—a trait in Peter's character

after *the ascension of Jesus that was very remarkable. Before the death of Jesus he was rash, headlong, variable; and it is one proof of the omniscience of Jesus that he saw that Peter* would *possess a character that would be expressed appropriately by the word* stone *or* rock. *The word* Jonas *is a Hebrew word, whose original signification is a* dove

. It may be that Jesus had respect to that when he gave Simon the name Peter. "You now bear a name emblematic of timidity and inconstancy. You shall be called by a name denoting firmness and constancy."

{k} "thou shalt be called Cephas" Mt 16:18 {7} "A Stone" or, "Peter"

Verse 43.

Would go forth

.

Into Galilee

. He was now in Judea, where he went to be baptized by John. He was now about to return to his native country.

Findeth Philip. *This does not refer to his calling these disciples to be apostles, for that took place at the Sea of Tiberias (*Mt 4:18), but it refers to their being convinced that he was the Christ. This is the object of this evangelist, to show how and when they were convinced of this. Matthew states the time and occasion in which they were called to be

apostles

; John, the time in which they first became acquainted with Jesus, and were convinced that he was the Messiah. There is, therefore, no contradiction in the evangelists.

Verse 44.

Of Bethsaida. See Barnes "Mt 11:21".

The city of

. The place where Andrew and Peter dwelt.

Verse 45.

Moses, in the law. *Moses, in that part of the Old Testament which he wrote, called by the Jews the law. See* De 18:15,18

Ge 49:10; 3:15. And the prophets, Isa 53:1-12; 9:6,7; Da 9:24-27; Jer 13:5,6; &c.

Jesus of Nazareth

, &c. They spoke according to common apprehension. They spoke of him as the son of Joseph because he was commonly supposed to be. They spoke of him as dwelling at Nazareth, though they might not have been ignorant that he was born at Bethlehem.

{1} "Moses in the law" Lu 24:27,44

Verse 46.

Can any good thing, *&c. The character of Nazareth was proverbially bad. To be a Galilean or a Nazarene was an expression of decided contempt,* Joh 7:52.

See Barnes "Mt 2:23".

Nathanael asked, therefore, whether it was possible that the Messiah should come from a place proverbially wicked. This was a mode of judging in the case not uncommon. It is not by examining evidence, but by prejudice. Many persons suffer their minds to be filled with prejudice against religion, and then pronounce at once without examination. They refuse to examine the subject, for they have set it down that it

cannot

be true. It matters not where a teacher comes from, or what is the place of his birth, provided he be authorized of God and qualified for his work.

Come and see. *This was the best way to answer Nathanael. He did not sit down to* reason *with him, or speculate about the possibility that a good thing could come from Nazareth; but he asked him to go and examine for himself, to see the Lord Jesus, to hear him converse, to lay aside his prejudice, and to judge from a fair and candid personal inquiry. So we should beseech sinners to lay aside their prejudices against religion, and* to be Christians, *and thus make trial for themselves. If men can be persuaded to come to Jesus, all their petty and foolish objections*

against religion will vanish. *They will be satisfied from their* own experience
that it is true, and in this way only will they ever be satisfied.

{m} "Can there be any good thing" Joh 7:41

THE GOSPEL ACCORDING TO JOHN-Chapter 1-Verse 47

Verse 47.

An Israelite indeed. *One who is really an Israelite—not by birth only, but one worthy of the name. One who possesses the spirit, the piety, and the integrity which become a man who is really a Jew, who fears God and obeys his law. Comp.* Ro 9:6; 2:28,29.

No guile

. No deceit, no fraud, no hypocrisy. He is really what he professes to be—a Jew, a descendant of the patriarch Jacob, fearing and serving God. He makes no profession which he does not live up to. He does not say that Nathanael was without guilt or sin, but that he had no disguise, no trick, no deceit—he was sincere and upright. This was a most honourable testimony. How happy would it be if he, who knows the hearts of all as he did that of Nathanael, could bear the same testimony of all who profess the religion of the gospel!

{n} "Behold" Ps 32:2; Ro 2:28,29

THE GOSPEL ACCORDING TO JOHN-Chapter 1-Verse 48

Verse 48.

Whence knowest thou me

? Nathanael was not yet acquainted with the divinity of Christ, and supposed that he had been a stranger to him. Hearing him express a favourable opinion of him, he naturally inquired by what means he had any knowledge of him. His conscience testified to the truth of what Jesus said—that he had no guile, and he was anxious to know whence he had learned his character.

Before that Philip called thee. *See* Joh 1:45.

When thou wast under the fig tree. *It is evident that it was from something that had occurred under the fig-tree that Jesus judged of his character. What that was is not recorded. It is not improbable that Nathanael was accustomed to retire to the shade of a certain tree, perhaps in his garden or in a grove, for the purpose of meditation and prayer. The Jews were much in the habit of selecting such places for private devotion, and in such scenes of stillness and retirement there is something peculiarly favourable for meditation and prayer. Our Saviour also worshipped in such places. Comp.* Joh 18:2; Lu 6:12.

In that place of retirement it is not improbable that Nathanael was engaged in private devotion.

xxxvii

I saw thee

. It is clear, from the narrative, that Jesus did not mean to say that he was bodily present with Nathanael and saw him; but he knew his thoughts, his desires, his secret feelings and wishes. In this sense Nathanael understood him. We may learn—

1st. That Jesus sees what is done in secret, and is therefore divine.

2nd. That he sees us when we little think of it.

3rd. That he sees us especially in our private devotions, hears our prayers, and marks our meditations. And

4th. That he judges of our

character *chiefly by our private devotions. Those are secret; the world sees them not; and in our closets we show what we are. How does it become us, therefore, that our secret prayers and meditations should be without* guile

and hypocrisy, and such as Jesus will approve!

{o} "I saw thee" Ps 139:1,2

Verse 49.

Rabbi. *Master. Applied appropriately to Jesus, and to no one else,* Mt 23:10.

The Son of God

. By this title he doubtless meant that he was the Messiah. His conscience told him that he had judged right of his character, and that therefore he must know the heart and the desires of the mind. If so, he could not be a mere man, but must be the long-expected Messiah.

The King of Israel. *This was one of the titles by which the Messiah was expected, and this was the title which was affixed to his cross,* Joh 19:18.

This case of Nathanael John adduces as another evidence that Jesus was the Christ. The great object he had in view in writing this gospel was to collect the evidence that he was the Messiah, Mt 20:31. A case, therefore, where Jesus searched the heart, and where his knowledge of the heart convinced a pious Jew that he was the Christ, is very properly adduced as important testimony.

{p} "the Son" Mt 14:33; Joh 20:28,29

{q} "the King of Israel" Mt 21:5; 27:11

Verse 50.

Greater things

. Fuller proof of his Messiahship, particularly what is mentioned in the following verse.

Verse 51.

Verily, verily. *In the Greek,* Amen, amen. *The word* amen

means truly, certainly, so be it—from the verb to confirm, to establish, to be true. It is often used in this gospel. When repeated it expresses the speaker's sense of the importance of what he is saying, and the certainty that it is as he affirms.

Ye shall see

. Not, perhaps, with the bodily eyes, but you shall have evidence that it is so. The thing shall take place, and you shall be a witness of it.

Heaven open. *This is a figurative expression, denoting the conferring of favours.* Ps 78:23,24

: "He opened the doors of heaven, and had rained down manna." It also denotes that God was about to work a miracle in attestation of a particular thing. See Mt 3:16. In the language, here, there is an evident allusion to the ladder that Jacob saw in a dream, and to the angels ascending and descending on it, Ge 18:12. It is not probable that Jesus referred to any particular instance in which Nathanael should literally see the heavens opened, The baptism of Jesus had taken place, and no other instance occurred in his life in which it is said that the

heavens were

opened.

Angels of God. *Those pure and holy beings that dwell in heaven, and that are employed as ministering spirits to our world,* Heb 1:14.

Good men are represented in the Scriptures as being under their protection, Ps 91:11,12; Ge 28:12.

They are the agents by which God often expressed his will to men, Heb 2:2; Ga 3:19. They are represented as strengthening the Lord Jesus, and ministering unto him. Thus they aided him in the wilderness (Mr 1:13), and in the garden (Lu 22:43), and they were present when he rose from the dead, Mt 28:2-4; Joh 20:12,13.

By their ascending and descending upon him it is probable that he meant that Nathanael would have evidence that they came to his aid, and that he would have

the *KIND of protection and assistance from God which would show* more fully that he was the Messiah

. Thus his life, his many deliverances from dangers, his wisdom to confute his skilled and cunning adversaries, the scenes of his death, and the attendance of angels at his resurrection, may all be represented by the angels descending upon him, and all would show to Nathanael and the other disciples most clearly that he was the Son of God.

The Son of man. *A term by which he often describes himself. It shows his humility, his love for man, his willingness to be esteemed* as a man, Php 2:6,7.

From this interview with Nathanael we may learn,

1st. That Jesus searches the heart.

2nd. That he was truly the Messiah.

3rd. That he was under the protection of God.

4th. That if we have faith in Jesus, it will be continually strengthened—the evidence will grow brighter and brighter.

5th. That if we believe his

word

, we shall yet see full proof that his word is true.

6th. As Jesus was under the protection of God, so will all his friends be. God will defend and save us also if we put our trust in him.

7th. Jesus applied to himself terms expressive of humility. He was not solicitous even to be called by titles which he

might *claim. So we should not be ambitious of titles and honours. Ministers of the gospel must resemble him when they seek for the fewest titles, and do not aim at distinctions from each other or their brethren.* See Barnes "Mt 23:8".

{r} "heaven open" Eze 1:1 {s} "the angels of God" Ge 28:12; Da 7:9,10; Ac 1:10,11

THE GOSPEL ACCORDING TO JOHN- Chapter 2

Verse 1.

And the third day

. On the third day after his conversation with Nathanael.

Cana\@. This was a small town about 15 miles north-west of Tiberias and 6 miles north-east of Nazareth. It is now called Kefr Kenna, is under the government of a Turkish officer, and contains perhaps three hundred inhabitants, chiefly Catholics. The natives still pretend to show the place where the water was turned into wine, and even one of the large stone water-pots.

"A Greek church," says Professor Hackett

(*Illustrations of Scripture*, p. 322),

"stands at the entrance of the town, deriving its
special sanctity, as I understood, from its
being supposed to occupy the site of the house in which
the marriage was celebrated to which Jesus and his
friends were invited. A priest to whom we were referred
as the custodian soon arrived, in obedience to our call,
and unlocked the doors of the church. It is a low stone
building, wretchedly neglected and out of repair."

"The houses," says Dr. Thomson (*The Land and the Book*,
vol. 2. p. 126),

"were built of limestone, cut and laid up after the fashion
still common in this region, and some of them may have been
inhabited within the last fifty years. There are many
ancient cisterns about it, and fragments of water-jars
in abundance, and both reminded us of the beginning
of miracles. Some of my companions gathered bits of
these water-jars as mementoes—witnesses they could
hardly be, for those of the narrative were of *stone*,
while these were baked earth."

"The place is now quite deserted. Dr. Thomson (ibid.) says:
"There is not now a habitable house in the humble village
where our blessed Lord sanctioned, by his presence and
miraculous assistance, the all-important and world-wide
institution of marriage."

It was called *Cana of Galilee* to distinguish it from another Cana in the tribe of Ephraim, Jos 16:9. This was the native place of Nathanael, Joh 21:2.

The mother of Jesus. Mary. It is not improbable that she was a relative of the family where the marriage took place.

{a} "Cana of Galilee" Jos 19:28; Joh 4:46

THE GOSPEL ACCORDING TO JOHN-Chapter 2-Verse 2

Verse 2. *His disciples*. Those that he had made when in Judea. These were Peter, Andrew, Philip, and Nathanael. They were not yet called to be *apostles*, but they believed that he was the Messiah. The miracle wrought here was doubtless to convince them more fully that he was the Christ.

{b} "the marriage" Heb 13:4

THE GOSPEL ACCORDING TO JOHN-Chapter 2-Verse 3

Verse 3. *When they wanted wine*. A marriage feast among the Jews was commonly observed for seven or eight days. It is not probable that there would be a want of wine at the marriage itself, and it is possible, therefore, that Jesus came there some time during the marriage feast.

They have no wine. It is not known why Mary told this to Jesus. It would seem that she had a belief that he was able to supply it, though he had as yet worked no miracle.

{c} "And when they wanted wine" Ec 10:19; Isa 24:11

THE GOSPEL ACCORDING TO JOHN-Chapter 2-Verse 4

Verse 4. *Woman*. This term, as used here, seems to imply reproof, as if she was interfering in that which did not properly concern her; but it is evident that no such reproof or disrespect was intended by the use of the term *woman* instead of *mother*. It is the same term by which he tenderly addressed Mary Magdalene after his resurrection (Joh 20:15), and his mother when he was on the cross, Joh 19:26. Comp. also Mt 15:28; Joh 4:21; 1 Co 7:16.

What have I to do with thee? See Barnes "Mt 8:29".

This expression is sometimes used to denote indignation or contempt. See Jud 11:12; 2 Sa 16; 1 Ki 17:18.

But it is not probable that it denoted either in this place; if it did, it was a mild reproof of Mary for attempting to control or direct him in his power of working miracles. Most of the ancients supposed this to be the intention of Jesus. The words sound to us harsh, but they might have been spoken in a *tender* manner, and not have been intended as a reproof. It is clear that he did not intend to *refuse* to provide wine, but only to delay it a little; and the design was, therefore, to compose the anxiety of Mary, and to prevent her being solicitous about it. It may, then, be thus expressed:

"My mother, be not anxious. To you and to me this
should not be a matter of solicitude. The proper
time of my interfering has not yet come. When that
is come I will furnish a supply, and in the
meantime neither you nor I should be solicitous."

Thus understood, it is so far from being a harsh reproof, that it was a mild exhortation for her to dismiss her fears and to put proper trust in him.

Mine hour, &c. My time. The proper time for my interposing. Perhaps the wine was not yet entirely exhausted. The wine had begun to fail, but he would not work a miracle until it was entirely gone, that the miracle might be free from all possibility of suspicion. It does not mean that the proper time for his working a miracle, or entering on his public work had not come, but that the proper time for his interposing there had not arrived.

THE GOSPEL ACCORDING TO JOHN-Chapter 2-Verse 5

Verse 5. *His mother saith*, &c. It is evident from this verse that his mother did not understand what he had said as a harsh reproof and repulse, but as an indication of his willingness at the proper time to furnish wine. In all this transaction he evinced the appropriate feelings of a son toward a mother.

{d} "Whatsoever he sayeth" Lu 5:5,6

THE GOSPEL ACCORDING TO JOHN-Chapter 2-Verse 6

Verse 6. *Six water-pots of stone*. Made of stone; or, as we should say, stoneware.

After the manner. After the usual custom.

Of the purifying. Of the washings or ablutions of the Jews. They were for the purpose of washing the hands before and after eating (Mt 15:2), and for the formal washing of vessels, and even articles of furniture, Lu 11:39; Mr 7:3,4.

Two or three firkins. It is not quite certain what is meant here by the word *firkins*. It is probable that the measure intended is the Hebrew *bath*, containing about 7« gallons.

THE GOSPEL ACCORDING TO JOHN-Chapter 2-Verse 7

Verse 7. *With water*. This was done by the servants employed at the feast. It was done by them, so that there might be no opportunity of saying that the disciples of Jesus had filled them

xliii

with wine to produce the *appearance* of a miracle. In this case there could be no deception. The quantity was very considerable. The servants would know whether the wine or water had been put in these vessels. It could not be believed that *they* had either the power or the disposition to impose on others in this manner, and the way was therefore clear for the proof that Jesus had really changed what was known to be *water* into *wine*.

To the brim. To the top. So full that no wine could be *poured in* to give the *appearance* of a mixture. Farther, vessels were used for this miracle in which wine had not been kept. These pots were never used to put wine in, but simply to keep *water* in for the various purposes of ablution. A large number was used on this occasion, because there were many guests.

THE GOSPEL ACCORDING TO JOHN-Chapter 2-Verse 8

Verse 8. *Draw out now*. This command was given to the servants. It showed that the miracle had been *immediately* wrought. As soon as they were filled the servants were directed to take to the governor of the feast. Jesus made no parade about it, and it does not even appear that he approached the water-pots. He willed it, and it was done. This was a clear exertion of divine power, and made in such a manner as to leave no doubt of its reality.

The governor. One who presided on the occasion. The one who stood at the head or upper end of the table. He had the charge of the entertainment, provided the food, gave directions to the servants, etc.

{e} "Draw out" Ec 9:7 {f} "governor of the feast" Ro 13:7

THE GOSPEL ACCORDING TO JOHN-Chapter 2-Verse 9

Verse 9. *And knew not whence it was*. This is said, probably, to indicate that his judgment was not biased by any favour, or any *want* of favour, toward Jesus. Had he known what was done, he would have been less likely to have judged impartially. As it is, we have his testimony that this was *real* wine, and of so fine a body and flavour as to surpass that which had been provided for the occasion. Everything in this miracle shows that there was no collusion or understanding between Jesus and any of the persons at the feast.

{g} "servants" Ps 119:100; Joh 7:17

THE GOSPEL ACCORDING TO JOHN-Chapter 2-Verse 10

Verse 10. *Every man*. It is customary, or it is generally done.

When men have well drunk. This word does not of necessity mean that they were *intoxicated*, though it is usually employed in that sense. It may mean when they have drunk sufficient, or to satiety; or have drunk so much as to produce hilarity, and to destroy the keenness of their taste, so that they could not readily distinguish the good from that which was worse. But this cannot be adduced in favour of drunkenness, even if it means to be intoxicated; for,

1st. It is not said of those who were present at that feast, but of what generally occurred. For anything that appears, at that feast all were perfectly temperate and sober.

2nd. It is not the saying of Jesus that is here recorded, but of the governor of the feast, who is declaring what usually occurred as a fact.

3rd. There is not any expression of opinion in regard to its *propriety*, or in approval of it, even by that governor.

4th. It does not appear that our Saviour even *heard* the observation.

5th. Still less is there any evidence that he *approved* such a state of things, or that he designed that it should take place here. Farther, the word translated "*well drunk*" cannot be shown to mean intoxication; but it *may* mean when they had drunk as much as they judged proper or as they desired, then the other was presented. It is clear that neither our Saviour, nor the sacred writer, nor the speaker here expresses any *approbation* of intemperance, nor is there the least evidence that anything of the kind occurred here. It is not proof that we approve of intemperance when we mention, as this man did, what occurs usually among men at feasts.

Is worse. Is of an inferior quality.

The good wine. This shows that this had all the qualities of real wine. We should not be deceived by the phrase "*good wine.*" We often use the phrase to denote that it is good in proportion to its strength and its power to intoxicate; but no such sense is to be attached to the word here. Pliny, Plutarch, and Horace describe wine as good, or mention that as the best wine, which was *harmless* or *innocent*—poculo vini *innocentis*. The most useful wine — *utilissimum vinum*— was that which had little strength; and the most wholesome wine—*saluberrimum vinum*— was that which had not been adulterated by "the addition of anything to the *must* or juice." Pliny expressly says that a "good wine" was one that was destitute of spirit (lib. iv. c. 13). It should not be assumed, therefore, that the "good wine" was *stronger* than the other: it is rather to be presumed that it was milder. The wine referred to here was doubtless such as was commonly drunk in Palestine. That was the pure juice of the grape. It was not brandied wine, nor drugged wine, nor wine compounded of various substances, such as we drink in this land. The common wine drunk in Palestine was that which was the simple juice of the grape. We use the word *wine* now to denote the kind of liquid which passes under that name in this country— always containing a considerable portion of alcohol —not only the alcohol produced by fermentation, but alcohol *added* to keep it or make it stronger. But we have no right to take that sense of the word, and go with it to the interpretation of the Scriptures. We should endeavour to place ourselves in the exact circumstances of those times, ascertain precisely what idea the word would convey to those who used it then, and apply *that* sense to the word in the interpretation of the Bible; and there is not the slightest evidence that the word so used would have conveyed any idea but that of the pure juice of the grape, nor the slightest circumstance mentioned in this account that would not be fully met by such a supposition. No man should adduce *this* instance in favour of drinking wine unless he can prove that the wine made in the" water-pots" of Cana was *just like* the wine which he proposes to drink. The Saviour's example may be always pleaded JUST AS IT WAS; but it is a matter of obvious and simple justice that we should find out exactly what the example was before we plead it. There is, moreover, no evidence that any other part of the water was converted into wine than that which was *drawn out* of the water-casks for the use of the guests. On this supposition, certainly, all the circumstances of the case are met, and the miracle would be more striking. All that was needed was to furnish a *supply* when the wine that had been prepared was nearly exhausted. The object was not to furnish a large quantity for future use. The miracle, too, would in this way be more apparent and impressive. On this supposition, the casks would *appear* to be filled with water *only*; as it was drawn out, it was pure wine. Who could doubt, then, that there was the exertion of miraculous power? All, therefore, that has been said about the Redeemer's furnishing a large quantity of wine for the newly-married pair, and about his benevolence in doing it, is wholly gratuitous. There is no evidence of it whatever; and it is not necessary to suppose it in order to an explanation of the circumstances of the case.

{h} "kept" Ps 104:15; Pr 9:2,5

THE GOSPEL ACCORDING TO JOHN-Chapter 2-Verse 11

Verse 11. *This beginning of miracles.* This his first public miracle. This is declared by the sacred writer to be a miracle— that is, an exertion of divine power, producing a change of the substance of water into wine, which no human power could do.

Manifested forth. Showed; exhibited.

His glory. His power, and proper character as the Messiah; showed that he had divine power, and that God had certainly commissioned him. This is shown to be a real miracle by the following considerations: 1st. Real water was placed in the vessels. This the servants believed, and there was no possibility of deception.

2nd. The water was placed where it was not *customary* to keep wine. It could not be *pretended* that it was merely a mixture of water and wine.

3rd. It was judged to be wine without knowing whence it came. There was no agreement between Jesus and the governor of the feast to impose on the guests.

4th. It was a change which nothing but divine power could effect. He that can change water into a substance like the juice of the grape must be clothed with divine power.

Believed on him. This does not mean that they did not *before* believe on him, but that their faith was confirmed or strengthened. They saw a miracle, and it satisfied them that he was the Messiah. *Before* this they believed on the testimony of John, and from conversation with Jesus (Joh 1:35-51); *now* they saw that he was invested with almighty power, and their faith was established. From this narrative we may learn,

1st. That marriage is honourable, and that Jesus, if sought, will not refuse his presence and blessing on such an occasion.

2nd. On such an occasion the presence and approbation of Christ should be sought. No compact formed on earth is more important; none enters so deeply into our comfort in this world;

perhaps none will so much affect our destiny in the world to come. It should be entered into, then, in the fear of God.

3rd. On all such occasions our conduct should be such that the presence of Jesus would be no interruption or disturbance. He is holy. He is always present in every place; and on all festival occasions our deportment should be such as that we should welcome the presence of the Lord Jesus Christ. *That is not a proper state of feeling or employment which would be interrupted by the presence of the Saviour.*

4th. Jesus delighted to do good. In the very beginning of his ministry he worked a miracle to show his benevolence. This was the appropriate commencement of a life in which he was to go about doing good. He seized every opportunity of doing it; and at a marriage feast, as well as among the sick and poor, he showed the character which he always sustained —that of a benefactor of mankind.

5th. An argument cannot be drawn from this instance in favour of intemperate drinking. There is no evidence that any who were present on that occasion drank too freely.

6th. Nor can an argument be drawn from this case in favour even of drinking wine such as we have. The common wine of Judea was the pure juice of the grape, without any mixture of alcohol, and was harmless. It was the common drink of the people, and did not tend to produce intoxication. *Our* wines are a *mixture* of the juice of the grape and of brandy, and often of infusions of various substances to give it colour and taste, and the appearance of wine. Those wines are little less injurious than brandy, and the habit of drinking them should be classed with the drinking of all other liquid fires.

The following table will show the danger of drinking the wines that are in common use:

```
Brandy has fifty-three parts and 39 hundredths in a hundred
of
    alcohol; or........................53.39 per cent.
    Rum...............................53.68 "
    Whisky, Scotch....................54.32 "
    Holland Gin.......................51.60 "
    Port Wine, highest kind...........25.83 "
```

lowest...............21.40 "

Madeira, highest.............. 29.42 "

lowest............. 19.34 " Lisbon...........................18.94 " Malaga..........................17.26 "
Red   Champagne....................11.30   "   White   ".................... 12.80   "   Currant Wine.....................20.25 "

It follows that a man who drinks two glasses of most of the wines used has taken as much alcohol as if he had taken one glass of brandy or whisky, and why should he not as well drink the alcohol in the brandy as in the Wine? What difference can it make in morals? What difference in its effects on his system? The experience of the world has shown that water, pure water, is the most wholesome, safe, and invigorating drink for man.

{i} "manifested forth his glory" Joh 1:14 {k} "and his disciples" Joh 5:13

THE GOSPEL ACCORDING TO JOHN-Chapter 2-Verse 12

Verse 12. *To Capernaum*. See Barnes "Mt 4:13".

Not many days. The reason why he remained there no longer was that the Passover was near, and they went up to Jerusalem to attend it.

THE GOSPEL ACCORDING TO JOHN-Chapter 2-Verse 13

Verse 13. *The Jews' passover*. The feast among the Jews called the Passover. See Barnes "Mt 26:2, also Mt 26:3-17.

And Jesus went up to Jerusalem. Every male among the Jews was required to appear at this feast. Jesus, in obedience to the law, went up to observe it. This is the *first* Passover on which he attended after he entered on the work of the ministry. It is commonly supposed that he observed three others— one recorded Lu 6:1, another Joh 6:4, and the last one on the night before he was crucified, Joh 11:55. As his baptism when he entered on his ministry had taken place some time before this —probably not far from six months— it follows that the period of his ministry was not far from three years and a half, agreeably to the prophecy in Da 9:27.

{l} "passover" Ex 12:14 {m} "Jesus" Joh 2:23; 5:1; 6:4; 11:55

THE GOSPEL ACCORDING TO JOHN-Chapter 2-Verse 14

Verse 14. *Found in the temple*, &c. The transaction here recorded is in almost all respects similar to that which has been explained in the See Barnes "Mt 21:12".

This took place at the *commencement* of his public ministry; that *at the close*. On each occasion he showed that his great regard was for the *pure worship* of his Father; and one great design of his coming was to reform the abuses which had crept into that worship, and to bring man to a proper regard for the glory of God. If it be asked how it was that those engaged in this traffic so *readily* yielded to Jesus of Nazareth, and that they left their gains and their property, and fled from the temple at the command of one so obscure as he was, it may be replied,

1st. That their *consciences* reproved them for their impiety, and they could not set up the *appearance* of self-defence.

2nd. It was customary in the nation to cherish a profound regard for the authority of a prophet; and the appearance and manner of Jesus—so fearless, so decided, so authoritative—led them to suppose *he* was a prophet, and they were afraid to resist him.

3rd. He *had* even then a wide reputation among the people, and it is not improbable that many supposed him to be the Messiah.

4th. Jesus on all occasions had a most wonderful control over men. None could resist him. There was something in his manner, as well as in his doctrine, that awed men, and made them tremble at his presence. Comp. Joh 18:5,6. On this occasion he had the *manner* of a prophet, the authority of God, and the testimony of their own consciences, and they could not, therefore, resist the authority by which he spoke.

Though Jesus thus purified the temple at the commencement of his ministry, yet in three years the same scene was to be repeated. See Mt 21:12. And from this we may learn,

1st. How soon men forget the most solemn reproofs, and return to evil practices.

2nd. That no sacredness of time or place will guard them from sin. In the very temple, under the very eye of God, these men soon returned to practices for which their consciences reproved them, and which they knew God disapproved.

3rd. We see here how strong is the love of gain—the ruling passion of mankind. Not even the sacredness of the temple, the presence of God, the awful ceremonials of religion, deterred them from this unholy traffic. So wicked men and hypocrites will always turn *religion*, if possible, into gain; and not even the sanctuary, the Sabbath, or the most awful and sacred scenes, will deter them from schemes of gain. Comp. Am 8:5. So strong is this grovelling passion, and so deep is that depravity which fears not God, and regards not his Sabbaths, his sanctuary, or his law.

{n} "And found in the temple" Mt 21:12; Mr 11:15; Lu 19:45

THE GOSPEL ACCORDING TO JOHN-Chapter 2-Verse 15

Verse 15. *A scourge.* A whip.

Of small cords. This whip was made as an emblem of authority, and also for the purpose of driving from the temple the cattle which had been brought there for sale. There is no evidence that he used any violence to the men engaged in that unhallowed traffic. The original word implies that these *cords* were made of twisted *rushes* or *reeds*— probably the ancient material for making ropes.

THE GOSPEL ACCORDING TO JOHN-Chapter 2-Verse 16

Verse 16. No Barnes text on this verse.

THE GOSPEL ACCORDING TO JOHN-Chapter 2-Verse 17

Verse 17. *It was written,* &c. This is recorded in Ps 69:9. Its meaning is, that he was affected with great zeal or concern for the pure worship of God.

The zeal of thine house. Zeal is intense ardour in reference to any object. The zeal of thine house means extraordinary concern for the temple of God; intense solicitude that the worship there should be pure, and such as God would approve.

Hath eaten me up. Hath absorbed me, or engaged my entire attention and affection; hath surpassed all other feelings, so that it may be said to be the one great absorbing affection and desire of the mind. Here is an example set for ministers and for all Christians. In Jesus this was the great commanding sentiment of his life. In us it should be also. In this manifestation of zeal he began and ended his ministry. In this we should begin and end our lives. We learn, also, that ministers of religion should aim to purify the church of God. Wicked men, conscience-smitten, will tremble when they see proper zeal in the ministers of Jesus Christ; and there is no combination of wicked men, and no form of depravity, that can stand before the faithful, zealous, pure preaching of the gospel. The preaching of every minister should be such that wicked men will feel that they must either become Christians or leave the house of God, or spend their lives there in the consciousness of guilt and the fear of hell.

{o} "The zeal" Ps 69:9

THE GOSPEL ACCORDING TO JOHN-Chapter 2-Verse 18

Verse 18. *What sign, &c.* What *miracle* dost thou work? He assumed the character of a prophet. He was reforming, by his authority, the temple. It was natural to ask by what *authority* this was done; and as they had been accustomed to miracles in the life of Moses, and Elijah, and the other prophets, so they demanded evidence that *he* had authority thus to cleanse the house of God.

Seeing that thou doest. Rather "by what *title or authority* thou doest these things." Our translation is ambiguous. They wished to know *by what miracle* he had shown, or could show, his right to do those things.

{p} "What sign" Mt 12:38; Joh 6:30

THE GOSPEL ACCORDING TO JOHN-Chapter 2-Verse 19

Verse 19. *Destroy this temple.* The evangelist informs us (Joh 2:21) that by *temple*, here, he meant his body. It is not improbable that he pointed with his finger to his body as he spoke. The word *destroy*, used here in the imperative, has rather the force of the *future*. Its meaning may thus be expressed:

"You are now profaners of the temple of God. You have
defiled the sanctuary; you have made it a place of
traffic. You have also despised my authority, and
been unmoved by the miracles which I have already
wrought. But your wickedness will not end here.
You will oppose me more and more; you will reject
and despise me, until in your wickedness you will
take my life and destroy my body."

Here was therefore a distinct prediction both of his death and the cause of it. The word *temple*, or *dwelling*, was not unfrequently used by the Jews to denote the body as being the residence of the spirit, 2 Co 5:1. Christians are not unfrequently called the temple of God, as being those in whom the Holy Spirit dwells on earth, 1 Co 3:16,17; 1 Co 6:19; 2 Co 6:16. Our Saviour called his body a temple in accordance with the common use of language, and more particularly because in him the fulness of the Godhead dwelt bodily, Col 2:9. The temple at Jerusalem was the appropriate dwelling-place of God. His visible presence was there peculiarly manifested, 2 Ch 36:15; Ps 76:2. As the Lord Jesus was divine—as the fulness of the Godhead dwelt in him—so his body might be called a temple.

In three days I will raise it up. The Jews had asked a miracle of him in proof of his authority—that is, a proof that he was the Messiah. He tells them that a full and decided proof of that would be his *resurrection from the dead.* Though they would not be satisfied by any other miracle, yet by this they ought to be convinced that he came from heaven, and was the long-expected Messiah. To the same evidence that he was the Christ he refers them on other occasions. See Mt 12:38,39. Thus early did he foretell his death and resurrection, for at the beginning of his work he had a clear foresight of all that was to take place. This knowledge shows clearly that he came from heaven, and it evinces, also, the extent of his love—that he was *willing* to come to save us, knowing clearly what it would cost him. Had he come *without* such an expectation of suffering, his love might have been far less; but when he fully knew all that was before him, when he saw that it would involve him in contempt and death, it shows compassion "worthy of a God" that he was willing to endure the load of all our sorrows, and die to save us from death everlasting. When Jesus says, "*I* will raise it up," it is proof, also, of divine power. A mere man could not say this. No deceased man can have such power over his body; and there must have been, therefore, in the person of Jesus a nature superior to human to which the term "I" could be applied, and which had power to raise the dead—that is, which was divine.

{q} "Destroy this temple" Mt 26:61; 27:40

THE GOSPEL ACCORDING TO JOHN-Chapter 2-Verse 20

Verse 20. *Then said the Jews,* &c. The Jews, either from the ambiguity of his language, or more probably from a design to cavil, understood him as speaking of the temple at Jerusalem. What he said here is all the evidence that they could adduce on his trial (Mt 26:61; Mr 14:58), and they reproached him with it when on the cross, Mt 27:40. The Jews frequently perverted our Saviour's meaning. The language which he used was often that of parables or metaphor; and as they sought to misunderstand him and pervert his language, so he often left them to their own delusions, as he himself says, "that seeing they might not see, and hearing they might not understand," Mt 13:13. This was a case which they *might*, if they had been disposed, have easily understood. They were in the temple; the conversation was about the temple; and though he probably pointed to his body, or designated it in some plain way, yet they chose to understand him as referring to the temple itself; and as it appeared so improbable that he could raise up that in three days, they sought to pervert his words and pour ridicule on his pretensions.

Forty and six years, &c. The temple in which they then were was that which was commonly called the *second temple*, built after the return of the Jews from Babylon. See Barnes "Mt 21:12".

This temple Herod the Great commenced repairing, or began to rebuild, in the eighteenth year of his reign—that is, *sixteen years* before the birth of Christ (Jos. Ant., b. xv. 1). The main body of the temple he completed in *nine years and a half* (Jos. Ant., xv. 5, 6), yet the temple, with its outbuildings, was not entirely complete in the time of our Saviour. Herod continued to ornament it and to perfect it even till the time of Agrippa (Jos. Ant., b. xx. ch. viii. § 11). As Herod began to rebuild the temple sixteen years before the birth of Jesus, and as what is here mentioned happened in the thirtieth year of the age of Jesus, so the time which had been occupied in it was *forty-six years*. This circumstance is one of the many in the New Testament which show the accuracy of the evangelists, and which prove that they were well acquainted with what they recorded. It demonstrates that their narration is true. Impostors do not trouble themselves to be very accurate about names and dates, and there is nothing in which they are more liable to make mistakes.

Wilt thou, &c. This is an expression of contempt. Herod, with all his wealth and power, had been engaged in this work almost half a century. Can you, an obscure and unknown Galilean, accomplish it in three days? The thing, in their judgment, was ridiculous, and showed, as they supposed, that he had no authority to do what he had done in the temple.

THE GOSPEL ACCORDING TO JOHN-Chapter 2-Verse 21

Verse 21. No Barnes text on this verse.

{r} "temple" Eph 2:21,22; Col 2:9; He 8:2

THE GOSPEL ACCORDING TO JOHN-Chapter 2-Verse 22

Verse 22. *When he was risen from the dead*, &c. This saying of our Saviour at that time seemed obscure and difficult. The disciples did not understand it, but they treasured it up in their memory, and the event showed what was its true meaning. Many prophecies are obscure when spoken which are perfectly plain when the event takes place. We learn from this, also, the importance of treasuring up the truths of the Bible *now*, though we may not perfectly understand them. Hereafter they may be plain to us. It is therefore important that*children* should learn the truths of the sacred Scriptures. Treasured up in their memory, they may not be understood *now*, but hereafter they may be clear to them. Every one engaged in teaching a Sunday-school, therefore, may be imparting instruction which may be understood, and may impart comfort, long after the teacher has gone to eternity.

They believed. That is, after he rose from the dead.

The scripture. The Old Testament, which predicted his resurrection. Reference here must be made to Ps 16:10, comp. Ac 2:27-32, Ac 13:35-37; Ps 2:7, comp. Ac 13:33. They understood those Scriptures in a sense different from what they did before.

The word which Jesus had said. The prediction which he had made respecting his resurrection in this place and on other occasions. See Mt 20:19; Lu 18:32,33.

{s} "his disciples" Lu 24:8

THE GOSPEL ACCORDING TO JOHN-Chapter 2-Verse 23

Verse 23. *Feast-day.* Feast. During the celebration of the Passover, which continued eight days.

Miracles which he did. These miracles are not particularly recorded. Jesus took occasion to work miracles, and to preach at that time, for a great multitude were present from all parts of Judea. It was a favourable opportunity for making known his doctrines and showing the evidence that he was the Christ, and he embraced it. We should always seek and embrace opportunities of doing good, and we should not be deterred, but rather excited, by the multitude around us to make known our real sentiments on the subject of religion.

THE GOSPEL ACCORDING TO JOHN-Chapter 2-Verse 24

Verse 24. *Did not commit himself.* The word translated *commit* here is the same which in Joh 2:23 is translated *believed.* It means to put *trust* or *confidence in.* Jesus did not put trust or reliance in them. He did not leave himself in their hands. He acted cautiously and prudently. The proper time for him to die had not come, and he secured his own safety. The reason why he did not commit himself to them is that he knew all men. He knew the inconstancy and fickleness of the multitude. He knew how easily they might be turned against him by the Jewish leaders, and how unsafe he would be if they should be moved to sedition and tumult.

{t} "he knew all men" 1 Sa 16:7; 1 Ch 28:9; 29:17; Jer 17:9,10; Mt 9:4
Lu 16:30; Ac 1:24; Re 2:23

THE GOSPEL ACCORDING TO JOHN-Chapter 2-Verse 25

Verse 25. *Should testify of man.* Should give him the character of any man.

He knew what was in man. This he did because he had made all Joh 1:3, and because he was God, Joh 1:1. There can be no higher evidence than this that he was omniscient, and was therefore divine. To search the heart is the prerogative of God alone (Jer 17:10); and as Jesus knew what was in these disciples, and as it is expressly said that he knew what was in man—that is, in all men— so it follows that he must be equal with God. As he knows *all*, he is acquainted with the *false* pretentions and professions of hypocrites. None can deceive him. He also knows the wants and desires of all his real friends. He hears their groans, he sees their sighs, he counts their tears, and in the day of need will come to their relief.

liii

THE GOSPEL ACCORDING TO JOHN- Chapter 3

Verse 1. *A man of the Pharisees*. A Pharisee. See Barnes "Mt 3:3".

Nicodemus, a ruler of the Jews. One of the *Sanhedrim*, or great council of the nation. He is twice mentioned after this as being friendly to our Saviour; in the first instance as advocating his cause, and defending him against the unjust suspicion of the Jews Joh 7:50, and in the second instance as one who came to aid in embalming his body, Joh 19:39. It will be recollected that the design of *John* in writing this gospel was to show that Jesus was the Messiah. To do this he here adduces the testimony of one of the *rulers* of the Jews, who early became convinced of it, and who retained the belief of it until the death of Jesus.

{a} "Nicodemus" Joh 7:50,51; 19:39

Verse 2. *The same came to Jesus*. The design of his coming seems to have been to inquire more fully of Jesus what was the doctrine which he came to teach. He seems to have been convinced that he was the Messiah, and desired to be farther instructed *in private* respecting his doctrine. It was not usual for a man of rank, power, and riches to come to inquire of Jesus in this manner; yet we may learn that the most favourable opportunity for teaching such men the nature of personal religion is when they are alone. Scarcely any man, of any rank, will refuse to converse on this subject when addressed respectfully and tenderly *in private*. In the midst of their companions, or engaged in business, they may refuse to listen or may cavil. When alone, they will hear the voice of entreaty and persuasion, and be willing to converse on the great subjects of judgment and eternity. Thus Paul says (Ga 2:2), *"privately to them which are of reputations;"* evincing his consummate prudence, and his profound knowledge of human nature.

By night. It is not mentioned why he came by night. It might have been that, being a member of the Sanhedrim, he was engaged all the day; or it may have been because the Lord Jesus was occupied all the day in teaching publicly and in working miracles, and that there was no opportunity for conversing with him as freely as he desired; or it may have been that he was afraid of the ridicule and contempt of those in power, and fearful that it might involve him in danger if publicly known; or it may have been that he was afraid that if it were publicly known that he was disposed to favour the Lord Jesus, it might provoke more opposition against *him* and endanger his life. As no *bad* motive is imputed to him, it is most in accordance with Christian charity to suppose that his motives were such as God would approve, especially as the Saviour did not reprove him. We should not be disposed to blame men where Jesus did not, and we should desire to find *goodness* in every man rather than be ever on the search for evil motives. 1 Co 13:4-7. We may learn here,

1st. That our Saviour, though engaged during the day, did not refuse to converse with an inquiring sinner at night. Ministers of the gospel at all times should welcome those who are asking the way to life.

2nd. That it is *proper* for men, even those of elevated rank, to *inquire* on the subject of religion. Nothing is so important as religion, and no temper of mind is more lovely than a disposition to ask the way to heaven. *At all times* men should seek the way of salvation, and especially in times of great religious excitement they should make inquiry. At Jerusalem, at the time referred to here, there was great solicitude. Many believed on Jesus. He wrought miracles, and preached, and many were converted. There was what would now be called *a revival off religion*, having all the features of a work of grace. At such a season it was proper, as it is now, that not only the poor, but the rich and great, should inquire the path to life.

Rabbi. This was a title of respect conferred on distinguished Jewish teachers, somewhat in the way that the title *doctor of divinity* is now conferred. See Barnes "Joh 1:38".

Our Saviour forbade his disciples to wear that title (See Barnes "Joh 1:38"), though it was proper for him to do it, as being the great Teacher of mankind. It literally signifies great, and was given by Nicodemus, doubtless, because Jesus gave distinguished proofs that he came as a teacher from God.

We know. I know, and those with whom I am connected. Perhaps he was acquainted with some of the Pharisees who entertained the same opinion about Jesus that he did, and *he*came to be more fully confirmed in the belief.

Come from God. Sent by God. This implies his readiness to hear him, and his desire to be instructed. He acknowledges the divine mission of Jesus, and delicately asks him to instruct him in the truth of religion. When we read the words of Jesus in the Bible, it should be with a belief that he came from God, and was therefore qualified and authorized to teach us the way of life.

These miracles. The miracles which he wrought in the temple and at Jerusalem, Joh 2:23.

Except God be with him. Except God *aid* him, and except his instructions are approved by God. Miracles show that a prophet or religious teacher comes from God, because God would not work a miracle in attestation of a falsehood or to give countenance to a false teacher. If God gives a man power to work a miracle, it is proof that he approves the teaching of that man, and the miracle is the proof or the credential that he came from God.

{b} "for no man" Joh 9:16,33; Ac 2:22

{c} "God be with him" Ac 10:38

THE GOSPEL ACCORDING TO JOHN-Chapter 3-Verse 3

Verse 3. *Verily, verily.* An expression of strong affirmation, denoting the *certainty* and the *importance* of what he was about to say. Jesus proceeds to state one of the fundamental and indispensable doctrines of his religion. It may seem remarkable that he should introduce this subject in this manner; but it should be remembered that Nicodemus acknowledged that he was a teacher come from God; that he implied by that his readiness and desire to receive instruction; and that it is not wonderful, therefore, that Jesus should *commence* with one of the fundamental truths of his religion. It is no part of Christianity to *conceal* anything. Jesus declared to every man, high or low, rich or poor, the most humbling truths of the gospel. Nothing was kept back for fear of offending men of wealth or power; and for them, as well as the most poor and lowly, it was declared to be indispensable to experience, as the first thing in religion, a change of heart and of life.

Except a man. This is a universal form of expression designed to include all mankind. Of *each and every man* it is certain that unless he is born again he cannot see the kingdom of God. It includes, therefore, men of every character and rank, and nation, moral and immoral, rich and poor, in office and out of office, old and young, bond and free, the slave and his master, Jew and Gentile. It is clear that our Saviour intended to convey to *Nicodemus* the idea, also, that *he* must be born again. It was not sufficient to be a Jew, or to acknowledge him to be a teacher sent by God—that is, the Messiah; it was necessary, in addition to this, to experience in his own soul that great change called the *new birth* or regeneration.

Be born again. The word translated here *again* means also *from above*, and is so rendered in the margin. It is evident, however, that Nicodemus understood it not as referring to a birth from above, for if he had he would not have asked the question in Joh 3:4. It is probable that in the language which he used there was not the same ambiguity that there is in the Greek. The ancient versions all understood it as meaning again, or the *second time*. Our natural birth introduces us to light, is the commencement of life, throws us amid the works of God, and is the beginning of our existence; but it also introduces us to a world of sin. We early go astray. All men transgress. The imagination of the thoughts of the heart is evil from the youth up. We are conceived in sin and brought forth in iniquity, and there is none that doeth good, no, not one. The carnal mind is enmity against God, and by nature we are dead in trespasses and sins, Ge 8:21; Ps 14:2,3; Ps 51:5; Ro 1:29-32; 3:10-20; 8:7.

All sin exposes men to misery here and hereafter. To escape from sin, to be happy in the world to come, it is necessary that man should be changed in his principles, his feelings, and his manner of life. This change, or the beginning of this new life, is called the *new birth*, or regeneration. It is so called because in many respects it has a striking analogy to the natural birth. It is the beginning of spiritual life. It introduces us to the light of the gospel. It is the moment when we really begin to live to any purpose. It is the moment when God reveals himself to us as our reconciled Father, and we are adopted into his family as his sons. And as every man is a sinner, it is necessary that each one should experience this change, or he cannot be happy or saved. This doctrine was not unknown to the Jews, and was particularly predicted as a doctrine that would be taught in the times of the Messiah. See De 10:16; Jer 4:4; 31:4,33; Eze 11:19;

36:25

Ps 51:12. The change in the New Testament is elsewhere called the *new creation* (2 Co 5:17; Ga 6:15), and *life from the dead*, or a resurrection, Eph 2:1; Joh 5:21,24.

He cannot see. To *see*, here, is put evidently for enjoying ——or he cannot be fitted for it and partake of it.

The kingdom of God. Either in this world or in that which is to come—that is, heaven. See Barnes "Mt 3:2".

The meaning is, that the kingdom which Jesus was about to set up was so pure and holy that it was indispensable that every man should experience this change, or he could not partake of its blessings. This is solemnly declared by the Son of God by an affirmation equivalent to an oath, and there can be no possibility, therefore, of entering heaven without experiencing the change which the Saviour contemplated by the *new birth.* And it becomes every man, as in the presence of a holy God before whom he must soon appear, to ask himself whether he has experienced this change, and if he has not, to give no rest to his eyes until he has sought the mercy of God, and implored the aid of his Spirit that his heart may be renewed.

{d} "Except" Joh 1:13; Ga 6:15; Eph 2:1; Tit 3:5; Jas 1:18; 1 Pe 1:23

1 Jo 2:29; 3:9

{1} "born again" or, "from above"

THE GOSPEL ACCORDING TO JOHN-Chapter 3-Verse 4

Verse 4. *How can a man,* &c. It may seem remarkable that Nicodemus understood the Saviour *literally,* when the expression *to be born again* was in common use among the Jews to denote a change from *Gentilism* to *Judaism* by becoming a proselyte by *baptism.* The word with them meant a change from the state of a heathen to that of a Jew. But they never used it as applicable to a Jew, because they supposed that by his birth every Jew was entitled to all the privileges of the people of God. When, therefore, our Saviour used it of a Jew, when he affirmed its necessity of *every man,* Nicodemus supposed that there was an absurdity in the doctrine, or something that surpassed his comprehension, and he therefore asked whether it was possible that Jesus could teach so absurd a doctrine—as he could conceive no other sense as applicable to a Jew—as that he should, when old, enter a second time into his mother's womb and be born. And we may learn from this—

1st. That prejudice leads men to misunderstand the plainest doctrines of religion.

2nd. That things which are at first incomprehensible or apparently absurd, may, when explained, become clear. The doctrine of regeneration, so difficult to Nicodemus, is plain to a child that is born of the Spirit.

3rd. Those in high rank in life, and who are learned, are often most ignorant about the plainest matters of religion. It is often wonderful that they exhibit so little acquaintance with the most simple subjects pertaining to the soul, and so much absurdity in their views.

4th. A doctrine is not to be *rejected* because the rich and the great do not believe or understand it. The doctrine of regeneration was not false because Nicodemus did not comprehend it.

THE GOSPEL ACCORDING TO JOHN-Chapter 3-Verse 5

Verse 5. *Be born of water.* By *water*, here, is evidently signified *baptism*. Thus the word is used in Eph 5:26; Tit 3:5. Baptism was practised by the Jews in receiving a Gentile as a proselyte. It was practised by John among the Jews; and Jesus here says that it is an ordinance of his religion, and the sign and seal of the renewing influences of his Spirit. So he said (Mr 16:16), "He that believeth and is baptized shall be saved." It is clear from these places, and from the example of the apostles (Ac 2:38,41; 8:12-13,36-38; 9:18

Ac 10:47,48; 16:15,33; 18:8; 22:16; Ga 3:27), that they considered this ordinance as binding on all who professed to love the Lord Jesus. And though it cannot be said that none who are not baptized can be saved, yet Jesus meant, undoubtedly, to be understood as affirming that this was to be the regular and uniform way of entering into his church; that it was the appropriate mode of making a profession of religion; and that a man who neglected this, when the duty was made known to him, neglected a plain command of God. It is clear, also, that any other command of God might as well be neglected or violated as this, and that it is the duty of everyone not only to love the Saviour, but to make an acknowledgment of that love by being baptized, and by devoting himself thus to his service. But, lest Nicodemus should suppose that this was all that was meant, he added that it was necessary that he should *be born of the Spirit also.* This was predicted of the Saviour, that he should *baptize with the Holy Ghost and with fire,* Mt 3:11. By this is clearly intended that the heart must be changed by the agency of the Holy Spirit; that the love of sin must be abandoned; that man must repent of crime and turn to God; that he must renounce all his evil propensities, and give himself to a life of prayer and holiness, of meekness, purity, and benevolence. This great change is in the Scripture ascribed uniformly to the Holy Spirit, Tit 3:5; 1 Th 1:6 Ro 5:5; 1 Pe 1:22.

Cannot enter into. This is the way, the appropriate way, of entering into the kingdom of the Messiah here and hereafter. He cannot enter into the true church here, or into heaven in the world to come, except in connection with a change of heart, and by the proper expression of that change in the ordinances appointed by the Saviour.

{e} "water" Mr 16:16; Ac 2:38 {f} "of the Spirit" Ro 8:2; 1 Co 2:12

THE GOSPEL ACCORDING TO JOHN-Chapter 3-Verse 6

Verse 6. *That which is born of the flesh.* To show the necessity of this change, the Saviour directs the attention of Nicodemus to the natural condition of man. By that which is born of the flesh he evidently intends man as he is by nature, in the circumstances of his natural birth. Perhaps, also, he alludes to the question asked by Nicodemus, whether a man could be born when he was old? Jesus tells him that if this could be, it would not answer any valuable purpose; he would still have the same propensities and passions. Another change was therefore indispensable.

Is flesh. Partakes of the nature of the parent. Comp. Ge 5:3. As the parents are corrupt and sinful, so will be their descendants. See Job 14:4. And as the parents are *wholly* corrupt by nature, so their children will be the same. The word *flesh* here is used as meaning *corrupt, defiled, sinful.* The flesh in the Scriptures is often used to denote the sinful propensities and passions of our nature, as those propensities are supposed to have their seat in the animal nature.

"The works of the flesh are manifest, which are these:
adultery, fornication, uncleanness, lasciviousness," &c.,
Ga 5:19,20. See also Eph 2:3; 1 Pe 3:21; 2:18; 1 Jo 2:16; Re 8:5

Is born of the Spirit. Of the Spirit of God, or by the agency of the Holy Ghost.

Is spirit. Is spiritual, like the spirit, that is, holy, pure. Here we learn,

1st. That all men are by nature sinful.

2nd. That none are renewed but by the Spirit of God. If man did the work himself, it would be still carnal and impure.

3rd. That the effect of the new birth is to make men holy. And,

4th. That no man can have evidence that he is born again who is not holy, and just in proportion as he becomes pure in his life will be the evidence that he is born of the Spirit.

{g} "That which is born of the Spirit" 1 Co 15:47-49; 2 Co 5:17

THE GOSPEL ACCORDING TO JOHN-Chapter 3-Verse 7

Verse 7. *Marvel not.* Wonder not. It is possible that Nicodemus in some way still expressed a doubt of the doctrine, and Jesus took occasion in a very striking manner to illustrate it.

{2} "born again" or, "from above"

THE GOSPEL ACCORDING TO JOHN-Chapter 3-Verse 8

Verse 8. *The wind bloweth,* &c. Nicodemus had objected to the doctrine because he did not understand how *it could be.* Jesus shows him that he ought not to reject it on that account, for he constantly believed things quite as difficult. It might appear incomprehensible, but it was to be judged of by its *effects.* As in this case of the wind, the *effects* were seen, the sound was heard, important changes were produced by it, trees and clouds were moved, yet the wind is *not seen,* nor do we know whence it comes, nor by what laws it is governed; so it is with the operations of the Spirit. We see the changes produced, Men just now sinful become holy; the thoughtless become serious; the licentious become pure; the vicious, moral; the moral, religious; the prayerless, prayerful; the rebellious and obstinate, meek, and mild, and gentle. When we see such changes, we ought no more to doubt that they are produced by some *cause*—by some mighty agent, than when we see the trees moved, or the waters of the ocean piled on heaps, or feel the cooling effects of a summer's breeze. In those cases we attribute it to the *wind*, though we see it not, and though we do not understand its operations. We may learn, hence,

1st. That the proper evidence of conversion is the *effect* on the life.

2nd. That we are not too curiously to search for the *cause* or *manner* of the change.

3rd. That God has power over the most hardened sinner to change him, as he has power over the loftiest oak, to bring it down by a sweeping blast.

4th. That there may be great *variety* in the modes of the operation of the Spirit. As the wind sometimes sweeps with a tempest, and prostrates all before it, and sometimes breathes upon us in a mild evening zephyr, so it is with the operations of the Spirit. The sinner sometimes trembles and is prostrate before the truth, and sometimes is sweetly and gently drawn to the cross of Jesus.

Where it listeth. Where it *wills* or pleases. *So is every one,* &c. Every one that is born of the Spirit is, in some respects, like the effects of the wind. You see it not, you cannot discern its laws, but you see *its effects*, and you know therefore that it does exist and operate. Nicodemus's objection was, that he could not *see* this change, or perceive *how* it could be. Jesus tells him that he should not reject a doctrine merely because he could not understand it. Neither could the *wind* be seen, but its effects were well known, and no one doubted the existence or the power of the agent. Comp. Ec 11:5.

{h} "so is every one" 1 Co 2:11

THE GOSPEL ACCORDING TO JOHN-Chapter 3-Verse 9

Verse 9. *How can these things be?* Nicodemus was still unwilling to admit the doctrine unless he understood it; and we have here an instance of a man of rank stumbling at one of the plainest doctrines of religion, and unwilling to admit a truth because he could not understand *how* it could be, when he daily admitted the truth of facts in other things which he could as little comprehend. And we may learn,

1st. That men will often admit facts on other subjects, and be greatly perplexed by similar facts in religion.

2nd. That no small part of men's difficulties are because they cannot understand *how* or *why* a thing is.

3rd. That men of rank and learning are as likely to be perplexed by these things as those in the obscurest and humblest walks of life.

4th. That this is one reason why such men, particularly, so often reject the truths of the gospel. And,

5th. That this is a very *unwise* treatment of truth, and a way which they do not apply to other things. If the wind cools and refreshes me in summer—if it prostrates the oak or lashes the sea into foam—if it destroys my house or my grain, it matters little *how* it does this; and so of the Spirit. If it renews my heart, humbles my pride, subdues my sin, and comforts my soul, it is a matter of little importance how it does all this. Sufficient for me is it to know that it is done, and to taste the blessings which flow from the renewing and sanctifying grace of God.

Verse 10. *A master of Israel.* A *teacher* of Israel; the same word that in the second verse is translated *teacher.* As such a *teacher* he ought to have understood this doctrine. It was not *new,* but was clearly taught in the Old Testament. See particularly Ps 51:10,16-17; Eze 11:19; 36:26.

It may seem surprising that a man whose business it was to teach the people should be a stranger to so plain and important a doctrine; but when worldly-minded men are placed in offices of religion—when they seek those offices for the sake of ease or reputation, it is no wonder that they are strangers to the plain truths of the Bible; and there have been many, and there are still, who are in the ministry itself, to whom the plainest doctrines of the gospel are obscure. No man can understand the Bible fully unless he is a humble Christian, and the easiest way to comprehend the truths of religion is to give the heart to God and live to his glory. A child thus may have more real knowledge of the way of salvation than many who are pretended masters and teachers of Israel, Joh 7:17; Mt 11:25; Ps 8:2

compared with Mt 21:16.

Of Israel. Of the Jews; of the Jewish nation.

Verse 11. *We speak.* Jesus here speaks in the plural number, including himself and those engaged with him in preaching the gospel. Nicodemus had said (Joh 3:2), "We know that thou art," &c., including himself and those with whom he acted. Jesus in reply said, We, who are engaged in spreading the new doctrines about which you have come to inquire, speak what we know. We do not deliver doctrines which we do not *practically* understand. This is a positive affirmation of Jesus, which he had a right to make about his new doctrine. *He* knew its truth, and those who came into his kingdom knew it also. We learn here,

1st. That the Pharisees taught doctrines which they did not practically understand. They taught much truth (Mt 23:2), but they were deplorably ignorant of the plainest matters in their practical application.

2nd. Every minister of the gospel ought to be able to appeal to his own experience, and to say that he knows the truth which he is communicating to others.

3rd. Every Sunday-school teacher should be able to say, "I *know* what I am communicating; I have experienced what is meant by the new birth, and the love of God, and the religion which I am teaching."

Testify. Bear witness to.

That we have seen. Jesus had seen by his omniscient eye all the operations of the Spirit on the hearts of men. His ministers have seen its effects as we see the effects of the wind, and, having seen men changed from sin to holiness, they are qualified to bear witness to the truth and reality of the change. Every successful minister of the gospel thus becomes a witness of the saving power of the gospel.

Ye receive not. Ye Pharisees. Though we give evidence of the truth of the new religion; though miracles are wrought, and proof is given that this doctrine came from heaven, yet you reject it.

Our witness. Our testimony. The *evidence* which is furnished by miracles and by the saving power of the gospel. Men reject revelation though it is attested by the strongest evidence, and though it is constantly producing the most desirable changes in the hearts and lives of men.

{i} "We speak that we do know" 1 Jo 1:1-8.

THE GOSPEL ACCORDING TO JOHN-Chapter 3-Verse 12

Verse 12. *If I have told you earthly things.* Things which occur on earth. Not *sensual* or *worldly* things, for Jesus had said nothing of these; but he had told him of *operations of the Spirit* which had occurred *on earth*, whose effects were visible, and which *might be*, therefore, believed. These were the *plainest* and most obvious of the doctrines of religion.

How shall ye believe. How *will* you believe. Is there any probability that you will understand them?

Heavenly things. Things pertaining to the government of God and his doings in the heavens; things which are removed from human view, and which cannot be subjected to human sight; the more profound and inscrutable things pertaining to the redemption of men. Learn hence,

1st. The height and depth of the doctrines of religion. There is much that we cannot yet understand.

2nd. The feebleness of our understandings and the corruptions of our hearts are the real causes why doctrines of religion are so little understood by us.

3rd. There is before us a vast eternity, and there are profound wonders of God's government, to be the study of the righteous, and to be seen and admired by them for ever and ever.

THE GOSPEL ACCORDING TO JOHN-Chapter 3-Verse 13

Verse 13. *And no man hath ascended into heaven.* No man, therefore, is qualified to speak of heavenly things, Joh 3:12. To speak of those things requires intimate acquaintance with them—demands that we have seen them; and as no one has ascended into heaven and returned, so no one is qualified to speak of them but He who came down from heaven. This does not mean that no one had *gone* to heaven or had been saved, for Enoch and Elijah had been borne there (Ge 5:24; comp. Heb 11:5; 2 Ki 2:11), and Abraham, Isaac, and Jacob, and others were there; but it means that no one had ascended and *returned*, so as to be qualified to speak of the things there.

But he that came down, &c. The Lord Jesus. He is represented as coming down, because, being equal with God, he took upon himself our nature, Joh 1:14; Php 2:6,7.

He is represented as *sent* by the Father, Joh 3:17,34; Ga 4:4; 1 Jo 4:9,10.

The Son of man. Called thus from his being *a man*; from his interest in man; and as expressive of his regard for man. It is a favourite title which the Lord Jesus gives to himself.

Which is in heaven. This is a very remarkable expression. Jesus, the Son of man, was then bodily on earth conversing with Nicodemus; yet he declares that he is *at the same time* in heaven. This can be understood only as referring to the fact that he had two natures—that his *divine nature* was in heaven, and his *human nature* on earth. Our Saviour is frequently spoken of in this manner. Comp. Joh 6:62; Joh 6:62; 17:5; 2 Co 8:9.

As Jesus was *in* heaven—as his proper abode was there—he was fitted to speak of heavenly things, and to declare the will of God to man. And we may learn,

1st. That the truth about the deep things of God is not to be learned of *men*. No one has ascended to heaven and returned to tell us what is there; and no infidel, no mere man, no prophet, is qualified of himself to speak of them.

2nd. That all the light which we are to expect on those subjects is to be sought in the Scriptures. It is only Jesus and his inspired apostles and evangelists that can speak of those things.

3rd. It is not wonderful that some things in the Scriptures are mysterious. They are about things which we have not seen, and we must receive them on the *testimony* of one who *has* seen them.

4th. The Lord Jesus is divine. He was in heaven while on earth. He had, therefore, a nature far above the human, and is equal with the Father, Joh 1:1.

THE GOSPEL ACCORDING TO JOHN-Chapter 3-Verse 14

Verse 14. *And as Moses.* Jesus proceeds in this and the following verses to state the reason why he came into the world; and, in order to this, he illustrates his design, and the efficacy of his coming, by a reference to the case of the brazen serpent, recorded in Nu 21:8,9. The people were bitten by flying fiery serpents. There was no cure for the bite. Moses was directed to make an *image* of the serpent, and place it in sight of the people, that they might look on it and be healed. There is no evidence that this was intended to be a *type* of the Messiah, but it is used by Jesus as strikingly *illustrating* his work. Men are sinners. There is no cure by human means for the maladies of the soul; and as the people who were bitten might look on the image of the serpent and be healed, so may sinners look to the Saviour and be cured of the moral maladies of our nature.

Lifted up. Erected on a pole. Placed on high, so that it might be seen by the people.

The serpent. The *image* of a serpent made of brass.

In the wilderness. Near the land of Edom. In the desert and desolate country to the south of Mount Hor, Nu 21:4.

Even so. In a similar manner and with a similar design. He here refers, doubtless, to his own death. Comp. Joh 12:32; 8:28. The points of resemblance between his being lifted up and that of the brazen serpent seem to be these:

1st. In each case those who are to/be benefited can be aided in no other way. The bite of the serpent was deadly, and could be healed only by looking on the brazen serpent; and sin is deadly in its nature, and can be removed only by looking on the cross.

2nd. The mode of their being lifted up. The brazen serpent was in the sight of the people, So Jesus was exalted from the earth—raised on a tree or cross.

3rd. The design was similar. The one was to save the life, the other the soul; the one to save from temporal, the other from eternal death.

4th. The manner of the cure was similar. The people of Israel were to look on the serpent and be healed, and so sinners are to look on the Lord Jesus that they may be saved.

Must. It is proper; necessary; indispensable, if men are saved. Comp. Lu 24:26; 22:42.

The Son of man. The Messiah.

{l} "as Moses" Nu 21:9

THE GOSPEL ACCORDING TO JOHN-Chapter 3-Verse 15

Verse 15. *That whosoever.* This shows the fulness and freeness of the gospel. All may come and be saved.

Believeth in him. Whosoever puts *confidence* in him as able and willing to save. All who feel that they are sinners, that they have no righteousness of their own, and are willing to look to him as their only Saviour.

Should not perish. They are in danger, by nature, of perishing—that is, of sinking down to the pains of hell; of "being *punished with everlasting destruction* from the presence of the Lord and from the glory of his power," 2 Th 1:9. All who believe on Jesus shall be saved from this condemnation and be raised up to eternal life. And from this we learn,

1st. That there is salvation in no other.

2nd. That salvation is here full and free for all who will come.

3rd. That it is easy. What was more easy for a poor, wounded, dying Israelite, bitten by a poisonous serpent, than to *look up* to a brazen serpent? So with the poor, lost, dying sinner. And what more foolish than for such a wounded, dying man to *refuse* to look on a remedy so easy and effectual? So nothing is more foolish than for a lost and dying sinner to refuse to look on God's only Son, exalted on a cross to die for the sins of men, and able to save to the uttermost all who come to God by him.

{m} "That whosoever" Joh 3:36; Heb 7:25

THE GOSPEL ACCORDING TO JOHN-Chapter 3-Verse 16

Verse 16. *For God so loved.* This does not mean that God *approved* the conduct of men, but that he had *benevolent* feelings toward them, or was *earnestly desirous* of their happiness. God hates wickedness, but he still desires the happiness of those who are sinful. *He hates the sin, but loves the sinner.* A parent may love his child and desire his welfare, and yet be strongly opposed to the conduct of that child. When we approve the *conduct* of another, this is the love of *complacency*; when we desire simply their *happiness*, this is the love of *benevolence*.

The world. All mankind. It does not mean any particular *part* of the world, but *man as man*—the race that had rebelled and that deserved to die. See Joh 6:33; 17:21. His love for the world, or for all mankind, in giving his Son, was shown by these circumstances:

1st. All the world was in ruin, and exposed to the wrath of God.

2nd. All men were in a hopeless condition.

3rd. God *gave* his Son. Man had no *claim* on him; it was a gift—an undeserved gift.

4th. He gave him up to extreme sufferings, even the bitter pains of death on the cross.

5th. It was for all the world. He tasted "death for every man," He 2:9. He "died for all," 2 Co 5:15. "He is the propitiation for the sins of the whole world," 1 Jo 2:2.

That he gave. It was a free and unmerited gift. Man had no claim; and when there was no eye to pity or arm to save, it pleased God to give his Son into the hands of men to die in their stead, Ga 1:4; Ro 8:32; Lu 22:19. It was the mere movement of love; the expression of eternal compassion, and of a desire that sinners should not perish forever.

His only-begotten Son. See Barnes "Joh 1:14".

This is the highest expression of love of which we can conceive. A parent who should give up his only son to die for others who are guilty—if this could or might be done—would show higher love than could be manifested in any other way. So it shows the depth of the love of God, that he was willing to give his only Son into the hands of sinful men that he might be slain, and thus redeem them from eternal sorrow.

{n} "For God" 1 Jo 4:9

THE GOSPEL ACCORDING TO JOHN-Chapter 3-Verse 17

Verse 17. *To condemn the world.* Not to *judge*, or pronounce sentence on mankind. God *might* justly have sent him for this. Man deserved condemnation, and it would have been right to have pronounced it; but God was willing that there should be an offer of pardon, and the sentence of condemnation was delayed. But, although Jesus did not come *then* to condemn mankind, yet the time is coming when he will return to judge the living and the dead, Ac 17:31; 2 Co 5:10; Mt 25:31-46.

{o} "For God" Lu 9:56

THE GOSPEL ACCORDING TO JOHN-Chapter 3-Verse 18

Verse 18. *He that believeth.* He that has confidence in him; that relies on him; that trusts to his merits and promises for salvation. To believe on him is to *feel* and *act* according to truth—that is, to go as lost sinners, and act toward him as a Saviour from sins; relying on him, and looking to him *only* for salvation. See Barnes "Mr 16:16".

Is not condemned. God pardons sin, and delivers us from deserved punishment, *because* we believe on him. Jesus died in our stead; he suffered for us, and by his sufferings our sins are expiated, and it is consistent for God to forgive. When a sinner, therefore, believes on Jesus, he trusts in him as having died in his place, and God having accepted the offering which Christ made in our stead, as being an equivalent for *our* sufferings in hell, there is now no farther condemnation, Ro 8:1.

He that believeth not. All who do not believe, whether the gospel has come to them or not. All men by nature.

Is condemned already. By conscience, by law, and in the judgment of God. God disapproves of their character, and this feeling of disapprobation, and the expression of it, is the condemnation. There is no condemnation so terrible as this—that *God disapproves* our conduct, and that he will *express* his disapprobation. He will judge according to truth, and woe to that man whose conduct God *cannot* approve.

Because. This word does not imply that the *ground* or *reason* of their condemnation is that they have not believed, or that they are condemned *because* they do not believe on him, for there are millions of sinners who have never heard of him; but the meaning is this: There is but *one* way by which men can be freed from condemnation. All men without the gospel are condemned. They who do not believe are still under this condemnation, not having embraced the *only way* by which they can be delivered from it. The verse may be thus paraphrased:

"All men are by nature condemned. There is but one way of
being delivered from this state—by believing on the Son
of God. They who do not believe or remain in that state
are still condemned, FOR they have not embraced the only
way in which they can be freed from it."

Nevertheless, those to whom the gospel comes greatly heighten their guilt and condemnation by rejecting the offers of mercy, and trampling under foot the blood of the Son of God,Lu 12:47; Mt 11:23; Heb 10:29

Pr 1:24-30. And there are thousands going to eternity under this double condemnation—

1st. For positive, open sin; and,

2nd. For rejecting God's mercy, and despising the gospel of his Son. This it is which will make the doom of sinners in Christian lands so terrible.

{p} "He that believeth" Joh 6:40,47

THE GOSPEL ACCORDING TO JOHN-Chapter 3-Verse 19

Verse 19. *This is the condemnation.* This is the *cause* of condemnation; or this is the reason why men are punished.

That light is come. Light often denotes instruction, teaching, doctrine, as that by which we see clearly the path of duty. *All* the instruction that God gives us by conscience, reason, or

lxvi

revelation may thus be called light; but this word is used peculiarly to denote the Messiah or the Christ, who is often spoken of as the *light*. See Isa 60:1; 9:2. Compare Mt 4:16; also See Barnes "Joh 1:4".

It was doubtless this light to which Jesus had particular reference here.

Men loved darkness. Darkness is the emblem of ignorance, iniquity, error, superstition—whatever is opposite to truth and piety. Men are said to love darkness more than they do light when they are better pleased with error than truth, with sin than holiness, with Belial than Christ.

Because their deeds are evil. Men who commit crime commonly choose to do it in the night, so as to escape detection. So men who are wicked prefer false doctrine and error to the truth. Thus the Pharisees cloaked their crimes under the errors of their system; and, amid their false doctrines and superstitions, they attempted to convince others that they had great zeal for God.

Deeds. Works; actions.

{q} "light is come into the world" Joh 1:4,9-11

THE GOSPEL ACCORDING TO JOHN-Chapter 3-Verse 20

Verse 20. *That doeth evil.* Every wicked man.

Hateth the light. This is true of all wicked men. They choose to practise their deeds of wickedness in darkness. They are afraid of the light, because they could be easily detected. Hence most crimes are committed in the night. So with the sinner against God. He hates the gospel, for it condemns his conduct, and his conscience would trouble him if it were enlightened.

His deeds should be reproved. To *reprove* here means not only to *detect* or make manifest, but also includes the idea of condemnation when his deeds are detected. The gospel would make his wickedness manifest, and his conscience would condemn him. We learn from this verse,

1st. That one design of the gospel is *to reprove men.* It convicts them of sin in order that it may afford consolation.

2nd. That men by nature *hate* the gospel. No man who is a sinner loves it; and no man by nature is disposed to come to it, any more than an adulterer or thief is disposed to come to the daylight, and do his deeds of wickedness there.

3rd. The reason why the gospel is hated is that men are sinners. "Christ is hated because sin is loved."

4th. The sinner must be convicted or convinced of sin. If it be not in this world, it will be in the next. There is no escape for him; and the only way to avoid condemnation in the world to come is to come humbly and acknowledge sin here, and seek for pardon.

{r} "neither cometh to the light" Job 24:23,17; Pr 4:18,19

{3} "reproved" or, "discovered"

THE GOSPEL ACCORDING TO JOHN-Chapter 3-Verse 21

Verse 21. *He that doeth truth.* He who does right, or he that *obeys* the truth. *Truth* here is opposed to error and to evil. The sinner acts from falsehood and error. The good man acts according to truth. The sinner believes a lie that God will not punish, or that there is no God, or that there is no eternity and no hell. The Christian believes all these, and acts as if they were true. This is the difference between a Christian and a sinner.

Cometh to the light. Loves the truth, and seeks it more and more. By prayer and searching the Scriptures he endeavours to as certain the truth, and yield his mind to it.

May be made manifest. May be made clear or plain; or that it may be made plain that his deeds are wrought in God. He searches for truth and light that he may have evidence that his actions are right.

Wrought in God. That they are performed according to the will of God, or perhaps by the assistance of God, and are such as God will approve. The actions of good men are performed by the influence and aid of God, Php 2:12. Of course, if they are performed by his aid, they are such as he will approve. Here is presented the character of a good man and a sincere Christian. We learn respecting that character,

1st. He does truth. He loves it, seeks it, follows it.

2nd. He comes to the light. He does not attempt to deceive himself or others.

3rd. He is willing to know himself, and aims to do it. He desires to know the true state of his heart before God.

4th. An especial object of his efforts is that his deeds may be wrought in God. He desires to be a good man; to receive continual aid from God, and to perform such actions as he will approve. This is the close of our Lord's discourse with Nicodemus—a discourse condensing the gospel, giving the most striking exhibition and illustration of truth, and representing especially the fundamental doctrine of regeneration and the evidence of the change. It is clear that the Saviour regarded this as lying at the foundation of religion. Without it we cannot possibly be saved. And now it becomes every reader, as in the presence of God, and in view of the judgment-seat of Christ, solemnly to ask himself whether he has experienced this change? whether he knows by experience what it is to be born of that Spirit? If he does he will be saved. If not, he is in the gall of bitterness and in the bond of iniquity, and should give no sleep to his eyes till he has made his peace with God.

{s} "doeth truth" 1 Jo 1:6 {t} "they are wrought" 3 Jo 1:11

THE GOSPEL ACCORDING TO JOHN-Chapter 3-Verse 22

Verse 22. *Land of Judea.* The region round about Jerusalem.

And baptized. Jesus did not himself administer the ordinance of baptism, but his disciples did it by his direction and authority, Joh 4:2.

{u} "and baptized" Joh 4:2

THE GOSPEL ACCORDING TO JOHN-Chapter 3-Verse 23

Verse 23. *In Enon.* The word *Enon,* or *AEnon,* means a *fountain,* and was doubtless given to this place because of the fountains there. On the situation of the place nothing certain has been determined. Eusebius places it 8 Roman miles south of Scythopolis or Bethshen, and 53 northeast of Jerusalem.

Near to Salim. It would seem from this that Salim was better known then than Enon, but nothing can be determined now respecting its site. These places are believed to have been on the west side of the Jordan.

Because there was much water there. John's preaching attracted great multitudes. It appears that they remained with him probably many days. In many parts of that country, particularly in the hilly region near where John preached, it was difficult to find water to accommodate the necessities of the people, and perhaps, also, of the camels with which those from a distance would come. To meet their necessities, as well as for the purpose of baptizing, he selected a spot that was well watered, probably, with springs and rivulets. Whether the ordinance of baptism was performed by immersion or in any other mode, the selection of a place well watered was proper and necessary. The mention of the fact that there was much water there, and that John selected that as a convenient place to perform his office as a baptizer, proves nothing in regard to the *mode* in which the ordinance was administered, since he would naturally select such a place, whatever was the mode. Where numbers of people came together to remain any time, it is necessary to select such a place, whatever their employment. An encampment of soldiers is made on the same principles, and in every camp-meeting that I have ever seen, a place is selected where there is a good supply of water, though not one person should be *immersed* during the whole services. As all the facts in the case are fully met by the supposition that John might have baptized in some other way besides immersion, and as it is easy to conceive *another* reason that is sufficient to account for the fact that such a place was selected, *this* passage certainly should not be adduced to prove that he performed baptism only in that manner.

{v} "Salim" 1 Sa 9:4 {w} "and they came there" Mt 3:5,6

THE GOSPEL ACCORDING TO JOHN-Chapter 3-Verse 24

Verse 24. *For John was not yet cast into prison.* See Lu 3:20. The mention of this shows that John was not imprisoned till some time after our Lord entered on his ministry. The design of John was to call men to repentance, and to prepare them for the Messiah, and this he continued to do after our Saviour commenced *his* work. It shows that a minister of religion should be industrious to the day of his death. John still toiled in his work not the *less* because the Messiah had come. So ministers should not labour less when Christ appears by his Spirit, and takes the work into his own hands, and turns many to himself.

{x} "For John was" Mt 14:3

THE GOSPEL ACCORDING TO JOHN-Chapter 3-Verse 25

Verse 25. *A question.* Rather a controversy —a dispute.

John's disciples. Those who had been baptized by him, and who attached great efficacy and importance to the teaching of their master. Comp. See Barnes "Ac 19:1, also Ac 19:2-5.

And the Jews. Many manuscripts, some of the fathers, and the ancient Syriac version, read this in the singular number— "with a *Jew*," one who, it is commonly supposed, had been baptized by the disciples of Jesus.

About purifying. What the precise subject of this dispute was we do not know. From what follows, it would seem probable that it was about the comparative value and efficacy of the baptism performed by John and by the disciples of Jesus. The word *purifying* may be applied to baptism, as it was an emblem of repentance and purity, and was thus used by the Jews, by John, and by Jesus. About this subject it seems that a dispute arose, and was carried to such a length that complaint was made to John. From this we may learn,

1st. That even in the time of Jesus, when the gospel began to be preached, there was witnessed—what has been ever since —unhappy disputings on the subject of religion. Even young converts may, by overheated zeal and ignorance, fall into angry discussion.

2nd. That such discussions are commonly about some unimportant matter of religion— something which they may not yet be qualified to understand, and which does not materially affect them if they could.

3rd. That such disputes are often connected with a spirit of proselytism— with boasting of the superior excellence of the sect with which *we* are connected, or in connection with whom *we* have been converted, and often with a desire to persuade others to join with us.

4th. That such a spirit is eminently improper on such occasions. Love should characterize the feelings of young converts; a disposition to *inquire* and not to *dispute*; a willingness that all should follow the dictates of their own consciences, and not a desire to *proselyte* them to *our* way of thinking or to our church. It may be added that there is scarcely anything which so certainly and effectually arrests a revival of religion as such a disposition to *dispute*, and to make proselytes to particular modes of faith, and of administering the ordinances of the gospel.

THE GOSPEL ACCORDING TO JOHN-Chapter 3-Verse 26

Verse 26. *Came unto John.* Came to him with their complaint; envious and jealous at the success of Jesus, and evidently irritated from the discussion, as if their master was about to lose his popularity.

Rabbi. Master. See Barnes "Mt 23:7".

Acknowledging him as their master and teacher.

That was with thee. Who was baptized by thee.

Thou barest witness. See Joh 1:29-35.

All men come to him. This was the source of their difficulty. It was that Jesus was gaining popularity; that the people flocked to him; that they feared that John would be forsaken, and his followers be diminished in numbers and influence. Thus many love their sect more than they do Christ, and would be more rejoiced that a man became a Presbyterian, a Methodist, a Baptist, than that he became a sincere and humble Christian. This is not the spirit of the gospel. True piety teaches us to rejoice that sinners turn to Christ and become holy, whether they follow us or not. See Mr 9:38,39. Let Jesus be exalted, and let men turn to him, is the language of religion, whatever denomination they may feel it their duty to follow.

{y} "to whom thou barest witness" Joh 1:7,15 {z} "all *men* come to him" Ps 65:2; Isa 45:23

THE GOSPEL ACCORDING TO JOHN-Chapter 3-Verse 27

Verse 27. *John answered*, &c. John did not enter into their feelings or sympathize with their love of party. He came to honour Jesus, not to build up a sect. He rejoiced at the success of the Messiah, and began to teach them to rejoice in it also.

A man can receive nothing, &c. All success is from heaven. All my success was from God. All the success of Jesus is from God. As success comes from the same source, we ought not to be envious. It is designed to answer the same end, and, by whomsoever accomplished, the hand of God is in it, and we should rejoice. If Jesus and his disciples are successful, if all men flee to him, it is proof that God favours him, and you should rejoice.

{a} "A man" 1 Co 2:12-14; 4:7; Heb 5:4; Jas 1:17

{4} "receive nothing" or, "take unto himself"

THE GOSPEL ACCORDING TO JOHN-Chapter 3-Verse 28

Verse 28. *Bear me witness.* You remember that at first I told you I was not the Messiah. As he had been *witness* to Jesus—as he came for no other end but to point him out to the Jews, they ought not to suppose that he was his superior. It was but reasonable to expect that Christ himself would be more successful than his forerunner. "I came, not to form a *separate party*, a peculiar sect, but to prepare the way that *he* might be more successful, and that the people might be ready for his coming, and that he might have the success which he has actually met with. You should rejoice, therefore, at that success, and not enter it, for *his success* is the best proof of the greatness of *my* word, and of *its success* also."

{b} "I am not the Christ" Joh 1:20,27 {c} "I am sent before him" Lu 1:17

THE GOSPEL ACCORDING TO JOHN-Chapter 3-Verse 29

Verse 29. *He that hath the bride*, &c. This is an illustration drawn from marriage. The bride belongs to her husband. So the church, the bride of the Messiah, belongs to him. It *is to be expected*, therefore, and *desired*, that the people should flock to him.

But the friend of the bridegroom. He whose office it is to attend him on the marriage occasion. This was commonly the nearest friend, and was a high honour.

Rejoiceth greatly. Esteems himself highly honoured by the proof of friendship.

The bridegroom's voice. His commands, requests, or conversation.

This is my joy, &c.

"I sustain to the Messiah the relation which a

groomsman does to the groom. The chief honour and the chief joy is not mine, but his. It is to be expected, therefore, that the people will come to him, and that his success will be great."

The relation of Christ to the church is often compared with the marriage relation, denoting the tenderness of the union, and his great love for his people. Comp. Isa 62:5; Re 21:2,9;22:17; Eph 5:26,27,32

2 Co 11:2.

{d} "bride" So 4:8-12; Jer 2:2; Eze 16:8; Hos 2:19,20; Mt 22:2

2 Co 11:2; Eph 5:25,27; Re 21:9

{e} "friend of the bridegroom" Joh 6:33; 8:23; Eph 1:20,21

Verse 30. *He must increase.* His authority and influence among the people must grow. *His doctrine shall continue to spread till it extends through all the earth.*

I must decrease.

"The purpose of my ministry is to point men to him. When that is done my work is done. I came not to form a party of my own, nor to set up a religion of my own; and my teaching must cease when he is fully established, as the light of the morning star fades away and is lost in the beams of the rising sun."

This evinced John's humility and willingness to be esteemed as nothing if he could honour Christ. It shows us, also, that it is sufficient honour for man if he may be permitted to point sinners to the Lord Jesus Christ. No work is so honourable and joyful as the ministry of the gospel; none are so highly honoured as those who are permitted to stand near the Son of God, to hear his voice, and to lead perishing men to his cross. Comp. Da 12:3.

Verse 31. *He that cometh from above.* The Messiah, represented as coming down from heaven. See Joh 3:13; 6:33; 8:23.

It has been doubted whether the remainder of this chapter contains the words of *John the Baptist* or of the *evangelist.* The former is the more probable opinion, but it is difficult to decide it, and it is of very little consequence.

Is above all. In nature, rank, and authority. *Is superior to all prophets* (Heb 1:1,2); *to all angels* (Heb 1:4-14), *and is over all the universe as its sovereign Lord,* Re 9:5; Eph 1:21,22;Col 1:15-19; 1 Co 15:25.

He that is of the earth. He who has no higher nature than the human nature. The prophets, apostles, and John were men like others, born in the same way, and sinking, like others, to the dust. See Ac 14:15. Jesus had a nature superior to man, and ought, therefore, to be exalted above all.

Is earthly. Is human. Is *inferior* to him who comes from heaven. Partakes of his *origin,* which is inferior and corrupt.

Speaketh of the earth. His teaching is inferior to that of him who comes from heaven. It is comparatively obscure and imperfect, not full and clear, like the teaching of him who is from above. This was the case with all the prophets, and even with John the Baptist, as compared with the teaching of Christ.

Verse 32. *And what he hath seen,* &c. See Joh 3:11.

No man receiveth his testimony. The words *no man* are here to be under stood in the sense of *few*. Though his doctrine is pure, plain, sublime, yet few, comparatively, received it in faith. Though multitudes came to him, drawn by various motives (Joh 6:26), yet few became his real disciples, Mt 26:56; 7:22.

His testimony. His doctrine. The truth to which he bears *witness* as having seen and known it, Joh 3:11. Often many persons *appear* for a time to become the followers of Christ, who in the end are seen to have known nothing of religion, Mt 13:6; Lu 8:13.

{h} "no man" Joh 1:11

Verse 33. *He that hath received his testimony.* Hath received and fully believed his doctrine. Hath yielded his heart to its influence.

Hath set to his seal. To seal an instrument is to make it sure; to acknowledge it as ours; to pledge our veracity that it is true and binding, as when a man seals a bond, a deed, or a will. Believing a doctrine, therefore, in the heart, is expressed by *sealing* it, or by believing it we express our firm conviction that it is true, and that God who has spoken it is true. We vouch for the veracity of God, and assume as our own the proposition that it is the truth of God.

God is true. Is faithful; is the author of the system of doctrines, and will fulfil all that he has promised. We learn here,

1st. That to be a true believer is something more than to hold a mere speculative belief of the truth.

2nd. That to be a believer is to *pledge ourselves* for the truth, to seal it as our own, to adopt it, to choose it, and solemnly assent to it, as a man does in regard to an instrument of writing that is to convey his property, or that is to dispose of it when he dies.

3rd. Every Christian is a witness for God, and it is his business to show by his life that he believes that God is true to his threatenings and to his promises. Barnes "Is 43:10".

4th. It is a solemn act to become a Christian. It is a surrender of all to God, or giving away body, soul, and spirit to him, with a belief that he is *true*, and alone is able to save.

5th. The man that does not do this— that is not willing to pledge his belief that God is true, sets to *his* seal that God is a liar and unworthy of confidence, 1 Jo 5:10.

{i} "set to his seal" 1 Jo 5:10

Verse 34. *Whom God hath sent*. The Messiah.

Speaketh the words of God. The truth, or commands of God.

For God giveth not the Spirit. The Spirit of God. Though Jesus was God as well as man, yet, as *Mediator*, God anointed him, or endowed him with the influences of his Spirit, so as to be completely qualified for his great work.

By measure. Not in a small degree, but fully, completely. The prophets were inspired on particular occasions to deliver special messages. The Messiah was continually filled with the Spirit of God. "The Spirit dwelt in him, not as a vessel, but as in a fountain, as in a bottomless ocean" (Henry).

{k} "For he whom God" Joh 7:16 {l} "Fro God giveth" Ps 45:7; Isa 11:2; 59:21; 1:16; Col 1:19

Verse 35. *Loveth the Son*. Loves him eminently, above all the prophets and all the other messengers of God.

Hath given all things into his hand. See Barnes "Mt 28:18".

{m} "The Father" Mt 28:18

Verse 36. *Hath everlasting life*. Has or is in possession of that which is a recovery from spiritual death, and which will result in eternal life in heaven. Piety here is the same that it will be there, except that it will be expanded, matured, purified, made more glorious. It is here life begun—the first breathings and pantings of the soul for immortality; yet it is life, though at first feeble and faint, which is eternal in its nature, and which shall be matured in the full and perfect bliss of heaven. The Christian here has a foretaste of the world of glory, and enjoys the same *kind* of felicity, though not the same *degree*, that he will there.

Shall not see life. Shall neither enjoy true *life* or happiness here nor in the world to come. Shall never enter heaven.

The wrath of God. The anger of God for sin. His opposition to sin, and its terrible effects in this world and the next.

Abideth on him. This implies that he is now under the wrath of God, or under condemnation. It implies, also, that it will *continue* to remain on him. It will *abide* or *dwell* there as its appropriate habitation. As there is no way of escaping the wrath of God but by the Lord Jesus Christ, so those who will not believe must go to eternity *as they are*, and bear alone and unpitied all that God may choose to inflict as the expression of *his* sense of sin. Such is the miserable condition of the sinner! Yet thousands choose to remain in this state, and to encounter *alone* all that is terrible in the wrath of Almighty God, rather than come to Jesus, who has borne their sins in his own body on the tree, and who is willing to bless them with the peace, and purity, and joy of immortal life.

{n} "He that believeth" Heb 2:4; Joh 3:15,16

{o} "wrath of God" Ro 1:18

THE GOSPEL ACCORDING TO JOHN-Chapter 4

Verse 1. *The Lord knew.* When Jesus knew. *How* he knew this we are not informed; whether by that power of omniscience by which he knew all things, or whether some person had informed him of it.

How the Pharisees had heard. The *Pharisees,* here, seem to denote either the members of the Sanhedrim or those who were in authority. They claimed the authority to regulate the rites and ceremonies of religion, and hence they supposed they had a right to inquire into the conduct of both John and our Lord. They had on a former occasion sent to inquire of John to know by what authority he had introduced such a rite into the religion of the Jewish people. See Barnes "Joh 1:25".

More disciples than John. Though many of the Pharisees came to his baptism-(Matthew Chapter 3.), yet those who were in authority were displeased with the success of John, Joh 1:25. The reasons of this were, probably, the severity and justness of his reproofs Mt 3:7, and the fact that by drawing many after him he weakened their authority and influence. As they were displeased with *John,* so they were with *Jesus,* who was doing the same thing on a larger scale— not only making disciples, but *baptizing* also without their authority, and drawing away the people after him.

{a} "baptized" Joh 3:22,26

Verse 2. *Though Jesus himself baptized not.* The reason why Jesus did not baptize was probably because, if he had baptized, it might have made unhappy divisions among his followers: those might have considered themselves most worthy or honoured who had been baptized by *him.* Comp. 1 Co 1:17.

Verse 3. *He left Judea.* The envy and malice of the Pharisees he might have known were growing so rapidly as to endanger his life. As his time to die had not yet come, he retired to Galilee, a country farther from Jerusalem, and much less under their control than Judea. See Mr 2:22; Lu 3:1. Though he feared not death and did not shrink from suffering, yet he did not *needlessly* throw himself into danger or provoke opposition. He could do as much *good* in Galilee, probably, as in Judea, and he therefore withdrew himself from immediate danger.

Verse 4. *And he must needs go through Samaria.* Samaria was between Judea and Galilee. The direct and usual way was to pass through Samaria. Sometimes, however, the Jews took a circuitous route on the east side of the Jordan, See Barnes "Mt 2:22".

{b} "must needs go" Lu 2:49

Verse 5. *Sychar.* This city stood about eight miles south-east of the city called Samaria, between Mount Ebal and Mount Gerizim. It was one of the oldest cities of Palestine, and was formerly known by the name of *Shechem*, or Sichem, Ge 33:18; 12:6. The city was in the tribe of Ephraim, Jos 21:21. It was at this place that Joshua assembled the people before his death, and here they renewed their covenant with the Lord, Joshua chapter 24. After the death of Gideon it became a place of idolatrous worship, the people worshipping *Baal-berith*, Jud 9:46. It was destroyed by Abimelech, who beat down the city and sowed it with salt, Jud 9:45. It was afterward rebuilt, and became the residence of Jeroboam, the King of Israel, 1 Ki 12:25. It was called by the Romans *Flavia Neapolis*, and this has been corrupted by the Arabs into *Nablus*, its present name. It is still a considerable place, and its site is remarkably pleasant and productive.

The parcel of ground. The *piece* of ground; or the land, &c.

That Jacob gave, &c. Jacob bought one piece of ground near to Shalem, a city of Shechem, of the children of Hamor, the father of Shechem, for an hundred pieces of silver, Ge 33:19. In this place the bones of Joseph were buried when they were brought up from Egypt, Jos 24:32. He also gave to Joseph an additional piece of ground which he took from the hand of the Amorite by his own valour, "with his sword and his bow," as a portion above that which was given to his brethren, Ge 48:22. Possibly these pieces of ground lay near together, and were a part of the *homestead* of Jacob. The well was "near" to this. There is now, the Rev. E. Smith mentioned to me in conversation, a place near this well called *Shalem*.

{c} "gave to his son Joseph" Ge 38:19; 48:22; Jos 24:32

Verse 6. *Jacob's well.* This is not mentioned in the Old Testament. It was called *Jacob's well*, probably, either because it was handed down by tradition that he dug it, or because it was near to the land which he gave to Joseph. There is still a well a few miles to the east of Nablus, which is said by the people there to be the same. The Rev. Eli Smith, missionary to Syria, stated to me that he had visited this well. It is about 100 feet deep. It is cut through solid rock of limestone. It is now dry, probably from having been partly filled with rubbish, or perhaps because the water has been diverted by earthquakes. The well is covered with a large stone, which has a hole in the centre large enough to admit a man. It is at the foot of Mount Gerizim, and has a plain on the east.

Sat thus. Jesus was weary, and, being thus weary, sat down on the well. The word translated *on* here may denote also *by*—he sat down by the well, or near it.

The sixth hour. About twelve o'clock. This was the common time of the Jewish meal, and this was the reason why his disciples were gone away to buy food.

THE GOSPEL ACCORDING TO JOHN-Chapter 4-Verse 7

Verse 7. *Of Samaria*. Not of the city of Samaria, for this was at a distance of 8 miles, but a woman who was a Samaritan, and doubtless from the city of Sychar.

Give me to drink. This was in the heat of the day, and when Jesus was weary with his journey. The request was also made that it might give him occasion to discourse with her on the subject of religion, and in this instance we have a specimen of the remarkably happy manner in which he could lead on a conversation so as to introduce the subject of religion.

THE GOSPEL ACCORDING TO JOHN-Chapter 4-Verse 8

Verse 8. *Buy meat*. Buy food.

THE GOSPEL ACCORDING TO JOHN-Chapter 4-Verse 9

Verse 9. *No dealings with the Samaritans*. For an account of the Samaritans, and of the differences between them and the Jews, See Barnes "Mt 10:5".

{d} "for the Jews" Ac 10:28

THE GOSPEL ACCORDING TO JOHN-Chapter 4-Verse 10

Verse 10. *The gift of God*. The word *gift*, here denotes *favour*. It may refer to Jesus *himself*, as the *gift* of God to the world, given to save men from death Joh 3:16; 2 Co 9:15 or it may refer to the opportunity then afforded her of seeking salvation. If thou knewest how favourable an opportunity God now gives thee to gain a knowledge of himself, &c. *And who it is*, &c. If thou knewest that the Messiah was speaking.

Living water. The Jews used the expression *living water* to denote springs, fountains, or running streams, in opposition to dead and stagnant water. Jesus here means to denote by it his doctrine, or his grace and religion, in opposition to the impure and dead notions of the Jews and the Samaritans. Joh 4:14. This was one of the many instances in which he took occasion from common topics of conversation to introduce religious discourse. None ever did it so happily as he did, but, by studying his example and manner, we may learn also to do it. One way to acquire the art is to have the mind full of the subject; to make religion our first and main thing; to carry it with us into all employments and into all society; to look upon everything in a religious light, and out of the abundance of the heart the mouth will speak, Mt 12:34.

{e} "the gift of God" Eph 2:8 {f} "living water" Isa 12:3; 41:17,18; Jer 2:13; Zec 13:1; 14:8; Re 22:17

THE GOSPEL ACCORDING TO JOHN-Chapter 4-Verse 11

Verse 11. *Hast nothing to draw with*. It seems that there were no means of drawing water *affixed* to the well, as with us. Probably each one took a pail or pitcher and a cord for the purpose. In travelling this was indispensable. The woman, seeing that Jesus had no means of drawing water, and not yet understanding his design, naturally inquired whence he could obtain the water.

The well is deep. If the same one that is there now, it was about 100 feet deep.

THE GOSPEL ACCORDING TO JOHN-Chapter 4-Verse 12

Verse 12. *Art thou greater?* Art thou wiser, or better able to find water, than Jacob was? It seems that she supposed that he meant that he could direct her to some living spring, or to some better well in that region, and that this implied more knowledge or skill than Jacob had. To find water and to furnish a good well was doubtless considered a matter of signal skill and success. It was a subject of great importance in that region. This shows how ready sinners are to misunderstand the words of Christ, and to pervert the doctrines of religion. If she had had any proper anxiety about her soul, she would at least have *suspected* that he meant to direct her thoughts to spiritual objects.

Our father Jacob. The Samaritans were composed partly of the remnant of the ten tribes, and partly of people sent from Chaldea; still, they considered themselves descendants of Jacob.

Which gave us. This was doubtless the tradition, though there is no evidence that it was true.

And drank thereof, &c. This was added in commendation of the water of the well. A well from which Jacob, and his sons, and cattle had drank must be pure, and wholesome, and honoured, and quite as valuable as any that Jesus could furnish. Men like to commend that which their ancestors used as superior to anything else. The world over, people love to speak of that which their ancestors have done, and boast of titles and honours that have been handed down from them, even if it is nothing better than existed here—because Jacob's cattle had drunk of the water.

THE GOSPEL ACCORDING TO JOHN-Chapter 4-Verse 13

Verse 13. *Shall thirst again*. Jesus did not directly answer her question, or say that he was *greater* than Jacob, but he gave her an answer by which she might infer that he was. He did not despise or undervalue Jacob or his gifts; but, however great might be the value of that well, the water could not altogether remove thirst.

THE GOSPEL ACCORDING TO JOHN-Chapter 4-Verse 14

Verse 14. *The water that I shall give him*. Jesus here refers, without doubt, to his own teaching, his grace, his spirit, and to the benefits which come into the soul that embraces his gospel. It is a striking image, and especially in Eastern countries, where there are vast deserts, and often a great want of water. The soul by nature is like such a desert, or like a traveller wandering through such a desert. It is thirsting for happiness, and seeking it everywhere, and finds it not. It looks in all directions and tries all objects, but in vain. Nothing meets its desires. Though a sinner seeks for joy in wealth and pleasures, yet he is not satisfied. He still thirsts for more, and seeks still for happiness in some new enjoyment. To such a weary and unsatisfied sinner the grace of Christ is *as cold waters to a thirsty soul*.

Shall never thirst. He shall be *satisfied* with this, and will not have a sense of want, a distressing feeling that it is not adapted to him. He who drinks this will not wish to seek for happiness in other objects. *Satisfied* with the grace of Christ, he will not desire the pleasures and amusements of this world. And this will be for ever—in this world and the world to come. *Whosoever* drinketh of this—all who partake of the gospel—shall be *for ever* satisfied with its pure and rich joys.

Shall be in him. The grace of Christ shall be in his heart; or the principles of religion shall abide with him.

A well of water. There shall be a constant supply, an unfailing fountain; or religion shall *live* constantly with him.

Springing up. This is a beautiful image. It shall bubble or spring up like a fountain. It is not like a stagnant pool—not like a deep well, but like an ever-living fountain, that flows at all seasons of the year, in heat and cold, and in all external circumstances of weather, whether foul or fair, wet or dry. So religion always lives; and, amid all changes of external circumstances—in heat and cold, hunger and thirst, prosperity and adversity, life, persecution, contempt, or death—it still lives on, and refreshes and cheers the soul.

Into everlasting life. It is not temporary, like the supply of our natural wants; it is not changing in its nature; it is not like a natural fountain or spring of water, to play a while and then die away, as all natural springs will at the end of the world. It is eternal in its nature and supply, and will continue to live on for ever. We may learn here—

1st. That the Christian has a never-failing source of consolation adapted to all times and circumstances.

2nd. That religion has its seat in the heart, and that it should constantly *live* there.

3rd. That it sheds its blessings on a world of sin, and is manifest by a continual *life* of piety, like a constant flowing spring.

4th. That its end is everlasting life. It will continue for ever; and *whosoever drinks of this shall never thirst*, but his piety shall be in his heart a pure fountain *springing up to eternal joy*.

{g} "whosoever drinketh" Joh 6:35,58 {h} "I shall give him" Joh 17:2,3; Ro 6:23

{i} "in him a well" Joh 7:38

THE GOSPEL ACCORDING TO JOHN-Chapter 4-Verse 15

Verse 15. *The woman said*, &c. It may seem strange that the woman did not yet understand him, but it shows how slow sinners are to understand the doctrines of religion.

Verse 16. *Go call thy husband.* We may admire the manner which our Saviour took to lead her to perceive that he was the Christ. His instructions she did not understand. He therefore proceeded to show her that he was acquainted with her life and with her sins. His object, here, was to lead her to consider her own state and sinfulness—a delicate and yet pungent way of making her see that she was a sinner. By showing her, also, that he knew her life, though a stranger to her, he convinced her that he was qualified to teach her the way to heaven, and thus prepared her to admit that he was the Messiah, Joh 4:29.

Verse 17. *I have no husband.* This was said, evidently, to evade the subject. Perhaps she feared that if she came there with the man that she lived with, the truth might be exposed. It is not improbable that by this time she began to suspect that Jesus was a prophet.

Hast well said. Hast said the truth.

Verse 18. *Hast had five husbands.* Who have either died; or who, on account of your improper conduct, have divorced you; or whom you have left improperly, without legal divorce. Either of these might have been the case.

Is not thy husband. You are not lawfully married to him. Either she might have left a former husband without divorce, and thus her marriage with this man was unlawful, or she was living with him without the form of marriage, in open guilt.

Verse 19. *A prophet.* One sent from God, and who understood her life. The word here does not denote one who *foretells future events*, but one who knew her heart and life, and who must therefore have come from God. She did not yet suppose him to be the Messiah, Joh 4:25. Believing him now to be a man sent from God, she proposed to him a question respecting the proper place of worship. This point had been long a matter of dispute between the Samaritans and the Jews. She submitted it to him because she thought he could settle the question, and perhaps because she wished to divert the conversation from the unpleasant topic respecting her husbands. The conversation about her manner of life was a very unpleasant topic to her—as it is always unpleasant to sinners to talk about their lives and the necessity of religion—and she was glad to *turn the conversation* to something else. Nothing is more common than for sinners to *change* the conversation when it begins to bear too hard upon their consciences; and no way of doing it is more common than to direct it to some *speculative*inquiry having some sort of connection with religion, as if to show that they are willing to talk about religion, and do not wish to appear to be opposed to it. Sinners do not love direct religious conversation, but many are too well-bred to refuse altogether to talk to consider her own state and sinfulness—a delicate and yet pungent way of making her see that she was a sinner. By showing her, also, that he knew her life, though a stranger to her, he convinced her that he was qualified to teach her the way to heaven, and thus prepared her to admit that he was the Messiah. Joh 4:29.

{k} "perceive" Joh 1:48,49

Verse 20. *Our fathers.* The Samaritans; perhaps also meaning to intimate that the patriarchs had done it also. See Ge 12:6; 33:20.

Worshipped. Had a place of worship.

In this mountain. Mount Gerizim, but a little way from Sychar. On this mountain they had built a temple somewhat similar to the one in Jerusalem. This was one of the main subjects of controversy between them and the Jews. The old Samaritan Pentateuch, or five books of Moses, has the word *Gerizim* instead of *Ebal* in De 27:4. On this account, as well as because the patriarchs are mentioned as having worshipped in Shethem, they supposed that that was the proper place on which to erect the temple.

Ye say. Ye Jews.

In Jerusalem. The place where the temple was built. This was built in accordance with the promise and command of God, De 12:5,11. In building this, David and Solomon were under the divine direction, 2 Sa 7:2,3,13; 1 Ki 5:5,12; 8:15-22.

As it was contemplated in the law of Moses that there should be but *one* place to offer sacrifice and to hold the great feasts, so it followed that the Samaritans were in error in supposing that *their* temple was the place. Accordingly, our Saviour decided in favour of the Jews, yet in such a manner as to show the woman that the question was of much *less*consequence than *they* supposed it to be.

{l} "this mountain" Jud 9:7 {m} "in Jerusalem" De 12:5-11; 1 Ki 9:3

Verse 21. *Believe me.* As she had professed to believe that he was a prophet, it was right to require her to put faith in what he was about to utter. It also shows the importance of what he was about to say.

The hour cometh. The *time* is coming, or is near.

When neither in this mountains, &c. Hitherto the public solemn worship of God has been confined to one place. It has been a matter of dispute whether that place should be Jerusalem or Mount Gerizim. That controversy is to be of much less importance than you have supposed. The old dispensation is about to pass away. The *peculiar* rites of the Jews are to cease. The worship of God, so long confined to a single place, is soon to be celebrated everywhere, and with as much acceptance in one place as in another. He does not say that there would be no worship of God in that place or in Jerusalem, but that the worship of God would not be *confined* there. He would be worshipped in other places as well as there.

{n} "when ye shall neither" Mal 1:11; Mt 18:20

THE GOSPEL ACCORDING TO JOHN-Chapter 4-Verse 22

Verse 22. *Ye worship ye know not what.* This probably refers to the comparative ignorance and corruption of the Samaritan worship. Though they received the five books of Moses, yet they rejected the prophets, and of course all that the prophets had said respecting the true God. Originally, also, they had joined the worship of idols to that of the true God. See 2 Ki 17:26-34. They had, moreover, *no authority* for building their temple and conducting public worship by sacrifices there. On all these accounts they were acting in an unauthorized manner. They were not obeying the true God, nor offering the worship which he had commanded or would approve. Jesus thus *indirectly* settled the question which she had proposed to him, yet in such a way as to show her that it was of much less importance than she had supposed.

We know. We Jews. This they knew because God had commanded it; because they worshipped in a place appointed by God, and because they did it in accordance with the direction and teaching of the prophets.

Salvation is of the Jews. They have the true religion and the true form of worship; and the *Messiah*, who will bring salvation, is to proceed from them. See Lu 2:30; 3:6. Jesus thus affirms that the Jews had the true form of the worship of God. At the same time he was sensible how much they had corrupted it, and on various occasions reproved them for it.

{o} "Ye worship" 2 Ki 17:29 {p} "for salvation" Isa 2:3; Ro 9:5

THE GOSPEL ACCORDING TO JOHN-Chapter 4-Verse 23

Verse 23. *But the hour cometh, and now is.* The old dispensation is about to pass away, and the new one to commence. *Already* there is so much light that God may be worshipped acceptably in any place.

The true worshippers. All who truly and sincerely worship God. They who do it with the heart, and not merely *in form*.

In spirit. The word *spirit*, here, stands opposed to rites and ceremonies, and to the pomp of external worship. It refers to the *mind*, the *soul*, the *heart*. They shall worship God with a sincere mind; with the simple offering of gratitude and prayer; with a desire to glorify him, and without external pomp and splendour. *Spiritual* worship is that where the *heart* is offered to God, and where we do not depend on external forms for acceptance.

In truth. Not through the medium of shadows and types, not by means of sacrifices and bloody offerings, but in the manner represented or typified by all these, Heb 9:9,24. In the *true* way of direct access to God through Jesus Christ.

For the Father seeketh, &c. Jesus gives two reasons why this kind of worship should take place. *One* is that God *sought* it, or desired it. He had appointed the old mode, but he did it because he sought to lead the mind to himself even *by those forms*, and to prepare the people for the purer system of the gospel, and *now* he sought or *desired* that those who worshipped him should worship him in that manner. He intimated his will by Jesus Christ.

{q} "in spirit" Php 3:3

Verse 24. *God is a spirit.* This is the *second* reason why men should worship him in spirit and in truth. By this is meant that God is without a body; that he is not material or composed of parts; that he is invisible, in every place, pure and holy. This is one of the first truths of religion, and one of the sublimest ever presented to the mind of man. Almost all nations have had some idea of God as gross or material, but the Bible declares that he is a pure spirit. As he is such a spirit, he dwells not in temples made with hands (Ac 7:48), neither is worshipped with men's hands as though he needed anything, seeing he giveth to all life, and breath, and all things, Ac 17:25. A pure, a holy, a spiritual worship, therefore, is such as he seeks—the offering of the *soul* rather than the formal offering of *the body*—the homage of the *heart* rather than that of the *lips*.

{r} "is a spirit" Php 3:3

Verse 25. *I know that Messias cometh.* As the Samaritans acknowledged the five books of Moses, so they expected, also, the coming of the Messiah.

Which is called Christ. These are probably the words of the evangelist, as it is not likely that the woman would explain the name on such an occasion.

Will tell us all things. Jesus had decided the question proposed to him (Joh 4:20) in favour of the Jews. The woman does not seem to have been satisfied with this answer, and said that the Messiah would tell them all about this question. Probably she was expecting that he would soon appear.

Verse 26. *I that speak unto thee am he.* I am the Messiah. This was the first time that he openly professed it. He did not do it yet to the Jews, for it would have excited envy and opposition. But nothing could be apprehended in Samaria; and as the woman seemed reluctant to listen to him as a prophet, and professed her willingness to listen to the Messiah, he openly declared that he was the Christ, that by some means he might save her soul. From this we may learn,

1st. The great wisdom of the Lord Jesus in leading the thoughts along to the subject of practical personal religion.

2nd. His knowledge of the heart and of the life. He must be therefore divine.

3rd. He gave evidence here that he was the Messiah. This was the design of John in writing this gospel. He has therefore recorded this narrative, which was omitted by the other evangelists.

4th. We see *our* duty. It is to seize on all occasions to lead sinners to the belief that Jesus is the Christ, and to make use of all topics of conversation to teach them the nature of religion.

There never was a model of so much wisdom in this as the Saviour, and we shall be successful only as we diligently study his character.

5th. We see the nature of religion. It does not consist merely in external forms. It is pure, spiritual, active, an ever-bubbling fountain. It is the worship of a pure and holy God, where the *heart* is offered, and where the desires of an humble soul are breathed out for salvation.

{s} "I that speak" Joh 9:37

THE GOSPEL ACCORDING TO JOHN-Chapter 4-Verse 27

Verse 27. *Upon this.* At this time.

Marvelled. Wondered. They wondered because the Jews had no intercourse with the Samaritans, and they were surprised that Jesus was engaged with her in conversation.

Yet no man said. No one of the disciples. They had such respect and reverence for him that they did not dare to ask him the reason of his conduct, or even to appear to reprove him. We should be confident that Jesus is right, even if we cannot fully understand all that he does.

THE GOSPEL ACCORDING TO JOHN-Chapter 4-Verse 28

Verse 28. *Left her water-pot.* Her mind was greatly excited. She was disturbed, and hastened to the city in great agitation to make this known. She seems to have been convinced that he was the Messiah, and went immediately to make it known to others. Our first business, when we have found the Saviour, should be to make him known also to others.

THE GOSPEL ACCORDING TO JOHN-Chapter 4-Verse 29

Verse 29. *Is not this the Christ?* Though she probably believed it, yet she proposed it modestly, lest she should appear to dictate in a case which was so important, and which demanded so much attention. The evidence on which *she* was satisfied that he was the Messiah was that he had told her all things that she had done—perhaps much more than is here recorded. The question which she submitted to them was whether this was not satisfactory proof that he was the Messiah.

THE GOSPEL ACCORDING TO JOHN-Chapter 4-Verse 30

Verse 30. *They went out of the city.* The men of the city left it and went to Jesus, to hear and examine for themselves.

THE GOSPEL ACCORDING TO JOHN-Chapter 4-Verse 31

Verse 31. *Prayed him.* Asked him.

THE GOSPEL ACCORDING TO JOHN-Chapter 4-Verse 32

Verse 32. *I have meat to eat.* See Barnes "Joh 4:34".

THE GOSPEL ACCORDING TO JOHN-Chapter 4-Verse 33

Verse 33. *Hath any man brought him,* &c. This is one of the many instances in which the disciples were slow to understand the Saviour.

Verse 34. *My meat, &c.* Jesus here explains what he said in Joh 4:32. His great object—the great design of his life—was to do the will of God. He came to that place weary and thirsty, and at the usual time of meals, probably an hungered; yet an opportunity of doing good presented itself, and he forgot his fatigue and hunger, and found comfort and joy in doing good—in seeking to save a soul. This one great object absorbed all his powers, and made him forget his weariness and the wants of nature. The mind may be so absorbed in doing the will of God as to forget all other things. Intent on this, we may rise above fatigue, and hardship, and want, and bear all with pleasure in seeing the work of God advance. See Job 23:12: "I have esteemed the words of his mouth more than my necessary food." We may learn, also, that the main business of life is not to avoid fatigue or to seek the supply of our temporal wants, but to do the will of God. The mere supply of our temporal necessities, though most men make it an object of their chief solicitude, is a small consideration in the sight of him who has just views of the great design of human life.

The will of him that sent me. The will of God in regard to the salvation of men. See Joh 6:38.

To finish his work. To *complete* or fully to do the work which he has commanded in regard to the salvation of men. It is *his* work to provide salvation, and his to redeem, and his to apply the salvation to the heart. Jesus came to *do it* by teaching, by his example, and by his death as an expiation for sin. And he shows us that we should be diligent. If *he* was so diligent for our welfare, if he bore fatigue and want to benefit us, then we should be diligent, also, in regard to our own salvation, and also in seeking the salvation of others.

{t} "My meat" Job 23:12; Joh 6:38 {u} "finish his work" Joh 17:4

Verse 35. *Say not ye.* This seems to have been a proverb. Ye say—that is, men say.

Four months and, &c. The common time from sowing the seed to the harvest, in Judea, was about *four months.* The meaning of this passage may be thus expressed:

"The husband-man, when he sows his seed, is
compelled to wait a considerable period before it
produces a crop. He is encouraged in sowing it; he
expects fruit; his labour is lightened by that
expectation; but it is not immediate—it is remote.
But it is not so with my preaching. The seed has
already sprung up. Scarce was it sown before it
produced an abundant harvest. The gospel was just
preached to a woman, and see how many of the
Samaritans come to hear it also. There is therefore

more encouragement to labour in this field than

the farmer has to sow his grain."

Lift your eyes. See the Samaritans coming to hear the gospel.

They are white. Grain, when ripe, turns from a green to a yellow or light colour, indicating that it is time to reap it. So here were indications that the gospel was effectual, and that the harvest was to be gathered in. Hence we may learn,

1st. That there is as much encouragement to attempt to save souls as the farmer has to raise a crop.

2nd. That the gospel is fitted to make an *immediate impression* on the minds of men. We are to expect that it will. We are not to *wait* to some future period, as if we could not expect immediate results. This wicked and ignorant people—little likely, apparently, to be affected—turned to God, heard the voice of the Saviour, and came in multitudes to him.

3rd. We are to expect *revivals* of religion. Here was one instance of it under the Saviour's own preaching. Multitudes were excited, moved, and came to learn the way of life.

4th. We know not how much good may be done by conversation with even a single individual. This conversation with a woman resulted in a deep interest felt throughout the city, and in the conversion of many of them to God. So a single individual may often be the means, in the hand of God, of leading many to the cross of Jesus.

5th. What evils may follow from *neglecting* to do our duty! How easily might Jesus have alleged, if he had been like many of his professed disciples, that he was weary, that he was hungry, that it was esteemed improper to converse with a woman alone, that she was an abandoned character, and there could be little hope of doing her good! How many consciences of ministers and Christians would have been satisfied with reasoning like this? Yet Jesus, in spite of his fatigue and thirst, and all the difficulties of the case, seriously set about seeking the conversion of this woman. And behold what a glorious result! The city was moved, and a great harvest was found ready to be gathered in! *Let us not be weary in well-doing, for in due season we shall reap if we faint not.*

{v} "white already" Mt 9:37

THE GOSPEL ACCORDING TO JOHN-Chapter 4-Verse 36

Verse 36. *He that reapeth.* He that gathers the harvest, or he who so preaches that souls are converted to Christ.

Receiveth wages. The labourer in the harvest receives his hire. Jesus says it shall be thus with those who labour in the ministry—he will not suffer them to go unrewarded. See Da 12:3; Mt 19:28.

Gathereth fruit unto life eternal. Converts souls, who shall inherit eternal life. The harvest is not temporary, like gathering grain, but shall result in eternal life.

That both he that soweth, &c. It is a united work. It matters little whether we sow the seed or whether we reap the harvest. It is part of the same work, and whatever part we may do, we should rejoice. God gives the increase, while Paul may plant and Apollos water. The teacher in the Sunday-school, who sows the seed in early life, shall rejoice with the minister of the gospel who may gather in the harvest, and both join in giving all the praise to God.

{w} "gathereth" Ro 6:22 {x} "both he that soweth" 1 Co 3:5-9

Verse 37. *That saying.* That proverb. This proverb is found in some of the *Greek* writers (Grotius). Similar proverbs were in use among the Jews. See Isa 65:21,22; Le 26:16; Mic 6:15.

One soweth, &c. One man may preach the gospel, and with little apparent effect; another, succeeding him, may be crowned with eminent success. The seed, long buried, may spring up in an abundant harvest.

{y} "one soweth" Mic 6:15

Verse 38. *I sent you.* In the commission given you to preach the gospel. You have not labored or toiled in preparing the way for the great harvest which is now to be gathered in.

Other men labored.

(1.) The prophets, who long labored to prepare the way for the coming of the Messiah.

(2.) The teachers among the Jews, who have read and explained the law and taught the people.

(3.) John the Baptist, who came to prepare the way. And,

(4.) The Saviour himself, who by his personal ministry taught the people, and prepared them for the success which was to attend the preaching of the apostles. Especially did Jesus lay the foundation for the rapid and extensive spread of the gospel. *He* saw comparatively little fruit of his ministry. He confined his labours to Judea, and even there he was occupied in sowing seed which chiefly sprang up after his death. From this we may learn,

1st. That the man who is crowned with eminent success has no cause of *boasting* over others, any more than the man who *reaps* a field of grain should boast over the man who sowed it. The labour of both is equally necessary, and the labour of both would be useless if GOD did not give the increase. Comp. 1 Co 3:6.

2nd. We should not be discouraged if we do not meet with immediate success. The man that *sows* is not disheartened because he does not see the harvest *immediately* spring up. We are to sow our seed in the morning, and in the evening we are not to withhold our hand, for we know not whether shall prosper, this or that; and we are to go forth bearing precious seed, though *weeping*, knowing that we shall come again rejoicing, bearing our sheaves with us, Ec 11:4; Ps 126:6

3rd. Every part of the work of the ministry and of teaching men is needful, and we should rejoice that we are permitted to bear any part, however humble, in bringing sinners to the knowledge of our Lord and Saviour Jesus Christ, 1 Co 12:21-24.

THE GOSPEL ACCORDING TO JOHN-Chapter 4-Verse 39

Verses 39-42. *And many of the Samaritans of that city believed on him*, &c. There is seldom an instance of so remarkable success as this. From a single conversation, in Circumstances, in a place, and with an individual little likely to be attended with such results, many sinners were converted; many believed on the testimony of the woman; many more came to hear, and believed because they heard him themselves. We should never despair of doing good in the most unpromising circumstances, and we should seize upon every opportunity to converse with sinners on the great subject of their souls' salvation.

{a} "for the testimony" Joh 4:29

THE GOSPEL ACCORDING TO JOHN-Chapter 4-Verse 40

Verse 40. No Barnes text on this verse.

THE GOSPEL ACCORDING TO JOHN-Chapter 4-Verse 41

Verse 41. No Barnes text on this verse.

THE GOSPEL ACCORDING TO JOHN-Chapter 4-Verse 42

Verse 42. No Barnes text on this verse.

THE GOSPEL ACCORDING TO JOHN-Chapter 4-Verse 43

Verse 43. *Into Galilee* Into some of the parts of Galilee, though evidently not into Nazareth, but probably direct to *Cana*, Joh 4:46.

THE GOSPEL ACCORDING TO JOHN-Chapter 4-Verse 44

Verse 44. *For Jesus himself testified*, &c. See Barnes "Mt 13:57".

The connection of this verse with the preceding may be thus explained: "Jesus went to Galilee, but not to Nazareth, for he testified," &c. Or, "Jesus went to Galilee, *although* he had said that a prophet had no honour in his own country; yet, because he foreknew that the Galileans would many of them believe on him, he went at this time."

{c} "a prophet" Mt 13:57; Mr 6:4; Lu 4:24

THE GOSPEL ACCORDING TO JOHN-Chapter 4-Verse 45

Verse 45. *Received him.* Received him kindly, or as a messenger of God. They had seen his miracles, and believed on him.

{d} "having seen" Joh 2:23 {e} "for they also went" De 16:16

THE GOSPEL ACCORDING TO JOHN-Chapter 4-Verse 46

A certain nobleman. One who was of the royal family, connected by birth with Herod Antipas; or one of the officers of the court, whether by birth allied to him or not. It seems that his ordinary residence was at Capernaum. Capernaum was about a day's journey from Cana, where Jesus then was.

{f} "he made the water wine" Joh 2:1,11 {1} "nobleman" or, "courtier" or, "ruler"

THE GOSPEL ACCORDING TO JOHN-Chapter 4-Verse 47

Verse 47. *He went unto him.* Though high in office, yet he did not refuse to go personally to Jesus to ask his aid. He felt as a father; and believing, after all that Jesus had done, that he could cure his son, he travelled to meet him. If men receive benefits of Christ, they must come in the same manner. The rich and the poor, the high and the low, must come personally as humble suppliants, and must be willing to bear all the reproach that may be cast on them for thus coming to him. This man showed strong faith in being willing thus to *go* to Jesus, but he erred in supposing that Jesus could heal only by his being present with his son.

Would come down. It is probable that the miracles of Jesus heretofore had been performed only on those who were present with him, and this nobleman seems to have thought that this was necessary. One design of Jesus in working this miracle was to show him that this was not necessary. Hence he did not go down to Capernaum, but healed him where he was.

THE GOSPEL ACCORDING TO JOHN-Chapter 4-Verse 48

Verse 48. *Except ye see signs,* &c. This was spoken not to the nobleman only, but to the Galileans generally. The Samaritans had believed without any miracle. The Galileans, he said, were less disposed to believe him than even they were; and though he had wrought miracles *enough* to convince them, yet, unless they continually saw them, they would not believe.

{g} "signs and wonders" 1 Co 1:22

THE GOSPEL ACCORDING TO JOHN-Chapter 4-Verse 49

Verse 49. *Come down,* &c. The earnestness of the nobleman evinces the deep and tender anxiety of a father. So anxious was he for his son that he was not willing that Jesus should delay a moment —not even to address the people. He still seems to have supposed that Jesus had no power to heal his son except he was *present* with him.

THE GOSPEL ACCORDING TO JOHN-Chapter 4-Verse 50

Verse 50. *Go thy way.* This was a kind and tender address. It was designed to convince him that he could word a miracle though not personally present.

Thy son liveth. Thy son shall recover; or he shall be restored to health, according to thy request.

The man believed. The manner in which Jesus spoke it, and the assurance which he gave, convinced the man that he could heal him there as well as to go to Capernaum to do it. This is an instance of the power of Jesus to convince the mind, to soothe doubts, to confirm faith, and to meet our desires. He blesses not always in the *manner* in which we ask, but he grants us our *main* wish. The father wished his son healed by Jesus *going down* to Capernaum. Jesus healed him, but not in *the way* in which he asked it to be done. God will hear our prayers and grant our requests, but often not in the precise *manner* in which we ask it. It is *his* to judge of the best way of doing us good.

{h} "Go thy way" Mt 8:13; Mr 7:29,30; Lu 17:14

THE GOSPEL ACCORDING TO JOHN-Chapter 4-Verse 51

Verse 51. No Barnes text on this verse.

THE GOSPEL ACCORDING TO JOHN-Chapter 4-Verse 52

Verse 52. *The seventh hour*. About one o'clock in the afternoon.

THE GOSPEL ACCORDING TO JOHN-Chapter 4-Verse 53

Verse 53. *The same hour*. The very time when Jesus spoke.

The fever left him. It seems that it left him suddenly and entirely; so much so that his friends went to inform the father, and to comfort him, and also, doubtless, to apprise him that it was not necessary to ask aid from Jesus. From this miracle we may learn,

1st. That Jesus has an intimate knowledge of all things. He knew the case of this son-the extent of his disease—where he was—and thus had power to heal him.

2nd. That Jesus has almighty power. Nothing else could have healed this child. Nor could it be pretended that he did it by any natural means. He was far away from him, and the child knew not the source of the power that healed him. It could not be pretended that there was any collusion or jugglery. The father came in deep anxiety. The servants saw the cure. Jesus was at a distance. Everything in the case bears the mark of being the simple energy of God—put forth with equal ease to heal, whether far or near. Thus he can save the sinner.

3rd. We see the benevolence of Jesus. Ever ready to aid, to heal, or to save, he may be called on at all times, and will never be called on in vain.

Himself believed. This miracle removed all his doubts, and he became a real disciple and friend of Jesus.

His whole house. His whole family. We may learn from this,

1st. That sickness or any deep affliction is often the means of great good. Here the sickness of the son resulted in the faith of all the family. God often takes away earthly blessings that he may impart rich spiritual mercies.

2nd. The father of a family may be the means of the salvation of his children. Here the effort of a parent resulted in their conversion to Christ.

3rd. There is great beauty and propriety when sickness thus results in piety. For that it is sent. God does not willingly grieve or afflict the children of men; and when afflictions thus terminate, it will be cause of eternal joy, of ceaseless praise.

4th. There is a peculiar charm when piety thus comes into the families of the rich and the noble. It is so unusual; their example and influence go so far; it overcomes so many temptations, and affords opportunities of doing so much good, that there is no wonder that the evangelist selected this instance as one of the effects of the power and of the preaching of the Lord Jesus Christ.

{i} "the same hour" Ps 107:20 {k} "and himself believed" Ac 16:34; 18:8

THE GOSPEL ACCORDING TO JOHN-Chapter 4-Verse 54

Verse 54. No Barnes text on this verse.

THE GOSPEL ACCORDING TO JOHN- Chapter 5

Verse 1. *A feast.* Probably the Passover, though it is not certain. There were two other feasts—the Pentecost and the Feast of Tabernacles—at which all the males were required to be present, and it might have been one of them. It is of no consequence, however, which of them is intended.

{a} "A feast" Le 23:2; De 16:16; Joh 2:3

Verse 2. *The sheep*-market. This might have been rendered the *sheep-gate,* or the gate through which the sheep were taken into the city for sacrifice. The marginal rendering is *gate,* and the word "*market*" is not in the original, nor is a "*sheep-market*" mentioned in the Scriptures or in any of the Jewish writings. A *sheep-gate* is repeatedly mentioned by Nehemiah (Ne 3:1,32; 12:39) being that by which sheep and oxen were brought into the city. As these were brought mainly for sacrifice, the gate was doubtless near the temple, and near the present place which is shown as the pool of Bethesda.

A pool. This word may either mean a small lake or pond in which one can swim, or a place for fish, or any waters collected for bathing or washing.

Hebrew tongue. Hebrew language. The language then spoken, which did not differ essentially from the ancient Hebrew.

Bethesda. The house of mercy. It was so called on account of its strong healing properties— the property of restoring health to the sick and infirm.

Five porches. The word *porch* commonly means a covered place surrounding a building, in which people can walk or sit in hot or wet weather. Here it probably means that there were five covered places, or apartments, in which the sick could remain, from each one of which they could have access to the water. This "pool" is thus described by Professor Hackett (*Illustrations of Scripture,* p. 291, 292)

"Just to the east of the Turkish garrison, and under
the northern wall of the mosque, is a deep excavation,
supposed by many to be the ancient pool of Bethesda,
into which the sick descended `after the troubling of
the water,' and were healed, Joh 5:1, sq. It is
360 feet long, 130 feet wide, and 75 deep. The evangelist
says that this pool was near the sheep-gate, as the
Greek probably signifies, rather than sheep-market, as

rendered in the English version. That gate, according to
Ne 3:1, sq., was on the north side of the temple,
and hence the situation of this reservoir would agree
with that of Bethesda. The present name, Birket Israil,
Pool of Israil, indicates the opinion of the native
inhabitants in regard to the object of the excavation.
The general opinion of the most accurate travellers
is that the so-called pool was originally part of a
trench or fosse which protected the temple on the
north. Though it contains no water at present except
a little which trickles through the stones at the
west end, it has evidently been used at some period
as a reservoir. It is lined with cement, and adapted
in other respects to hold water."

Dr. Robinson established by personal inspection the fact of the subterranean connection of the pool of *Siloam* with the *Fountain of the Virgin*, and made it probable that the fountain under the mosque of Omar is connected with them. This spring is, as he himself witnessed, an *intermittent one*, and there may have been some artificially constructed basin in connection with this spring to which was given the name of *Bethesda*. He supposes, however, that there is not the slightest evidence that the place or reservoir now pointed out as *Bethesda* was the Bethesda of the New Testament (*Bib. Res., i. 501,506, 509*). In the time of Sandys (1611) the spring was found running, but in small quantities; in the time of Maundrell (1697) the stream did not run. Probably in his time, as now, the water which had formerly filtered through the rocks was dammed up by the rubbish.

{1} "sheep-*market*", or "gate", Ne 3:1; 12:39

THE GOSPEL ACCORDING TO JOHN-Chapter 5-Verse 3

Verse 3. *Impotent folk.* Sick people; or people who were *weak* and feeble by long disease. The word means those who were *feeble* rather than those who were afflicted with acute disease.

Halt. Lame.

Withered. Those who were afflicted with one form of the palsy that withered or dried up the part affected. See Barnes "Mt 4:24".

Moving of the water. It appears that this pool had medicinal properties only when it was *agitated* or *stirred*. It is probable that at regular times or intervals the fountain put forth an unusual quantity of water, or water of peculiar properties, and that about these times the people assembled in multitudes who were to be healed.

Verse 4. *An angel.* It is not affirmed that the angel did this *visibly*, or that they saw him do it. They judged by the *effect*, and when they saw the waters agitated, they concluded that they had healing properties, and descended to them. The Jews were in the habit of attributing all favours to the minis try of the angels of God, Ge 19:15; Heb 1:14; Mt 4:11;18:10; Lu 16:22; Ac 7:53; Ga 3:19; Ac 12:11. This fountain, it seems, had strong medicinal properties. Like many other waters, it had the property of healing certain diseases that were incurable by any other means. Thus the waters of Bath, of Saratoga, &c., are found to be highly medicinal, and to heal diseases that are otherwise incurable. In the case of the waters of Bethesda there does not appear to have been anything *miraculous*, but the waters seem to have been endued with strong medicinal properties, especially after a periodical agitation. All that is peculiar about them in the record is that this was produced by the ministry of an angel. This was m accordance with the common sentiment of the Jews, the common doctrine of the Bible, and the belief of the sacred writers. Nor can it be shown to be absurd or improbable that such blessings should be imparted to man by the ministry of an angel. There is no more absurdity in the belief that a pure spirit or holy angel should aid man, than that a physician or a parent should; and no more absurdity in supposing that the healing properties of such a fountain should be produced by his aid, than that any other blessing should be, Heb 1:12. What man can prove that all his temporal blessings do not come to him through the medium of others—of parents, of teachers, of friends, of *angels*? And who can prove that it is unworthy the *benevolence* of angels to minister to the wants of the poor, the needy, and the afflicted, when man does it, and Jesus Christ did it, and God himself does it daily?

Went down. Descended to the pool.

At a certain season. At a certain time; periodically. The people knew about the time when this was done, and assembled in multitudes to partake of the benefits. Many medicinal springs are more strongly impregnated at some seasons of the year than others.

Troubled the water. Stirred or *agitated* the water. There was probably an increase, and a bubbling and agitation produced by the admission of a fresh quantity.

Whosoever then first. This does not mean that but *one* was healed, and that the *first* one, but that those who first descended into the pool were healed. The strong medicinal properties of the waters soon subsided, and those who could not at first enter into the pool were obliged to wait for the return of the agitation.

Stepped in. Went in.

Was made whole. Was healed. It is not implied that this was done instantaneously or by a miracle. The water had such properties that he was healed, though probably gradually. It is not less the gift of God to suppose that this fountain restored gradually, and in accordance with what commonly occurs, than to suppose, what is not affirmed, that it was done at once and in a miraculous manner.

In regard to this passage, it should be remarked that the account of the angel in the 4th verse is wanting in many manuscripts, and has been by many supposed to be spurious. There is not conclusive evidence, however, that it is not a part of the genuine text, and the best critics suppose that it should not be rejected. One difficulty has been that no such place as this spring is mentioned by Josephus. But John is as good a historian, and as worthy to be believed as Josephus. Besides, it is known that many important places and events have not been mentioned by the Jewish historian, and it is no evidence that there was no such place as this because *he* did not mention it. When this fountain was discovered, or how long its healing properties continued to be known, it is impossible now to ascertain. All that we know of it is what is mentioned here, and conjecture would be useless. We may remark, however, that *such* a place anywhere is an evidence of the great goodness of God. Springs or fountains having healing properties abound on earth, and nowhere more than in our own country. Diseases are often healed in such places which no human skill could remove. The Jews regarded such a provision as proof of the mercy of God. They gave this healing spring the name of a "house of mercy." They regarded it as under the care of an angel. And there is no place where man should be more sensible of the goodness of God, or be more disposed to render him praise as in a "house of mercy," than when at such a healing fountain. And yet how lamentable is it that such places—watering places—should be mere places of gaiety and thoughtlessness, of balls, and gambling, and dissipation! How melancholy that amid the very places where there is most evidence of the goodness of God, and of the misery of the poor, the sick, the afflicted, men should forget all the goodness of their Maker, and spend their time in scenes of dissipation, folly, and vice!

{b} "first after" Pr 8:17; Ec 9:10; Mt 11:12

{c} "was made whole" Eze 47:8,9; Zec 13:1

THE GOSPEL ACCORDING TO JOHN-Chapter 5-Verse 5

Verse 5. *An infirmity* A weakness. We know not what his disease was. We know only that it disabled him from walking, and that it was of very long standing. It was doubtless regarded as incurable.

{d} "had an infirmity" Lu 8:43; 13:16

THE GOSPEL ACCORDING TO JOHN-Chapter 5-Verse 6

Verse 6. No Barnes text on this verse.

THE GOSPEL ACCORDING TO JOHN-Chapter 5-Verse 7

Verse 7. *Sir, I have no man*, &c. The answer of the man implied that he did wish it, but, in addition to all his other trials, he had no friend to aid him. This is an additional circumstance that heightened his affliction.

{f} "I have no man" De 32:36; Ps 72:12; 142:4; Ro 5:6; 2 Co 1:9,10

Verse 8. *Rise, take up*, &c. Jesus not only restored him to health, but he gave evidence to those around him that this was a real miracle, and that he was really healed. For almost forty years he had been afflicted. He was not even able to walk. Jesus commanded him not only to *walk*, but to take up his *bed* also, and carry that as proof that he was truly made whole. In regard to this we may observe,

1st. That it was a remarkable command. The poor man had been long infirm, and it does not appear that he expected to be healed except by being put into the waters. Yet Jesus, when he gives a commandment, can give strength to obey it.

2nd. It is our business to obey the commands of Jesus, however feeble we feel ourselves to be. His grace will be sufficient for us, and his burden will be light.

3rd. The weak and helpless sinner should put forth his efforts in obedience to the command of Jesus. Never was a sinner more *helpless* than was this man. If God gave *him* strength to do his will, so he can all others; and the plea that we can do nothing could have been urged with far more propriety by this man than it can be by any impenitent sinner.

4th. This narrative should not be *abused*. It should not be supposed as intended to teach that a sinner should delay repentance, as if *waiting for God*. The narrative neither teaches nor implies any such thing. It is a simple record of a fact in regard to a man who had no power to heal himself, and who was under no obligation to heal himself. There is no reference in the narrative to the difficulties of a sinner— no intimation that it was intended to refer to his condition; and to make this example an excuse for *delay*, or an argument for *waiting*, is to abuse and pervert the Bible. Seldom is more mischief done than by attempting to draw from the Bible what it was not intended to teach, and by an effort to make that convey spiritual instruction which God has not declared designed for that purpose.

Thy bed. Thy couch; or the mattress or clothes on which he lay.

{g} "Rise" Mt 9:6; Mr 2:11; Lu 5:24

Verse 9. *The Sabbath*. To carry burdens on the Sabbath was forbidden in the Old Testament, Jer 17:21; Ne 13:15; Ex 20:8-10.

If it be asked, then, why Jesus commanded a man to do on the Sabbath what was understood to be a violation of the day, it may be answered,

1st. That the Son of man was Lord of the Sabbath, and had a right to declare what might be done, and even to dispense with a positive law of the Jews, Mt 12:8; Joh 5:17.

2nd. This was a poor man, and Jesus directed him to secure his property.

3rd. The Jews extended the obligation of the Sabbath beyond what was intended by the appointment. They observed it superstitiously, and Jesus took every opportunity to convince them of their error, and to restore the day to its proper observance, Mt 12:6-11; Lu 6:9; Lu 13:14;

14:5. This method he took to show them what the law of God really *permitted* on that day, and that works of necessity and mercy were lawful.

{h} "and on the same day" Joh 9:14

THE GOSPEL ACCORDING TO JOHN-Chapter 5-Verse 10

Verse 10. *Not lawful.* It was forbidden, they supposed, in the Old Testament. The Jews were very strenuous in the observation of the external duties of religion.

{i} "It is the sabbath day" Jer 17:21; Mt 12:2

THE GOSPEL ACCORDING TO JOHN-Chapter 5-Verse 11

Verse 11. *He that made me whole.* The man reasoned correctly. If Jesus had power to work so signal a miracle, he had a right to explain the law. If he had conferred so great a favour on him, he had a right to expect obedience; and we may learn that the mercy of God in pardoning our sins, or in bestowing any signal blessing, imposes the obligation to obey him. We should yield obedience to him according to what we know to be his will, whatever may be the opinions of men, or whatever interpretation *they* may put on the law of God. *Our* business is a simple, hearty, child-like obedience, let the men of the world say or think of us as they choose.

THE GOSPEL ACCORDING TO JOHN-Chapter 5-Verse 12

Verse 12. *What man is he,* &c. In this verse there is a remarkable instance of the *perverseness* of men, of their want of candour, and of the manner in which they often look at a subject. Instead of looking at the miracle, and at the man's statement of the manner in which he was healed, they look only at what they thought to be a violation of the law. They assumed it as certain that nothing could make his conduct, in carrying his bed on the Sabbath-day, proper; and they meditated vengeance, not only on the man who was carrying his bed, but on him, also, who had told him to do it. Thus men often assume that a certain course or opinion is proper, and when anyone differs from them they look only *at the difference,* but not *at the reasons for it.* One great source of dispute among men is that they look only at the points in which they *differ,* but are unwilling to listen to the reasons why others do not believe as they do. It is always enough to condemn one in the eyes of a bigot that he differs from *him,* and he looks upon him who holds a different opinion, as the Jews did at this man, as *certainly wrong*; and such a bigot looks at the reasons why others differ from him just as the Jews did at the reason why this man bore his bed on the Sabbath—as not worth regarding or hearing, or as if they could not possibly be right.

THE GOSPEL ACCORDING TO JOHN-Chapter 5-Verse 13

Verse 13. *Wist not.* Knew not.

Had conveyed himself away. Was lost in the crowd. He had silently mingled with the multitude, or had passed on with the crowd unobserved, and the man had been so rejoiced at his cure that he had not even inquired the name of his benefactor.

{1} "for Jesus" Lu 4:30 {2} "a multitude" or, "from the multitude that was"

Verse 14. *Findeth him*. Fell in with him, or saw him.

In the temple. The man seems to have gone at once to the temple—perhaps a privilege of which he had been long deprived. They who are healed from sickness should seek the sanctuary of God and give him thanks for his mercy. Comp. See Barnes "Is 38:20".

There is nothing more improper, when we are raised up from a bed of pain, than to forget God our benefactor, and neglect to praise him for his mercies.

Thou art made whole. Jesus calls to his remembrance the fact that he was healed, in order that he might admonish him not to sin again.

Sin no more. By this expression it was implied that the infirmity of this man was caused by sin—perhaps by vice in his youth. His crime or dissipation had brought on him this long and distressing affliction. Jesus shows him that he knew the cause of his sickness, and takes occasion to warn him not to repeat it. No man who indulges in vice can tell what may be its consequences. It must always end in evil, and not unfrequently it results in loss of health, and in long and painful disease. This is always the case with intemperance and all gross pleasures. Sooner or later, sin will always result in misery.

Sin no more. Do not repeat the vice. You have had dear-bought experience, and if repeated it will be worse. When a man has been restored from the effects of sin, he should learn to avoid the very appearance of evil. He should shun the place of temptation; he should not mingle again with his old companions; he should touch not, taste not, handle not. God visits with heavier judgment those who have been once restored from the ways of sin and who return again to it. The drunkard that has been reformed, and that returns to his habits of drinking, becomes more beastly; the man that professes to have experienced a change of heart, and who then indulges in sin, sinks deeper into pollution, and is seldom restored. The only way of safety in all such cases is to *sin no more*; not to be in the way of temptation; not to expose ourselves; not to touch or approach that which came near to working our ruin. The man who has been intemperate and is reformed, if he tastes the poison *at all*, may expect to sink deeper than ever into drunkenness and pollution.

A worse thing. A more grievous disease, or the pains of hell. "The doom of apostates is a worse thing than thirty-eight years' lameness" (Henry).

{m} "sin no more" Joh 8:11

THE GOSPEL ACCORDING TO JOHN-Chapter 5-Verse 15

Verse 15. No Barnes text on this verse.

THE GOSPEL ACCORDING TO JOHN-Chapter 5-Verse 16

Verse 16. *Persecuted Jesus*. They opposed him; attempted to ruin his character; to destroy his popularity; and probably held him up before the people as a violator of the law of God. Instead of making inquiry whether he had not given proof that he was the Messiah, they *assumed* that he must be wrong, and ought to be punished. Thus every bigot and persecutor does in regard to those who differ from them.

To slay him. To put him to death. This they attempted to do because it was directed in the law of Moses, Ex 31:15; 35:2; Lu 6:7,11; 13:14.

We see here,

1st. How full of enmity and how bloody was the purpose of the Jews. All that Jesus had done was to restore an infirm man to health—a thing which they would have done for their cattle (Lu 6:7; 13:14), and yet they sought his life because he had done it for a sick man.

2nd. Men are often extremely envious because good is done by others, especially if it is not done according to the way of *their* denomination or party.

3rd. Here was an instance of the common feelings of a hypocrite. He often covers his enmity against the *power* of religion by great zeal for the form of it. He hates and persecutes those who do good, who seek the conversion of sinners, who love revivals of religion and the spread of the gospel, because it is not according to some matter of form which has been established, and on which he supposes the whole safety of the church to hang. There was nothing that Jesus was more opposed to than hypocrisy, and nothing that he set himself more against than those who suppose all goodness to consist in *forms*, and all piety in the *shibboleths* of a party.

THE GOSPEL ACCORDING TO JOHN-Chapter 5-Verse 17

Verse 17. *My Father*. God.

Worketh hitherto. Worketh *until now*, or till this time. God has not ceased to work on the Sabbath. He makes the sun to rise; he rolls the stars; he causes the grass, the tree, the flower to grow. He has not suspended his operations on the Sabbath, and the obligation to *rest* on the Sabbath does not extend to him. He *created* the world in six days, and ceased the work of creations; but he has not ceased to *govern* it, and to carry forward, by his providence, his great plans on the Sabbath.

And I work. "As God does good on that day; as he is not bound by the law which requires his creatures to rest on that day, so I do the same. The law on that subject may be dispensed with, also, in my case, for the Son of man is Lord of the Sabbath." In this reply it is implied that he was equal with God from two circumstances:

1st. Because he called God his Father, Joh 5:18.

2nd. Because he claimed the same *exemption* from law which God did, asserting that the law of the Sabbath did not bind him or his Father, thus showing that he had a right to impose and repeal laws in the same manner as God. He that has a right to do this must be God.

{n} "My father" Joh 9:4; 14:10

THE GOSPEL ACCORDING TO JOHN-Chapter 5-Verse 18

Verse 18. *The more to kill him*. The answer of Jesus was fitted greatly to irritate them. He did not *deny* what he had done, but he *added* to that what he well knew would highly, offend them. That he should claim the right of *dispensing* with the law, and affirm that, in regard to its observance, he was in the same condition with God, was eminently fitted to enrage them, and he doubtless knew that it might endanger his life. We may learn from his answer, That we are not to keep back truth because it may endanger us.

2nd. That we are not to keep back truth because it will irritate and enrage sinners. The fault is not in the *truth*, but in the sinner.

3rd. That when any one portion of truth enrages hypocrites, they will be enraged the more they hear.

Had broken the sabbath. They supposed he had broken it.

Making himself equal with God. This shows that, in the view of the Jews, the name Son of God, or that calling God his Father, implied equality with God. The Jews were the best interpreters of their own language, and as Jesus did not deny the correctness of their interpretations, it follows that he meant to be so understood. See Joh 10:29-38. The interpretation of the Jews was a very natural and just one. He not only said that God was his Father, but he said that he had the same right to work on the Sabbath that God had; that by the same authority, and in the same manner, he could dispense with the obligation of the day. They had now *two* pretences for seeking to kill him—one for making himself equal with God, which they considered blasphemy, and the other for violating the Sabbath. For each of these the law denounced death, Nu 15:35; Le 24:11-14.

{p} "making himself equal with God" Zec 13:7; Joh 10:30,33; Php 2:6

THE GOSPEL ACCORDING TO JOHN-Chapter 5-Verse 19

Verse 19. *The Son can do nothing of himself.* Jesus, having stated the *extent* of his authority, proceeds here to show its *source and nature*, and *to prove* to them that what he had said was true. The first explanation which he gives is in these words: *The Son*—whom he had just impliedly affirmed to be equal with God— did nothing *of himself*; that is, nothing without the appointment of the Father; nothing contrary to the Father, as he immediately explains it. When it is said that he CAN do nothing OF HIMSELF, it is meant that such is the union subsisting between the Father and the Son that he can do nothing independently or separate from the Father. Such is the nature of this union that he can do nothing which has not the concurrence of the Father, and which he does not command. In all things he must, from the necessity of his nature, act in accordance with the nature and will of God. Such is the intimacy of the union, that the fact that *he* does anything is proof that it is by the concurring agency of God. There is no separate action—no separate existence; but, alike in being and in action, there is the most perfect oneness between him and the Father. Comp. Joh 10:30; Joh 17:21.

What he seeth the Father do. In the works of creation and providence, in making laws, and in the government of the universe. There is a peculiar force in the word seeth here. No man can see God acting in his works; but the word here implies that the Son sees him act, as we see our fellow-men act, and that he has a knowledge of him, therefore, which no mere mortal could possess.

What things soever. In the works of creation and of providence, and in the government of the worlds. The word is without limit—ALL that the Father does the Son likewise does. This is as high an assertion as possible of his being *equal* with God. If one does all that another does or can do, then there must be equality. If the Son does all that the Father does, then, like him, he must be almighty, omniscient, omnipresent, and infinite in every perfection; or, in other words, he must be God. If he had this *power*, then he had authority, also, to do on the Sabbath-day what God did.

{q} "The Son can do nothing of himself" Joh 5:30

THE GOSPEL ACCORDING TO JOHN-Chapter 5-Verse 20

Verse 20. *The Father loveth the Son.* This authority he traces to the love which the Father has for him—that peculiar, ineffable, infinite love which God has for his only-begotten Son, feebly and dimly illustrated by the love which an earthly parent has for an only child.

Showeth him. Makes him acquainted with. Conceals nothing from him. From apostles, prophets, and philosophers no small part of the doings of God are concealed. From the *Son* nothing is. And as God shows him *all* that he does, he must be possessed of omniscience, for to no finite mind could be imparted a knowledge of all the works of God.

Will show Him. Will appoint and direct him to do greater works than these.

Greater works than these. Than healing the impotent man, and commanding him to carry his bed on the Sabbath-day. The greater works to which he refers are those which he proceeds to specify—he will raise the dead and judge the world, &c.

May marvel. May wonder, or be amazed.

THE GOSPEL ACCORDING TO JOHN-Chapter 5-Verse 21

Verse 21. *As the Father raiseth up the dead.* God has power to raise the dead. By his power it had been done in at least two instances—by the prophet Elijah, in the case of the son of the widow of Sarepta (1 Ki 17:22), and by the prophet Elisha, in the case of the Shunamite's son, 2 Ki 4:32-35. The Jews did not doubt that God had power to raise the dead. Jesus here expressly affirms it, and says he has the same power.

Quickeneth them. Gives them *life.* This is the sense of the word *quickeneth* throughout the Bible.

Even so. In the same manner. By the same authority and power. The power of raising the dead must be one of the highest attributes of the divinity. As Jesus affirms that he has the power to do this *in the same manner* as the Father, so it follows that he must be equal with God.

The Son quickeneth. Gives life to. This may either refer to his raising the dead from their graves, or to his giving spiritual life to those who are dead in trespasses and sins. The former he did in the case of Lazarus and the widow's son at Nain, Joh 11:43,44; Lu 7:14,15. The latter he did in the case of all those who were converted by his power, and still does it in any instance of conversion. *Whom he will.* It was in the power of Jesus to raise up any of the dead as well as Lazarus. It depended on his will whether Lazarus and the widow's son should come to life. So it depends on his will whether sinners shall live. He has power to renew them, and the renewing of the heart is as much the result of his *will* as the raising of the dead.

{s} "the Son quickeneth" Lu 8:54; Joh 11:25; 17:2

THE GOSPEL ACCORDING TO JOHN-Chapter 5-Verse 22

Verse 22. *Judgeth no man.* Jesus in these verses is showing his *equality with God.* He affirmed (Joh 5:17) that he had the same power over the Sabbath that his Father had; in Joh 5:19 that he did the same things as the Father; in Joh 5:21 particularly that he had the same power to raise the dead. He now adds that God has given him the authority to *judge* men. The Father pronounces judgment on no one. This office he has committed to the Son. The power of judging the world implies ability to search the heart, and omniscience to understand the motives of all actions. This is a work which none but a divine being can do, and it shows, therefore, that the Son is equal to the Father.

Hath committed, Hath appointed him to be the judge of the world. In the previous verse he had said that he had power to raise the dead; he here adds that it will be his, also, to judge them when they are raised. See Mt 25:31-46; Ac 17:31.

{t} "hath committed" Mt 11:27; Ac 17:31; 2 Co 5:10

THE GOSPEL ACCORDING TO JOHN-Chapter 5-Verse 23

Verse 23. *That all men should honour,* &c. To honour is to esteem, reverence, praise, do homage to. We honour one when we ascribe to him in our hearts, and words, and actions the praise and obedience which are due to him. We honour God when we obey him and worship him aright. We honour the Son when we esteem him to be as he is; when we have right views and feelings toward him. As he is declared to be God (Joh 1:1), as he here says he has power and authority equal with God, so we honour him when we regard him as such. The primitive Christians are described by Pliny, in a letter to the Emperor Trajan, as meeting together to sing hymns to Christ *as God.* So we honour him aright when we regard him as possessed of wisdom, goodness, power, eternity, omniscience — equal with God.

Even as. To the same extent; in the same manner. Since the Son is to be honoured EVEN AS the Father, it follows that he must be equal with the Father. To *honour the Father* must denote religious homage, or the rendering of that honour which is due to God; so to honour the Son must also denote *religious* homage. If our Saviour here did not intend to teach that he ought to be worshipped, and to be esteemed as *equal* with God, it would be difficult to teach it by any language which we could use.

He that honoureth not the Son. He that does not believe on him, and render to him the homage which is his due as the equal of God.

Honoureth not the Father. Does not worship and obey the Father, the first person of the Trinity—that is, does not worship *God.* He may imagine that he worships God, but there *is* no God but the God subsisting as Father, Son, and Holy Ghost. He that withholds proper homage from one, withholds it from all. He that should refuse to honour *the Father,* could not be said to honour *God;* and in the like manner, he that honoureth not the *Son,* honoureth not the *Father.* This appears farther from the following considerations:—

1st. The Father wills that the Son should be honoured. He that refuses to do it disobeys the Father.

2nd. They are equal. He that denies the one denies also the other.

3rd. The same feeling that leads us to honour the *Father* will also lead us to honour the Son, for he is "the brightness of his glory, and the express image of his person," Heb 1:3.

4th. The evidence of the existence of the Son is the same as that of the Father. He has the same wisdom, goodness, omnipresence, truth, power.

And from these verses we may learn —

1st. That those who do not render proper homage to Jesus Christ do not worship the true God.

2nd. There is no such God as the infidel professes to believe in. There can be but one God; and if the God of the Bible be the true God, then all other gods are false gods.

3rd. Those who withhold proper homage from Jesus Christ, who do not honour him EVEN AS they honour the Father, cannot be Christians.

4th. One evidence of piety is when we are willing to render proper praise and homage to Jesus Christ —to love him, and serve and obey him, with all our hearts.

5th. As *a matter of fact,* it may be added that they who do not honour the Son do not worship God at all. The infidel has no form of worship; he has no place of secret prayer, no temple of worship, no family altar. Who ever yet heard of an infidel that prayed? Where do such men build houses of worship? Where do they meet to praise God? Nowhere. As certainly as we hear the name infidel, we are certain at once that we hear the name of a man who has no form of religion in his family, who never prays in secret, and who will do nothing to maintain the public worship of God. Account for it as men may, it is a fact that no one can dispute, that it is only they who do honour to the Lord Jesus that have any form of the worship of God, or that honour him; *and their veneration for God is just in proportion to their love for the Redeemer—just as they honour him.*

THE GOSPEL ACCORDING TO JOHN-Chapter 5-Verse 24

Verse 24. *He that heareth my word.* To hear, in this place, evidently denotes not the outward act of hearing, but to receive in a proper manner; to suffer it to make its proper impression on the mind; to obey. The word *hear* is often used in this sense, Mt 11:15; Joh 8:47;

Ac 3:23.

Many persons outwardly hear the gospel who neither understand nor obey it.

My word. My doctrine, my teaching. All that Jesus taught about *himself*, as well as about the Father.

On him that sent me. On the Father, who, in the plan of redemption, is represented as *sending* his Son to save men. See Joh 3:17. Faith in God, who sent his Son, is here represented as being connected with everlasting life; but there can be no faith in him who *sent* his Son, without faith also in him who is *sent*. The belief of *one* of the true doctrines of religion is connected with, and will lead to, the belief of *all*.

Hath everlasting life. The state of man by nature is represented as death in sin, Eph 2:1. Religion is the opposite of this, or is *life*. The *dead* regard not anything. They are unaffected by the cares, pleasures, amusements of the world. They hear neither the voice of merriment nor the tread of the living over their graves. So with sinners. They are unmoved with the things of religion. They hear not the voice of God; they see not his loveliness; they care not for his threatenings. But religion is *life*. The Christian lives with God, and feels and acts as if there was a God. Religion, and its blessings here and hereafter, are one and the same. The happiness of heaven is *living* unto God—being sensible of his presence, and glory, and power—and rejoicing in that. There shall be no more *death* there, Re 21:4. This *life*, or this religion, whether on earth or in heaven, is the same—the same joys extended and expanded for ever. Hence, when a man is converted, it is said that he *has* everlasting life; not merely *shall have*, but is already *in possession* of that life or happiness which shall be everlasting. It is life begun, expanded, ripening for the skies. He has already entered on his inheritance—that inheritance which is everlasting.

Shall not come into condemnation. He was by nature under condemnation. See Joh 3:18. Here it is declared that he shall not return to that state, or he will not be again condemned. This promise is sure; it is made by the Son of God, and there is no one that can pluck them out of his hand, Joh 10:28. Comp. See Barnes "Re 8:1".

But is passed from death unto life. Has *passed over* from a state of spiritual death to the life of the Christian. The word translated *is passed* would be better expressed by *has passed*. It implies that he has done it voluntarily; that none compelled him; and that the passage is made unto *everlasting* life. Because Christ is the *author* of this life in the soul, he is called the *life* (Joh 1:4); and as he has always existed, and is the source of *all life*, he is called the *eternal* life, 1 Jo 5:20.

{v} "passed from death" 1 Jo 3:14

THE GOSPEL ACCORDING TO JOHN-Chapter 5-Verse 25

Verse 25. *The hour*. The time.

Is coming. Under the preaching of the gospel, as well as in the resurrection of the dead.

Now is. It is now taking place. Sinners were converted under his ministry and brought to spiritual life.

The dead. Either the dead in sins, or those that are in their graves. The words of the Saviour will apply to either. Language, in the Scriptures, is often so used as to describe two similar events. Thus the destruction of Jerusalem and the end of the world are described by Jesus in the same language, Matthew 24 and 25. The return of the Jews from Babylon, and the coming of the Messiah, and the spread of his gospel, are described in the same language by Isaiah, Isaiah 40-41. Comp. See Barnes "Is 7:14".

The renewal of the heart, and the raising of the dead at the judgment, are here also described in similar language, because they so far resemble each other that the same language will apply to both.

The voice of the Son of God. The voice is that by which we give command. Jesus raised up the dead by his command, or by his authority. When he did it he spoke, or, commanded it to be done. Mr 5:41, "He took the damsel by the hand, and said, `Talitha cumi.'" Lu 7:14: "And he came and touched the bier, and said, `Young man, I say unto thee, Arise.'" Joh 11:43: "He cried with a loud voice, `Lazarus, come forth.'" So it is by his command that those who are dead in sins are quickened or made alive, Joh 5:21. And so at the day of judgment the dead will be raised by his command or voice, though there is no reason to think that his voice will be audibly heard, Joh 5:28.

Shall live. Shall be restored to life.

{w} "the dead shall hear" Joh 5:28; Eph 2:1.

THE GOSPEL ACCORDING TO JOHN-Chapter 5-Verse 26

Verse 26. *As the Father hath life.* God is the source of all life. He is thence called the *living* God, in opposition to idols which have no life. Ac 14:15: "We preach unto you that ye should turn from these vanities (idols) *unto the living God*," Jos 3:10; 1 Sa 17:26; Jer 10:10. See also Isa 40:18-31.

In himself. This means that life in God, or existence, is not *derived* from any other being. *Our* life is derived from God. Ge 2:7: God "breathed into his nostrils the breath of life, and man became a living soul"—that is, a living being. All other creatures derive their life from him. Ps 104:29,30: "Thou sendest forth thy spirit, they are created; thou takest away their breath, they die and return to their dust." But God is underived. He always existed as he is. Ps 90:2 "From everlasting to everlasting thou art God." He is unchangeably the same, Jas 1:17. It cannot be said that he is *self-existent,* because that is an absurdity; no being can originate or create himself; but he is not dependent on any other for *life.* Of course, no being can take away his existence; and of course, also, no being can take away his *happiness.* He has in himself infinite sources of happiness, and no other being, no change in his universe can destroy that happiness.

So. In a manner like his. It corresponds to the first "as," implying that one is the same as the other; life in the one is the same, and possessed in the *same manner*, as in the other.

Hath he given. This shows that the power or authority here spoken of was *given* or committed to the Lord Jesus. This evidently does not refer to the manner in which the second person of the Trinity exists, for the power and authority of which Christ here speaks is that which he exercises as *Mediator*. It is the power of raising the dead and judging the world. In regard to his divine nature, it is not affirmed here that it is in any manner derived; nor does the fact that God is said to have given him this power prove that he was inferior in his nature or that his existence was derived. For,

1st. It has reference merely *to office.* As Mediator, he may be said to have been appointed by the Father.

2nd. Appointment to office does not prove that the one who is appointed is inferior in nature to him who appoints him. A son may be appointed to a particular work by a parent, and yet, in regard to talents and every other qualification, may be equal or superior to the father. He sustains the relation of a son, and in this relation there is an official inferiority. General Washington was not inferior in nature and talents to the men who commissioned him. He simply derived *authority* from them to do what he was otherwise fully able to do. So the Son, as Mediator, is subject to the Father; yet this proves nothing about his nature.

To have life. That is, the right or authority of imparting life to others, whether dead in their graves or in their sins.

In himself. There is much that is remarkable in this expression. It is IN *him* as it is IN *God.* He has the control of it, and can exercise it as he will. The prophets and apostles are never represented as having such power in themselves. They were dependent; they performed miracles in the name of God and of Jesus Christ (Ac 3:6; 4:30; 16:18); but Jesus did it by his own name, authority, and power. He had but to speak, and it was done, Mr 5:41; Lu 7:14; Joh 11:43.

This wonderful commission he bore from God to raise up the dead as he pleased; to convert sinners when and where he chose; and finally to raise up *all* the dead, and pronounce on them an eternal doom according to the deeds done in the body. None could do this but he who had the power of creation—equal in omnipotence to the Father, and the power of searching all hearts—equal in omniscience to God.

{x} "life in himself" 1 Co 15:45

THE GOSPEL ACCORDING TO JOHN-Chapter 5-Verse 27

Verse 27. *Hath given him authority.* Hath appointed him to do this. Has made him to be judge of all. This is represented as being the appointment of the Father, Ac 17:31. The word*authority* here (commonly rendered *power*) implies all that is necessary to execute judgment—all the physical power to raise the dead, and to investigate the actions and thoughts of the life; and all the *moral right* or authority to sit in judgment on the creatures of God, and to pronounce their doom.

To execute judgment. To *do* judgment—that is, to judge. He has appointment to do justice; to see that the universe suffers no wrong, either by the escape of the guilty or by the punishment of the innocent.

Because he is the Son of man. The phrase *Son of man* here seems to be used in the sense of "because he is a man," or because he has human nature. The term is one which Jesus often gives to himself, to show his union with man and his interest in man. See Barnes "Mt 8:19,20".

It is to be remarked here that the word *son* has not the article before it in the original: "Because he is *a* Son of man"—that is, because he is a man. It would seem from this that there is a propriety that one in our nature should judge us. What this propriety is we do not certainly know. It may be,

1st. Because one who has experienced our infirmities, and who possesses our nature, may be supposed by those *who are judged* to be better qualified than one in a different nature.

2nd. Because he is to decide between *man* and *God*, and it is proper that *our* feelings, and nature, and views should be represented in the judge, as well as those of God.

3rd. Because Jesus has all the feelings of compassion we could ask—all the benevolence we could desire in a judge; because he has *shown* his disposition to defend us by giving his life, and it can never be alleged by those who are condemned that their judge was a distant, cold, and unfriendly being. Some have supposed that the expression *Son of man* here means the same as *Messiah* Da 7:13,14, and that the meaning is that God hath made him judge because he was the Messiah. Some of the ancient versions and fathers connected this with the following verse, thus: "Marvel not because I am a man, or because this great work is committed to a man apparently in humble life. You shall see greater things than these." Thus the Syriac version reads it, and Chrysostom, Theophylact, and some others among the fathers.

{y} "authority" Joh 5:22

THE GOSPEL ACCORDING TO JOHN-Chapter 5-Verse 28

Verse 28. *Marvel not.* Do not wonder or be astonished at this.

The hour is coming. The time is approaching or will be.

All that are in the graves. All the dead, of every age and nation. They are described as in the graves. Though many have turned to their native dust and perished from human view, yet God sees them, and can regather their remains and raise them up to life. The phrase *all that are in the graves* does not prove that the same particles of matter will be raised up, but it is equivalent to saying *all the dead*. See Barnes "1 Co 15:35-38".

Shall hear his voice. He will restore them to life, and command them to appear before him. This is a most sublime description, and this will be a wonderful display of almighty power. None but God can *see* all the dead, none but he could remould their frames, and none else could command them to return to life.

Verse 29. *Shall come forth.* Shall come out of their graves. This was the language which he used when he raised up Lazarus, Joh 11:43,4.

They that have done good. That is, they who are righteous, or they who have by their good works shown that they were the friends of Christ. See Mt 25:34-36.

Resurrection of life. Religion is often called life, and everlasting life. See Barnes "Joh 5:24".

In the resurrection the righteous will be raised up to the full enjoyment and perpetual security of that life. It is also called the resurrection of life, because there shall be no more *death*, Re 21:4. The enjoyment of God himself and of his works; of the society of the angels and of the redeemed; freedom from sickness, and sin, and dying, will constitute the life of the just in the resurrection. The resurrection is also called the resurrection of the just (Lu 14:14), and the first resurrection, Re 20:5,6.

The resurrection of damnation. The word *damnation* means the sentence passed on one by a judge—judgment or condemnation. The word, as we use it, applies only to the judgment pronounced by God on the wicked; but this is not its meaning always in the Bible. Here it has, however, that meaning. Those who have done evil will be raised up to be *condemned* or *damned*. This will be the object in raising them up—this the sole design. It is elsewhere said that they shall then be condemned to everlasting punishment (Mt 25:46), and that they shall be punished with everlasting destruction (2 Th 1:8,9); and it is said of the unjust that they are reserved unto the day of judgment to be punished, 2 Pe 2:9. That this refers to the future judgment—to the resurrection then, and not to anything that takes place in this life— is clear from the following considerations:

1st. Jesus had just spoken of what would be done in this life—of the power of the gospel, Joh 5:25. He adds here that something still more wonderful—something *beyond* this—would take place. *All that are in the graves* shall hear his voice.

2nd. He speaks of those who are in their graves, evidently referring to the dead. Sinners are sometimes said to be dead in sin. This is applied in the Scriptures only to those who are deceased.

3rd. The language used here of the *righteous* cannot be applied to anything in this life. When God converts men, it is not because they *have been good.*

4th. Nor is the language employed of the evil applicable to anything here. In what condition among men can it be said, with any appearance of sense, that they are brought forth from their graves to the resurrection of damnation? The doctrine of those Universalists who hold that all men will be saved immediately at death, therefore, cannot be true. This passage proves that at the day of judgment the wicked will be condemned. Let it be added that if *then* condemned they will be lost for ever. Thus (Mt 25:46) it is said to be *everlasting* punishment; 2 Th 1:8,9, it is called *everlasting* destruction. There is no account of redemption in hell—no Saviour, no Holy Spirit, no offer of mercy there.

Verse 30. *Of mine own self.* See Joh 5:19. The Messiah, the Mediator, does nothing without the concurrence and the authority of God. Whatever he does, he does according to the will of God.

As I hear I judge. To *hear* expresses the condition of one who is commissioned or instructed. Thus (Joh 8:26), "I speak to the world those things which I have *heard* of him;" Joh 8:18, "As the father hath taught me, I speak those things." Jesus here represents himself as commissioned, taught, or sent of God. When he says, "as I *hear*," he refers to those things which the Father had *showed* him Joh 5:20—that is, he came to communicate the will of God; to show to man what God wished man to know.

I judge. I determine or decide. This was true respecting the institutions and doctrines of religion, and it will be true respecting the sentence which he will pass on mankind at the day of judgment. He will decide their destiny according to what the Father will and wishes—that is, according to justice.

Because I seek, &c. This does not imply that his own judgment would be wrong if he sought his own will, but that he had no *private* ends, no selfish views, no improper bias. He came not to aggrandize himself, or to promote his own views, but he came to do the will of God. Of course his decision would be impartial and unbiased, and there is every security that it will be according to truth. See Lu 22:42 where he gave a memorable instance, in the agony of the garden, of his submission to his Father's will.

{c} "the will of the Father" Ps 40:7,8; Mt 26:39; Joh 4:34; 6:38

Verse 31. *If I bear witness of myself.* If I have no other evidence than my own testimony about myself.

My witness. My testimony; my evidence. The proof would not be decisive.

Is not true. The word *true.* here, means worthy of belief, or established by suitable evidence. See Mt 22:16: "We *know* that thou art *true*"—that is, worthy of confidence, or that thou hast been truly sent from God, Lu 20:21; Joh 8:13,17.

The law did not admit a man to testify in his own case, but required *two* witnesses, De 17:6. Though what Jesus said *true* Joh 8:13,17, yet he admitted it was not sufficient testimony *alone* to claim their belief. They had a right to expect that his statement that he came from God would be confirmed by other evidence. This evidence he gave in the miracles which he wrought as proof that God had sent him.

{d} "If I bear witness" Ps 27:2; Joh 8:14; Re 3:14

Verse 32. *There is another.* That is, God. See Joh 5:36.

{e} "another" Joh 8:18; Ac 10:43; 1 Jo 5:7-9

Verse 33. *Ye sent unto John.* See Joh 1:19.

He bare witness, &c. This testimony of John *ought* to have satisfied them. John was an eminent man; many of the Pharisees believed on him; he was candid, unambitious, sincere, and his evidence was impartial. On this Jesus *might* have rested the proof that he was the Messiah, but he was willing, also, to adduce evidence of a higher order.

{f} "he bare witness" Joh 1:7,32

Verse 34. *I receive not testimony from men.* I do not depend for proof of my Messiahship on the testimony of men, nor do I pride myself on the commendations or flattery of men.

But these thing, &c. "This testimony of John I adduce that you might be convinced. It was evidence of your own seeking. It was clear, full, explicit. You *sent* to make inquiry, and he gave you a candid and satisfactory answer. Had you believed that, you would have believed in the Messiah and been saved."

Men are often dissatisfied with the very evidence of the truth of religion which they sought, and on which they professed themselves willing to rely.

{g} "but these things" Joh 20:31; Ro 3:3

Verse 35. *He was.* It is probable that John had been cast into prison before this, Hence his public ministry had ceased, and our Saviour says he *was* such a light.

Light. The word in the original properly means a *lamp,* and is not the same which in Joh 1:4,5 is translated *light.* That is a word commonly applied to the sun, the fountain of light; this means a *lamp,* or a light that is lit up or kindled artificially from oil or tallow. A teacher is often called a *light,* because he guides or illuminates the minds of others. Ro 2:19. "Thou art confident that thou art a guide of the blind, *a light* of them that sit in darkness;" Joh 8:12; 12:46; Mt 5:14.

A burning. A lamp lit up that burns with a steady lustre.

Shining. Not dim, not indistinct. The expression means that he was an eminent teacher; that his doctrines were clear, distinct, consistent.

Ye were willing. You willed, or you chose; you went out voluntarily. This shows that some of those whom Jesus was now addressing were among the great multitudes of Pharisees that came unto John in the wilderness, Mt 3:7. As *they* had at one time admitted John to be a prophet, so Jesus might with great propriety adduce his testimony in his favour.

For a season. In the original, for an *hour*—denoting only a short time. They did it, as many others do, while he was popular, and it was the *fashion* to follow him.

To rejoice in his light. To rejoice in his doctrines, and in admitting that he was a distinguished prophet; perhaps, also, to rejoice that he professed to be sent to introduce the Messiah, until they found that he bore testimony to Jesus of Nazareth.

{h} "ye were willing" Mt 21:26; Mr 6:20

THE GOSPEL ACCORDING TO JOHN-Chapter 5-Verse 36

Verse 36. *Greater witness.* Stronger, more decisive evidence.

The works. The miracles—healing the sick and raising the dead.

Hath given me. Hath committed to me, or appointed me to do. Certain things he intrusted in his hands to accomplish.

To finish. To do or to perform until the task is completed. the word is applied to the *termination* of anything, as we say a task is *ended* or a work is completed. So Jesus said, when he expired, It is *"finished,"* Joh 19:30. From this it appears that Jesus came to *accomplish* a certain work; and hence we see the reason why he so often guarded his life and sought his safety until the task was fully completed. These works or miracles bore witness of him; that is, they showed that he was sent from god, because none but God could perform them, and because God would not give such power to any whose life and doctrines he did not approve. They were more decisive proof than the testimony of John, because,

1st. John worked no miracles Joh 10:41

2nd. It was possible that *a man* might be deceived or be an imposter. It was *not* possible for *God* to deceive.

3rd. The miracles which Jesus wrought were such as no *man* could work, and no angel. He that could raise the dead must have all power, and he who commissioned Jesus, therefore, must be God.

{i} "the works" Joh 10:25; 15:24; Ac 2:22

{k} "the Father" Mt 3:17; 17:5

THE GOSPEL ACCORDING TO JOHN-Chapter 5-Verse 37

Verse 37. *The Father himself—hath borne witness of me.* This God had done,

1st. By the miracles which Jesus had wrought, and of which he was conversing.

2nd. At the baptism of Jesus, where he said, "This is my beloved Son," Mt 3:17.

3rd. In the prophecies of the Old Testament. It is not easy to say here to which of these he refers. Perhaps he has reference to all.

Ye have neither heard his voice. This difficult passage has been interpreted in various ways. The main design of it seems to be clear—to reprove the Jews for not believing the evidence that he was the Messiah. In doing this he says that they were indisposed to listen to the testimony of God. He affirmed that God had given sufficient evidence of his divine mission, but they had disregarded it. The *first* thing that he notices is that they had not heard his voice. The word *hear*, in this place, is to be understood in the sense of *obey* or listen to.See Barnes "Joh 5:25".

The voice of God means his *commands* or his declarations, however made; and the Saviour said that it had been the *characteristic* of the Jews that they had not listened to the voice or command of God. As this had been their general characteristic, it was not wonderful that they disregarded now his testimony in regard to the Messiah. The voice of God had been literally heard on the mount. See De 4:12: "Ye heard the voice of the words." *At any time.* This has been the uniform characteristic of the nation that they have disregarded and perverted the testimony of God, and it was as true of that generation as of their fathers.

Nor seen his shape. No man hath seen God at any time, Joh 1:18. But the word *shape*, here, does not mean God himself. It refers to the visible *manifestation* of himself; to the*appearance* which he assumed. It is applied in the Septuagint to his manifesting himself to Moses, Nu 12:8: "With him will I speak mouth to mouth, *even apparently;*" in Greek, *in a form or shape*—the word used here. It is applied to the visible symbol of God that appeared in the cloud and that rested on the tabernacle, Nu 9:15,16. It is the same word that is applied to the Holy Spirit appearing in bodily *shape* like a dove, Lu 3:22. Jesus does not here deny that God had *appeared* in this manner, but he says they had not seen—that is, had not *paid attention to*, or *regarded*, the appearance of God. He had manifested himself, but they disregarded it, and, in particular, they had disregarded his manifestations in attestation of the Messiah. As the word *hear* means to obey, to listen to, so the word see means to pay attention to, to regard (2 Jo 1:8; 1 Jo 3:6), and thus throws light on Joh 14:9: "He that hath seen me hath seen the Father." "I am a *manifestation* of God—God appearing in human flesh, as he appeared formerly in the symbol of the cloud; and he that *regards me*, or attends to me, regards the Father."

{m} "Ye have neither heard" De 4:12; 1 Ti 6:16

THE GOSPEL ACCORDING TO JOHN-Chapter 5-Verse 38

Verse 38. *His word abiding in you.* His law does not abide in you—that is, you do not regard or obey it. This was the *third* thing that he charged them with.

1st. They had not obeyed the command of God.

2nd. They had not regarded his manifestations, either in the times of the old dispensation, or now through the Messiah.

3rd. They did not yield to what he had said in the revelation of the Old Testament.

For whom he hath sent. God had foretold that the Messiah would come. He had now given evidence that Jesus was he; but now they rejected him, and this was proof that they did not regard the word of God.

{n} "And you have not" 1 Jo 2:14

THE GOSPEL ACCORDING TO JOHN-Chapter 5-Verse 39

Verse 39. *Search the scriptures.* The word translated *search* here means to *search diligently* or *anxiously.* It is applied to miners, who search for precious metals—who look anxiously for the *bed* of the ore with an intensity or anxiety proportionate to *their sense* of the value of the metal. Comp. See Barnes "Job 28:3".

It is applied by Homer to a lioness robbed of her whelps, and who *searches* the plain to *trace out* the footsteps of the man who has robbed her. It is also applied by him to dogs tracing their game by searching them out by the scent of the foot. It means a diligent, faithful, anxious investigation. The word *may* be either in the indicative or imperative mood. In our translation it is in the imperative, as if Jesus *commanded* them to search the Scriptures, Cyril, Erasmus, Beza, Bengel, Kuinoel, Tholuck, De Wette, and others, give it as in the indicative; Chrysostom, Augustine, Luther, Calvin, Wetstein, Stier, Alford, and others, regard it as in the imperative, or as a command. It is impossible to determine which is the true interpretation. Either of them makes good sense, and it is proper to use the passage in either signification. There is abundant evidence that the Jews *did* search the books of the Old Testament. It is equally clear that all men *ought* to do it.

The scriptures. The writings or books of the Old Testament, for those were all the books of revelation that they then possessed.

In them ye think ye have eternal life. The meaning of this is: "Ye think that by studying the Scriptures you will obtain eternal life. You suppose that they teach the way to future blessedness, and that by diligently studying them you will attain it." We see by this—

1. That the Jews in the time of Jesus were expecting a future state.

2. The Scriptures teach the way of life, and it is our duty to study them. The Bereans are commended for searching the Scriptures (Ac 17:11); and Timothy is said from a child to have "known the holy scriptures, which are able to make us wise unto salvation," 2 Ti 3:15. Early life is the proper time to search the Bible, for they who seek the Lord early shall find him.

They are they, &c. They bear witness to the Messiah. They predict his coming, and the manner of his life and death, Isa 53:1-12; Da 9:26,27, &c. See Barnes "Lu 24:27".

{p} "they are" Lu 24:27; 1 Pe 1:10,11

THE GOSPEL ACCORDING TO JOHN-Chapter 5-Verse 40

Verse 40. *And ye will not come,* &c. Though the Old Testament bears evidence that I am the Messiah; though you professedly search it to learn the way to life, and though my works prove it, yet you will not come to me to obtain life. From this we may learn,

1st. That life is to be obtained in Christ. He is the way, the truth, and the life, and he only can save us.

2nd. That, in order to do that, we must *come to him*—that is, must come in the way appointed, as lost sinners, and be willing to be saved by him alone.

3rd. That the reason why sinners are not saved lies in the will. "The only reason why sinners die is because they *will not come* to Christ for life and happiness: it is not because they *cannot,* but because they *will not*" (Henry).

4th. Sinners have a particular opposition to going to Jesus Christ for eternal life. They would prefer any other way, and it is commonly not until all other means are tried that they are willing to submit to him.

{q} "ye will not come to me" Joh 3:19

THE GOSPEL ACCORDING TO JOHN-Chapter 5-Verse 41

Verses 41,42. *I receive not honour*, &c. "I do not say these things because I am desirous of human applause, but to account for the fact that you do not believe on me. The reason is, that you have not the love of God in you." In this passage we see,

1st. That we should not seek for human applause. It is of very little value, and it often keeps men from the approbation of God, Joh 5:44.

2nd. They who will not believe on Jesus Christ give evidence that they have no love for God.

3rd. The reason why they do not believe on him is because they have no regard for his character, wishes, or law.

Love of God. Love to God.

In you. In your hearts. You do not love God.

{r} "honour from men" Joh 5:34; 1 Th 2:6

THE GOSPEL ACCORDING TO JOHN-Chapter 5-Verse 42

Verse 42. No Barnes text on this verse.

THE GOSPEL ACCORDING TO JOHN-Chapter 5-Verse 43

Verse 43. *I am come in my Father's name.* By the authority of God; or giving proof that I am sent by him.

If another shall come in his own name. A false teacher setting up himself, and not even pretending to have a divine commission. The Jews were much accustomed to receive and follow particular teachers. In the time of Christ they were greatly divided between the schools of Hillel and Shammai, two famous teachers.

Ye will receive. You will follow, or obey him as a teacher.

THE GOSPEL ACCORDING TO JOHN-Chapter 5-Verse 44

Verse 44. *Which receive honour one of another.* Who are studious of praise, and live for pride, ambition, and vainglory. This desire, Jesus says, was the great reason, why they would not believe on him. They were unwilling to renounce their worldly honours, and become the followers of one so humble and unostentatious as he was. They expected a Messiah of pomp and splendour, and would not submit to one so despised and of so lowly a rank. Had the Messiah come, as they expected, with pomp and power, it would have been an honour, in their view, to follow him; as it was, they despised and rejected him. The great reason why multitudes do not

cxv

believe is their attachment to human honours, or their pride, and vanity, and ambition. These are so strong, that while they continue they cannot and will not believe. They might, however, renounce these things, and then, the obstacles being removed, they would believe. Learn,

1. A man *cannot* believe the gospel while he is wholly under the influence of ambition. The two are not compatible. The religion of the gospel is humility, and a man who has not that cannot be a Christian.

2. Great numbers are deterred from being Christians by pride and ambition. Probably there is no single thing that prevents so many young men from becoming Christians as this passion. The proud and ambitious heart refuses to bow to the humiliating terms of the gospel.

3. Though while a man is under this governing principle he *cannot* believe the gospel, yet this proves nothing about his *ability* to lay that aside, and to yield to truth. *That* is another question. A child CANNOT open a trunk when he gets on the lid and attempts to raise his own weight and the cover of the trunk too; but that settles nothing about the inquiry whether he might not get off and then open it. The true question is whether a man can or cannot lay aside his ambition and pride, and about that there ought not to be any dispute. No one doubts that it may be done; and if that can be done, he can become a Christian.

Seek not the honour. The praise, the glory, the approbation of God. The honour which comes from men is their praise, flattery, commendation; the honour that comes from God is his approbation for doing his will. God alone can confer the honours of heaven—the reward of having done our duty here. That we should seek, and if we seek that, we shall come to Christ, who is the way and the life.

{t} "seek not the honour" Ro 2:10

THE GOSPEL ACCORDING TO JOHN-Chapter 5-Verse 45

Verses 45,46. *Do not think that I will accuse you.* Do not suppose that I intend to follow your example. They had accused Jesus of breaking the law of God, Joh 5:16. He says that he will not imitate their example, though he implies that he *might* accuse them.

To the Father. To God.

There is one that accuseth you. Moses might be said to accuse or reprove them. He wrote of the Messiah, clearly foretold his coming, and commanded them to hear him. As they did*not* do it, it might be said that they had disregarded his command; and as Moses was divinely commissioned and had a right to be obeyed, so his command reproved them: they were disobedient and rebellious.

He wrote of me. He wrote of the Messiah, and I am the Messiah, Ge 3:15; 12:3; comp. Joh 8:56; Ge 49:10; De 18:15

{u} "there is *one*" Ro 2:12.

Verse 46. No Barnes text on this verse.

{v} "he wrote of me"

Ge 3:15; 22:18; De 18:15,18; Ac 26:22

Verse 47. *If ye believe not his writings.* If you do not credit what he has written which you profess to believe, it is not to be expected that you will believe my declarations. And from this we may learn,

1st. That many men who *profess* to believe the Bible have really no regard for it when it crosses their own views and inclinations.

2nd. It is our duty to study the Bible, that we may be established in the belief that Jesus is the Messiah.

3rd. The prophecies of the Old Testament are conclusive proofs of the truth of the Christian religion.

4th. He that rejects one part of the Bible, will, for the same reason, reject all.

5th. The Saviour acknowledged the truth of the writings of Moses, built his religion upon them, appealed to them to prove that he was the Messiah, and commanded men to search them. We have the testimony of Jesus, therefore, that the Old Testament is a revelation from God. He that rejects his testimony on *this* subject must reject his authority altogether; and it is vain for any man to profess to believe in the New Testament, or in the Lord Jesus, without also acknowledging the authority of the Old Testament and of Moses.

We have in this chapter an instance of the profound and masterly manner in which Jesus could meet and silence his enemies. There is not anywhere a more conclusive argument, or a more triumphant meeting of the charges which they had brought against him. No one can read this without being struck with his profound wisdom; and it is scarcely possible to conceive that there could be a more distinct declaration and proof that he was equal with God.

{w} "if you believe not" Lu 16:31

THE GOSPEL ACCORDING TO JOHN-Chapter 6

Verse 1. *Jesus went over.* Went to the east side of the sea. The place to which he went was Bethsaida, Lu 9:10. The account of this miracle of feeding the five thousand is recorded also in Mt 14:13-21; Mr 6:32-44; Lu 9:10-17. John has added a few circumstances omitted by the other evangelists.

{a} "after these things" Mt 14:15; Mr 6:34; Lu 9:12

Verse 2. *Because they saw his miracles,* &c. They saw that he had the power to supply their wants, and they therefore followed him. See Joh 6:26. Comp. also Mt 14:14.

Verse 3. No Barnes text on this verse.

Verse 4. *The passover.* See Barnes "Mt 26:2,17".

A feast of the Jews. This is one of the circumstances of explanation thrown in by John which show that he wrote for those who were unacquainted with Jewish customs.

Verse 5. No Barnes text on this verse.

Verse 6. *To prove him.* To try him; to see if he had faith, or if he would show that he believed that Jesus had power to supply them.

Verse 7. No Barnes text on this verse.
{b} "Two hundred pennyworth" Nu 11:21,22; 2 Ki 4:43

Verse 8. No Barnes text on this verse.

Verse 9. No Barnes text on this verse.

Verse 10. No Barnes text on this verse.

Verse 11. No Barnes text on this verse.

Verse 12. *Gather up the fragments*. This command is omitted by the other evangelists. It shows the care of Jesus that there should be no waste. Though he had power to provide any quantity of God, yet he has here taught us that the bounties of Providence are not to be squandered. In all things the Saviour set us an example of frugality, though he had an infinite supply at his disposal; he was himself economical, though he was Lord of all. If *he* was thus saving, it becomes us dependent creatures not to waste the bounties of a beneficent Providence. And it especially becomes the rich not to squander the bounties of Providence. They often *feel* that they are rich. They have enough. They have no fear of want, and they do not feel the necessity of studying economy. Yet let them remember that what they have is the gift of God— just as certainly as the loaves and fishes created by the Saviour were his gift. It is not given them to waste, nor to spend in riot, nor to be the means of injuring their health or of shortening life. It is given to sustain life, to excite gratitude, to fit for the active service of God. Everything should be applied to its appropriate end, and nothing should be squandered or lost.

{c} "When the were filled" Ne 9:25 {d} "that nothing be lost" Ne 8:10

Verse 13. No Barnes text on this verse.

Verse 14. *That Prophet*, &c. The Messiah. The power to work the miracle, and the benevolence manifested in it, showed that he was the long-expected Messiah.

{e} "that Prophet" Ge 49:10; De 18:15-18

Verse 15. *When Jesus perceived*, &c. They were satisfied by the miracle that he was the Messiah. They supposed that the Messiah was to be a temporal prince. They saw that Jesus was retiring, unambitious, and indisposed to assume the ensigns of office. They thought, therefore, that they would proclaim him as the long-expected king, and constrain him to assume the character and titles of an earthly prince. Men often attempt to dictate to God, and suppose that they understand what is right better than he does. They are fond of pomp and power, but Jesus sought retirement, and evinced profound humility. Though he had *claims* to the honour and gratitude of the nation, yet he sought it not in this way; nor did it evince a proper spirit in his followers when they sought to advance him to a place of external splendour and regal authority.

Verses 16-21. See this miracle of walking on the sea explained in See Barnes "Mt 14:22, also Mt 14:23-33. Comp. Mr 6:45-52.

{f} "And when even was now come" Mt 14:23; Mr 6:47

Verse 17. No Barnes text on this verse.

Verse 18. No Barnes text on this verse.

{g} "the sea arose"

Ps 107:25

Verse 19. No Barnes text on this verse.

Verse 20. No Barnes text on this verse.

{h} "It is I"

Ps 35:3; Isa 43:1,2; Re 1:17,18

Verse 21. *Immediately*. Quickly. Before a long time. How far they were from the land we know not, but there is no evidence that there was a *miracle* in the case. The word translated*immediately* does not of necessity imply that there was no interval of time, but that there was not a long interval. Thus in Mt 13:5, in the parable of the sower, "and forthwith (the same word in Greek) they sprung up," &c., Mr 4:17; Mt 24:29; 3 Jo 1:14.

Verse 22. *The people which stood on the other side of the sea.* That is, on the east side, or on the same side with Jesus. The country was called the region beyond or on the other side of the sea, because the writer and the people lived on the west side.

Jesus went not with his disciples. He had gone into a mountain to pray alone, Joh 6:15. Comp. Mr 6:46.

Verse 23. *There came other boats.* After the disciples had departed. This is added because, from what follows, it appears that they supposed that he had entered one of those boats and gone to Capernaum after his disciples had departed.

From Tiberias. This town stood on the western borders of the lake, not far from where the miracle had been wrought. It was so called in honour of the Emperor Tiberius. It was built by Herod Antipas, and was made by him the capital of Galilee. The city afterward became a celebrated seat of Jewish learning. It is now called *Tabaria*, and is a considerable place. It is occupied chiefly by Turks, and is very hot and unhealthy. Mr. Fisk, an American missionary, was at Tiberias (Tabaria) in 1823. The old town is surrounded by a wall, but within it is very ruinous, and the plain for a mile or two south is strewed with ruins. The Jordan, where it issues from the lake, was so shallow that cattle and asses forded it easily. Mr. Fisk was shown a house called the house of Peter, which is used as the Greek Catholic church, and is the only church in the place. The number of Christian families is thirty or forty, all Greek Catholics. There were two sects of Jews, each of whom had a synagogue. The Jewish population was estimated at about one thousand. On the 1st of January, 1837, Tiberias was destroyed by an earthquake. Dr. Thomson (*The Land and the Book*, vol. it. p. 76, 77) says of this city: \-

"Ever since the destruction of Jerusalem, it has been
chiefly celebrated in connection with the Jews, and
was for a long time the chief seat of rabbinical
learning. It is still one of their four holy cities.
Among the Christians it also early rose to
distinction, and the old church, built upon the spot
where our Lord gave his last charge to Peter, is a
choice bit of ecclesiastical antiquity. The present
city is situated on the shore, at the north-east
corner of this small plain. The walls inclose an
irregular parallelogram, about 100 rods from north
to south, and in breadth not more than 40.
They were strengthened by ten round towers on the west,
five on the north, and eight on the south. There were
also two or three towers along the shore to protect the
city from attack by sea. Not much more than one-half of
this small area is occupied by buildings of any kind,
and the north end, which is a rocky hill, has nothing
but the ruins of the old palace. The earthquake of
1837 prostrated a large part of the walls, and they
have not yet been repaired, and perhaps never will be.
There is no town in Syria so utterly filthy as Tiberias,
or so little to be desired as a residence. Being 600 feet
below the level of the ocean, and overhung on the west
by a high mountain, which effectually shuts off the
Mediterranean breezes, it is fearfully hot in summer.
The last time I was encamped at the Baths the
thermometer stood at 100 at midnight, and a steam

went up from the surface of the lake as from some
huge smouldering volcano. Of course it swarms with
all sorts of vermin. What can induce human beings
to settle down in such a place? And yet some two
thousand of our race make it their chosen abode.
They are chiefly Jews, attracted hither either to
cleanse their leprous bodies in her baths, or to
purify their unclean spirits by contact with her
traditionary and ceremonial holiness."
{i} "nigh unto the place" Joh 6:11

Verse 24. *Took shipping.* Went into the boats.

Came to Capernaum. This was the ordinary place of the residence of Jesus, and they therefore expected to find him there.

Verse 25. No Barnes text on this verse.

Verse 26. *Ye seek me, not because,* &c. The miracles which Jesus wrought were proofs that he came from God. To seek him because they had seen them, and were convinced by them that he was the Messiah, would have been proper; but to follow him simply because their wants were supplied was mere selfishness of a gross kind. Yet, alas! many seek religion from no better motive than this. They suppose that it will add to their earthly happiness, or they seek *only* to escape from suffering or from the convictions of conscience, or they seek for heaven *only* as a place of enjoyment, and regard religion as valuable only for this. All this is mere selfishness. Religion does not forbid our regarding our own happiness, or seeking it in any proper way; but when this is the only or the prevailing motive, it is evident that we have never yet sought God aright. We are aiming at the loaves and fishes, and not at the honour of God and the good of his kingdom; and if this is the only or the main motive of our entering the church, we cannot be Christians.

Verse 27. *Labour not.* This does not mean that we are to make *no effort* for the supply of our wants (comp. 1 Ti 5:1; 2 Th 3:10), but that we are not to manifest anxiety, we are not to make this the main or supreme object of our desire. See Barnes "Mt 6:25".

The meat that perisheth. The food for the supply of your natural wants. It perishes. The strength you derive from it is soon exhausted, and your wasted powers need to be reinvigorated.

That meat which endureth. The supply of your spiritual wants; that which supports, and nourishes, and strengthens the soul; the doctrines of the gospel, that are to a weak and guilty soul what needful food is to the weary and decaying body.

To everlastingly life. The strength derived from the doctrines of the gospel is not exhausted. It endures without wasting away. It nourishes the soul to everlasting life. "They that wait upon the Lord shall renew their strength; they shall run and not be weary, and shall walk and not faint," Isa 40:31.

Him hath God the Father sealed. To *seal* is to confirm or approve as ours. This is done when we set our seal to a compact, or deed, or testament, by which we ratify it as *our act.* So God the Father, by the *miracles* which had been wrought by Jesus, had shown that he had sent him, that he approved his doctrines, and ratified his works. The *miracles* were to his doctrine what a *seal* is to a written instrument. See Barnes "Joh 3:33".

{1} "Labour" or, "Work not" {k} "that meat which endureth" Jer 15:16; Joh 4:14; Joh 6:54,58

{l} "him hath God" Ps 2:7; 40:7; Isa 42:1; Joh 8:18; Ac 2:22; 2 Pe 1:17

THE GOSPEL ACCORDING TO JOHN-Chapter 6-Verse 28

Verse 28. *What shall we do, that we might work the world's of God?* That is, such things as God will approve. This was the earnest inquiry of men who were seeking to be saved. They had crossed the Sea of Tiberias to seek him; they supposed him to be the Messiah, and they sincerely desired to be taught the way of life; yet it is observable that they expected to find that way as other sinners commonly do—by *their works.* The idea of doing something. to merit salvation is one of the last that the sinner ever surrenders.

THE GOSPEL ACCORDING TO JOHN-Chapter 6-Verse 29

Verse 29. *This is the work of God.* This is the thing that will be acceptable to God, or which you are to do in order to be saved. Jesus did not tell them they had *nothing to do,* or that they were to sit down and wait, but that there was a work to perform, and that was a duty that was imperative. It was to believe on the Messiah. This is the work which sinners are to do; and doing this they will be saved, for Christ is the end of the law for righteousness to every one that believeth, Ro 10:4.

{m} "This is the work of God" 1 Jo 3:23

THE GOSPEL ACCORDING TO JOHN-Chapter 6-Verse 30

Verse 30. *What sign showest thou?* On the word *sign* compare See Barnes "Is 7:14".

What miracle dost thou work to prove that thou art the Messiah? They had just seen the miracle of the loaves in the desert, which was sufficient to show that he was the Messiah, and it would seem from the preceding narrative that those who crossed the lake to see him supposed that he was the Christ. It seems wonderful that they should so soon ask for farther evidence that he was sent from God; but it is not improbable that this question was put by *other Jews*, rulers of the synagogue, who happened to be present, and who had not witnessed his miracles. Those men were continually asking for *signs* and proofs that he was the Messiah. See Mt 12:38,39; Mr 8:11; Lu 9:29.

As Jesus claimed the right of teaching them, and as it was manifest that he would teach them differently from what *they* supposed Moses to teach, it was natural to ask him by what authority he claimed the right to be heard.

{n} "sign?" Mt 12:38; 1 Co 1:22

Verse 31. *Our fathers.* The Jews who were led by Moses through the wilderness.

Did eat manna. This was the name given by the Jews to the food which was furnished to them by God in their journey. It means literally, "What is this?" and was the question which they asked when they first saw it, Ex 16:14,15. It was small like frost, and of the size of coriander-seed, and had a sweetish taste like honey. It fell in great quantities, and was regarded by the Jews as proof of a continued miracle during forty years, and was incontestable evidence of the interposition of God in favour of their fathers. The manna which is sold in the shops of druggists is a different substance from this. It is obtained from the bark of certain trees in Armenia, Georgia, Persia, and Arabia. It is procured, as resin is, by making an incision in the bark, and it flows out or distils from the tree.

As it is written. The substance of this is written in Ps 78:24,25.

He gave them. This was regarded as a miraculous interference in their behalf, and an attestation of the divine mission of Moses, and hence they said familiarly that *Moses* gave it to them.

Bread from heaven. The word *heaven*, in the Scriptures, denotes often the region of the air, the atmosphere, or that region in which the clouds are. See Mt 16:3. "The sky (heaven) is red and lowering." Also Mt 3:16; Lu 4:15; 5:18.

The Jews, as appears from their writings (see Lightfoot), expected that the Messiah would provide his followers with plenty of delicious food; and as *Moses* had provided for the Jews in the wilderness, so they supposed that Christ would make provision for the temporal wants of his friends. This was the sign, probably, which they were now desirous of seeing.

{q} "my Father" Ga 4:4

Verse 32. *Moses gave you not that bread from heaven.* This might be translated, "Moses gave you not *the* bread of heaven." The word "that," which makes some difference in the sense, is not necessary to express the meaning of the original. It does not appear that Jesus intended to call in question the fact that their fathers were fed by the instrumentality of Moses, but to state that he did not give them the true bread that was adapted to the wants of the *soul*. He fed the body, although his food did not keep the body alive (Joh 6:59), but he did not give that which would preserve the soul from death. God gave, in his Son Jesus, the true bread from heaven which was fitted to man, and of far more value than any supply of their temporal wants, He tells them, therefore, that they are not to seek from him any such supply of their temporal wants as they had supposed. A better gift had been furnished in his being given for the life of the world.

My father giveth you. In the gospel; in the gift of his Son.

The true bread. The *true* or *real* support which is needed to keep the soul from death. It is not false, deceitful, or perishing. Christ is called *bread*, because, as bread supports life, so his doctrine supports, preserves, and saves the soul from death. He is the *true* support, not only in opposition to the mere supply of *temporal* wants such as Moses furnished, but also in opposition to all false religion which deceives and destroys the soul.

{q} "my Father" Ga 4:4

THE GOSPEL ACCORDING TO JOHN-Chapter 6-Verse 33

Verse 33. *The bread of God.* The means of support which God furnishes. That which, in his view, in needful for man.

Is he, &c. Is the Messiah who has come from heaven.

And giveth life, &c. See Barnes "Joh 1:4".

{r} "bread" Joh 6:48,58

THE GOSPEL ACCORDING TO JOHN-Chapter 6-Verse 35

Verse 35. *I am the bread of life.* I am the support of spiritual life; or my doctrines will give life and peace to the soul.

Shall never hunger. See Barnes "Joh 4:14".

{s} "he that cometh to me" Re 7:16 {t} "he that believeth on me" Joh 4:14; 7:38

THE GOSPEL ACCORDING TO JOHN-Chapter 6-Verse 36

Verse 36. *But I said unto you.* This he said, not in so many words, but in substance, in Joh 6:26. Though they saw him, and had full proof of his divine mission, yet they did not believe. Jesus then proceeds to state that, although they did not believe on him, yet his work would not be in vain, for others would come to him and be saved.

{u} "That ye also have seen me" Joh 6:64

THE GOSPEL ACCORDING TO JOHN-Chapter 6-Verse 37

Verse 37. *All.* The original word is in the neuter gender, but it is used, doubtless, for the masculine, or perhaps refers to his people considered as a *mass* or *body*, and means that every individual that the Father had given him should come to him.

The Father giveth me. We here learn that those who come to Christ, and who will be saved, are *given* to him by God.

1st. God promised him that he should see of the travail of his soul—that is, "the fruit of his wearisome toil" (Lowth), and should be satisfied, Isa 53:11.

2nd. All men are sinners, and none have any claim to mercy, and he may therefore bestow salvation on whom he pleases.

3rd. All men of themselves are disposed to reject the gospel, Joh 5:40.

4th. God enables those who do believe to do it. He draws them to him by his Word and Spirit; he opens their hearts to understand the Scriptures (Ac 16:14); and he grants to them repentance, Ac 11:18; 2 Ti 2:25.

5th. All those who become Christians may therefore be said to be *given* to Jesus as the reward of his sufferings, for his death was the price by which they were redeemed. Paul says (Eph 1:4,5) that, "he hath chosen us in him (that is, in Christ) before the foundation of the world, that we should be holy and without blame before him in love; having predestinated us unto the adoption of children to himself, according to the good pleasure of his will."

Shall come to me. This is an expression denoting that they would *believe* on him. To come to one implies our need of help, our confidence that he can aid us, and our readiness to trust to him. The sinner comes to Jesus feeling that he is poor, and needy, and wretched, and casts himself on his mercy, believing that he alone can save him. This expression also proves that men are not *compelled* to believe on Christ. Though they who believe are *given* to him, and though his Spirit works in them faith and repentance, yet they are made willing in the day of his power, Ps 110:3. No man is compelled to go to heaven against his will, and no man is compelled to go to hell against his will. The Spirit of God inclines the will of one, and he comes freely as a moral agent. The other chooses the way to death; and, though God is constantly using means to save him, yet he prefers the path that leads down to woe.

Him that cometh. Every one that comes—that is, every one that comes in a proper manner, feeling that he is a lost and ruined sinner. This invitation is wide, and full, and free. It shows the unbounded mercy of God; and it shows, also, that the reason, and the only reason, why men are not saved, is that they will not come to Christ. Of any sinner it may be said that if he had been willing to come to Christ he *might* have come and been saved. As he chooses not to come, he cannot blame God because he saves others who are willing, no matter from what cause, and who thus are made partakers of everlasting life.

In no wise. In no manner, or at no time. The original is simply, "I will not cast out."

Cast out. Reject, or refuse to save. This expression does not refer to the doctrine of perseverance of the saints, but to the fact that Jesus will not *reject* or *refuse* any sinner who comes to him.

{w} "him who comes" Ps 102:17; Isa 1:18; 55:7; Mt 11:28; Lu 23:42,43
1 Ti 1:15,16; Re 22:17

Verse 38. *For I came down*, &c. This verse shows that he came for a specific purpose, which he states in the next verse, and means that, as he came to do his Father's will, he would be faithful to the trust. Though his hearers should reject him, yet the will of God would be accomplished in the salvation of some who should come to him.

Mine own will. See Barnes "Joh 5:30".

{x} "but the will" Ps 40:7; Joh 5:30

Verse 39. *Father's will.* His purpose; desire; intention. As this is the Father's will, and Jesus came to execute his will, we have the highest security that it will be done. God's will is always right, and he has power to execute it. Jesus was always faithful, and all power was given to him in heaven and on earth, and he will therefore most certainly accomplish the will of God.

Of all which. That is, of every one who believes on him, or of all who become Christians. See Joh 6:37.

I should lose nothing. Literally, "I should not *destroy*." He affirms here that he will keep it to life eternal; that, though the Christian will die, and his body return to corruption, yet he will not be *destroyed*. The Redeemer will watch over him, though in his grave, and keep him to the resurrection of the just. This is affirmed of all who are given to him by the Father; or, as in the next verse, "*Every one that believeth on him shall have everlasting life.*"

At the last day. At the day of judgment. The Jews supposed that the righteous would be raised up at the appearing of the Messiah. See Lightfoot. Jesus directs them to a *future*resurrection, and declares to them that they will be raised at the *last* day—the day of judgment. It is also supposed and affirmed by some Jewish writers that they did not believe that the *wicked* would be raised. Hence, to speak of being raised up in the last day was the some as to say that one was righteous, or it was spoken of as the peculiar privilege of the righteous. In accordance with this, Paul says, "If by any means I might attain unto the resurrection of the dead," Php 3:11.

{y} "Father's will" Mt 18:14; Joh 10:28; 17:12; 18:9; 2 Ti 2:19

Verse 40. *Everyone which seeth the Son, and believeth on him.* It was not sufficient to see him and hear him, but it was necessary, also, to *believe on him.* Many of the Jews had seen him, but few believed on him. Jesus had said in the previous verse that all that the Father *had given him* should be saved. But he never left a doctrine so that men *must*misunderstand it. Lest it should be supposed that if a man was given to him this was all that was needful, and lest anyone should say, "If I am to be saved I shall be, and my efforts will be useless," he states here that it is necessary that a man should *believe* on him. This would be the *evidence* that he was given to

God, and this would be evidence conclusive that he would be saved. If this explanation of the Saviour had always been attended to, the doctrine of election would not have been abused as it has been. Sinners would not sit down in unconcern, saying that if they are given to Christ all will be well. They would have arisen like the prodigal, and would have gone to God; and, having *believed* on the Saviour, they would then have had evidence that they were given to him—the evidence resulting from an humble, penitent, believing heart—and then they might rejoice in the assurance that Jesus would lose none that were given to him, but would raise it up at the last day. All the doctrines of Jesus, as *he* preached them, are safe, and pure, and consistent; as *men* preach them, they are, unhappily, often inconsistent and open to objection, and are either fitted to produce despair on the one hand, or presumptuous self-confidence on the other. Jesus teaches men to strive to enter heaven, as if they could do the work themselves; and yet to depend on the help of God, and give the glory to him, as if he had done it all.

{z} "him that sent me" Joh 6:47,54; 3:15,16

{a} "I will raise him up" Joh 11:25

THE GOSPEL ACCORDING TO JOHN-Chapter 6-Verse 41
Verse 41. No Barnes text on this verse.

THE GOSPEL ACCORDING TO JOHN-Chapter 6-Verse 42
Verse 42. No Barnes text on this verse.

{b} "Is not this"

Mt 13:55; Mr 6:3; Lu 4:22

THE GOSPEL ACCORDING TO JOHN-Chapter 6-Verse 43
Verse 43. No Barnes text on this verse.

THE GOSPEL ACCORDING TO JOHN-Chapter 6-Verse 44
Verse 44. *No man can come to me.* This was spoken by Jesus to reprove their murmurings—"Murmur not among yourselves." They objected to his doctrine, or murmured against it, because he claimed to be greater than Moses, and because they supposed him to be a mere man, and that what he said was impossible. Jesus does not deny that these things appeared difficult, and hence he said that if any man believed, it was proof that God had inclined him. It was not to be expected that *of themselves* they would embrace the doctrine. If any man believed, it would be because he had been influenced by God. When we inquire what the reasons were why they did not believe, they appear to have been—

1st. Their improper regard for Moses, as if no one could be superior to him.

2nd. Their unwillingness to believe that Jesus, whom they knew to be the reputed son of a carpenter, should be superior to Moses.

3rd. The difficulty was explained by Jesus (Joh 5:40) as consisting in the opposition of their will; and (Joh 5:44) when he said that their love of *honour* prevented their believing on him. The difficulty in the case was not, therefore, a want of natural faculties, or of power to do their duty, but erroneous opinions, pride, obstinacy, self-conceit, and a deep-felt contempt for Jesus. The word "cannot" is often used to denote a strong and violent opposition of the will. Thus we say a man is so great a liar that he cannot speak the truth, or he is so profane that he cannot but swear. We mean by it that he is so wicked that while he has that disposition the other effects will follow, but we do not mean to say that he could not break off from the habit. Thus it is said (Ge 37:4) of the brethren of Joseph that they *hated him, and could not speak peaceably to him*. Thus (Mt 12:34), "How can, ye, being evil, speak good things?" See Lu 14:33; 1 Sa 16:2.

Come to me. The same as believe on me.

Draw him. This word is used here, evidently, to denote such an influence from God as to secure the result, or as to incline the mind to believe; yet the manner in which this is done is not determined by the use of the word. It is used in the New Testament six times. Once it is applied to a compulsory drawing of Paul and Silas to the market-place, Ac 16:19. Twice it is used to denote the drawing of a net, Joh 21:6,11. Once to the drawing of a sword (Joh 18:10); and once in a sense similar to its use here (Joh 12:32): "And I, if I be lifted up from the earth, will *draw* all men unto me." What is its meaning here must be determined by the facts about the sinner's conversion. See Barnes "Joh 6:40".

In the conversion of the sinner God enlightens the mind (Joh 6:45), he inclines the will (Ps 110:3), and he influences the soul by motives, by just views of his law, by his love, his commands, and his threatenings; by a desire of happiness, and a consciousness of danger; by the Holy Spirit applying truth to the mind, and urging him to yield himself to the Saviour. So that, while God inclines him, and will have all the glory, man yields without compulsion; the obstacles are removed, and he becomes a willing servant of God.

{c} "draw him" So 1:4

THE GOSPEL ACCORDING TO JOHN-Chapter 6-Verse 45

Verse 45. *In the prophets*. Isa 54:13. A similar sentiment is found in Mic 4:1-4; Jer 31:34; but by the *prophets*, here, is meant *the book of the prophets*, and it is probable that Jesus had reference only to the place in Isaiah, as this was the usual way of quoting the prophets.

Shall be all taught of God. This explains the preceding verse. It is by the *teaching* of his Word and Spirit that men are *drawn* to God. This shows that it is not *compulsory*, and that there is no obstacle in the way but a strong voluntary ignorance and unwillingness.

{d} "in the prophets" Isa 54:13; Jer 31:34; Mic 4:2
{e} "Every man" Mt 11:27

THE GOSPEL ACCORDING TO JOHN-Chapter 6-Verse 46

Verse 46. *Not that any man hath seen the Father*. Jesus added this, evidently, to guard against mistake. He had said that all who came to him were *taught* of God. The *teacher* was commonly *seen* and *heard* by the pupil; but, lest it should be supposed that he meant to say that a man to come to him must *see* and *hear* God, visibly and audibly, he adds that he did not intend to affirm this. It was still true that no man had seen God at any time. They were not, therefore, to *expect* to see God, and his words were not to be *perverted* as if he meant to teach that.

Save he which is of God. Jesus here evidently refers to himself as the Son of God. He had just said that no *man* had seen the Father. When he affirms that *he* has seen the Father, it implies that he is more than man. He is the only-begotten Son who is in the bosom of the Father, Joh 1:18; the brightness of his glory, and the express image of his person, Heb 1:3; God over all, blessed for ever, Re 9:5. By his being *of God* is meant that he is the only-begotten Son of God, and sent as the Messiah into the world.

Hath seen. Hath intimately known or perceived him. He knows his nature, character, plans. This is a claim to knowledge superior to what man possesses, and it cannot be understood except by supposing that Jesus is equal with God.

{f} "Not that any" Joh 5:37 {g} "save he which is of the God" Lu 10:22

THE GOSPEL ACCORDING TO JOHN-Chapter 6-Verse 47

Verse 47. No Barnes text on this verse.

{h} "He that believeth"

Joh 6:40

THE GOSPEL ACCORDING TO JOHN-Chapter 6-Verse 48

Verse 48. *I am that bread of life.* My doctrines and the benefits of my mediation are that real support of spiritual life of which the manna in the wilderness was the faint emblem. SeeJoh 6:32,33.

{i} "I am that bread" Joh 6:33,35,51

THE GOSPEL ACCORDING TO JOHN-Chapter 6-Verse 49

Verse 49. *Your fathers did eat manna.* There was a real miracle wrought in their behalf; there was a perpetual interposition of God which showed that they were his chosen people.

And are dead. The bread which they ate could not save them from death. Though God interfered in their behalf, yet they died. We may learn,

1st. That that is not the most valuable of God's gifts which merely satisfies the temporal wants.

2nd. That the most distinguished temporal blessings will not save from death. Wealth, friends, food, raiment, will not preserve life.

3rd. There is need of something better than mere earthly blessings; there is need of that bread which cometh down from heaven, and which giveth life to the world.

{k} "and are dead" Zec 1:5

THE GOSPEL ACCORDING TO JOHN-Chapter 6-Verse 50

Verse 50. No Barnes text on this verse.

{l} "not die"
Joh 3:16

Verse 51. *The bread that I will give is my flesh.* That is, his body would be offered as a sacrifice for sin, agreeably to his declaration when he instituted the Supper: "This is my body which is broken for you," 1 Co 11:24.

Life of the world. That sinners might, by his atoning sacrifice, be recovered from spiritual death, and be brought to eternal life. The use of the word *world* here shows that the sacrifice of Christ was full, free, ample, and designed for all men, as it is said in 1 Jo 2:2, "He is the propitiation for our sins, and not for ours only, but also for the sins of the whole world." In this verse Jesus introduces the subject of his *death* and atonement. It may be remarked that in the language which he used the transition from *bread* to his flesh would appear more easy than it does in our language. The same word which in Hebrew means *bread*, in the Syriac and Arabic means also *flesh*.

{m} "my flesh" He 10:5,10,20
{n} "the life of the world" Joh 3:16

Verse 52. No Barnes text on this verse.
{o} "saying, How"
Joh 3:9

Verses 53-55. In these verses Jesus repeats what he had in substance said before.

Except ye eat the flesh, &c. He did not mean that this should be understood *literally*, for it was never done, and it is absurd to suppose that it was intended to be so understood. Nothing can *possibly* be more absurd than to suppose that when he instituted the Supper, and gave the bread and wine to his disciples, they literally ate his flesh and drank his blood. Who *can* believe this? There he stood, a living man—his body yet alive, his blood flowing in his veins; and how can it be believed that this body was eaten and this blood drunk? Yet this absurdity must be held by those who hold that the bread and wine at the communion are "changed into the body, blood, and *divinity* of our Lord." So it is taught in the decrees of the Council of Trent; and to such absurdities are men driven when they depart from the simple meaning of the Scriptures and from common sense. It may be added that if the bread and wine used in the Lord's Supper were not changed into his literal body and blood when it was first instituted, they have never been since. The Lord Jesus would institute it just as he meant it should be observed, and there is nothing *now* in that ordinance which there was not when the Saviour first appointed it. His body was offered on the cross, and was raised up from the dead and received into heaven. Besides, there is no evidence that he had any reference in this passage to the Lord's Supper. That was not yet instituted, and in that there was no literal eating of his flesh and drinking of his blood. The plain meaning of the passage is, that by his bloody death—his body and his blood offered in sacrifice for sin—he would procure pardon and life for man; that they who partook of that, or had an interest in that, should obtain eternal life. He uses the figure of eating and drinking because that was the subject of discourse; because the Jews prided themselves much on the fact that their fathers had eaten *manna*; and because, as he had said that he was the *bread* of life, it was natural and easy, especially in the language which he used, to *carry out the figure*, and say that bread must be eaten in order to be of any avail in supporting and saving men. To eat and to drink, among the Jews, was also expressive of *sharing in* or *partaking of* the privileges of friendship. The happiness of heaven and all spiritual blessings are often represented under this image, Mt 8:11; 26:29; Lu 14:15, &c.

{p} "Except ye eat" Mt 26:26,28

THE GOSPEL ACCORDING TO JOHN-Chapter 6-Verse 54

Verse 54. No Barnes text on this verse.

{q} "eateth"
Joh 6:40

THE GOSPEL ACCORDING TO JOHN-Chapter 6-Verse 55

Verse 55. *Is meat indeed.* Is truly food. My doctrine is truly that which will give life to the soul.

{r} "meat indeed" Ps 4:7

THE GOSPEL ACCORDING TO JOHN-Chapter 6-Verse 56

Verse 56. *Dwelleth in me.* Is truly and intimately connected with me. To dwell or abide in him is to remain in the belief of his doctrine, and in the participation of the benefits of his death. Comp. Joh 15:1-6; 17:21-23.

I in him. Jesus dwells in believers by his Spirit and doctrine. When his Spirit is given them to sanctify them; when his temper, his meekness, his humility, and his love pervade their hearts; when his doctrine is received by them and influences their life, and when they are supported by the consolations of the gospel, it may be said that he *abides* or dwells in them.

{t} "dwelleth" Joh 15:4; 1 Jo 3:24; 4:15,16

THE GOSPEL ACCORDING TO JOHN-Chapter 6-Verse 57
Verse 57. *I live by the Father.* See Barnes "Joh 5:26".

{u} "so he that eateth me" 1 Co 15:22

THE GOSPEL ACCORDING TO JOHN-Chapter 6-Verse 58
Verse 58. *This is that bread*, &c. This is *the* true bread that came down. The word "that"

should not be in the translation.

Shall live for ever. Not on the earth, but in the enjoyments of a better world.

{v} "not as your fathers" Joh 6:49-51.

Verse 59. No Barnes text on this verse.

Verse 60. *Many of his disciples.* The word *disciple* means *learner.* It was applied to the followers of Christ because they were taught by him. It does not imply, of necessity, that those to whom it was given were real Christians, but simply that they were under his teaching, and were professed learners in his school. See Mt 17:16"; Mr 2:18; Joh 9:28; Mt 10:24.

It is doubtless used in this sense here. It is, however, often applied to those who are real Christians.

This is an hard saying. The word *hard* here means *offensive, disagreeable* —that which they could not bear. Some have understood it to mean "difficult to be understood," but this meaning does not suit the connection. The doctrine which he delivered was opposed to their prejudices; it seemed to be absurd, and they therefore rejected it.

Saying. Rather *doctrine* or *speech*—Greek, *logos.* It does not refer to any *particular part* of the discourse, but includes the whole.

Who can hear it? That is, who can hear it *patiently*—who can stay and listen to such doctrine or believe it. The effect of this is stated in Joh 6:66. The doctrines which Jesus taught that were so offensive appear to have been,

1st. That he was superior to Moses.

2nd. That God would save all that he had chosen, and those only.

3rd. That he said he was the bread that came from heaven.

4th. That it was necessary to partake of that; or that it was necessary that an *atonement* should be made, and that they should be saved by that. These doctrines have always been among the most offensive that men have been called on to believe, and many, rather than trust in them, have chosen to draw back to perdition.

Verse 61. No Barnes text on this verse.

Verse 62. What *and if,* &c. Jesus does not say that those who were then present would see him ascend, but he implies that he would ascend. They had taken offence because he said he came down from heaven. Instead of explaining that away, he proceeds to state another doctrine quite as offensive to them—that he would reascend to heaven. The apostles only were present at his ascension, Ac 1:9. As Jesus was to ascend to heaven, it was clear that he could not have intended literally that they should eat his flesh.

{w} "ascend" Joh 3:13; Mr 16:19; Eph 4:8-10

Verse 63. *It is the Spirit that quickeneth.* These words have been understood in different ways. The word "Spirit," here, evidently does not refer to the Holy Ghost, for he adds, "The words that I speak unto you, they are *spirit*." He refers here, probably, to the doctrine which he had been teaching in opposition to their notions and desires. "*My* doctrine is spiritual; it is fitted to quicken and nourish the soul. It is from heaven. Your doctrine or your views are *earthly*, and may be called *flesh*, or fleshly, as pertaining only to the support of the body. You place a great value on the doctrine that Moses fed the *body*; yet that did not permanently profit, for your fathers are dead. You seek also food from me, but your views and desires are gross and earthly."

Quickeneth. Gives life. See Barnes "Joh 5:21".

The flesh. Your carnal views and desires, and the *literal* understanding of my doctrine. By this Jesus shows them that he did not intend that his words should be taken literally.

Profiteth nothing. Would not avail to the *real* wants of man. The bread that Moses gave, the food which you seek, would not be of real value to man's highest wants.

They are spirit. They are spiritual. They are not to be understood *literally*, as if you were really to eat my flesh, but they are to be understood as denoting the need of that provision for the soul which God has made by my coming into the world.

Are life. Are fitted to produce or give life to the soul dead in sins.

{x} "It is the Spirit" 2 Co 3:6

Verse 64. *Jesus knew from the beginning,* &c. As this implied a knowledge of the heart, and of the secret principles and motives of men, it shows that he must have been omniscient.

{y} "knew" Ro 8:29; 2 Ti 2:19

Verse 65. No Barnes text on this verse.

Verse 66. *Many of his disciples.* Many who had followed him professedly as his disciples and as desirous of learning of him. See Barnes "Joh 6:60".

Went back. Turned away from him and left him. From this we may learn,

1st. Not to wonder at the apostasy of many who profess to be followers of Christ. Many are induced to become his professed followers by the prospect of some temporal benefit, or under some public excitement, as these were; and when that temporal benefit is not obtained, or that excitement is over, they fall away.

2nd. Many may be expected to be offended by the doctrines of the gospel. Having no spirituality of mind, and really understanding nothing of the gospel, they may be expected to take offence and turn back. The best way to understand the doctrines of the Bible is to be a sincere Christian, and aim to do the will of God, Joh 7:17.

3rd. We should examine ourselves. We should honestly inquire whether we have been led to make a profession of religion by the hope of any temporal advantage, by any selfish principle, or by mere excited animal feeling. If we have it will profit us nothing, and we shall either *fall away* of ourselves, or be cast away in the great day of judgment.

{a} "went" Zep 1:6; Lu 9:62; He 10:38

THE GOSPEL ACCORDING TO JOHN-Chapter 6-Verse 67

Verse 67. *The twelve.* The twelve apostles.

Will ye also go away? Many apostatized, and it was natural now for Jesus to submit the question to the twelve. "Will *you*, whom I have chosen, on whom I have bestowed the apostleship, and who have seen the evidence of my Messiahship, will you now also leave me?" This was the time to try them; and it is always a time to try *real* Christians when many professed disciples become cold and turn back; and *then* we may suppose Jesus addressing *us*, and saying, Will ye ALSO go away? Observe here, it was submitted to their choice. God compels none to remain with him against their will, and the question in such trying times is submitted to every man whether he will or will not go away.

THE GOSPEL ACCORDING TO JOHN-Chapter 6-Verse 68

Verse 68. *Simon Peter answered him.* With characteristic ardour and promptness. Peter was probably one of the oldest of the apostles, and it was his character to be *first* and most ardent in his professions.

To whom shall we go? This implied their firm conviction that Jesus was the Messiah, and that he alone was able to save them. It is one of Peter's noble confessions—the instinctive promptings of a pious heart and of ardent love. There was no one else who could teach them. The Pharisees, the Sadducees, and the scribes were corrupt, and unable to guide them aright; and, though the doctrines of Jesus were mysterious, yet they were the only doctrines that could instruct and save them.

Thou hast, &c. The meaning of this is, *thou teachest the doctrines which lead to eternal life.* And from this we may learn,

1st. That we are to expect that some of the doctrines of the Bible will be mysterious.

2nd. That, though they are difficult to be understood, yet we should not therefore reject them.

3rd. That nothing would be *gained* by rejecting them. The atheist, the infidel—nay, the philosopher, believes, or professes to believe, propositions quite as mysterious as any in the

Bible.

4th. That poor, lost, sinful man has nowhere else to go but to Jesus. He is the way, the truth, and the life, and if the sinner betakes himself to any other way he will wander and die.

5th. We should, therefore, on no account forsake the teachings of the Son of God. The words that he speaks are spirit and are life.

{b} "the words of eternal" Ac 5:20; 7:38

Verse 69. *We are sure*, &c. See a similar confession of Peter in Mt 16:16, and See Barnes "Mt 16:16".

Peter says *we* are sure, in the name of the whole of the apostles. Jesus immediately cautions him, as he did on other occasions, not to be too confident, for *one* of them actually had no such feelings, but was a traitor.

{c} "we believe" Mt 16:16; Joh 1:29; 11:27

Verse 70. *Have not I chosen you twelve?* There is much emphasis in these words. Have not I—I, the Saviour, the Messiah, chosen you in mercy and in love, and therefore it will be a greater sin to betray me? *Chosen.* Chosen to the apostolic office; conferred on you marks of peculiar favour, and treason is therefore the greater sin. *You twelve.* So small a number. Out of such a multitude as follow for the loaves and fishes, it is to be expected there should be apostates; but when the number is so small, chosen in such a manner, then it becomes every one, however confident he. may be, to be on his guard and examine his heart.

Is a devil. Has the spirit, the envy, the malice, and the treasonable designs of a devil. The word *devil* here is used in the sense of an *enemy*, or one hostile to him.

{d} "a devil" Joh 13:27

Verse 71. *He spake of Judas*, &c. There is no evidence that Jesus *designated* Judas so that the disciples *then* understood that it was he. It does not appear that the apostles even suspected Judas, as they continued to treat him afterward with the same confidence, for he carried the *bag*, or the purse containing their little property (Joh 12:6; 13:29); and at the table, when Jesus said that one of them would betray him, the rest did not suspect Judas until Jesus pointed him out particularly, Joh 13:26. Jesus spoke of *one*, to put them on their guard, to check their confidence, and to lead them to self-examination. So in every church, or company of professing Christians, we may know that it is probable that there may be some one or more deceived; but we may not know who it may be, and should therefore inquire prayerfully and honestly, "Lord, is it *I*?"

Should betray. Would betray. If it be asked why Jesus called a man to be an apostle who he knew had no love for him, who would betray him, and who had from the beginning the spirit of a "devil," we may reply,

1st. It was that Judas might be an important witness for the innocence of Jesus, and for the fact that he was not an impostor. Judas was with him more than three years. He was treated with the same confidence as the others, and in some respects even with superior confidence, as he had "the bag" (Joh 12:6), or was the treasurer. He saw the Saviour in public and in private, heard his public discourses and his private conversation, and he would have been just the witness which the high-priests and Pharisees would have desired, if he had known any reason why he should be condemned. Yet he alleged nothing against him. Though he betrayed him, yet he afterward said that he was innocent, and, under the convictions of conscience, committed suicide. If Judas had known anything *against* the Saviour he would have alleged it. If he had known that he was an impostor, and had alleged it, he would have saved his own life and been rewarded. If Jesus was an impostor, he *ought* to have made it known, and to have been rewarded for it.

2nd. It *may* have been, also, with a foresight of the necessity of having such a man among his disciples, in order that his own death might be brought about in the manner in which it was predicted. There were several prophecies which would have been unfulfilled had there been no such man among the apostles.

3rd. It showed the knowledge which the Saviour had of the human heart, that he could thus discern character before it was developed, and was able so distinctly to predict that he would betray him.

4th. We may add, what benevolence did the Saviour evince—what patience and forbearance-that he had with him for more than three years a man who he knew hated him at heart, and who would yet betray him to be put to death on a cross, and that during all that time he treated him with the utmost kindness!

THE GOSPEL ACCORDING TO JOHN-
Chapter 7

Verse 1. *After these things.* After the transactions which are recorded in the last chapters had taken place, and after the offence he had given the Jews. See Joh 5:18.

Jesus walked. Or Jesus *lived*, or *taught.* He travelled around Galilee teaching.

In Jewry. In Judea, the southern division of Palestine. Comp. See Barnes on "Joh 4:3".

The Jews sought. That is, the rulers of the Jews. It does not appear that the common people ever attempted to take his life.

Verse 2. *The Jews' feast of tabernacles.* Or the feast of *tents.* This feast was celebrated on the fifteenth day of the month Tisri, answering to the last half of our month September and the first half of October, Nu 29:12; De 16:13-15. It was so called from the *tents* or tabernacles which on that occasion were erected in and about Jerusalem, and was designed to commemorate their dwelling in *tents* in the wilderness, Ne 8:16-18. During the continuance of this feast they dwelt in booths or tents, as their fathers did in the wilderness, Le 23:42,43. The feast was continued *eight* days, and the eighth or last day was the most distinguished, and was called the *great day* of the feast, Joh 7:37; Nu 29:35. The Jews on this occasion not only dwelt in *booths*, but they carried about the branches of palms, willows, and other trees which bore a thick foliage, and also branches of the olive-tree, myrtle, &c., Ne 8:15. Many sacrifices were offered on this occasion (Nu 29:12-39; De 16:14-16), and it was a time of general joy. It is called by Josephus and Philo the *greatest* feast, and was one of the three feasts which every male among the Jews was obliged to attend.

{a} "feast of Tabernacles" Le 23:24

Verse 3. *His brethren.* See Barnes "Mt 12:47".

Thy disciples. The disciples which he had made when he was before in Judea, Joh 4:1-3.

The works. The miracles.

Verses 4,5. *For there is no man,* &c. The brethren of Jesus supposed that he was influenced as others are. As it is a common thing among men to seek popularity, so they supposed that he would also seek it; and as a great multitude would be assembled at Jerusalem at this feast, they supposed it would be a favourable time to make himself known. What follows shows that this was said, probably, not in sincerity, but in derision; and to the other sufferings of our Lord was to be added, what is so common to Christians, *derision* from his relatives and friends on account of his pretensions. If our Saviour was derided, we also may expect to be by our relatives; and, having his example, we should be content to bear it.

If thou do, &c. It appears from this that they did not really believe that he wrought miracles; or, if they *did* believe it, they did not suppose that he was the Christ. Yet it seems hardly credible that they could suppose that his miracles were *real*, and yet not admit that he was the Messiah. Besides, there is no evidence that these relatives had been present at any of his miracles, and all that they knew of them might have been from report. See Barnes "Mr 3:21".

On the word *brethren* in Joh 7:5, See Barnes "Mt 13:55"

See Barnes "Ga 1:19".

THE GOSPEL ACCORDING TO JOHN-Chapter 7-Verse 5

Verse 5. No Barnes text on this verse.

{b} "his brethren" Mr 3:21

THE GOSPEL ACCORDING TO JOHN-Chapter 7-Verse 6

Verse 6. *My time*, &c. The proper time for my going up to the feast. We know not *why* it was not yet a proper time for him to go. It might be because if he went *then*, in their company, while multitudes were going, it would have too much the appearance of parade and ostentation; it might excite too much notice, and be more likely to expose him to the envy and opposition of the rulers.

Your time, &c. It makes no difference to you when you go up. Your going will excite no tumult or opposition; it will not attract attention, and will not endanger your lives. Jesus therefore chose to go up more privately, and to remain until the multitude had gone. They commonly travelled to those feasts in large companies, made up of most of the families in the neighbourhood. See Barnes "Lu 2:44".

{c} "My time"

@Joh 2:4; 8:20; 7:8,30

THE GOSPEL ACCORDING TO JOHN-Chapter 7-Verse 7

Verse 7. *The world cannot hate you.* You profess no principles in opposition to the world. You do not excite its envy, or rouse against you the civil rulers. As you possess the same spirit and principles with the men of the world, they cannot be expected to hate you.

I testify of it. I bear witness against it. This was the main cause of the opposition which was made to him. He proclaimed that men were depraved, and the result was that they hated him. We may expect that all who preach faith-fully against the wickedness of men will excite opposition.

Yet this is not to deter us from doing our duty, and, after the example of Jesus, from proclaiming to men their sins, whatever may be the result.

{d} "the world" Joh 15:19

THE GOSPEL ACCORDING TO JOHN-Chapter 7-Verse 8

Verse 8. *I go not up yet.* Jesus remained until about the middle of the feast, Joh 7:14. That is, he remained about four days after his brethren had departed, or until the mass of the people had gone up, so that his going might excite no attention, and that it might not be said he chose such a time to excite a tumult. We have here a signal instance of our Lord's prudence and opposition to parade. Though it would have been *lawful* for him to go up at that time, and though it would have been a favourable period to make himself known, yet he chose to forego these advantages rather than to afford an occasion of envy and jealousy to the rulers, or to appear even to excite a tumult among the people.

THE GOSPEL ACCORDING TO JOHN-Chapter 7-Verse 9

Verse 9. No Barnes text on this verse.

THE GOSPEL ACCORDING TO JOHN-Chapter 7-Verse 10

Verse 10. No Barnes text on this verse.

THE GOSPEL ACCORDING TO JOHN-Chapter 7-Verse 11

Verse 11. No Barnes text on this verse.

{e} "Then the Jews" Joh 11:56

THE GOSPEL ACCORDING TO JOHN-Chapter 7-Verse 12

Verse 12. *Murmuring.* Contention, disputing.

He deceiveth the people. That is, he is deluding them, or drawing them away by pretending to be the Messiah.

{f} "there was much murmuring" Joh 9:16

THE GOSPEL ACCORDING TO JOHN-Chapter 7-Verse 13

Verse 13. *Spake openly of him.* The word translated *openly,* here, is commonly rendered *boldly.* This refers, doubtless, to those who really believed on him. His enemies were not silent; but his friends had not confidence to speak of him *openly* or *boldly*—that is, to speak what they really thought. Many supposed that he was the Messiah, yet even this they did not dare to profess. All that they could say in his favour was that he *was a good man.* There are always many such friends of Jesus in the world who are desirous of saying *something* good about him, but who, from fear or shame, refuse to make a full acknowledgement of him. Many will praise his *morals,* his *precepts,* and his *holy life,* while they are ashamed to speak of his *divinity* or his *atonement,* and still more to acknowledge that they are dependent on him for salvation.

Verse 14. *About the midst.* Or about the middle of the feast. It continued eight days. *The temple.* See Barnes "Mt 21:12"

And taught. Great multitudes were assembled in and around the temple, and it was a favourable time and place to make known his doctrine.

Verse 15. *Knoweth this man letters.* The Jewish *letters* or science consisted in the knowledge of their Scriptures and traditions. Jesus exhibited in his discourses such a profound acquaintance with the Old Testament as to excite their amazement and admiration.

Having never learned. The Jews taught their law and tradition in celebrated schools. As Jesus had not been instructed in those schools, they were amazed at his learning. What early human teaching the Saviour had we have no means of ascertaining, farther than that it was customary for the Jews to teach their children to read the Scriptures. 2 Ti 3:15: "From a child thou (Timothy) hast known the holy scriptures."

{1} "letters" or, "learning"

Verse 16. *My doctrine.* My *teaching,* or what I teach. This is the proper meaning of the word *doctrine.* It is what is *taught* us, and, as applied to religion, it is what is taught us by God in the holy Scriptures.

Is not mine. It is not *originated by me.* Though I have not learned in your schools, yet you are not to infer that the doctrine which I teach is devised or invented by me. I teach nothing that is contrary to the will of God, and which he has not ap-pointed me to teach.

His that sent me. God's. It is such as he approves, and such as he has commissioned me to teach. The doctrine is divine in its origin and in its nature.

{h} "not mine" Joh 8:28; 12:49

Verse 17. *If any man will do his will.* Literally, if any man *wills* or is *willing* to do the will of God. If there is a disposition in anyone to do that will, though he should not be able perfectly to keep his commandments. To do the will of God is to obey his commandments; to yield our hearts and lives to his requirements. A disposition to do his will is a readiness to yield our intellects, our feelings, and all that we have entirely to him, to be governed according to his pleasure.

He shall know. He shall have *evidence,* in the very attempt to do the will of God, of the truth of the doctrine. This evidence is internal, and to the individual it is satisfactory and conclusive. It is of two kinds.

1st. He will find that the doctrines which Jesus taught are such as commend themselves to his reason and conscience, and such as are consistent with all that we know of the perfections of God. His doctrines commend themselves to us as fitted to make us pure and happy, and of course they are such as must be from God.

2nd. An honest desire to obey God will lead a man to embrace the great doctrines of the Bible. He will find that his heart is depraved and inclined to evil, and he will see and feel the truth of the doctrine of *depravity*; he will find that he is a sinner and needs to be born again; he will learn his own weakness, and see his need of a Saviour, of an atonement, and of pardoning mercy; he will feel that he is polluted, and needs the purifying influence of the Holy Spirit. Thus we may learn,

1st. That an honest effort to obey God is the easiest way to become acquainted with the doctrines of the Bible.

2nd. Those who make such an effort will not cavil at any of the doctrines of the Scriptures.

3rd. This is evidence of the truth of revelation which every man can apply to his own case.

4th. It is such evidence as to lead to *certainty*. No man who has ever made an honest effort to live a pious life, and to do all the will of God, has ever had any doubt of the truth of the Saviour's doctrines, or any doubt that his religion is true and is fitted to the nature of man. They only doubt the truth of religion who wish to live in sin.

5th. We see the goodness of God in giving us evidence of his truth that may be within every man's reach. It does not require great learning to be a Christian, and to be convinced of the truth of the Bible. It requires an honest heart, and a willingness to obey God.

Whether it be of God. Whether it be *divine*.

Or whether *I speak of myself.* Of myself without being commissioned or directed by God.

{i} "if any man do his will" Joh 8:43

THE GOSPEL ACCORDING TO JOHN-Chapter 7-Verse 18

Verse 18. *That speaketh of himself.* This does not mean about or concerning himself, but he that speaks by his own authority, without being sent by God, as mere human teachers do.

Seeketh his own glory. His own *praise*, or seeks for reputation and applause. This is the case with mere human teachers, and as Jesus in his discourses manifestly sought to honour God, they ought to have supposed that he was sent by him.

No unrighteousness. This word here means, evidently, there is no falsehood, no deception in him. He is not an impostor. It is used in the same sense in 2 Th 2:10-12. It is true that there was no unrighteousness, no sin in Jesus Christ, but that is not the truth taught here. It is that he was not an *impostor*, and the evidence of this was that he sought not his own glory, but the honour of God. This evidence was furnished,

1st. In his retiring, unobtrusive disposition; in his not seeking the applause of men.

2nd. In his teaching such doctrines as tended to exalt God and humble man.

3rd. In his ascribing all glory and praise to God.

{l} "but he that seeketh" Pr 25:27

THE GOSPEL ACCORDING TO JOHN-Chapter 7-Verse 19

Verse 19. *Did not Moses give you the law?* This they admitted, and on this they prided themselves. Every violation of that law they considered as deserving of death. They had accused Jesus of violating it because he had healed a man on the Sabbath, and for that they had sought his life, Joh 5:10-16. He here recalls that charge to their recollection, and shows them that, though they pretended great reverence for that law, yet they were really its violators in having sought his life.

None of you, &c. None of you Jews. They had sought to kill him. This was a pointed and severe charge, and shows the great faithfulness with which he was accustomed to proclaim the truth.

Why go ye about to kill me? Why do ye *seek* to kill me? See Joh 5:16.

{m} "Moses" Joh 1:17; Ga 3:19 {n} "none of you" Ro 3:10-19 {o} "to kill me" Mt 12:14; Joh 5:16,18

THE GOSPEL ACCORDING TO JOHN-Chapter 7-Verse 20

Verse 20. *The people.* Perhaps some of the people who were not aware of the designs of the rulers.

Thou hast a devil. Thou art deranged or mad. See Joh 10:20. As they saw no effort to kill him, and as they were ignorant of the designs of the rulers, they supposed that this was the effect of derangement.

THE GOSPEL ACCORDING TO JOHN-Chapter 7-Verse 21

Verse 21. *One work.* The healing of the man on the Sabbath, John chapter 5.

Ye all marvel. You all wonder or are amazed, and particularly that it was done on the Sabbath. This was the *particular* ground of astonishment, that he should dare to do what they esteemed a violation of the Sabbath.

Verse 22. *Moses therefore gave unto you circumcision.* Moses commanded you to circumcise your children, Le 12:3. The word "therefore" in this place—literally *"on account of this"*—means, "Moses *on this account* gave you circumcision, not because it is of Moses, but of the fathers;" that is, the reason was not that he himself appointed it as a new institution, but he found it already in existence, and incorporated it in his institutions and laws.

Not because, &c. Not *that* it is of Moses. Though Jesus spoke in accordance with the custom of the Jews, who ascribed the appointment of circumcision to Moses, yet he is careful to remind them that it was in observance long before Moses. So, also, the *Sabbath* was kept before Moses, and alike in the one case and the other they ought to keep in mind the *design* of the appointment.

Of the fathers. Of the patriarchs, Abraham, Isaac, and Jacob, Ge 17:10.

Ye on the sabbath-day, &c. The law required that the child should be circumcised on the *eighth* day. If that day happened to be the *Sabbath,* yet they held that he was to be circumcised, as there was a positive law to that effect; and as this was *commanded,* they did not consider it a breach of the Sabbath.

A man. Not an *adult* man, but a man-child. See Joh 16:21: "She remembereth no more the anguish for joy that *a man* is born into the world."

{q} "Moses" Le 12:3 {r} "but of the fathers" Ge 17:10

Verse 23. *That the law of Moses' should not be broken.* In order that the law requiring it to be done at a specified time, though that might occur on the Sabbath, should be kept.

Are ye angry, &c. The argument of Jesus is this:
"You yourselves, in interpreting the law about the
Sabbath, allow a work of necessity to be done. You
do that which is necessary as an ordinance of religion
denoting *separation* from other nations, or external
purity. As you allow this, you ought also, for the
same reason, to allow that a man should be completely
restored to health—that a work of much more importance
should be done."

We may learn here that it would be happy for all if they would not condemn others in that thing which they allow. Men often accuse others of doing things which they themselves do in other ways.

Every whit whole. Literally, "I have restored the whole man to health," implying that the man's *whole body* was diseased, and that he had been *entirely* restored to health.

{2} "that the law of Moses" or, "without breaking the law of Moses"

THE GOSPEL ACCORDING TO JOHN-Chapter 7-Verse 24

Verse 24. *Judge not according to the appearance.* Not as a thing first offers itself to you, without reflection or candour. In *appearance*, to circumcise a child on the Sabbath might be a violation of the law; yet you do it, and it is right. So, to appearance, it might be a violation of the Sabbath to heal a man, yet it is right to do works of necessity and mercy.

Judge righteous judgment. Candidly; looking at the law, and inquiring what its spirit really requires.

{t} "judge" De 1:16,17

THE GOSPEL ACCORDING TO JOHN-Chapter 7-Verse 25

Verse 25. No Barnes text on this verse.

THE GOSPEL ACCORDING TO JOHN-Chapter 7-Verse 26

Verse 26. *Do the rulers know indeed,* &c. It seems from this that they supposed that the *rulers* had been convinced that Jesus was the Messiah, but that from some cause they were not willing yet to make it known to the people. The reasons of this opinion were these:

1st. They knew that they *had* attempted to kill him.

2nd. They now saw him speaking boldly to the people without interruption from the rulers. They concluded, therefore, that some change had taken place in the sentiments of the rulers in regard to him, though they had not yet made it public.

The rulers. The members of the *Sanhedrim*, or great council of the nation, who had charge of religious affairs.

Indeed. Truly; certainly. Have they certain evidence, as would appear from their suffering him to speak without interruption?

The very Christ. Is *truly or really* the Messiah.

{u} "Do the rulers" Joh 7:48

THE GOSPEL ACCORDING TO JOHN-Chapter 7-Verse 27

Verse 27. *Howbeit.* But. They proceeded to state a reason why *they* supposed that he could not be the Messiah, whatever the rulers might think.

We know this man whence he is. We know the place of his birth and residence.

No man knoweth whence he is. From Mt 2:5, it appears that the common expectation of the Jews was that the Messiah would be born at Bethlehem; but they had also reigned that after his birth he would be *hidden* or taken away in some mysterious manner, and appear again from some unexpected quarter. We find allusions to this expectation in the New Testament, where our Saviour *corrects* their common notions, Mt 24:23: "Then if any man shall say unto you, Lo, here is Christ, or there, believe it not." And again (Mt 24:26), "If they shall say unto you, Behold, he is in the desert, go not forth; behold, he is in the secret chambers, believe it not." The following extracts from Jewish writings show that this was the common expectation: "The Redeemer shall manifest himself, and afterward be hid. So it was in the redemption from Egypt. Moses showed himself and then was hidden." So on the passage, So 2:9— "My beloved is like a roe or a young hart"—they say: "A roe appears and then is hid; so the Redeemer shall first appear and then be concealed, and then again be concealed and then again appear." "So the Redeemer shall first appear and then be hid, and then, at the end of forty-five days, shall reappear, and cause *manna* to descend." See Lightfoot. Whatever may have been the source of this opinion, it explains the passage, and shows that the writer of this gospel was well acquainted with the opinions of the Jews, however improbable those opinions were.

{v} "Howbeit" Mt 13:55

THE GOSPEL ACCORDING TO JOHN-Chapter 7-Verse 28

Verse 28. *Ye know whence I am.* You have sufficient evidence of my divine mission, and that I am the Messiah.

Is true. Is worthy to be believed. He has given evidence that I came from him, and he is worthy to be believed. Many read this as a question—Do ye know me, and know whence I am? I am not come of myself, &c.

{w} "and I am not come" Joh 5:43 {x} "he that sent" Ro 3:4 {y} "whom ye know now" Joh 1:18; 8:55

THE GOSPEL ACCORDING TO JOHN-Chapter 7-Verse 29

Verse 29. No Barnes text on this verse.

{z} "But I know him"

Mt 11:27; Joh 10:15

THE GOSPEL ACCORDING TO JOHN-Chapter 7-Verse 30

Verse 30. *Then they sought to take him.* The rulers and their friends. They did this —

1st. Because of his reproof; and,

2nd. For professing to be the Messiah.

His hour. The proper and the appointed time for his death. See Mt 21:46.

{a} "Then" Mr 11:18; Lu 20:19; Joh 8:37

THE GOSPEL ACCORDING TO JOHN-Chapter 7-Verse 31

Verse 31. *Will he do more miracles?* It was a common expectation that the Messiah would work many miracles. This opinion was founded on such passages as Isa 35:5,6, &c.: "Then the eyes of the blind shall be opened, and the ears of the deaf shall be unstopped; then shall the lame man leap as an hart," &c. Jesus had given abundant evidence of his power to work such miracles, and they therefore believed that he was the Messiah.

{b} "many of the people" Joh 4:39

Verse 32. *The people murmured such things.* That is, that the question was agitated whether he was the Messiah; that it excited debate and contention; and that the consequence was, he made many friends. They chose, therefore, if possible, to remove him from them.

Verse 33. *Yet a little while am I with you.* It will not be long before my death. This is supposed to have been about six months before his death. This speech of Jesus is full of tenderness. They were seeking his life. He tells them that he is fully aware of it; that he will not be long with them; and *implies* that they should be diligent to seek him while he was yet with them. He was about to die, but they might now seek his favour and find it. When we remember that this was said to his persecutors and murderers; that it was said even while they were seeking his life, we see the peculiar tenderness of his love. Enmity, and hate, and persecution did not prevent his offering salvation to them.

I go unto him that sent me. This is one of the intimations that he gave that he would ascend to God. Comp. Joh 6:62.

{c} "Yet a little while" Joh 13:33; 16:16

Verse 34. *Ye shall seek me.* This probably means simply, Ye shall seek *the Messiah.* Such will be your troubles, such the calamities that will come on the nation, that you will earnestly desire the coming of the Messiah. You will seek for a deliverer, and will look for *him,* that he may bring deliverance. This does not mean that they would seek for Jesus and not be able to find him, but that they would desire the aid and comfort of *the Messiah,* and would be disappointed. Jesus speaks of himself as the Messiah, and his own name as synonymous with the Messiah. See Barnes "Mt 23:39".

Shall not find me. Shall not find the Messiah. He will not come, according to your expectations, to aid you. See Barnes "Mt 24:1"

and following.

Where I am. This whole clause is to be understood as future, though the words "am" and "cannot" are both in the present tense. The meaning is, Where I shall be you will not be able to come. That is, he, the Messiah, would be in heaven; and though they would earnestly desire his presence and aid to save the city and nation from the Romans, yet they would not be able to obtain it—represented here by their not being able to *come to him.* This does not refer to their individual salvation, but to the deliverance of their nation. It is not true of individual sinners that they seek Christ in a proper manner and are not able to find him; but it was true of the Jewish nation that they looked for the Messiah, and sought his coming to deliver them, but he did not do it.

{d} "Ye shall seek me" Ho 5:6; Joh 8:21

Verse 35. *The dispersed among the Gentiles.* To the *Jews* scattered among the Gentiles, or living in distant parts of the earth. It is well known that at that time there were Jews dwelling in almost every land. There were multitudes in Egypt, in Asia Minor, in Greece, in Rome, &c., and in all these places they had synagogues. The question which they asked was whether he would leave an ungrateful country, and go into those distant nations and teach them.

Gentiles. In the original, *Greeks.* All those who were not *Jews* were called *Greeks,* because they were chiefly acquainted with those heathens only who spake the Greek language. It is remark able that Jesus returned no answer to these inquiries. He rather chose to turn off their minds from a speculation about the place to which he was going, to the great affairs of their own personal salvation.

{e} "dispersed" Isa 11:12; Jas 1:1; 1 Pe 1:1

{3} "Gentiles" or, "Greeks"

Verse 36. No Barnes text on this verse.

Verse 37. *In the last day.* The eighth day of the festival.

That great day. The day of the holy convocation or solemn assembly, Le 23:36. This seems to have been called the *great* day,

1st. Because of the solemn assembly, and because it was the closing scene.

2nd. Because, according to their traditions, on the previous days they offered sacrifices for the *heathen* nations as well as for themselves, but on this day for the Jews only (Lightfoot).

3rd. Because on this day they abstained from all servile labour (Le 23:39), and regarded it as a holy day.

4th. On this day they finished the reading of the law, which they commenced at the beginning of the feast.

5th. Because on this day probably occurred the ceremony of drawing water from the pool of Siloam. On the last day of the feast it was customary to perform a solemn ceremony in this manner: The priest filled a golden vial with water from the fount of Siloam (See Barnes "Joh 9:7"), which was borne with great solemnity, attended with the clangour of trumpets, through the gate of the temple, and being mixed with wine, was poured on the sacrifice on the altar. What was the origin of this custom is unknown. Some suppose, and not improbably, that it arose from an improper understanding of the passage in Isa 12:3: "With joy shall ye draw water out of the wells of salvation." It is certain that no such ceremony is commanded by Moses. It is supposed to be probable that Jesus stood and cried while they were performing this ceremony, that he might,

1st. illustrate the nature of his doctrine by this; and

2nd. call off their attention from a rite that was uncommanded, and that could not confer eternal life.

Jesus stood. In the temple, in the midst of thousands of the people.

If any man thirst. Spiritually. If any man feels his need of salvation. See Joh 4:13,14; Mt 5:6; Re 22:17.

The invitation is full and free to all.

Let him come unto me, &c. Instead of depending on *this* ceremony of drawing water let him come to me, the Messiah, and he shall find an ever-abundant supply for all the wants of his soul.

{f} "last day" Le 23:36 {g} "If any man thirst" Isa 55:1; Re 22:17

THE GOSPEL ACCORDING TO JOHN-Chapter 7-Verse 38

Verse 38. *He that believeth* on me. He that acknowledges me as the Messiah, and trusts in me for salvation.

As the scripture hath said. This is a difficult expression, from the fact that no such expression as follows is to be found literally in the Old Testament. Some have proposed to connect it with what precedes—"He that believeth on me, as the Old Testament has *commanded* or required"— but to this there are many objections. The natural and obvious meaning here is, doubtless, the true one; and Jesus probably intended to say, not that there was any *particular* place in the Old Testament that affirmed this in so many words, but that this was the*substance* of what the Scriptures taught, or this was the spirit of their declarations. Hence the *Syriac* translates it in the plural—*the Scriptures.* Probably there is a reference more particularly to Isa 58:11, than to any other single passage: "Thou shalt be like a watered garden, and like a spring of water whose waters fail not." See also Isa 44:3,4; Joe 3:18.

Out of his belly. Out of his midst, or out of his heart. The word *belly* is often put for the midst of a thing, the centre, and the heart, Mt 12:40. It means here that from the man shall flow; that is, his piety shall be of such a nature that it will extend its blessings to others. It shall be like a running fountain— perhaps in allusion to statues or ornamented reservoirs in gardens, in which pipes were placed from which water was continually flowing. The Jews used the same figure: "His two reins are like fountains of water, from which the law flows." And again: "When a man turns himself to the Lord, he shall be as a fountain filled with living water, and his streams shall flow to all the nations and tribes of men" (Kuinoel).

Rivers. This word is used to express abundance, or a full supply. It means here that those who are Christians shall diffuse large, and liberal, and constant blessings on their fellow-men; or, as Jesus immediately explains it, that they shall be the *instruments* by which the Holy Spirit shall be poured down on the world.

Living water. Fountains, ever-flowing streams. That is, the gospel shall be constant and life-giving in its blessings. We learn here,

1st. That it is the nature of Christian piety to be diffusive.

2nd. That no man can believe on Jesus who does not desire that others should also, and who will not seek it.

3rd. That the desire is large and liberal—that the Christian desires the salvation of all the world.

4th. That the *faith* of the believer is to be connected with the influence of the Holy Spirit, and *in that way* Christians are to be like rivers of living water.

{h} "out if his belly" Pr 18:4; Isa 58:11; Joh 4:14

THE GOSPEL ACCORDING TO JOHN-Chapter 7-Verse 39

Verse 39. *Of the Spirit.* Of the Holy Spirit, that should be sent down to attend their preaching and to convert sinners.

For the Holy Ghost was not yet given. Was not given in such full and large measures as should be after Jesus had ascended to heaven. Certain measures of the influences of the Spirit had been always given in the conversion and sanctification of the ancient saints and prophets; but that abundant and full effusion which the apostles were permitted afterward to behold had not yet been given. See Ac 2:1-12; 10:44,45.

Jesus was not yet glorified. Jesus had not yet ascended to heaven—to the glory and honour that awaited him there. It was a part of the arrangement in the work of redemption that the influences of the Holy Spirit should descend chiefly after the death of Jesus, as that death was the procuring cause of this great blessing. Hence he said (Joh 16:7), "It is expedient for you that I go away; for if I go not away the Comforter will not come unto you; but if I depart I will send him unto you." See also Joh 16:8-12; 14:15,16,26.

Comp. Eph 4:8-11.

{i} "the Spirit" Isa 44:3; Joe 2:28; Joh 16:7; Ac 2:17,33

THE GOSPEL ACCORDING TO JOHN-Chapter 7-Verse 40

Verse 40. *The Prophet.* That is, the prophet whom they expected to precede the coming of the Messiah—either Elijah or Jeremiah. See Mt 16:14.

{k} "the prophet" De 18:15; Joh 6:14

THE GOSPEL ACCORDING TO JOHN-Chapter 7-Verse 41

Verses 41,42. See Barnes "Mt 2:4, and following.

Where David was 1 Sa 16:1-4.

{l} "This is the" Joh 4:42; 6:69 {m} "Shall Christ come out of Galilee?" Joh 1:46; 7:52

THE GOSPEL ACCORDING TO JOHN-Chapter 7-Verse 42

Verse 42. No Barnes text on this verse.

{n} "Christ cometh"

Ps 132:11

{o} "town of Bethlehem" Mic 5:2; Lu 2:4 {p} "where David was" 1 Sa 16:1,4

THE GOSPEL ACCORDING TO JOHN-Chapter 7-Verse 43

Verse 43. No Barnes text on this verse.

THE GOSPEL ACCORDING TO JOHN-Chapter 7-Verse 44

Verse 44. No Barnes text on this verse.

THE GOSPEL ACCORDING TO JOHN-Chapter 7-Verse 45

Verses 45,46. *The officers.* Those who had been appointed (Joh 7:32) to take him. It seems that Jesus was in the midst of the people addressing them, and that they happened to come at the very time when he was speaking. They were so impressed and awed with what he said that they dared not take him. There have been few instances of eloquence like this. His speaking had so much evidence of truth, so much proof that he was from God, and was so impressive and persuasive, that they were convinced of his innocence, and they *dared* not touch him to execute their commission. We have here,

1st. A remarkable testimony to the commanding eloquence of Jesus.

2nd. Wicked men may be awed and restrained by the presence of a good man, and by the evidence that he speaks that which is true.

3rd. God can preserve his friends. Here were men sent for a particular purpose. They were armed with power. They were commissioned by the highest authority of the nation. On the other hand, Jesus was without arms or armies, and without external protection. Yet, in a manner which the officers and the high-priests would have little expected, he was preserved. So, in ways which we little expect, God will defend and deliver us when in the midst of danger.

4th. No prophet, apostle, or minister has ever spoken the truth with as much power, grace, and beauty as Jesus. It should be *ours*, therefore, to listen to his words, and to sit at his feet and learn heavenly wisdom.

THE GOSPEL ACCORDING TO JOHN-Chapter 7-Verse 46

Verse 46. No Barnes text on this verse.

{q} "Never man spake like this man" Lu 4:22.

THE GOSPEL ACCORDING TO JOHN-Chapter 7-Verse 47

Verse 47. *Are ye also deceived?* They set down the claims of Jesus as of course an imposture. They did not examine, but were, like thousands, determined to believe that he was a deceiver. Hence they did not ask them whether they were *convinced*, or had seen evidence that he was the Messiah; but, with mingled contempt, envy, and anger, they asked if they were also *deluded.* Thus many assume religion to be an imposture; and when one becomes a Christian, they assume at once that he is deceived, that he is the victim of foolish credulity or superstition, and treat him with ridicule or scorn. Candour would require them to inquire whether such changes were not proof of the power and truth of the gospel, as candour in the case of the rulers required them to inquire whether Jesus had not given them evidence that he was from God.

Verse 48. *The rulers*. The members of the Sanhedrim, who were supposed to have control over the religious rites and doctrines of the nation.

The Pharisees. The sect possessing wealth, and office, and power. The name *Pharisees* sometimes denotes those who were high in honour and authority.

Believed on him. Is there any instance in which those who are high in rank or in office have embraced him as the Messiah? This shows the rule by which they judged of religion.

1st. They claimed the right of regulating the doctrines and rites of religion.

2nd. They repressed the liberty of private judgment, stifled investigation, assumed that a *new* doctrine *must* be heresy, and laboured to keep the people in inglorious bondage.

3rd. They treated the new doctrine of Jesus with *contempt*, and thus attempted to put it down, not by argument, but by *contempt*, and especially because it was embraced by the common people. This is the way in which doctrines contrary to the truth of God have been uniformly supported in the world; this is the way in which new views of truth are met; and this the way in which those in ecclesiastical power often attempt to *lord it over God's heritage*, and to repress the investigation of the Bible.

{r} "any of the rulers" Jer 5:4,5; Joh 12:42; 1 Co 1:26

Verse 49. *This people*. The word here translated *people* is the one commonly rendered *the multitude*. It is a word expressive of contempt, or, as we would say, *the rabble*. It denotes the scorn which they felt that the *people* should presume to judge for themselves in a case pertaining to their own salvation.

Who knoweth not the law. Who have not been *instructed* in the schools of the Pharisees, and been taught to interpret the Old Testament as they had. They supposed that any who believed on the humble and despised Jesus must be, of course, ignorant of the true doctrines of the Old Testament, as they held that a very *different* Messiah from him was foretold. Many instances are preserved in the writings of the Jews of the great contempt in which the Pharisees held the common people. It may here be remarked that Christianity is the only system of religion ever presented to man that in a proper manner regards the poor, the ignorant, and the needy. Philosophers and Pharisees, in all ages, have looked on them with contempt.

Are cursed. Are execrable; are of no account; are worthy only of contempt and perdition. Some suppose that there is reference here to their being worthy to be cut off from the people for believing on him, worthy to be put out of the synagogue (See Joh 9:22); but it seems to be an expression only of *contempt*; a declaration that they were a rabble, ignorant, unworthy of notice, and going to ruin. Observe, however,

1st. That of this despised people were chosen most of those who became Christians.

2nd. That if the people were ignorant, it was the fault of the Pharisees and rulers. It was their business to see that they were taught.

3rd. There is no way so common of attempting to oppose Christianity as by ridiculing its friends as poor, ignorant, and weak, and credulous. As well night food, and raiment, and friendship, and patriotism be held in contempt because the poor need the one or possess the other.

Verse 50. *Nicodemus.* See Joh 3:1.

One of them. That is, one of the great council or Sanhedrim. God often places one or more pious men in legislative assemblies to vindicate his honour and his law; and he often gives a man grace on such occasions boldly to defend his cause; to put men *upon their proof,* and to confound the proud and the domineering. We see in this case, also, that a man, at one time timid and fearful (comp.) Joh 3:1), may on other occasions be bold, and fearlessly defend the truth as it is in Jesus. This example should lead every man intrusted with authority or office fearlessly to defend the truth of God, and, when the rich and the mighty are pouring contempt on Jesus and his cause, to stand forth as its fearless defender.

{s} "he that came" Joh 3:2 {4} "to Jesus", "to him"

Verse 51. *Doth our law,* &c. The law required *justice* to be done, and gave every man the right to claim a fair and impartial trial, Le 19:15,16; Ex 23:1,2; De 19:15,18.

Their condemnation of Jesus was a violation of every rule of right. He was not arraigned; he was not heard in self-defence, and not a single witness was adduced. Nicodemus demanded that *justice* should be done, and that he should not be condemned until he had had a fair trial. Every man should be presumed innocent until he is proved to be guilty. This is a maxim of law, and a most just and proper precept in our judgments in private life.

{t} "Doth our law" De 17:8; Pr 18:13

Verse 52. *Art thou also of Galilee?* Here is another expression of contempt. To be a *Galilean* was a term of the highest reproach. They knew well that he was not of Galilee, but they meant to ask whether *he* also had become a follower of the despised Galilean. Ridicule is not argument, and there is no demonstration in a gibe; but, unhappily, this is the only weapon which the proud and haughty often used in opposing religion.

Ariseth no prophet. That is, there is no prediction that any prophet should come out of Galilee, and especially no prophet that was to attend or precede the Messiah. Comp. Joh 1:46.

They assumed, therefore, that Jesus could not be the Christ.

{u} "Out of Galilee" Isa 9:1,2

Verse 53. *And every man went unto his own house.* There is every mark of confusion and disorder in this breaking up of the Sanhedrim. It is possible that some of the Sadducees might have joined Nicodemus in opposing the Pharisees, and thus increased the disorder. It is a most instructive and melancholy exhibition of the influence of pride, envy, contempt, and anger, when brought to bear on an inquiry, and when they are manifestly opposed to candour, to argument, and to truth. So wild and furious are the passions of men when they oppose the person and claims of the Son of God! It is remarkable, too, how God accomplishes his purposes. *They* wished to destroy Jesus. God suffered their passions to be excited, a tumult to ensue, the assembly thus to break up in disorder, and Jesus to be safe, for his time had not yet come. "The wrath of man shall praise thee; the remainder of wrath shalt thou restrain,"Ps 76:10.

THE GOSPEL ACCORDING TO JOHN-Chapter 8

Verse 1. *Mount of Olives.* The mountain about a mile directly east of Jerusalem. See Barnes "Mt 21:1".

This was the place in which he probably often passed the night when attending the feasts at Jerusalem. The Garden of Gethsemane, to which he was accustomed to resort (Joh 18:2), was on the western side of that mountain, and Bethany, the abode of Martha and Mary, on its east side, Joh 11:1.

Verse 2. No Barnes text on this verse.

Verse 3. No Barnes text on this verse.

Verse 4. No Barnes text on this verse.

Verse 5. *Moses in the law,* &c. The punishment of adultery commanded by Moses was death, Le 20:10; De 22:22. The particular manner of the death was not specified in the law. The Jews had themselves, in the time of Christ, determined that it should be by stoning. See this described in See Barnes "Mt 21:35".

See Barnes "Mt 21:44".

The punishment for adultery varied. In some cases it was strangling. In the time of Ezekiel Eze 16:38-40 it was stoning and being thrust through with a sword. If the adulteress was the daughter of a priest, the punishment was being burned to death.

{a} "Now Moses" Le 20:10

Verse 6. *Tempting him.* Trying him, or laying a plan that they might have occasion to accuse him. If he decided the case, they expected to be able to bring an accusation against him; for if he decided that she ought to die, they might accuse him of claiming power which belonged to the Romans—the power of life and death. They might allege that it was not the giving an opinion about an abstract case, but that she was formally before him, that he decided her case *judicially,* and that without authority or form of trial. If he decided otherwise, they would have alleged that he denied the authority of the law, and that it was his intention to abrogate it. They had had a controversy with him about the authority of the Sabbath, and they perhaps supposed that he would decide this case as he did that—against them. It may be farther added that they knew that Jesus admitted publicans and sinners to eat with him; that one of their charges was that he was friendly to sinners (see Lu 15:2); and they wished, doubtless, to make it appear that he was *gluttonous*, and a *wine-bibber*, and *a friend of sinners*, and disposed to relax all the laws of morality, even in the case of adultery. Seldom was there a plan more artfully laid, and never was more wisdom and knowledge of human nature displayed than in the manner in which it was met.

Wrote on the ground. This took place in the *temple.* The "ground," here, means the pavement, or the dust on the pavement. By this Jesus showed them clearly that he was not*solicitous* to pronounce an opinion in the case, and that it was not his wish or intention to intermeddle with the civil affairs of the nation.

As though he heard them not. This is added by the translators. It is not in the original, and should not have been added. There is no intimation in the original, as it seems to be implied by this addition, that the object was to convey the impression that he did not hear them. What was his object is unknown, and conjecture is useless. The most probable reason seems to be that he did not wish to intermeddle; that he designed to show no solicitude to decide the case; and that he did not mean to decide it unless he was *constrained* to.

THE GOSPEL ACCORDING TO JOHN-Chapter 8-Verse 7

Verse 7. *They continued asking him.* They pressed the question upon him. They were determined to extort an answer from him, and showed a perseverance in evil which has been unhappily often imitated.

Is without sin. That is, without this particular sin; he who has not himself been guilty of this very crime—for in this place the connection evidently demands this meaning.

Let him first cast a stone at her. In the punishment by death, one of the witnesses threw the culprit from the scaffold, and the other threw the first stone, or rolled down a stone to crush him. See De 17:6,7. This was in order that the witness might feel his responsibility in giving evidence, as he was also to be the executioner. Jesus therefore put them to the test. Without pronouncing on her case, he directed them, if any of them were innocent, to perform the office of executioner. This was said, evidently, well knowing their guilt, and well knowing that no one would dare to do it.

{b} "He that is" De 17:7; Ro 2:1,2

THE GOSPEL ACCORDING TO JOHN-Chapter 8-Verse 8

Verse 8. No Barnes text on this verse.

THE GOSPEL ACCORDING TO JOHN-Chapter 8-Verse 9

Verse 9. *Beginning at the eldest.* As being conscious of more sins, and, therefore, being desirous to leave the Lord Jesus. The word *eldest* here probably refers not to age, but to *honour*— from those who were in highest reputation to the lowest in rank. This consciousness of crime showed that the state of the public morals was exceedingly corrupt, and justified the declaration of Jesus that it was an *adulterous and wicked generation*, Mt 16:4.

Alone. Jesus only was left with the woman, &c.

In the midst. Her *accusers* had gone out, and left Jesus and the woman; but it is by no means probable that the people had left them; and, as this was in the temple on a public occasion, they were doubtless surrounded still by many. This is evident from the fact that Jesus immediately (Joh 8:12) addressed a discourse to the people present.

THE GOSPEL ACCORDING TO JOHN-Chapter 8-Verse 10

Verse 10. *Hath no man condemned thee?* Jesus had directed them, if innocent, to cast a stone, thus *to condemn her*, or to use the power which he gave them to condemn her. No one of them had done that. They had *accused her*, but they had not proceeded to the act expressive of *judicial condemnation*.

THE GOSPEL ACCORDING TO JOHN-Chapter 8-Verse 11

Verse 11. *Neither do I condemn thee.* This is evidently to be taken in the sense of *judicial* condemnation, or of passing sentence as a *magistrate*, for this was what they had arraigned her for. It was not to obtain his opinion about adultery, but to obtain the *condemnation* of the woman. As he claimed no *civil* authority, he said that he did not exercise it, and should not *condemn her to die*. In this sense the word is used in the previous verse, and this is the only sense which the passage demands. Besides, what follows shows that this was his meaning.

Go, and sin no more. You have sinned. You have been detected and accused. The sin is great. But I do not claim power to condemn you to die, and, as your *accusers* have left you, my direction to you is that you *sin* no more. This passage therefore teaches us,

1st. That Jesus claimed no civil authority.

2nd. That he regarded the action of which they accused her as sin.

3rd. That he knew the *hearts* and *lives* of men.

4th. That men are often very zealous in accusing others of that of which they themselves are guilty. And,

5th. That Jesus was endowed with wonderful wisdom in meeting the devices of his enemies, and eluding their deep-laid plans to involve him in ruin. It should be added that this passage, together with the last verse of the preceding chapter, has been by many critics thought to be spurious. It is wanting in many of the ancient manuscripts and versions, and has been rejected by Erasmus, Calvin, Beza, Grotius, Wetstein, Tittman, Knapp, and many others. It is not easy to decide the question whether it be a genuine part of the New Testament or not. Some have supposed that it was not *written* by the evangelists, but was often *related* by them, and that after a time it was recorded and introduced by Papias into the sacred text.

{c} "Neither do I condemn" Joh 3:17 {d} "and sin no more" Joh 5:14

Verse 12. *I am the light of the world.* See Barnes "Joh 1:4"
See Barnes "Joh 1:9"

{e} "I am the light of the world" Joh 1:4; 9:5 {f} "He that followeth" Joh 12:35,46

Verse 13. *Thou bearest record of thyself.* Thou art a *witness* for thyself, or in thy own case. See Joh 5:31. The law required two witnesses in a criminal case, and they alleged that as the only evidence which Jesus had was his own assertion, it could not be entitle to belief.

Is not true. Is not worthy of belief, or is not substantiated by sufficient evidence.

{g} "Thou bearest record" Joh 5:31

Verse 14. *Jesus answered,* &c. To this objection Jesus replied by saying, first, that the case was such that his testimony alone ought to be received; and, secondly, that he had the evidence given him by his Father. Though, in common life, in courts, and in mere human transactions, it was true that a man ought not to give evidence in his own case, yet in this instance, such was the nature of the case that his word was worthy to be believed.

My record. My evidence, my testimony.

Is true. Is worthy to be believed.

For I know whence I came—but ye, &c. I know by what authority I act; I know by whom I am sent, and what commands were given me; but you cannot determine this, for you do not know these unless *I* bear witness of them to you. We are to remember that Jesus came not of himself (Joh 6:38); that he came not to do his own will, but the will of his Father. He came as a *witness* of those things which he had seen and known (Joh 3:11), and no man could judge *of those things,* for no man had seen them. As he came from heaven; as he knew his Father's will; as he had seen the eternal world, and known the counsels of his Father, so his testimony was worthy of confidence. As *they* had not seen and known these things, they were not qualified to judge. An ambassador from a foreign court knows the will and purposes of the sovereign who sent him, and is competent to bear witness of it. The court to which he is sent has no way of judging but by his testimony, and he is therefore competent to testify in the case. All that can be demanded is that he give *his* credentials that he is appointed, and this Jesus had done both by the nature of his doctrine and his miracles.

{h} "but you cannot tell" Joh 7:28; 9:29,30

Verse 15. *After the flesh.* According to appearance; according to your carnal and corrupt mode; not according to the spiritual nature of the doctrines. By your preconceived opinions and prejudices you are determined not to believe that I am the Messiah.

I judge no man. Jesus came not to condemn the world, Joh 3:17. They were in the habit of judging rashly and harshly of all; but this was not the purpose or disposition of the Saviour. This expression is to be understood as meaning that he judged no one *after their manner*; he did not come to censure and condemn men after the appearance, or in a harsh, biased, and unkind manner.

{i} "I judge no man" Joh 3:17; 12:47

THE GOSPEL ACCORDING TO JOHN-Chapter 8-Verse 16

Verse 16. *And yet, if I judge.* If I should express my judgment of men or things. He was not *limited,* nor forbidden to do it, nor restrained by any fear that his judgment would be erroneous.

My judgment is true. Is worthy to be regarded.

For I am not alone. I concur with the Father who hath sent me. His judgment *you* admit would be right, and *my* judgment would accord with his. He was commissioned by his Father, and his judgment would coincide with all that God had purposed or revealed. This was shown by the evidence that God gave that he had sent him into the world.

{k} "my judgment" 1 Sa 16:7; Ps 45:6,7; 72:2

{i} "for I am not alone" Joh 8:29; 16:32

THE GOSPEL ACCORDING TO JOHN-Chapter 8-Verse 17

Verse 17. *In your law.* De 17:6; 19:15. Comp. Mt 18:16. This related to cases in which the life of an individual was involved. Jesus says that if, in such a case, the testimony of two men were sufficient to *establish* a fact, his own testimony and that of his Father ought to be esteemed ample evidence in the case of religious doctrine.

Two men.. If two men could confirm a case, the evidence of Jesus and of God ought not to be deemed insufficient.

Is true. In Deuteronomy, "established." This means the same thing. It is confirmed; is worthy of belief.

THE GOSPEL ACCORDING TO JOHN-Chapter 8-Verse 18

Verse 18. *I am one that bear witness of myself.* In human courts a man is not allowed to bear witness of himself, because he has a personal interest in the case, and the court could have no proof of the *impartiality* of the evidence; but in the case of Jesus it was otherwise. When one has no party ends to serve; when he is willing to deny himself; when he makes great sacrifices; and when, by his life, he gives every evidence of sincerity, his own testimony may be admitted in evidence of his motives and designs. This was the case with Jesus and his apostles. And though in a legal or criminal case such testimony would not be admitted, yet, in an argument on moral subjects, about the will and purpose of him who sent him, it would not be right to reject the testimony of one who gave so many proofs that he came from God.

The Father—beareth witness of me. By the voice from heaven at his baptism (Mt 3:17), and by the miracles which Jesus wrought, as well as by the prophecies of the Old Testament. We may here remark,

1st. That there is a distinction between the Father and the Son. They are both represented as bearing testimony; yet,

2nd. They are not divided. They are not different beings. They bear testimony to the same thing, and are *one* in counsel, in plan, in essence, and in glory.

{n} "the Father" Joh 5:37

Verse 19. *Where is thy Father?* This question was asked, doubtless, in derision. Jesus had often given them to understand that by his Father he meant God, Joh 5:1-6:71. They *professed* to be ignorant of this, and probably looked round in contempt for his Father, that he might adduce him as a witness in the case.

If ye had known me, &c. If you had listened to my instructions, and had received me as the Messiah, you would also, at the same time, have been acquainted with God. We may here observe,

1st. The *manner* in which Jesus answered them. He gave no heed to their cavil; he was not *irritated* by their contempt; he preserved his *dignity*, and gave them an answer worthy of the Son of God.

2nd. We should meet the *cavils* and sneers of sinners in the same manner. We should not render railing for railing, but "in meekness instruct those that oppose themselves, if God peradventure will give them repentance to the acknowledging of the truth," 2 Ti 2:25.

3rd. The way to know God is to know Jesus Christ. "No man hath seen God at any time. The only-begotten Son which is in the bosom of the Father, he hath *declared* him," Joh 1:18. No sinner can have just views of God but in Jesus Christ, 2 Co 4:6.

{o} "Jesus answered" Joh 8:55; 16:3; 17:25

Verse 20. *The treasury.* See Barnes "Mt 21:12".

His hour was not yet come. The time for him to die had not yet arrived, and God restrained them, and kept his life. This proves that God has power over wicked men to control them, and to make them accomplish his own purposes.

{q} "treasury" Mr 12:41 {r} "for his hour" Joh 7:30

Verse 21. *I go my way.* See Barnes "Joh 7:33".

Ye shall die in your sins. That is, you will seek the Messiah; you will desire his coming, but the Messiah that *you* expect will not come; and, as you have rejected me, and there is no other Saviour, you must die in your sins. You will die unpardoned, and as you did not seek me where you might find me, you cannot come where I shall be. Observe,

1st. All those who reject the Lord Jesus must die unforgiven. There is no way of pardon but by him. See Barnes "Ac 4:12".

2nd. There will be a time when sinners will seek for a Saviour but will find none. Often this is done too late, in a dying moment, and in the future world they may seek a deliverer, but not be able to find one.

3rd. Those who reject the Lord Jesus must perish. Where he is they cannot come. Where he is is heaven. Where he is not, with his favour and mercy, there is hell; and the sinner that has no Saviour must be wretched for ever.

{s} "ye shall seek me" Joh 7:34 {t} "and shall die" Job 20:11

THE GOSPEL ACCORDING TO JOHN-Chapter 8-Verse 22

Verse 22. *Will he kill himself?* It is difficult to know whether this question was asked from ignorance or malice. Self-murder was esteemed then, as it is now, as one of the greatest crimes; and it is not improbable that they asked this question with mingled hatred and contempt. "He is a *deceiver*; he has broken the law of Moses; he is mad, and it is probable he *will* go on and kill himself." If this was their meaning, we see the wonderful patience of Jesus in enduring the contradiction of sinners; and as *he* bore contempt without rendering railing for railing, so should we.

THE GOSPEL ACCORDING TO JOHN-Chapter 8-Verse 23

Verse 23. *Ye are from bequeath.* The expression *from beneath*, here, is opposed to the phrase from above. It means, You are *of the earth*, or are influenced by earthly, sensual, and corrupt passions. You are governed by the lowest and vilest views and feelings, such as are opposed to heaven, and such as have their origin in earth or in hell.

I am from above. From heaven. My views are heavenly, and my words should have been so interpreted.

Ye are of this world. You think and act like the corrupt men of this world.

I am not of this world. My views are above these earthly and corrupt notions. The meaning of the verse is:

"Your reference to self-murder shows that you are
earthly and corrupt in your views. You are governed
by the mad passions of men, and can think only of these."

We see here how difficult it is to excite wicked men to the contemplation of heavenly

clxi

things. They interpret all things in a low and corrupt sense, and suppose all others to be governed as they are themselves.

THE GOSPEL ACCORDING TO JOHN-Chapter 8-Verse 24

Verse 24. *That I am*. That I am the Messiah.

{v} "I said" Joh 8:21

THE GOSPEL ACCORDING TO JOHN-Chapter 8-Verse 25

Verse 25. *Who art thou?* As Jesus did not expressly say in the previous verse that he was the Messiah, they professed still not to understand him. In great contempt, therefore, they asked him who *he was*. As if they had said, "Who art thou that undertakest to threaten us in this manner?" When we remember that they regarded him as a mere pretender from Galilee; that he was poor and without friends; and that he was persecuted by those in authority, we cannot but admire the patience with which all this was borne, and the coolness with which he answered them.

Even the same, &c. What he had professed to them was that he was the light of the world; that he was the bread that came down from heaven; that he was sent by his Father, &c. From all this they might easily gather that he claimed to be the Messiah. He assumed no *new* character; he made no *change* in his professions; he is the same yesterday, today, and for ever; and as he had once professed to be the light of the world, so, in the face of contempt, persecution, and death, he adhered to the profession.

The beginning. From his first discourse with them, or uniformly.

THE GOSPEL ACCORDING TO JOHN-Chapter 8-Verse 26

Verse 26. *I have many things to say*. There are many things which I *might* say to reprove and expose your pride and hypocrisy. By this he implied that he understood *well* their character, and that he was able to expose it. This, indeed, he had shown them in his conversations with them.

And to judge of you. To reprove in you. There are many things in you which I might condemn.

But he that sent me is true. Is worthy to be believed, and his declarations about men are to be credited. The meaning of this verse may be thus expressed:

"I have indeed many things to say blaming or
condemning you. I have already said many such things,
and there are many more that I might say; but I
speak only those things which God has commanded. I
speak not of myself I come to execute his commission,
and he is worthy to be heard and feared. Let it not be
thought, therefore, that my judgment is rash or harsh.
It is such as is commanded by God."

{x} "he that sent me" Joh 7:28

Verse 27. *They understood not.* They knew not, or they were unwilling to receive him as a messenger from God. They doubtless understood that he *meant* to speak of God, but they were unwilling to acknowledge that he really came from God.

Verse 28. *When ye have lifted up.* When you have crucified. See Barnes "Joh 3:14, See Barnes "Joh 12:32".

The Son of man. See Barnes "Mt 8:19,20".

Then shall ye know. Then shall you have evidence or proof.
That I am he. Am the Messiah, which I have professed to be.
And that I do nothing of myself. That is, you shall have proof that God has sent me; that I am the Messiah; and that God concurs with me and approves my doctrine. This proof was furnished by the miracles that attended the death of Jesus —the earthquake and darkness; but chiefly by his resurrection from the dead, which proved, beyond a doubt, that he was what he affirmed he was— the Messiah.
{y} "lifted up" Joh 3:14; 12:32

Verse 29. *Is with me.* In working miracles, &c.
Hath not left me alone. Though men had forsaken and rejected him, yet God attended him.
Those things that please him. See Mt 3:17: "This is my beloved Son, in whom I am well pleased," Php 2:8; Isa 53:10-12; 2 Pe 1:17; Lu 3:22; Mt 17:5.

His *undertaking* the work of redemption was pleasing to God, and he had the consciousness that in *executing* it he did those things which God approved. It is a small matter to have men opposed to us, if we have a conscience void of offence, and evidence that we please God. Comp. Heb 11:5 "Enoch —before his translation had this testimony that he pleased God." See also 1 Co 4:3.

Verse 30. *Many believed on him.* Such was the convincing nature and force of the truths which he presented, that they believed he was the Messiah and received his doctrine. While there were many that became more obstinate and hardened under his preaching, there were many, also, who by the same truth were made penitent and believing. "The same sun that hardens the clay, softens the wax" (Clarke).
{z} "many believed on him" Joh 10:42

Verse 31. *If ye continue in my word.* If you continue to obey my commandments and to receive my doctrines.

Then are ye, &c. This is the true test of Christian character. Joh 14:21. "He that hath my commandments and keepeth them, he it is that loveth me." See 1 Jo 2:4; 3:24; 2 Jo 1:6.

In this place Jesus cautions them against *too much confidence from their present feelings.* They were just converted—converted under a single sermon. They had had no time to test their faith. Jesus assures them that if their faith should abide the test, if it should produce obedience to his commandments and a holy life, it would be proof that their faith was genuine, for the tree is known by its fruit. So we may say to all new converts, Do not repress your love or your joy, but do not be too confident. Your faith has not yet been tried, and if it does not produce a holy life it is vain, Jas 2:17-26.

{a} "continue" Ro 2:7; Col 1:23; Heb 10:38,39

Verse 32. *Shall know the truth.* See Barnes "Joh 7:17".

The truth shall make you free. The *truth* here means the Christian religion. Comp. Ga 3:1; Col 1:6. The doctrines of the true religion shall make you free—that is, it will free you from the *slavery* of evil passions, corrupt propensities, and grovelling views. The condition of a sinner is that of a *captive* or a *slave* to sin. He is one who serves and obeys the dictates of an evil heart and the promptings of an evil nature, Ro 6:16,17: "Ye were the *servants* of sin;" Ro 6:19: "Ye have yielded your members servants unto iniquity; Ro 6:20; 7:6,8,11; 8:21; Ac 8:23.

"Thou art in the —bond of iniquity;" Ga 4:3,9. The effect of the gospel is to break this hard bondage to sin and to set the sinner free. We learn from this that religion is not slavery or oppression. It is true freedom.

"He is the freeman whom the truth makes free,
And all are slaves beside." —Cowper.

The service of God is freedom from degrading vices and carnal propensities; from the slavery of passion and inordinate desires. It is a cheerful and delightful surrender of ourselves to Him whose yoke is easy and whose burden is light.

{b} "know the truth" Ho 6:3 {c} "the truth" Ps 119:45; Joh 17:17; Ro 6:14,18,22; Jas 1:25; 2:12

Verse 33. *They answered him.* Not those who believed on him, but some who stood by and heard him.

We be Abraham's seed. We are the children or descendants of Abraham. Abraham was not a slave, and they pretended that they were his real descendants, inheriting his freedom as well as his spirit. They meant that they were the direct descendants of Abraham by Isaac, his heir. Ishmael, also Abraham's son, was the son of a bond-woman (Ga 4:21-23), but *they* were descended in a direct line from the acknowledged heir of Abraham.

Were never in bondage to any man. This is a most remarkable declaration, and one evidently false. Their fathers had been slaves in Egypt; their nation had been enslaved in Babylon; it had repeatedly been subject to the Assyrians; it was enslaved by Herod the Great; and was, at the very time they spoke, groaning under the grievous and insupportable bondage of the Romans. But we see here,

1st. That Jesus was right when he said (Joh 8:44), "Ye are of your father the devil; he is a liar, and the father of it."

2nd. Men will say anything, however false or ridiculous, to avoid and oppose the truth.

3rd. Men groaning under the most oppressive bondage are often unwilling to acknowledge it in any manner, and are indignant at being charged with it. This is the case with all sinners.

4th. Sin, and the bondage to sin, produces passion, irritation, and a troubled soul; and a man under the influence of passion regards little what he says, and is often a liar.

5th. There is need of the gospel. That only can make men free, calm, collected, meek, and lovers of truth; and as every man is by nature the servant of sin, he should without delay seek an interest in that gospel which can alone make him free.

{d} "never in bondage" Le 25:42

THE GOSPEL ACCORDING TO JOHN-Chapter 8-Verse 34

Verse 34. *Whosoever committeth sin*, &c. In this passage Jesus shows them that he did not refer to *political* bondage, but to the slavery of the soul to evil passions and desires.

Is the servant. Is the *slave* of sin. He is bound to it as a slave is to his master.

{e} "Whosever committeth sin" Ro 6:16,20; 2 Pe 2:19

THE GOSPEL ACCORDING TO JOHN-Chapter 8-Verse 35

Verse 35. *The servant abideth not*, &c. The servant does not, of course, remain for ever, or till his death, with his master. If he is disobedient and wicked, the master sells him or turns him away. He is not the heir, and may at any time be expelled from the house of his master. But a son is the heir. He cannot be in this manner cast off or sold. He is privileged with the right of remaining in the family. This takes place in common life. So said the Saviour to the Jews: "You, if you are disobedient and rebellious, may at any time be rejected from being the people of God, and be deprived of your peculiar privileges as a nation. You are in the condition of servants, and unless you are made *free* by the gospel, and become entitled to the privilege of the sons of God, you will be cast off like an unfaithful slave." Comp. He 3:5,6.

Abideth not. Remains not, or has not the legal right to remain. He may at any time be rejected or sold.

In the house. In the family of his master.

For ever. During the whole time of his life.

The Son. The heir. He remains, and cannot be sold or cast off.

Ever. Continually. Till the day of his death. This is the privilege of a son, to inherit and dispose of the property.

Verse 36. *If the Son*, &c. The Son of God —heir of all things—who is for ever with God, and who has therefore the right and power to liberate men from their thraldom.

Shall make you free. Shall deliver you from the bondage and dominion of sin.

Free indeed. Truly and really free. You shall be blessed with the most valuable freedom; not from the chains and oppressions of earthly masters and monarchs, but from the bondage of sin.

{g} "the Son" Ga 4:30 {h} "ye shall be free" Isa 61:1

Verse 37. *I know*, &c. I admit that you are the descendants of Abraham. Jesus did not wish to call that in question, but he endeavoured to show them that they might be his descendants and still lack entirely his spirit. See Barnes "Mt 3:9".

Ye seek to kill me. Joh 5:16; 7:32.

Because my word. My *doctrine*; the principles of my religion. You have not the spirit of my doctrine; you hate it, and you therefore seek to kill me.

Hath no place. That is, you do not embrace my doctrine, or it exerts no influence over you. The original word conveys the notion that there was *no room* for his doctrine in their minds. It met with *obstructions*, and did not penetrate into their hearts. They were so filled with pride, and prejudice, and false notions, that they would not receive his truth; and as they had not his truth or spirit, and could not bear it, they sought to kill him.

Verse 38. *I speak*, &c. Joh 3:11-13.

My Father. God.

Your father. The devil. See Joh 8:44. To see here means to learn of. They had learned of or been taught by the devil, and imitated him.

{i} "I speak that" Joh 14:10,24

Verse 39. *Abraham is our father.* We are descended from Abraham. Of this the Jews boasted much, as being descended from such an illustrious man. See Barnes "Mt 3:9".

As Jesus did not expressly say who he meant (Joh 8:38) when he said they did the works of their father, they obstinately persisted in pretending not to understand him, as if they had said, "We acknowledge no other father but Abraham, and to charge us with being the offspring of another is slander and calumny."

If ye were Abraham's children. The words *sons* and *children* are often used to denote those who imitate another or who have his spirit. See Barnes "Mt 1:1".

Here it means, "if you were worthy to be called the children of Abraham, or if you had his spirit."

{k} "Abraham" Mt 3:9 {l} "If ye were" Ro 2:28,29; 9:7; Ga 3:7,29

THE GOSPEL ACCORDING TO JOHN-Chapter 8-Verse 40

Verse 40. *Ye seek to kill me.* See Joh 8:37.

This did not Abraham. Or such things Abraham did not do. There are two things noted here in which they differed from Abraham:

1st. In seeking to kill him, or in possessing a murderous and bloody purpose.

2nd. In rejecting the truth as God revealed it. Abraham was distinguished for love to man as well as God. He liberated the captives (Ge 14:14-16); was distinguished for hospitality to strangers (Ge 18:1-8); and received the revelations of God to him, however mysterious, or however trying their observance, Ge 12:1-4; 15:4-6; Ge 22:1-24. It was for these things that he is so much commended in the New Testament (Ro 4:9; 9:9; Ga 3:6); and, as the Jews sought to kill Jesus instead of treating him hospitably and kindly, they showed that they had none of the spirit of Abraham.

{m} "this did not Abraham" Ro 4:12

THE GOSPEL ACCORDING TO JOHN-Chapter 8-Verse 41

Verse 41. *The deeds of your father.* See Joh 8:38. Jesus repeats the charge, and yet repeats it as if unwilling to name Satan as their father. He chose that they should *infer* whom he meant, rather than bring a charge so direct and repelling. When the Saviour delivered an awful or an offensive truth, he always approached the mind so that the truth might make the deepest impression.

We be not born of fornication. The people still professed not to understand him; and since Jesus had denied that they were the children of *Abraham,* they affected to suppose that he meant they were a mixed, spurious race; that they had no right to the covenant privileges of the Jews; that they were not worshippers of the true God. Hence they said, We are not thus descended. We have the evidence of our genealogy. We are worshippers of the true God, descended from those who acknowledged him, and we acknowledge no other God and Father than him. To be *children of fornication* is an expression denoting in the Scriptures idolatry, or the worship of other gods than the true God, Isa 1:21; 57:3; Ho 1:2; 2:4.

This they denied. They affirmed that they acknowledged no God for their Father but the true God.

{n} "we have one Father" Isa 63:16; 64:8

THE GOSPEL ACCORDING TO JOHN-Chapter 8-Verse 42

Verse 42. *If God were your Father.* If you had the spirit of God, or love to him, or were worthy to be called his children.

Ye would love me. Jesus was "the brightness of the Father's glory and the express image of his person," Heb 1:3. "Every one that loveth him that begat, loveth him also that is begotten of him," 1 Jo 5:1. From this we see,

1st. That all who truly love God, love his Son Jesus Christ.

2nd. That men that pretend that they love God, and reject his Son, have no evidence that they are the friends of God.

3rd. That those who reject the Bible cannot be the friends of God. If they loved God, they would love Him who came from him, and who bears his image.

{o} "If God" Joh 17:8,25

THE GOSPEL ACCORDING TO JOHN-Chapter 8-Verse 43

Verse 43. *Why do ye not.* My meaning is clear, if you were disposed to understand me.

Even *because ye cannot hear my word.* The word "hear" in this place is to be understood in the sense of *bear* or *tolerate,* as in Joh 6:60. His doctrine was offensive to them. They hated it, and hence they perverted his meaning, and were resolved *not* to understand him. Their pride, vanity, and wickedness opposed it. The reason why sinners do not understand the Bible and its doctrines is because they cannot *bear* them. They hate them, and their hatred produces want of candour, a disposition to cavil and to pervert the truth, and an obstinate purpose that it *shall not* be applied to their case. Hence they embrace every form of false doctrine, and choose error rather than truth, and darkness rather than light. A *disposition to believe God* is one of the best helps for understanding the Bible.

{q} "even because" Isa 6:9

THE GOSPEL ACCORDING TO JOHN-Chapter 8-Verse 44

Verse 44. *Ye are of your father the devil.* That is, you have the temper, disposition, or spirit of the devil. You are influenced by him, you imitate him, and ought therefore to be called his children. See also 1 Jo 3:8-10; Ac 13:10: "Thou child of the devil."

The devil. See Barnes "Mt 4:1".

The lusts. The desires or the wishes. You do what pleases him. *Ye will do.* The word *will,* here, is not an auxiliary verb. It does not simply express *futurity,* or that such a thing will take place, but it implies an act of volition. This you *will* or *choose* to do. The same mode of speech occurs in Joh 5:40. In what respects they showed that they were the children of the devil he proceeds to state:

1st. in their murderous disposition;

2nd. in rejecting the truth;

3rd. in being favourable to falsehood and error.

He was a murderer from the beginning. That is, from the beginning of the world, or in the first records of him he is thus represented. This refers to the seduction of Adam and Eve. Death was denounced against sin, Ge 2:17. The devil deceived our first parents, and they became subject to death, Ge 3:1-24. As he was the cause why death came into the world, he may be said to have been a murderer in that act, or from the beginning. We see here that the tempter mentioned in Ge 3:1 was Satan or the devil, who is here declared to have been the murderer. Comp. Re 5:12; 12:9:

"And the great dragon was cast out, that old serpent
called the devil, and Satan, which deceiveth the
whole world."

Besides, Satan has in all ages *deceived* men, and been the cause of their spiritual and eternal death. His work has been to destroy, and in the worst sense of the word he may be said to have been a *murderer*. It was by his instigation, also, that Cain killed his brother, 1 Jo 3:12: "Not as Cain, who was of that wicked one, and slew his brother." As the Jews endeavoured to kill the Saviour, so they showed that they had the spirit of the devil.

Abode not in the truth. He departed from the truth, or was false and a liar.

No truth in him. That is, he is a liar. It is his nature and his work to deceive.

He speaketh of his own. The word "own" is in the plural number, and means of the things that are appropriate to him, or that belong to his nature. His speaking falsehood is originated by his own propensities or disposition; he utters the expressions of his genuine character.

He is a liar. As when he deceived Adam, and in his deceiving, as far as possible, the world, and dragging man down to perdition.

The father of it. The father or *originator of falsehood.* The word "it" refers to *lie* or *falsehood* understood. From him falsehood first proceeded, and all liars possess his spirit and are under his influence. As the Jews refused to hear the truth which Jesus spoke, so they showed that they were the children of the father of lies.

{r} "Ye are" Mt 13:38; 1 Jo 3:8 {s} "abode not in the truth" Jude 1:6

THE GOSPEL ACCORDING TO JOHN-Chapter 8-Verse 45

Verse 45. No Barnes text on this verse.

{t} "because I tell you"

Ga 4:16; 2 Th 2:10

THE GOSPEL ACCORDING TO JOHN-Chapter 8-Verse 46

Verse 46. *Which of you convinceth me?* To *convince,* with us, means to satisfy a *man's own mind* of the truth of anything; but this, is not its meaning here. It rather means to *convict.* Which of you can *prove* that I am guilty of sin.

Of sin. The word *sin* here evidently means *error, falsehood*, or *imposture*. It stands opposed to *truth*. The argument of the Saviour is this: A doctrine might be rejected if it could be proved that he that delivered it was an *impostor*; but as you cannot prove this of me, you are bound to receive my words.

THE GOSPEL ACCORDING TO JOHN-Chapter 8-Verse 47

Verse 47. *He that is of God.* He that loves, fears, and honours God.

Heareth God's words. Listens to, or attends to the doctrines or commandments of God, as a child who loves his parent will regard and obey his commandments. This is an evidence of true piety. A willingness to receive all that God teaches us, and to obey all his commandments, is an undoubted proof that we are his friends, Joh 14:21; 1 Jo 2:4; 3:24.

As the Jews did *not* show a readiness to obey the commands of God, it proved that they were not of him, and to this was owing their rejection of the Lord Jesus.

THE GOSPEL ACCORDING TO JOHN-Chapter 8-Verse 48

Verse 48. *Say we not well.* Say we not *truly.*

Thou art a Samaritan. This was a term of contempt and reproach. See Barnes "Joh 4:9".

It had the force of charging him with being a *heretic* or a *schismatic*, because the Samaritans were regarded as such.

And hast a devil. See Joh 7:20. This charge they brought against him because he had said that they were not of God, or were not the friends of God. This they regarded as the same as taking sides with the Samaritans, for the question between the Jews and Samaritans was, which of them worshipped God aright, Joh 4:20. As Jesus affirmed that the *Jews* were not of God, and as he, contrary to all *their* views, had gone and preached to the Samaritans (John 4), they regarded it as a proof that he was disposed to take part with them. They also regarded it as evidence that he had a devil. The *devil* was an *accuser* or *calumniator*; and as Jesus charged them with being opposed to God, they considered it as proof that he was influenced by such an evil spirit.

Devil. In the original, *demon.* Not the prince or chief of the devils, but an evil spirit.

{v} "hast not a devil"

@Joh 7:20

THE GOSPEL ACCORDING TO JOHN-Chapter 8-Verse 49

Verse 49. *I have not a devil.* To the first part of the charge, that he was a Samaritan, he did not reply. To the other part he replied by saying that he *honoured his Father.* He taught the doctrines that tended to exalt God. He taught that he was holy and true. He sought that men should love him and obey him. All his teaching proved this. An evil spirit would not do this, and this was sufficient proof that he was not influenced by such a spirit.

Verse 50. *Mine own glory.* My own praise or honour. In all his teaching this was true. He did not seek to exalt or to vindicate himself. He was willing to lie under reproach and to be despised. He regarded little, therefore, their taunts and accusations; and even now, he says, he would not seek to vindicate himself.

There is one that seeketh and judgeth. God will take care of my reputation. He seeks my welfare and honour, and I may commit my cause into his hands without attempting my own vindication. From these verses (Joh 8:46-50) we may learn—

1st. That where men have no sound arguments, they attempt to overwhelm their adversaries by calling odious and reproachful names. Accusations of heresy and schism, and the use of reproachful terms, are commonly proof that men are not only under the influence of unchristian feeling, but that they have no sound reasons to support their cause.

2nd. It is right to vindicate ourselves from such charges, but it should not be done by rendering railing for railing.

"In meekness we should instruct those that oppose
themselves, if God peradventure will give them
repentance to the acknowledging of the truth,"
2 Ti 2:25.

3rd. We should not regard it as necessarily dishonourable if we lie under reproach. If we have a good conscience, if we have examined for ourselves, if we are conscious that we are seeking the glory of God, we Should be willing, as Jesus was, to bear reproach, believing that God will in due time avenge us, and bring forth our righteousness as the light, and our judgment as the noon-day, Ps 37:6.

{w} "I seek not" Joh 5:41

Verse 51. *If a man keep my saying.* If he believes on me and obeys my commandments.

He shall never see death. To *see death,* or to *taste of death,* is the same as *to die,* Lu 2:26; Mt 16:28; Mr 9:1.

The sense of this passage is, "He shall obtain eternal life, or he shall be raised up to that life where there shall be no death." See Joh 6:49,50; 3:36; 5:24; 11:25,26.

Verse 52. *Hast a devil.* Art deranged. Because he affirmed a thing which they supposed to be contrary to all experience, and to be impossible.

{x} "Abraham is dead" Zec 1:5

Verse 53. *Whom makest thou thyself?* Or, who dost thou pretend to be? Although the greatest of the prophets have died, yet *thou*—a Nazarene, a Samaritan, and a devil—pretendest that thou canst keep thy followers from dying! It would have been scarcely possible to ask a question implying more contempt and scorn.

Verse 54. *If I honour myself.* If I commend or praise myself. If I had no other honour and sought no other honour than that which proceeds from a desire to glorify myself.

My honour is nothing. My commendation or praise of myself would be of no value. See Barnes "Joh 5:31".

{y} "If I honour" Joh 5:31,41 {z} "it is my Father" Joh 17:1.

Verse 55. No Barnes text on this verse.

Verse 56. *Your father Abraham.* The testimony of Abraham is adduced by Jesus because the Jews considered it to be a signal honour to be his descendants, Joh 8:39. As they regarded the sayings and deeds of Abraham as peculiarly illustrious and worthy of their imitation, so they were bound, in consistency, to listen to what he had said of the Messiah.

Rejoiced. This word includes the notion of *desire* as well as *rejoicing.* It denotes that act when, impelled with strong desire for an object, we *leap forward* toward its attainment with joy; and it expresses —

1st. The fact that this was an object that filled the heart of Abraham with joy; and

2nd. That he *earnestly* desired to see it. We have no single word which expresses the meaning of the original.

In Mt 5:12 it is rendered "be exceeding glad."

To see. Rather, he earnestly and joyfully desired *that he might see.* To see here means to have a view or distinct conceptions of. It does not imply that Abraham *expected* that the Messiah would appear during his life, but that he might have a representation of, or a clear description and foresight of the times of the Messiah.

My day. The day of the Messiah. The word "day," here, is used to denote the *time*, the appearance, the advent, and the manner of life of the Messiah. Lu 17:26: "As it was in the days of Noah, so shall it be also in the days of the Son of man." See Joh 9:4; Mt 11:12. The day of judgment is also called *the day* of the Son of man, because it will be a remarkable time of his manifestation. Or perhaps in both those cases it is called HIS day because he will act the most conspicuous part; his person and work will characterize the times; as we speak of the days of Noah, &c., because he was the most conspicuous person of the age.

He saw it. See Heb 11:13: "These all died in faith, not having received (obtained the fulfillment of) the promises, *but having seen them afar off,* and were persuaded of them," &c.

Though Abraham was not permitted to live to see the times of the Messiah, yet he was permitted to have prophetic view of him, and also of the design of his coming; for,

1st. God foretold his advent clearly to him, Ge 12:3; 18:18 Comp. Ga 3:16: "Now to Abraham and his seed were the promises made. He saith not, And to seeds, as of many; but as of one, and to thy seed, which is Christ."

2nd. Abraham was permitted to have a view of the death of the Messiah as a sacrifice for sin, represented by the command to offer Isaac, Ge 22:1-13. Comp. Heb 11:19. The death of the Messiah as a sacrifice for the sins of men was that which characterized his work— which distinguished his times and his advent, and this was represented to Abraham clearly by the command to offer his son. From this arose the proverb among the Jews (Ge 22:14), "In the mount of the Lord it shall be seen," or it shall be provided for; a proverb evidently referring to the offering of the Messiah on the mount for the sins of men. By this event Abraham was impressively told that a parent would not be required to offer in sacrifice his sons for the sins of his soul—a thing which has often been done by heathen; but that God would provide a victim, and in due time an offering would be made for the world.

Was glad. Was glad in view of the promise, and that he was permitted so distinctly to see it represented. If the father of the faithful rejoiced so much to see him afar off, how should we rejoice that he has come; that we are not required to look into a distant futurity, but know that he has appeared; that we may learn clearly the manner of his coming, his doctrine, and the design of his death! Well might the eyes of a patriarch rejoice to be permitted to look in any manner on the sublime and glorious scene of the Son of God dying for the sins of men. And our chief honour and happiness is to contemplate the amazing scene of man's redemption, where the Saviour groaned and died to save a lost and ruined race.

{a} "he saw *it* and was glad" Ge 22:13,14; Heb 11:13

THE GOSPEL ACCORDING TO JOHN-Chapter 8-Verse 57

Verse 57. *Fifty years old.* Jesus is supposed to have been at this time about thirty-three. It is remarkable that when he was so young they should have mentioned the number fifty, but they probably designed to prevent the possibility of a reply. Had they said *forty* they might have apprehended a reply, or could not be so certain that they were correct.

Hast thou seen Abraham? It is remarkable, also, that they perverted his words. His affirmation was not that he had seen Abraham, but that Abraham had seen his day. The design of Jesus was to show that he was greater than Abraham, Joh 8:53. To do this, he says that Abraham, great as he was, earnestly desired to see his time, thus acknowledging his inferiority to the Messiah. The Jews perverted this, and affirmed that it was impossible that he and Abraham should have seen each other.

THE GOSPEL ACCORDING TO JOHN-Chapter 8-Verse 58

Verse 58. *Verily, verily.* This is an expression used only in John. It is a strong affirmation

clxxiii

denoting particularly the great importance of what was about to be affirmed. See Barnes "Joh 3:5".

Before Abraham was. Before Abraham lived.

I am. The expression I *am*, though in the *present* tense, is clearly designed to refer to a past time. Thus, in Ps 90:2, "From everlasting to everlasting thou *art* God." Applied to God, it denotes continued existence without respect to time, so far as he is concerned. We divide time into the past, the present, and the future. The expression, applied to God, denotes that he does not measure his existence in this manner, but that the word by which we express the present denotes his continued and unchanging existence. Hence he assumes it as his name, "I AM," and "I AM THAT I AM," Ex 3:14. Comp. Isa 44:6; 47:8. There is a remarkable similarity between the expression employed by Jesus in this place and that used in Exodus to denote the name of God. The *manner* in which Jesus used it would strikingly suggest the application of the same language to God. The question here was about his pre-existence. The objection of the Jews was that he was not fifty years old, and could not, therefore, have seen Abraham. Jesus replied to that that he existed before Abraham. As in his human nature he was not yet fifty years old, and could not, as a man, have *existed before Abraham*, this declaration must be referred to another nature; and the passage proves that, while he was a man, he was also endowed with *another nature* existing before Abraham, and to which he applied the term (familiar to the Jews as expressive of the existence of God) I AM; and this declaration corresponds to the affirmation of John (Joh 1:1), that he was in the beginning with God, and was God. This affirmation of Jesus is one of the proofs on which John relies to prove that he was the Messiah (Joh 20:31), to establish which was the design of writing this book.

{b} "I am" Ex 3:14; Is 43:13; Joh 1:1,2; Col 1:17; Re 1:8

THE GOSPEL ACCORDING TO JOHN-Chapter 8-Verse 59

Verse 59. *Then took they up stones.* It seems they understood him as blaspheming, and proceeded, even without a form of trial, to stone him as such, because this was the punishment prescribed in the law for blasphemy, Le 24:16. See Joh 10:31. The fact that the *Jews* understood him in this sense is strong proof that his words *naturally* conveyed the idea that he was divine. This was in the temple. Herod the Great had not yet completed its repairs, and Dr. Lightfoot has remarked that stones would be lying around the temple in repairing it, which the people could easily use in their indignation.

Jesus hid himself. See Lu 4:30. That is, he either by a miracle rendered himself invisible, or he so mixed with the multitude that he was concealed from them and escaped. Which is the meaning cannot be determined.

THE GOSPEL ACCORDING TO JOHN- Chapter 9

Verse 1. *As Jesus passed by.* As he was leaving the temple, Joh 8:59. This man was in the way in which Jesus was going to escape from the Jews.

Verse 2. *Master, who did sin?* &c. It was a universal opinion among the Jews that *calamities* of all kinds were the effects of sin. See Barnes "Lu 13:1-4".

The case, however, of this man was that of one that was blind from his *birth*, and it was a question which the disciples could not determine whether it was *his* fault or that of his parents. Many of the Jews, as it appears from their writings (see Lightfoot), believed in the doctrine of the *transmigration*, of souls; or that the soul of a man, in consequence of sin, might be compelled to pass into other bodies, and be punished there. They also believed that an infant might sin before it was born (see Lightfoot), and that consequently this blindness might have come upon the child as a consequence of that. It was also a doctrine with many that the crime of the parent might be the cause of deformity in the child, particularly the violation of the command in Le 20:18.

Verse 3. *Neither hath this man sinned,* &c. That is, his blindness is not the effect of his sin, or that of his parents. Jesus did not, evidently, mean to affirm that he or his parents were without any sin, but that this blindness was not the effect of sin. This answer is to be interpreted by the nature of the question submitted to him. The sense is, "his blindness is not to be traced to any fault of his or of his parents."

But that the works of God. This thing has happened that it might appear how great and wonderful are the works of God. By *the works of God*, here, is evidently intended the miraculous power which God would put forth to heal the man, or rather, perhaps, the *whole* that happened to him in the course of divine providence—first his blindness, as an act of his providence, and then his *healing* him, as an act of mercy and power. It has *all* happened, not by the fault of his parents or of himself, but by the wise arrangement of God, that it *might be seen* in what way calamities come, and in what way God meets and relieves them. And from this we may learn,

1st. To pity and not to despise and blame those who are afflicted with any natural deformity or calamity. While the Jews regarded it as the effect of sin, they looked upon it without compassion. Jesus tells us that it is not the fault of man, but proceeds from the wise arrangement of God.

2nd. All suffering in the world is not the effect of sin. In this case it is expressly so declared; and there may be many modes of suffering that cannot be traced to any particular transgression. We should be cautious, therefore, in affirming that there can be no calamity in the universe but by transgression.

3rd. We see the wise and wonderful arrangement of Divine Providence. It is a part of his great plan to adapt his mercies to the woes of men; and often calamity, want, poverty, and sickness are permitted, that he may show the provisions of his mercy, that he may teach us to prize his blessings, and that deep-felt gratitude for deliverance may bind us to him.

4th. Those who are afflicted with blindness, deafness, or any deformity, should be submissive to God. It is his appointment, and is right and best. God does no wrong, and the universe will, when *all* his works are seen, feel and know that he is just.

{a} "that the works of God" Joh 11:4

THE GOSPEL ACCORDING TO JOHN-Chapter 9-Verse 4

Verse 4. *The works of him*, &c. The works of beneficence and mercy which God has commissioned me to do, and which are expressive of his goodness and power. This was on the Sabbath-day (Joh 9:14); and though Jesus had endangered his life (Joh 5:1-16) by working a similar miracle on the Sabbath, yet he knew that this was the will of God that he should do good, and that he would take care of his life.

While it is day. The *day* is the proper time for work— night is not. This is the general, the universal sentiment. While the day lasts it is proper to labour. The term *day* here refers to the *life* of Jesus, and to the opportunity thus afforded of working miracles. His life was drawing to a close. It was probably but about six months after this when he was put to death. The meaning is, My life is near its close. While it continues I must employ it in doing the works which God has appointed.

The night cometh. Night here represents death. It was drawing near, and he must therefore do what he had to do soon. It is not improbable, also, that this took place near the close of the Sabbath, as the sun was declining, and the shades of evening about to appear. This supposition will give increased beauty to the language which follows.

No man can work. It is literally true that *day* is the appropriate time for toil, and that the *night of death* is a time when nothing can be done. Ec 9:10: "There is no work, nor device, nor knowledge, nor wisdom in the grave." From this we may learn,

1st. That it is our duty to employ all our time in doing the will of God.

2nd. That we should seek for opportunities of doing good, and suffer none to pass without improving it. *We go but once through the world, and we cannot return to correct errors, and recall neglected opportunities of doing our duty.*

3rd. We should be especially diligent in doing our Lord's work from the fact that the night of death is coming. This applies to the aged, for they must soon die; and to the young, for they *may* soon be called away from this world to eternity.

{b} "I am the light" Joh 1:5,9; 8:12; 12:35,46

THE GOSPEL ACCORDING TO JOHN-Chapter 9-Verse 5

Verse 5. *As long as I am in the world*, &c. As the sun is the natural light of the world, even while it sinks away to the west, so am I, although my days are drawing to a close, the light of the spiritual world. What a sublime description is this! Jesus occupied the same place, filled the same space, shed his beams as far, in the moral world, as the sun does on natural objects; and as all is dark when that sun sinks to the west, so when he withdraws from the souls of men all is midnight and gloom. When we look on the sun in the firmament or in the west, let us remember that such is the great Sun of Righteousness in regard to our souls; that his shining is as necessary, and his beams as mild and lovely on the soul, as is the shining of the natural sun to illumine the material creation. See Barnes "Joh 1:4".

THE GOSPEL ACCORDING TO JOHN-Chapter 9-Verse 6

Verse 6. *And made clay*, &c. Two reasons may be assigned for making this clay, and anointing the eyes with it. One is, that the Jews regarded *spittle* as medicinal to the eyes when diseased, and that they forbade the use of medicines on the Sabbath. They regarded the Sabbath so strictly that they considered the preparation and use of medicines as contrary to the law. Especially it was particularly forbidden among them to use spittle on that day to heal diseased eyes. See instances in Lightfoot. Jesus, therefore, by making this spittle, showed them that their manner of keeping the day was superstitious, and that he dared to do a thing which they esteemed unlawful. He showed that *their* interpretation of the law of the Sabbath was contrary to the intention of God, and that his disciples were not bound by their notions of the sacredness of that day. Another reason may have been that it was common for prophets to use some symbolical or expressive action in working miracles. Thus Elisha commanded his staff to be laid on the face of the child that he was about to restore to life, 2 Ki 4:29. See Barnes "Isa 8:18".

In such instances the prophet showed that the miracle was wrought by power communicated through *him*; so, in this case, Jesus by this act showed to the blind man that the power of *healing* came from him who anointed his eyes. He could not see him, and the act of anointing convinced him of what might have been known without such an act, could he have *seen*him— that Jesus had power to give sight to the blind.

{c} "he spat on the ground" Mr 8:23 {1} "anointed", or "spread the clay upon the eyes of the blind man"

THE GOSPEL ACCORDING TO JOHN-Chapter 9-Verse 7

Verse 7. *Wash in the pool*. In the *fountain*.

Of Siloam. See Barnes "Lu 13:4".

By interpretation, Sent. From the Hebrew verb *to send*—perhaps because it was regarded as a blessing *sent* or given by God. *Why* Jesus sent him to wash there is not known. It is clear that the waters had no efficacy themselves to open the eyes of a blind man, but it is probable that he directed him to go there to *test his obedience*, and to see whether he was disposed to obey him in a case where he could not see the reason of it. An instance somewhat similar occurs in the case of Naaman, the Syrian leper, 2 Ki 5:10. The proud Syrian despised the direction; the humble blind man obeyed and was healed. This case shows us that we should obey the commands of God, however unmeaning or mysterious they may appear. God has always a reason for all that he directs us to do, and our faith and willingness to obey him are often tried when we can see little of the reason of his requirements. In the first edition of these Notes it was remarked that the word "Siloam" is from the same verb as *Shiloh* in Ge 49:10. "The sceptre shall not depart from Judah—until Shiloh (that is, the Sent of God; the Messiah) come," and that John in this remark probably had reference to this prophecy. This was incorrect; and there is no evidence that John in this passage had reference to that prophecy, or that this fountain was emblematic of the Messiah. The original words Siloam and Shiloh are from different roots and mean different things. The former, Siloam (^greek^), is derived from ^greek^ (*to send*); the latter, *Shiloh* (^greek^), means *rest* or *quiet*, and was given to the Messiah, probably, because he would bring *rest*—that is, he would be the "prince of peace." Comp. Isa 9:6.

{d} "pool of Siloam" Ne 3:15 {e} "He went his way" 2 Ki 5:14

THE GOSPEL ACCORDING TO JOHN-Chapter 9-Verse 8
Verse 8. *The neighbours*, &c. This man seems to have been one who attracted considerable attention. The number of persons totally blind in any community is very small, and it is possible that this was the only blind beggar in Jerusalem. The case was one, therefore, likely to attract attention, and one where there could be no imposture, as he was generally known.

THE GOSPEL ACCORDING TO JOHN-Chapter 9-Verse 9
Verse 9. No notes from Barnes on this verse.

THE GOSPEL ACCORDING TO JOHN-Chapter 9-Verse 10
Verse 10. No notes from Barnes on this verse.

THE GOSPEL ACCORDING TO JOHN-Chapter 9-Verse 11
Verse 11. No notes from Barnes on this verse.
{f} "A man that is called Jesus" Joh 9:6,7

THE GOSPEL ACCORDING TO JOHN-Chapter 9-Verse 12
Verse 12. No notes from Barnes on this verse.

THE GOSPEL ACCORDING TO JOHN-Chapter 9-Verse 13
Verse 13. *To the Pharisees*. To the members of the Sanhedrim. They did this, doubtless, to

accuse Jesus of having violated the Sabbath, and not, as they ought to have done, to examine into the evidence that he was from God.

Verse 14. No notes from Barnes on this verse.

Verse 15. *The Pharisees asked him how*, &c. The proper question to have been asked in the case was whether he had *in fact* done it, and not in *what way*. The question, also, about a sinner's conversion is whether in fact it has been done, and not about the *mode* or *manner* in which it is effected; yet it is remarkable that no small part of the disputes and inquiries among men are about the *mode* in which the Spirit renews the heart, and not about the evidence that it is done.

Verse 16. *This man is not of God.* Is not *sent* by God, or cannot be a *friend* of God.

Because he keepeth not the sabbath-day. They assumed that *their views* of the Sabbath were correct, and by *those views* they judged others. It did not occur to them to inquire whether the interpretation which they put on the law might not be erroneous. Men often assume their own interpretations of the Scriptures to be infallible, and then judge and condemn all others by those interpretations.

A sinner. A deceiver; an impostor. They reasoned conclusively that God would not give the power of working such miracles to an impostor. The miracles were such as could not be denied, nor did even the enemies of Jesus attempt to deny them or to explain them away. They were open, public, frequent. And this shows that they *could* not deny their reality. Had it been possible, they would have done it; but the reality and power of those miracles had already made a party in favour of Jesus, even in the Sanhedrim (Joh 7:50; 12:42), and those opposed to them *could* not deny their *reality*. It may be added that the early opponents of Christianity never denied the reality of the miracles performed by the Saviour and his apostles. Celsus, Porphyry, and Julianas acute foes of the gospel as perhaps have ever lived—never call this in question. They attempted to show that it was by some evil influence, or to account for the miracles in some other way than by admitting the divine origin of the Christian religion, but about the *facts* they had no question. Were they not as well qualified to judge about those *facts* as men are now? They lived near the time; had every opportunity to examine the evidence; were skilful and talented disputants; and if they *could* have denied the reality of the miracles they would have done it. It is scarcely possible to conceive of more conclusive proof that those miracles were really performed, and, if so, then the Lord Jesus was sent by God.

A division. Greek, "A schism." A separation into two parties.

{g} "How can a man" Joh 9:31; 3:2 {h} "And there was a division" Joh 7:12,43

Verse 17. *What sayest thou of him*? &c. The translation here expresses the sense obscurely. The meaning is, "What sayest thou of him for giving thee sight?" (Campbell); or, "What opinion of him hath this work of power and mercy to thee wrought in thee?" (Hammond).

He is a prophet. That is, "I think that the power to work such a miracle proves that he is sent from God. And though this has been done on the Sabbath, yet it proves that he must have been sent by God, for such a power could never have proceeded from man." We see here,

1st. A noble confession made by the man who was healed, in the face of the rulers of the people, and when he doubtless knew that they were opposed to Jesus. We should never be ashamed, before any class of men, to acknowledge the favours which we have received from Christ, and to express our belief of his power and of the truth of his doctrine.

2nd. The works of Jesus were such as to prove that he came from God, however much he may have appeared to oppose the previous notions of men, the interpretation of the law by the Pharisees, or the deductions of reason. Men should *yield* their own views of religion to the teachings of God, and believe that he that could open the eyes of the blind and raise the dead was fitted to declare his will.

{i} "He is a prophet" Joh 4:19

Verses 18,19. *Is this your son*? &c. The Pharisees proposed *three* questions to the parents, by which they hoped to convict the man of falsehood.

1st. Whether he was their son?

2nd. Whether they would affirm that he was *born* blind? and,

3rd. Whether they knew by what means he now saw? They evidently intended to intimidate the parents, so that they might give an answer to one of these questions that would convict the man of deception. We see here the art to which men will resort rather than admit the truth. Had they been half as much disposed to believe on Jesus as they were to disbelieve, there would have been no difficulty in the case. And so with all men: were they as much *inclined* to embrace the truth as they are to reject it, there would soon be an end of cavils.

{k} "did not believe" Isa 26:11

Verse 19. No notes from Barnes on this verse.

Verses 20-22. *His parents answered*, &c. To the first *two* questions they answered without hesitation. They knew that he was their son, and that he was born blind. The third question they *could not* positively answer, as they had not witnessed the means of the cure, and were afraid to express their belief. It appears that they had themselves no doubt, but they were not eye-witnesses, and could not be therefore legal evidence.

He is of age. He is of sufficient age to give testimony. Among the Jews this age was fixed at thirteen years.

If any man did confess that he was Christ. Did acknowledge that he was the Messiah. They had prejudged the case, and were determined to put down all free inquiry, and not to be convinced by any means.

Put out of the synagogue. This took place in the *temple*, or near the temple. It does not refer, therefore, to any *immediate* and violent putting forth from the place where they were. It refers to *excommunication* from the synagogue. Among the Jews there were two grades of excommunication; the one for lighter offences, of which they mentioned twenty-four causes; the other for greater offences. The first excluded a man for thirty days from the privilege of entering a synagogue, and from coming nearer to his wife or friends than 4 cubits. The other was a solemn exclusion for ever from the worship of the synagogue, attended with awful maledictions and curses, and an exclusion from all intercourse with the people. This was called the *curse*, and so thoroughly excluded the person from all communion whatever with his countrymen, that they were not allowed to sell to him anything, even the necessaries of life (Buxtorf). It is probable that this *latter* punishment was what they intended to inflict if anyone should confess that Jesus was the Messiah; and it was the fear of this terrible punishment that deterred his parents from expressing their opinion.

THE GOSPEL ACCORDING TO JOHN-Chapter 9-Verse 21

Verse 21. No notes from Barnes on this verse.

THE GOSPEL ACCORDING TO JOHN-Chapter 9-Verse 22

Verse 22. No notes from Barnes on this verse.

{l} "they feared the Jews" Pr 29:25; Joh 7:13; 12:42

{m} "he should be put out of the synagogue" Joh 9:34; 16:2

THE GOSPEL ACCORDING TO JOHN-Chapter 9-Verse 23

Verse 23. No notes from Barnes on this verse.

THE GOSPEL ACCORDING TO JOHN-Chapter 9-Verse 24

Verse 24. *Give God the praise*. This expression seems to be a form of administering an oath. It is used in Jos 7:19, when Achan was put on his oath and entreated to confess his guilt. Joshua said, "My son, give, I pray thee, glory to the Lord God of Israel (in the Greek of the Septuagint, the very expression used in John, `Give God the praise'), and make confession unto him." It is equivalent to an adjuration in the presence of God to acknowledge the truth; as the truth would be giving God praise, confessing the case before him, and trusting to his mercy. Comp. 1 Sa 6:5. The meaning here is not "give God praise for healing you," for they were not willing to admit that *he had been cured* (Joh 9:18), but *confess* that there is imposture in the case; that you have declared to us a falsehood, that you have endeavoured to impose on us; and by thus confessing your sin, give praise and honour to God, who condemns all imposture and false-hood, and whom you will thus acknowledge to be *right* in your condemnation. To induce him to do this, they added that they *knew*, or were satisfied that Jesus was a sinner. As they considered *that point* settled, they urged him to confess that he had attempted to impose on them.

We know. We have settled that. He has broken the Sabbath, and that leaves no doubt.

A sinner. A violator of the law respecting the Sabbath, and an impostor. Joh 9:16.

{n} "Give God the praise" Jos 7:19; Ps 50:14,15

Verse 25. *Whether he be a sinner or no, I know not*. The man had just said that he believed Jesus to be *a prophet*, Joh 9:17. By his saying that he did not know whether he was a sinner *may be* meant that *though* he might be a prophet, yet that he might not be perfect; or that it did not become him, being an obscure and unlearned man, to attempt to determine that question. What follows shows that he did not believe that he was a sinner, and these words were probably spoken in irony to deride the Pharisees. They were perverse and full of cavils, and were determined not to believe. The man reminded them that the question was not whether Jesus was a sinner; that, though that *might* be, yet it did not settle the other question about opening his eyes, which was the chief point of the inquiry.

One thing I know, &c. About this *he* could have no doubt. He disregarded, therefore, their cavils. We may learn, also, here,

1st. That this declaration may be made by every converted sinner. He may not be able to meet the cavils of others. He may not be able to tell *how* he was converted. It is enough if he can say, "I *was* a sinner, but now love God; I *was* in darkness, but have now been brought to the light of truth."

2nd. We should not be *ashamed* of the fact that we are made to see by the Son of God. No cavil or derision of men should deter us from such an avowal.

3rd. Sinners are perpetually shifting the *real* point of inquiry. They do not inquire into *the facts*. They *assume* that a thing cannot be true, and then argue as if that was a conceded point. The proper way in religion is first to inquire *into the facts*, and then account for them as we can.

Verse 26. *How opened he thine eyes*? The reason why they asked this so often was doubtless to attempt to draw him into a contradiction; either to intimidate him, or throw him off his guard, so that he might be detected in denying what he had before affirmed. But God gave to this poor man grace and strength to make a bold confession of the truth, and sufficient common sense completely to confound his proud and subtle examiners.

Verse 27. No notes from Barnes on this verse.

Verse 28. *Thou art his disciple.* This they cast at him as a reproach. His defence of Jesus they regarded as proof that he was his follower, and this they now attempted to show was inconsistent with being a friend of Moses and his law. Moses had given the law respecting tho Sabbath; Jesus had healed a man contrary, in *their* view, to the law of Moses. They therefore held Jesus to be a violater and contemner of the law of Moses, and of course that his followers were also.

We are Moses' disciples. We acknowledge the authority of the law of Moses, which they alleged Jesus has broken by healing on that day.

{o} "reviled" 1 Pe 2:23

Verse 29. *We know,* &c. We know that God commanded Moses to deliver the law. In that they were correct; but they assumed *their* interpretation of the law to be infallible, and hence condemned Jesus.

As for *this* fellow. The word *fellow* is not in the original. It is simply "this." The word *fellow* implies contempt, which it cannot be proved they intended to express.

Whence he is. We know not his origin, his family, or his home. The contrast with the preceding member of the sentence shows that they intended to express their belief that he was not from God. They knew not whether he was mad, whether he was instigated by the devil, or whether he spoke of himself. See Joh 7:27; 8:48-52.

{p} "We know" Ps 103:7; Heb 3:5 {q} "we know not" Joh 8:14

Verse 30. *A marvellous thing.* This is wonderful and amazing.

Know not from whence he is. That you cannot perceive that he who has wrought such a miracle must be from God.

{r} "Why, herein" Joh 3:10 {s} "yet he hath" Ps 119:18; Isa 29:18,19; 35:5; 2 Co 4:6

Verse 31. *Now we know.* That is, it is an admitted or conceded point. No one calls it into question.

God heareth not. When a miracle was performed it was customary to invoke the aid of God. Jesus often did this himself, and it was by his power only that prophets and apostles could perform miracles. The word "heareth" in this place is to be understood as referring to such cases. God will not "hear"—that is, answer.

Sinners. Impostors. False prophets and pretenders to divine revelation. See Joh 9:24. The meaning of this verse is, therefore, "It is well understood that God will not give miraculous aid to impostors and false prophets," We may remark here,

1st. That the passage has no reference to the prayers which sinners make for salvation.

2nd. If it had it would not be of course true. It was the mere opinion of this man, in accordance with the common sentiment of the Jews, and there is no evidence that he was inspired.

3rd. The only prayers which God will not hear are those which are offered in mockery, or when the man loves his sins and is un-willing to give them up. Such prayers God will not hear, Ps 66:18: "If I regard iniquity in my heart, the Lord will not hear me;" Isa 1:14,15; Job 27:9; Jer 11:11; Eze 8:18; Mic 3:4; Zec 8:13.

A worshipper. A sincere worshipper; one who fears, loves, and adores him.

Doeth his will. Obeys his commandments. This is infallibly true. The Scripture abounds with promises to such that God will hear their prayer. See Ps 34:15; Mt 7:7,8.

{t} "God heareth not sinners" Job 27:9; Ps 66:18; Pr 28:9; Isa 1:15
Jer 11:11; Eze 8:18; Mic 3:4; Zec 7:13

{u} "but if any man" Ps 34:15; Pr 15:29

THE GOSPEL ACCORDING TO JOHN-Chapter 9-Verse 32

Verse 32. *Since the world began.* Neither Moses nor any of the prophets had ever done this. No instance of this kind is recorded in the Old Testament. As this was a miracle which had never been performed, the man argued justly that he who had done it must be from God. As Jesus did it not by surgical operations, but by *clay*, it showed that he had power of working miracles by any means. It may be also remarked that the restoration of sight to the blind by surgical operations was never performed until the year 1728. Dr. Cheselden, an English surgeon, was the first who attempted it successfully, who was enabled to remove a *cataract* from the eye of a young man, and to restore sight. This fact shows the difficulty of the operation when the most skilful natural means are employed, and the greatness of the miracle performed by the Saviour.

THE GOSPEL ACCORDING TO JOHN-Chapter 9-Verse 33

Verse 33. *Could do nothing.* Could do no such work as this. This reasoning was conclusive. The fact that Jesus could perform miracles like this was full proof that never has been and never can be refuted. One such miracle proves that he was from God. But Jesus gave *many* similar proofs, and thus put his divine mission beyond the possibility of doubt.

THE GOSPEL ACCORDING TO JOHN-Chapter 9-Verse 34

Verse 34. *Wast born in sins.* That is, thou wast born in a state of blindness—a state which proved that either thou or thy parents had sinned, and that this was the punishment for it. See Joh 9:2. Thou wast cursed by God with blindness for crime, and yet thou dost set up for a religious teacher! When men have no arguments, they attempt to supply their place by revilings. When they are pressed by argument, they reproach their adversaries with crime, and especially with being *blind, perverse, heretical, disposed to speculation, and regardless of the authority of God.* And especially do they consider it great presumption that one of an inferior age or rank should presume to advance an argument in opposition to prevailing opinions.

They cast him out. Out of the synagogue. They *excommunicated* him. See Barnes "Joh 9:22".

{v} "Thou was altogether" Joh 9:2 {w} "they" Isa 66:5 {2} "cast out", or "excommunicated"

THE GOSPEL ACCORDING TO JOHN-Chapter 9-Verse 35

Verse 35. *Dost thou believe on the Son of God?* Hitherto he had understood little of the true character of Jesus. He believed that he had *power* to heal him, and he *inferred* that he must be a prophet, Joh 9:17. He believed according to the *light he had*, and he *now* showed that he was prepared to believe all that Jesus said. This is the nature of true faith. It believes all that God has made known, and it is *prepared* to receive all that he *will* teach. The phrase *Son of God* here is equivalent to *the Messiah.* See Barnes "Mt 8:29".

{x} "believe" 1 Jo 5:13

THE GOSPEL ACCORDING TO JOHN-Chapter 9-Verse 36

Verse 36. *Who is he?* It is probable that the man did not know that ho who now addressed him was the same who had healed him. He had not yet *seen him* (Joh 9:7), but he was prepared to acknowledge him when he did see him. He inquired, therefore, *who* the person was, or wished that he might be pointed out to him, that he *might* see him. This passage shows that he was *disposed* to believe, and had a strong desire to see and hear the Son of God.

Lord. This word here, as in many other instances in the New Testament, means "Sir." It is clear that the man did not know that it was the Lord Jesus that addressed him, and he therefore replied to him in the common language of respect, and asked him to point out to him the Son of God. The word translated "Lord" here is rendered "Sir" in Joh 4:11 Joh 20:15;12:21; Ac 16:30; Mt 27:63.

It should have been also here, and in many other places.

THE GOSPEL ACCORDING TO JOHN-Chapter 9-Verse 37

Verse 37. No notes from Barnes on this verse.

Verse 38. *I believe.* This was the overflowing expression of gratitude and faith.

And he worshipped him. He did homage to him as the Messiah and as his gracious benefactor. See Barnes "Mt 2:2".

This shows,

1st. That it is right and natural to express thanks and praise for mercies.

2nd. All blessings should lead us to pour out our gratitude to Jesus, for it is from him that we receive them.

3rd. Especially is this true when the *mind* has been enlightened, when our spiritual eyes have been opened, and we are permitted to see the glories of the heavenly world.

4th. It is right to pay homage or worship to Jesus. He forbade it not. He received it on earth, and for all mercies of providence and redemption we should pay to him the tribute of humble and grateful hearts. The Syriac renders the phrase, "he worshipped him," thus: "and, casting himself down, he adored him." The Persic, "and he bowed down and adored Christ." The Arabic, "and he adored him." The Latin Vulgate, "and, falling down, he adored him."

{a} "For judgment" Joh 5:22,27; 12:47

{b} "they which see not" 1 Pe 2:9 {c} "they which see might" Mt 14:33

Verse 39. *For judgment.* The word *judgment,* here, has been by some understood in the sense of condemnation— "The effect of my coming is to condemn the world." But this meaning does not agree with those places where Jesus says that he came not to condemn the world, Joh 3:17; 12:47; 5:45.

To *judge* is to express *an opinion in a judicial manner,* and also to express any sentiment about any person or thing, Joh 7:24; 5:30; Lu 8:43.

The meaning here may be thus expressed:

"I came to *declare the condition of men*; to show them

their duty and danger. My coming will have this effect,

that some will be reformed and saved, and some more

deeply condemned."

That they, &c. The Saviour does not affirm that this was the *design* of his coming, but that such would be the effect or result. He came to declare the truth, and the effect *would be,* &c. Similar instances of expression frequently occur. Comp. Mt 11:25; 10:34: "I came not to send peace, but a sword "—that is, such will be the effect of my coming.

That they which see not. Jesus took this illustration, as he commonly did, from the case before him; but it is evident that he meant it to be taken in a *spiritual sense.* He refers to those who are blind and ignorant by sin; whose minds have been darkened, but who are desirous of seeing.

Might see. Might discern the path of truth, of duty, and of salvation, Joh 10:9.

They which see. They who suppose they see; who are proud, self-confident, and despisers of the truth. Such were evidently the Pharisees.

Might be made blind. Such would be the *effect* of his preaching.

It would exasperate them, and their pride and opposition to him would confirm them more and more in their erroneous views. This is always the effect of truth. Where it does not *soften* it *hardens* the heart; where it does not convert, it sinks into deeper blindness and condemnation.

{a} "For judgment" Joh 5:22,27; 12:47

{b} "they which see not" 1 Pe 2:9 {c} "they which see" Mt 13:13; Joh 3:19

THE GOSPEL ACCORDING TO JOHN-Chapter 9-Verse 40

Verse 40. No Barnes text on this verse.

{d} "Are we blind also"

Ro 2:19; Re 3:17

THE GOSPEL ACCORDING TO JOHN-Chapter 9-Verse 41

Verse 41. *If ye were blind.* If you were *really* blind—had had no *opportunities* of learning the truth. If you were truly ignorant, and were willing to confess it, and to come to me for instruction.

No sin. You would not be guilty. Sin is measured by the *capacities* or *ability* of men, and by their opportunities of knowing the truth. If men had no *ability* to do the will of God, they could incur no blame. If they have all proper *ability*, and no *disposition*, God holds them to be guilty. This passage teaches conclusively,

1st. That men are not condemned for what they cannot do.

2nd. That the reason why they are condemned is that they are not disposed to receive the truth.

3rd. That pride and self-confidence are the sources of condemnation.

4th. That if men are condemned, they, and not God, will be to blame.

We see. We have knowledge of the law of God. This they had pretended when they professed to understand the law respecting the Sabbath better than Jesus, and had condemned him for healing on that day.

Your sin remaineth. You *are* guilty, and your sin is unpardoned. Men's sins will always be unpardoned while they are proud, and self-sufficient, and confident of their own wisdom. If they will come with humble hearts and confess their ignorance, God will forgive, enlighten, and guide them in the path to heaven.

{e} "If ye were blind" Joh 15:22,24 {f} "therefore" Isa 5:21; Lu 18:14; 1 Jo 1:8-10

THE GOSPEL ACCORDING TO JOHN-Chapter 10

Verse 1. *Verily, verily*. See Barnes "Joh 3:3".

I say unto you. Some have supposed that what follows here was delivered on some other occasion than the one mentioned in the last chapter; but the expression *verily, verily*, is one which is not used at the *commencement* of a discourse, and the discourse itself seems to be a continuation of what was said before. The Pharisees professed to be the *guides or shepherds* of the people. Jesus, in the close of the last chapter, had charged them with being *blind*, and of course of being unqualified to lead the people. He proceeds here to state the character of a *true* shepherd, to show what was a hireling, and to declare that *he* was the true shepherd and guide of his people. This is called (Joh 10:6) *a parable*, and it is an eminently beautiful illustration of the office of the Messiah, drawn from an employment well known in Judea. The Messiah was predicted under the image of a *shepherd*, Eze 34:23; 37:24; Zec 13:7.

Hence at the close of the discourse they asked him whether he were the Messiah, Joh 10:24.

Into the sheepfold. The sheepfold was an inclosure made in fields where the sheep were collected by night to defend them from robbers, wolves, &c. It was not commonly covered, as the seasons in Judea were mild. By the figure here we are to understand the Jewish people, or the church of God, which is often likened to a flock, Eze 34:1-19 Jer 23:1-4; Zec 13:1. By the *door*, here, is meant the Lord Jesus Christ, Joh 10:7,9. He is"the way, the truth, and the life," Joh 14:6. And, as the only proper way of entering the fold was by the door, so the only way of entering the church of God is by believing on him and obeying his commandments. The particular application of this place, however, is to *religious teachers*, who cannot enter properly on the duties of teaching and guarding the flock except by the Lord Jesus—that is, in the way which he has appointed. The Pharisees claimed to be *pastors*, but not under his appointment. They entered some other way. The true *pastors* of the church are those who enter by the influences of the Spirit of Jesus, and in the manner which he has appointed.

Some other way. Either at a window or over the wall.

A thief. One who silently and secretly takes away the property of another.

A robber. One who does it by *violence* or *bloodshed*. Jesus here designates those pastors or ministers of religion who are influenced not by love to *him*, but who seek the office from ambition, or the love of power, or wealth, or ease; who come, not to promote the welfare of the church, but to promote their own interests. Alas! in all churches there have been many—many who for no better ends have sought the pastoral office. To all such Jesus gives the names of *thieves* and *robbers*.

{a} "He that entereth not" Ro 10:15; Heb 5:4

Verse 2. *He that entereth by the door*. This was the way in which a shepherd had access to his flock. In Joh 10:7 Jesus says he is the door. In this place he refers to those who *by him*—that is, in accordance with his spirit and law—become ministers of religion.

Is the shepherd of the sheep. Christ does not here refer to himself, for he is the way or door by which *others* enter; but he refers to all the ministers of the gospel who have access to the church *by* him. In the original, the article "the" is wanting before the word shepherd—"is a *shepherd*." By his entering in this manner he shows that he is a shepherd— one who cares for his flock, and does not come to kill and destroy.

{b} "the door is the shepherd" Joh 10:7,9

Verse 3. *To him the porter openeth*. The porter is the doorkeeper. It seems that the more wealthy Jews who owned flocks employed some person to take charge of the flock. At first*all* shepherds attended their flocks personally by day and by night, and this continued to be commonly the practice, but not always.

The sheep hear his voice. The voice of the shepherd. A flock will readily discern the well-known voice of one who is accustomed to attend them. The meaning is, that the people of God will be found disposed to listen to the instructions of those who are appointed by Christ, who preach his pure doctrines, and who show a real love for the church of God. There is scarcely any better test of fidelity in the pastoral office than the approbation of the humble and obscure people of God, when they discern in the preacher the very manner and spirit of the doctrines of the Bible.

He calleth his own sheep by name. It was customary, and is still, we are told by travellers, for shepherds to give particular *names* to their sheep, by which they soon learned to regard the voice of the shepherd. By this our Saviour indicates, doubtless, that it is the duty of a minister of religion to seek an intimate and personal acquaintance with the people of his charge; to feel an interest in them as *individuals*, and not merely to address them *together*; to learn their private wants; to meet them in their individual trials, and to administer to them personally the consolations of the gospel.

Leadeth them out. He leads them from the fold to pasture or to water. Perhaps there is here intended the care of a faithful pastor to provide suitable instruction for the people of his charge, and to feed them with the bread of life. See a beautiful and touching description of the care of the Great Shepherd in Ps 23:1-6.

{c} "To him" Re 3:20 {d} "calleth his own sheep" Eze 34:11; Ro 8:30 {e} "leadeth them out" Eze 34:11; Ro 8:30

Verse 4. *He putteth forth.* Or leads them out of the fold.

He goeth before them. He leads them, and guides them, and does not leave them. A shepherd spent his time with his flocks. He went before them to seek the best pastures and watering-places, and to defend them from danger. In this is beautifully represented the tender care of him who watches for souls as one that must give account.

{f} "they know his voice" So 2:8; 5:2

Verse 5. *A stranger,* &c. This was literally true of a flock. Accustomed to the voice and presence of a kind shepherd, they would not regard the command of a stranger. It is also true spiritually. Jesus by this indicates that the true people of God will not follow false teachers—those who are proud, haughty, and self-seeking, as were the Pharisees. Many *may* follow such, but humble and devoted Christians seek those who have the mild and self-denying spirit of their Master and Great Shepherd. It is also true in reference to those who are *pastors* in the churches. They have an influence which no stranger or wandering minister can have. A church learns to put confidence in a pastor; he knows the wants of his people, sees their danger, and can adapt his instructions to them. A stranger, however eloquent, pious, or learned, can have few of these commit the churches to the care of wandering strangers, of those who have no permanent relation to the church, than it would be for a flock to be committed to a foreigner who knew nothing of it, and who had no particular interest in it. The pastoral office is one of the wisest institutions of heaven. The following extract from *The Land and the Book* (Thomson) will show how strikingly this whole passage accords with what actually occurs at this day in Palestine:

"This is true to the letter. They are so tame
and so trained that they follow their keeper with the
utmost docility. He leads them forth from the fold, or
from their houses in the villages, just where he
pleases. As there are many flocks in such a place
as this, each one takes a different path, and it is his
business to find pasture for them. It is necessary,
therefore, that they should be taught to follow, and
not to stray away into the unfenced fields of corn
which lie so temptingly on either side. Any one that
thus wanders is sure to get into trouble. The shepherd
calls sharply from time to time to remind them of his
presence. They know his voice and follow on; but if a
stranger call, they stop short, lift up their heads

in alarm, and, if it is repeated, they turn and flee,
because they know not the voice of a stranger. This is
not the fanciful costume of a parable; it is simple fact.
I have made the experiment repeatedly. The shepherd goes
before, not merely to point out the way, but to see
that it is practicable and safe. He is armed in order
to defend his charge, and in this he is very courageous.
Many adventures with wild beasts occur not unlike that
recounted by David, and in these very mountains; for,
though there are now no lions here, there are wolves in
abundance; and leopards and panthers, exceedingly fierce,
prowl about these wild wadies. They not unfrequently
attack the flock in the very presence of the shepherd,
and he must be ready to do battle at a moment's warning.
I have listened with intense interest to their
graphic descriptions of downright and desperate fights
with these savage beasts. And when the thief and the
robber come (and come they do), the faithful shepherd
has often to put his life in his hand to defend his
flock. I have known more than one case in which he
had literally to lay it down in the contest. A poor
faithful fellow last spring, between Tiberias and Tabor,
instead of fleeing, actually fought three Bedouin robbers
until he was hacked to pieces with their khanjars, and
died among the sheep he was defending."

{g} "but will flee from him" 2 Ti 3:5; Re 2:2

THE GOSPEL ACCORDING TO JOHN-Chapter 10-Verse 6
Verse 6. *This parable*. See Barnes "Mt 13:3".

They understood not, &c. They did not understand the meaning or design of the illustration.

THE GOSPEL ACCORDING TO JOHN-Chapter 10-Verse 7
Verse 7. *I am the door*. I am the way by which ministers and people enter the true church. It is by his merits, his intercession, his aid, and his appointment that they enter.
Of the sheep. Of the church.
{h} "I am the door of the sheep" Eph 2:18

Verse 8. *All that ever came before me.* This does not refer to the prophets, but to those who came *pretending* to be the pastors or guides of the people. Some have supposed that he referred to those who pretended to be the Messiah before him; but there is not evidence that *any* such person appeared before the coming of Jesus. It is probable that he rather refers to the scribes and Pharisees, who claimed to be instructors of the people, who claimed the right to regulate the affairs of religion, and whose only aim was to aggrandize themselves and to oppress the people. See Barnes "Joh 1:18".

When the Saviour says that "*all*" were thieves, he speaks in a popular sense, using the word "all" as it is often used in the New Testament, to denote the great mass or the majority.

Thieves and robbers. See Joh 10:1; Jer 23:1: "Woe be unto the pastors that destroy and scatter the sheep of my pasture;" Eze 24:2,3: "Woe be to the shepherds of Israel that do feed themselves! Ye eat the fat, and ye clothe you with the wool, ye kill them that are fed; but ye feed not the flock." This had been the *general* character of the Pharisees and scribes. They sought wealth, office, ease at the expense of the people, and thus deserved the character of thieves and robbers. They insinuated themselves slyly as a thief, and they oppressed and spared not, like a robber.

The sheep. The people of God—the pious and humble portion of the Jewish nation. Though the great mass of the people were corrupted, yet there were always some who were the humble and devoted people of God. Comp. Ro 11:3,4. So it will be always. Though the great mass of teachers may be corrupt, yet the true friends of God will mourn in secret places, and refuse to "listen to the instruction that causeth to err."

Verse 9. *By me.* By my instruction and merits.

Shall be saved. See Joh 5:24.

Shall go in and out, &c. This is language applied commonly to flocks. It meant that he shall be well supplied, and defended, and led "beside the still waters of salvation."

Verse 10. *The thief cometh not,* &c. The thief has no other design in coming but to plunder. So false teachers have no other end in view but to enrich or aggrandize themselves.

I am come that they might have life. See Barnes "Joh 5:24".

Might have it more abundantly. Literally, that they may have *abundance,* or that which abounds. The word denotes that which is not absolutely essential to *life,* but which is superadded to make life happy. They shall not merely have *life*—simple, bare *existence*— but they shall have all those superadded things which are needful to make that life eminently blessed and happy. It would be vast mercy to keep men merely from annihilation or hell; but Jesus will give them eternal joy, peace, the society of the blessed, and all those exalted means of felicity which are prepared for them in the world of glory.

THE GOSPEL ACCORDING TO JOHN-Chapter 10-Verse 11

Verse 11. *The good shepherd.* The faithful and true shepherd, willing to do *all* that is necessary to defend and save the flock.

Giveth his life. A shepherd that regarded his flock would hazard his own life to defend them. When the wolf comes, he would still remain to protect them. To *give his life,* here, means the same as not to fly, or to forsake his flock; to be willing to expose his life, if necessary, to defend them. Comp. Jud 12:3 "I put my life in my hands and passed over," &c.; 1 Sa 19:5;28:21. See Joh 10:15. The Messiah was often predicted under the character of a shepherd.

{i} "I am the good shepherd" Heb 13:20; 1 Pe 2:25

THE GOSPEL ACCORDING TO JOHN-Chapter 10-Verse 12

Verse 12. *A hireling.* A man employed to take care of the sheep, to whom wages is paid. As he does not *own* the sheep, and guards them merely for pay, rather than risk his life he would leave the flock to the ravages of wild beasts. The word translated *hireling* is often employed in a good sense; but here it denotes one who is unfaithful to his trust; and especially those ministers who preach *only* for support, and who are unwilling to encounter any danger or to practise any self-denial for the welfare of the church of God. They are those who have no boldness in the cause of their Master, but who, rather than lose their reputation or place, would see the church corrupted and wasted by its spiritual foes.

Whose own the sheep are not. Who does not own the sheep.

{k} "leaveth the sheep" Eze 34:2-6; Zec 11:17

THE GOSPEL ACCORDING TO JOHN-Chapter 10-Verse 13

Verse 13. *Because he is a hireling.* Because he regards only his wages. He feels no special interest in the flock.

THE GOSPEL ACCORDING TO JOHN-Chapter 10-Verse 14

Verse 14. *Know my sheep.* Know my people, or my church. The word *know* here is used in the sense of *affectionate regard* or *love.* It implies such a knowledge of their wants, their dangers, and their characters, as to result in *a deep interest in their welfare.* Thus the word "knoweth," in Joh 10:15, is in Joh 10:17 explained by the word "loveth." Jesus *knows* the hearts, the dangers, and the wants of his people, and his kindness as their shepherd prompts him to defend and aid them.

Am known of mine. That is, he is known and loved as their Saviour and Friend. They have seen their sins, and dangers, and wants; they have felt their need of a Saviour; they have come to him, and they have found him and his doctrines to be such as they need, and they have loved him. And as a flock follows and obeys its kind shepherd, so they follow and obey him who leads them beside the still waters, and makes them to lie down in green pastures.

{l} "know my sheep" 2 Ti 2:19 {m} "and am known of mine" 1 Jo 5:20

Verse 15. *As the Father knoweth me*, &c. See Barnes "Mt 11:27"
See Barnes "Lu 10:22".

I lay down my life for the sheep. That is, I give my life as an atoning sacrifice for their sins. I die in their place, to redeem them from sin, and danger, and death. See Joh 10:17,18.

{n} "As the Father" Mt 11:27 {o} "I lay down" Joh 15:13; Isa 53:4,5

Verse 16. *Other sheep.* There are others who shall be members of my redeemed church.

I have. This does not imply that they were *then* his friends, but that they *would* be. There were others whom it was his *purpose* and *intention* to call to the blessings of the gospel and salvation. The purpose was so sure, and the fact that they would believe on him so certain, that he could use the present tense as if they were already his own. This purpose was in accordance with the promise (Isa 53:11), "He shall see of the travail of his soul, and shall be satisfied." An instance of a parallel expression occurs in Ac 18:10 "I *have much people* in this city" (Corinth). That is, it was the *purpose* of God to bless the preaching of Paul, and give him many souls as the seals of his ministry. It was so *certain* that they would believe in the Saviour, that it could be spoken of as if it were already done. This certainty could have existed only in consequence of the *intention* of God that it *should be* so. It did not consist in any disposition to embrace the gospel which was foreseen, for they were the most corrupt and licentious people of antiquity, and it must have been because God *meant* that it should be so. Declarations like these are full proof that God has a *plan* in regard to the salvation of men, and that the number is known and determined by him. Learn—

1. That it is not a question of chance or uncertainty whether men shall be saved.

2. That there is encouragement for preaching the gospel. There are those whom God means to save, and if he intends to do it it will be done.

Not of this fold. Not Jews. This is a distinct intimation that the gospel was to be preached to the Gentiles—a doctrine extremely offensive to the Jews. This prediction of the Saviour has been strikingly confirmed in the conversion of millions of the Gentiles to the gospel.

Them also I must bring. Bring into the church and kingdom of heaven. This was to be done, not by his personal ministry, but by the labour of his apostles and other ministers.

One fold. One church; there shall be no distinction, no peculiar national privileges. The partition between the Jews and the Gentiles shall be broken down, and there shall be no pre-eminence of rank or honour, Eph 2:14: "Christ hath broken down the middle wall of partition between us;" Ro 10:12: "There is no difference between the Jew and the Greek."

One shepherd. That is, the Lord Jesus—the common Saviour, deliverer, and friend of all true believers, in whatever land they were born and whatever tongue they may speak. This shows that Christians of all denominations and countries should feel that they are *one*—redeemed by the same blood, and going to the same eternal home. Comp. 1 Co 12:13; Ga 3:28;Col 3:11; Ac 17:26.

{p} "And other" Isa 49:6; 56:8 {q} "And there shall be one fold" Eze 37:22; Eph 2:14

THE GOSPEL ACCORDING TO JOHN-Chapter 10-Verse 17

Verse 17. *I lay down my life.* I give myself to die for my people, in Jewish and pagan lands. I offer myself a sacrifice to show the willingness of my Father to save them; to provide an atonement, and thus to open the way for their salvation. This proves that the salvation of man was an object dear to God, and that it was a source of peculiar gratification to him that his Son was *willing* to lay down his life to accomplish his great purposes of benevolence.

That I might take it again. Be raised up from the dead, and glorified, and still carry on the work of redemption. See this same sentiment sublimely expressed in Php 2:5-11.

{r} "because I lay down" Isa 53:7-12; He 2:9

THE GOSPEL ACCORDING TO JOHN-Chapter 10-Verse 18

Verse 18. *No man taketh it from me.* That is, no one could take it by force, or unless I was willing to yield myself into his hands. He had power to preserve his life, as he showed by so often escaping from the Pharisees; he voluntarily went up to Jerusalem, knowing that he would die; he knew the approach of Judas to betray him; and he expressly told Pilate at his bar that he could have no power at all against him except it were given him by his Father, Joh 19:11. Jesus had a right to lay down his life for the good of men. The patriot dies for his country on the field of battle; the merchant exposes his life for gain; and the Son of God had a right to put himself in the way of danger and of death, when a dying world *needed* such an atoning sacrifice. This shows the peculiar love of Jesus. His death was voluntary. His *coming* was voluntary-the fruit of love. His death was the fruit of love. He was permitted to choose the *time* and *mode* of his death. He did. He chose the most painful, lingering, ignominious manner of death then known to man, and THUS showed his love.

I have power. This word often means authority. It includes all necessary power in the case, and the commission or authority of his Father to do it.

Power to take it again. This shows that he was divine. A *dead* man has no power to raise himself from the grave. And as Jesus had this power *after* he was deceased, it proves that there was some other nature than that which had expired, to which the term "I" might be still applied. None but God can raise the dead; and as Jesus had this power over his own body it proves that he was divine.

This commandment. My Father has appointed this, and commissioned me to do it.

{s} "I lay it down" Php 2:6-8 {t} "I have power" Joh 2:19 {u} "This commandment" Joh 6:38

THE GOSPEL ACCORDING TO JOHN-Chapter 10-Verse 19

Verse 19. No Barnes text on this verse.

THE GOSPEL ACCORDING TO JOHN-Chapter 10-Verse 20

Verse 20. *He hath a devil.* Joh 7:20.

Is mad. Is deranged, or a maniac. His words are incoherent and unintelligible.

{v} "He hath a devil" Joh 7:20

THE GOSPEL ACCORDING TO JOHN-Chapter 10-Verse 21

Verse 21. *Not the words,* &c. His words are sober, grave, pious, full of wisdom. The preaching of Jesus always produced effect. It made bitter enemies or decided friends. So will all faithful preaching. It is not the fault of the gospel that there are divisions, but of the unbelief and mad passions of men.

{w} "open the eyes of the blind" Joh 9:6

THE GOSPEL ACCORDING TO JOHN-Chapter 10-Verse 22

Verse 22. *The feast of the dedication.* Literally, the feast of the *renewing,* or of the renovation. This feast was instituted by Judas Maccabaeus, in the year 164 B.C. The temple and city were taken by Antiochus Epiphanes in the year 167 B.C. He slew forty thousand inhabitants, and sold forty thousand more as slaves. In addition to this, he sacrificed a sow on the altar of burnt-offerings, and a broth being made of this, he sprinkled it all over the temple. The city and temple were recovered three years afterward by Judas Maccabaeus, and the temple was *purified* with great pomp and solemnity. The ceremony of purification continued through eight days, during which Judas presented magnificent victims, and celebrated the praise of God with hymns and psalms (Josephus, Ant., b. xii. ch. 11). "They decked, also, the forefront of the temple with crowns of gold and with shields, and the gates and chambers they *renewed* and hanged doors upon them," 1 Mac. iv. 52-59. On this account it was called the feast of renovation or dedication. Josephus calls it the feast of *lights,* because the city was illuminated, as expressive of joy. The feast began on the twenty-fifth day of *Chisleu,* answering to the fifteenth day of December. The festival continued for eight days, with continued demonstrations of joy.

It was winter. The feast was celebrated in the winter. The word here implies that it was cold and inclement, and it is given as a reason why he walked in Solomon's porch.

Solomon's porch. The porch or covered way on the east of the temple. See Barnes "Mt 21:12".

THE GOSPEL ACCORDING TO JOHN-Chapter 10-Verse 23

Verse 23. No Barnes text on this verse.

{x} "Solomon's porch" Ac 3:11; 5:12

Verse 24. *Tell us plainly.* The Messiah was predicted as a *shepherd.* Jesus had applied that prediction to himself. They supposed that that was an evidence that he claimed to be the Messiah. He also wrought miracles, which they considered as evidence that he was the Christ, Joh 7:31. Yet the rulers made a difficulty. They alleged that he was from Galilee, and that the Messiah could not come from thence, Joh 7:52. He was poor and despised. He came contrary to the common expectation. A splendid prince and conqueror had been expected. In this perplexity they came to him for a plain and positive declaration that he was the Messiah.

{1} "make us to doubt", or, "hold us in suspense"

Verse 25. *I told you.* It is not recorded that Jesus had told them in so many words that he was the Christ, but he had used expressions designed to convey the same truth, and which many of them understood as claiming to be the Messiah. See Joh 5:19; 8:36,56; 10:1.

The expression "the Son of God" they understood to be equivalent to the Messiah. This he had often used of himself in a sense not to be mistaken.

The works. The miracles, such as restoring the blind, curing the sick, &c.

In my Father's name. By the power and command of God. Jesus was either the Messiah or an impostor. The Pharisees charged him with being the latter (Mt 26:60,61; 27:63; Joh 4:36); but God would not give such power to an impostor. The power of working miracles is an attestation of God to what is taught. See Barnes "Mt 4:24".

{y} "the works that I do" Joh 5:36

Verse 26. *Are not of my sheep.* Are not my people, my followers. You do not possess the spirit of meek and humble disciples. Were it not for pride, and prejudice, and vainglory—for your false notions of the Messiah, and from a determination not to believe, you would have learned from my declarations and works that I am the Christ.

As I said unto you. Comp. Joh 8:47.

{z} "ye believe not" Joh 8:47; 1 Jo 4:6

Verse 27. *My sheep.* My church, my people, those who have the true spirit of my followers. The name is given to his people because it was an illustration which would be well understood in a country abounding in flocks. There is also a striking resemblance, which he proceeds to state, between them.

Hear my voice. See Joh 10:3,4. Applied to Christians, it means that they hear and obey his commandments.

I know them. See Joh 10:14.

They follow me. A flock follows its shepherd to pastures and streams, Joh 10:3. Christians not only *obey* Christ, but they *imitate* him; they go where his Spirit and providence lead them; they yield themselves to his guidance, and seek to be led by him. When Jesus was upon earth many of his disciples *followed* or *attended* him from place to place. Hence Christians are called his *followers*, and in Re 14:4 they are described as "they that follow the Lamb."

{a} "My sheep hear my voice" Joh 10:4

THE GOSPEL ACCORDING TO JOHN-Chapter 10-Verse 28

Verse 28. *I give unto them eternal life.* See Joh 5:24.

Shall never perish. To *perish* here means to be destroyed, or to be punished in hell. Mt 10:28: "Which is able to destroy (the same word) both soul and body in hell."

Mt 18:14: "It is not the will of your Father which is in heaven that one of these little ones should *perish*." Joh 3:15: "That whosoever believeth in him should not perish." Ro 2:12: "They who have sinned without law shall also *perish* without law." Joh 17:12; 1 Co 1:18. In all these places the word refers to *future punishment*, and the declaration of the Saviour is that his followers, his true disciples, shall never be cast away. The original is expressed with remarkable strength: "They shall not be destroyed for ever." Syriac: "They shall not perish to eternity." This is spoken of all Christians—that is, of all who ever possess the character of true followers of Christ, and who can be called his flock.

Shall any. The word *any* refers to any power that might attempt it. It will apply either to men or to devils. It is an affirmation that no man, however eloquent in error, or persuasive in infidelity, or cunning in argument, or mighty in rank; and that no devil with all his malice, power, cunning, or allurements, shall be able to pluck them from his hand.

Pluck them. In the original to *rob*; to seize and bear away as a robber does his prey. Jesus holds them so secure and so certainly that no foe can surprise him as a robber does, or overcome him by force.

My hand. The *hand* is that by which we *hold* or *secure* an object. It means that Jesus has them safely in his own care and keeping. Comp. Ro 8:38,39.

{b} "they shall never perish" Joh 17:12

THE GOSPEL ACCORDING TO JOHN-Chapter 10-Verse 29

Verse 29. *Which gave them me.* See Joh 6:37.

Is greater. Is more powerful.

Than all. Than all others—men, angels, devils. The word includes *everything*—everything that could *attempt* to pluck them away from God; in other words, it means that God is *supreme*. It implies, farther, that God will keep them, and will so control *all* other beings and things that they shall be safe.

None is able. None has power to do it. In these two verses we are taught the following important truths:

cxcviii

1st. That Christians are *given* by God the Father to Christ.

2nd. That Jesus gives to them eternal life, or *procures* by his death and intercession, and imparts to them by his Spirit, that religion which shall result in eternal life.

3rd. That both the Father and the Son are pledged to keep them so that they shall never fall away and perish. It would be impossible for any language to teach more explicitly that the saints will persevere.

4th. That there is no power in man or devils to defeat the purpose of the Redeemer to save his people. We also see our safety, if we truly, humbly, cordially, and *daily* commit ourselves to God the Saviour. In no other way can we have evidence that we are his people than by such a persevering resignation of ourselves to him, to obey his law, and to follow him through evil report or good report. If we do that we are safe. If we do not that we have no evidence of piety, and are not, cannot be safe.

{d} "gave them me" Joh 17:2

THE GOSPEL ACCORDING TO JOHN-Chapter 10-Verse 30

Verse 30. *I and my Father are one*. The word translated "one" is not in the *masculine*, but in the *neuter* gender. It expresses *union*, but not the precise nature of the union. It *may*express any union, and the particular kind intended is to be inferred from the connection. In the previous verse he had said that he and his Father were *united* in the same object—that is, in redeeming and preserving his people. It was *this* that gave occasion for this remark. Many interpreters have understood this as referring to union of design and of plan. The words may bear this construction. In this way they were understood by Erasmus, Calvin, Bucer, and others. Most of the Christian fathers understood them, however, as referring to the *oneness*or *unity of nature* between the Father and the Son; and that this was the design of Christ appears probable from the following considerations:

1st. The question in debate was not about his being united with the Father in *plan* and *counsel*, but in *power*. He affirmed that he was able to rescue and keep his people from *all*enemies, or that he had *power* superior to men and devils—that is, that he had *supreme* power over all creation. He affirmed the same of his Father. *In this*, therefore, they were *united*. But this was an attribute only of God, and they thus understood him as claiming equality to God in regard to *omnipotence*.

2nd. The Jews understood him as affirming his equality with God, for they took up stones to punish him for blasphemy (Joh 10:31,33), and they said *to him* that they understood him as affirming that he was God, Joh 10:33.

3rd. Jesus did not *deny* that it was his intention to be so understood. See Barnes "Joh 10:34, also on Mt 10:35-37.

4th. He *immediately made another* declaration implying the same thing, leaving the same impression, and which they attempted to punish in the same manner, Joh 10:37-39. If Jesus had not *intended* so to be understood, it cannot be easily reconciled with moral honesty that he did not distinctly *disavow* that such was his intention. The Jews were well acquainted with their own language. They understood him in this manner, and he left this impression on their minds.

{e} "I and *my* father" Joh 17:11,22

THE GOSPEL ACCORDING TO JOHN-Chapter 10-Verse 31

Verse 31. *The Jews took up stones.* Stoning was the punishment of a blasphemer, Le 24:14-16. They considered him guilty of blasphemy because he made himself equal with God,Joh 10:33.

Again. They had before plotted against his life (Joh 5:16,18) and once at least they had taken up stones to destroy him, Joh 8:59.

{f} "The Jews" Joh 8:59

THE GOSPEL ACCORDING TO JOHN-Chapter 10-Verse 32

Verse 32. *Many good works.* Many miracles of benevolence—healing the sick, &c. His miracles were *good works*, as they tended to promote the happiness of men, and were proofs of his benevolence. He had performed no other works than those of benevolence; he knew that they could charge him with no other, and he confidently appealed to *them* as witnesses of that. Happy would it be if all, when they are opposed and persecuted, could appeal even to their persecutors in proof of their own innocence.

THE GOSPEL ACCORDING TO JOHN-Chapter 10-Verse 33

Verse 33. *For blasphemy.* See Barnes "Mt 9:3".

Makest thyself God. See Barnes "Joh 5:18".

This shows how *they* understood what he had said.

Makest thyself. Dost *claim* to be God, or thy language implies this.

{g} "and because" Joh 5:16; 10:30; Ps 82:6; Ro 13:1

THE GOSPEL ACCORDING TO JOHN-Chapter 10-Verse 34

Verses 34-38. *Jesus answered them.* The answer of Jesus consists of two parts. The first (Joh 10:34-36) shows that *they* ought not to object to his use of the word God, *even* if he were no more than a man. The second (Joh 10:37,38) repeats substantially what he had before said, left the same impression, and in proof of it he appealed to his works.

Verse 34. *In your law.* Ps 82:6. The word *law* here, is used to include the Old Testament.

I said. The Psalmist said, or God said by the Psalmist.

Ye are gods. This was said of *magistrates* on account of the dignity and honour of their office, and it shows that the word translated "god" in that place *might* be applied to man. Such a use of the word is, however, rare. See instances in Ex 7:1; 4:16.

Verse 35. *Unto whom the word of God came.* That is, who were his servants, or who received their dignity and honour only because the law of God was intrusted to them. The *word of God* here means the command of God; his commission to them to do justice.

The scripture cannot be broken. See Mt 5:19. The authority of the Scripture is final; it *cannot be set aside.* The meaning is, \-

> "If, therefore, the Scripture uses the word god as
> applied to magistrates, it settles the question that
> it is *right* to apply the term to those in office and
> authority. If applied to *them*, it may be to others in
> similar offices. It can not, therefore, be *blasphemy*
> to use this word as applicable to a personage so much
> more exalted than mere magistrates as the Messiah."

Verse 36. *Whom the Father hath sanctified.* The word *sanctify* with us means to *make holy*; but this is not its meaning here, for the Son of God was always holy. The original word means to set apart from a common to a sacred use; to devote to a sacred purpose, and to designate or consecrate to a holy office. This is the meaning here. God has *consecrated* or appointed his Son to be his Messenger or Messiah to mankind. See Ex 28:41; Le 8:30.

And sent into the world. As the Messiah, an office far more exalted than that of magistrates. *I am the Son of God.* This the Jews evidently understood as the same as saying that he was equal with God. This expression he had often applied to himself. The meaning of this place may be thus expressed:

> "You charge me with blasphemy. The foundation of that
> charge is the use of the name *God*, or the
> *Son* of God, applied to myself; yet that same term
> is applied in the Scriptures to magistrates. The use
> of it there shows that it is *right* to apply it to
> those who sustain important offices. And especially
> *you*, Jews, ought not to attempt to found a charge
> of blasphemy on the application of a word to the
> Messiah which in your own Scriptures is applied to
> all magistrates."

And we may remark here,
1st. That Jesus did not deny that he meant to apply the term to himself.
2nd. He did not deny that it was *properly* applied to him.

3rd. He did not deny that it implied that he was God. He affirmed only that *they* were *inconsistent*, and *were not authorized* to bring a charge of blasphemy for the application of the*name* to himself.

{h} "hath sanctified" Isa 11:2,3; 49:1,3; Joh 6:27

THE GOSPEL ACCORDING TO JOHN-Chapter 10-Verse 37

Verse 37. *The works of my Father.* The very works that my Father does. See Joh 5:17: "My Father worketh hitherto, and I work." See Barnes "Joh 5:17".

The works of his Father are those which God only can do. As Jesus *did them*, it shows that the name "*Son of God*," implying *equality* with God, was properly applied to him. This shows conclusively that he meant to be understood as claiming to be equal with God. So the Jews naturally understood him Joh 10:39 and they were left with this impression on their minds.

{k} "If I do not the works" Joh 14:10,11; 15:24

THE GOSPEL ACCORDING TO JOHN-Chapter 10-Verse 38

Verse 38. *Believe the works.* Though you do not credit *me*, yet consider my *works*, for they prove that I came from God. No one could do them unless he was sent of God.

Father is in me, &c. Most intimately connected. See Joh 5:36. This expression denotes most intimate union—such as can exist in no other case. See Mt 11:27. See Barnes "Joh 17:21".

THE GOSPEL ACCORDING TO JOHN-Chapter 10-Verse 39

Verse 39. *Sought again to take him.* They evidently understood him as still claiming equality with God, and under this impression Jesus left them. Nor can it be doubted that he*intended* to leave them with this impression; and if so, then he is divine.

He escaped. See Joh 8:59.

THE GOSPEL ACCORDING TO JOHN-Chapter 10-Verse 40

Verse 40. *Where John at first baptized.* At Bethabara, or Bethany, Joh 1:28.

{l} "the place where John at first baptized" Joh 1:28

THE GOSPEL ACCORDING TO JOHN-Chapter 10-Verse 41

Verse 41. *No miracle.* He did not confirm his mission by working *miracles*, but he showed that he was a *prophet* by foretelling the character and success of Jesus. Either miracle or prophecy is conclusive proof of a divine mission, for no man can foretell a future event, or work a miracle, except by the special aid of God. It may be remarked that the people of that place were properly prepared by the ministry of John for the preaching of Jesus. The persecution of the Jews was the occasion of his going there, and thus the wrath of man was made to praise him. It has commonly happened that the opposition of the wicked has resulted in the increased success of the cause which they have persecuted. God takes the wise in their own craftiness, and brings glory to himself and salvation to sinners out of the pride, and passions, and rage of wicked men.

{m} "all things that John" Joh 3:30-36

Verse 42. No Barnes text on this verse.

THE GOSPEL ACCORDING TO JOHN-
Chapter 11

Verse 1. *A certain* man *was sick*. The resurrection of Lazarus has been recorded only by John. Various reasons have been conjectured why the other evangelists did not mention so signal a miracle. The most probable is, that at the time they wrote Lazarus was still living. The miracle was well known, and yet to have recorded it might have exposed Lazarus to opposition and persecution from the Jews. See Joh 12:10,11. Besides, John wrote for Christians who were out of Palestine. The other gospels were written chiefly for those who were in Judea. There was the more need, therefore, that he should enter minutely into the account of the miracle, while the others did not deem it necessary or proper to record an event so well known.

Bethany. A village on the eastern declivity of the Mount of Olives. See Barnes "Mt 21:1".

The town of Mary. The place where she lived. At that place also lived Simon the leper (Mt 26:6), and there our Lord spent considerable part of his time when he was in Judea. The transaction recorded in this chapter occurred nearly four months after those mentioned in the previous chapter. Those occurred in December, and these at the approach of the Passover in April.

{a} "Mary, and her sister Martha" Lu 10:38,39

Verse 2. *It was that Mary*, &c. See Barnes "Mt 26:6, See Barnes "Lu 7:36, also on Lu 7:37-50

{b} "which anointed the Lord" Mr 14:3; Joh 12:3

Verse 3. *Whom thou lovest*, Joh 11:5. The members of this family were among the few peculiar and intimate friends of our Lord. He was much with them, and showed them marks of special friendship Lu 10:38-42, and they bestowed upon him peculiar proof of affection in return. This shows that *special* attachments are lawful for Christians, and that those friendships are peculiarly lovely which are tempered and sweetened with the spirit of Christ. *Friendships* should always be cemented by religion, and one main end of those attachments should be to aid one another in the great business of preparing to die.

Sent unto him. They believed that he had power to heal him (Joh 11:21), though they did not *then* seem to suppose that he could raise him if he died. Perhaps there were two reasons why they sent for him; one, because they supposed he would be desirous of seeing his friend; the other, because they supposed he could restore him. In sickness we should implore the aid and presence of Jesus. He only can restore us and our friends; he only can perform for us the office of a friend when all other friends fail; and he only can cheer us with the hope of a blessed resurrection.

{c} "whom thou lovest" Heb 12:6; Re 3:19

THE GOSPEL ACCORDING TO JOHN-Chapter 11-Verse 4

Verse 4. *This sickness is not unto death.* The word *death* here is equivalent to *remaining render death*, Ro 6:23: "The wages of sin is *death*"—-permanent or unchanging death, opposed to eternal life. Jesus evidently did not intend to deny that he would die. The words which he immediately adds show that he would expire, and that he would raise him up to show forth the power and glory of God. Comp. Joh 11:11. Those words cannot be understood on any other supposition than that he *expected* to raise him up. The Saviour often used expressions similar to this to fix the attention on what he was about to say in explanation. The sense may be thus expressed: "His sickness is not fatal. It is not designed for his death, but to furnish an opportunity for a signal display of the glory of God, and to furnish a standing proof of the truth of religion. It is intended to exhibit the power of the Son of God, and to be a proof at once of the truth of his mission; of his friendship for this family; of his mild, tender, peculiar love as a man; of his power and glory as the Messiah; and of the great doctrine that the dead will rise."

For the glory of God. That God may be honoured See Joh 9:3.

That the Son of God, &c. The glory of God and of his Son is the same. That which promotes the one promotes also the other. Few things could do it more than the miracle which follows, evincing at once the lovely and tender character of Jesus as a man and a friend, and his power as the equal with God.

{d} "for the glory of God" Joh 9:3; 11:40

THE GOSPEL ACCORDING TO JOHN-Chapter 11-Verse 5

Verse 5. No Barnes text on this verse.

THE GOSPEL ACCORDING TO JOHN-Chapter 11-Verse 6

Verse 6. *He abode two days.* Probably Lazarus died soon after the messengers left him. Jesus knew that (Joh 11:11) and did not hasten to Judea, but remained two days longer where he was, that there might not be the possibility of doubt that he was dead, so that when he came there he had been dead four days, Joh 11:39. This shows, moreover, that he *intended* to raise him up. If he had not, it could hardly be reconciled with friendship thus to remain, without any reason, away from an afflicted family.

Where he was. At Bethabara (Joh 1:28; 10:40), about 30 miles from Bethany. This was about a day's journey, and it renders it probable that Lazarus died soon after the message was sent. One day would be occupied before the message came to him; two days he remained; one day would be occupied by him in going to Bethany; so that Lazarus had been dead four days (Joh

11:39) when he arrived.

Verse 7. No Barnes text on this verse.

Verse 8. *Of late*. About four months before, Joh 10:31
{e} "of late" Joh 10:31 {f} "goest thou thither again" Ac 20:24

Verses 9,10. *Twelve hours*. The Jews divided and the day from sunrise to sunset into twelve equal parts. A similar illustration our Saviour uses in Joh 9:4,5. See Barnes "Joh 9:4".

If any man walk. If any man *travels*. The illustration here is taken from a traveller. The conversation was respecting a *journey* into Judea, and our Lord, as was his custom, took the illustration from the case before him.

He stumbleth not. He is able, having light, to make his journey safely. He sees the obstacles or dangers and can avoid them.

The light of this world. The light by which the world is illuminated —that is, the light of the sun.

In the night. In darkness he is unable to see danger or obstacles, and to avoid them. His journey is unsafe and perilous, or, in other words, it is not a proper time to travel.

No light in him. He sees no light. It is dark; his eyes admit no light within him to direct his way. This description is figurative, and it is difficult to fix the meaning. Probably the intention was the following:

1st. Jesus meant to say that there was an allotted or appointed time for him to live and do his Father's will, represented here by the *twelve hours of the day*.

2nd. Though his life was nearly spent, yet it was not entirely; a remnant of it was left.

3rd. A traveller journeyed on till night. It was as proper for him to travel the *twelfth hour* as any other.

4th. So it was proper for Jesus to labour until the close. It was the proper time for him to work. The night of death was coming, and no work could then be done.

5th. God would defend him in this until the appointed time of his death. He had nothing to fear, therefore, in Judea from the Jews, until it was the will of God that he should die. He was safe in his hand, and he went fearlessly into the midst of his foes, trusting in him. This passage teaches us that we should be diligent to the end of life; fearless of enemies when we that God requires us to labour, confidently committing ourselves to Him who is able to shield us, and in whose hand, if we have a conscience void of offence, we are safe.

{g} "any man walk in the day" Joh 12:35

Verse 10. No Barnes text on this verse.

{h} "walk in the night"

Ec 2:14

Verse 11. *Lazarus sleepeth.* Is dead. The word *sleep* is applied to death,

1st. Because of the *resemblance* between them, as sleep is the "kinsman of death." In this sense it is often used by pagan writers. But,

2nd. In the Scriptures it is used to intimate that death will not be *final*: that there will be an awaking out of this sleep, or a resurrection. It is a beautiful and tender expression, removing all that is dreadful in death, and filling the mind with the idea of calm repose after a life of toil, with a reference to a future resurrection in increased rigour and renovated powers. In this sense it is applied in the Scriptures usually to the saints, 1 Co 11:30; 15:51; 1 Th 4:14; 5:10; Mt 9:24.

{i} "sleepeth" De 31:16; Ac 7:60; 1 Co 15:18,51

Verse 12. *If he sleep, he shall do well.* Sleep was regarded by the Jews, in sickness, as a favourable symptom; hence it was said among them, "Sleep in sickness is a sign of recovery, because it shows that the violence of the disease has abated" (Lightfoot.) This seems to have been the meaning of the disciples. They intimated that if had *this* symptom, there was no need of his going into Judea to restore him.

Verse 13. No Barnes text on this verse.

Verse 14. No Barnes text on this verse.

Verse 15. *I am glad,* &c. The meaning of this verse may be thus expressed:
"If I had been there during his sickness, the
entreaties of his sisters and friends would have
prevailed with me to restore him to health. I
could not have refused them without appearing
to be unkind. Though a restoration to *health*
would have been a miracle, and sufficient to
convince you, yet the miracle of raising him
after four days dead will be far more impressive, and
on that account I rejoice that an opportunity is

thus given so strikingly to confirm your faith."

To the intent. To furnish you *evidence* on which you might be established in the belief that I am the Messiah.

Verse 16. *Thomas, which is called Didymus*. These names express the same thing. One is Hebrew and the other Greek. The name means *a twin*.

Die with him. It has been much doubted by critics whether the word *him* refers to Lazarus or to Jesus. They who refer it to Lazarus suppose this to be the meaning:
"Let us go and die, for what have we to hope for
if Jesus returns into Judea? Lately they attempted
to stone him, and now they will put him to death,
and we also, like Lazarus, shall be dead."

This expression is supposed to be added by John to show the slowness with which Thomas believed, and his readiness to doubt without the fullest evidence. See Joh 20:25. Others suppose, probably more correctly, that it refers to Jesus:
"He is about to throw himself into danger. The Jews
lately sought his life, and will again. They will
put him to death. But let us not forsake him. Let
us attend him and die with him."

It may be remarked that this, not less than the other mode of interpretation, expresses the doubts of Thomas about the miracle which Jesus was about to work.

Verse 17. *In the grave*. It was sometimes the custom to *embalm* the dead, but in this case it does not seem to have been done. He was probably buried soon after death.

Verse 18. *Nigh unto Jerusalem*. This is added to show that it was easy for many of the Jews to come to the place. The news that Jesus was there, and the account of the miracle, would also be easily carried to the Sanhedrim.

Fifteen furlongs. Nearly two miles. It was directly east from Jerusalem. Dr. Thompson (*The Land and the Book*, vol. 2. p. 599) says of Bethany:
"It took half an hour to walk over Olivet to Bethany
this morning, and the distance from the city,
therefore, must be about two miles. This agrees with

what John says: 'Now Bethany was nigh unto Jerusalem,
about fifteen furlongs off.' The village is small,
and appears never to have been large, but it is
pleasantly situated near the south-eastern base of
the mount, and has many fine trees about and above it.
We, of course, looked at the remains of those old
edifices which may have been built in the age of
Constantine, and repaired or changed to a convent
in the time of the Crusades. By the dim light of a
taper we also descended very cautiously, by
twenty-five slippery steps, to the reputed sepulchre
of Lazarus, or El Azariyeh, as both tomb and village
are now called. But I have no description of it to
give, and no questions about it to ask. It is a
wretched cavern, every way unsatisfactory, and
almost disgusting."

{1} "about fifteen furlongs" or "about two miles"

Verse 19. *Many of the Jews.* Probably their distant relatives or their friends.

To comfort. These visits of consolation were commonly extended to seven days (Grotius; Lightfoot).

{k} "comfort" 1 Ch 7:22; Job 2:11; 42:11; Ro 12:15; 1 Th 4:18

Verse 20. *Then Martha, &c.* To Martha was intrusted the management of the affairs of the family, Lu 10:40. It is probable that she first heard of his coming, and, without waiting to inform her sister, went immediately out to meet him. See Joh 11:28.

Sat still in the house. The word *still* is not in the original. It means that she remained sitting in the house. The common posture of grief among the Jews was that of sitting, Job 2:8;Eze 8:14. Often this grief was so excessive as to fix the person in astonishment, and render him immovable, or prevent his being affected by any external objects. It is possible that the evangelist meant to intimate this of Mary's grief. Comp. Ezr 9:3,4; Ne 1:4; Is 47:1.

Verse 21. No Barnes text on this verse.

Verse 22. *Whatsoever thou wilt ask of God.* Whatever is necessary to our consolation that thou will ask, thou canst obtain. It is possible that she meant gently to intimate that he could raise him up and restore him again to them.

{l} "whatsoever thou wilt ask" Joh 9:31

THE GOSPEL ACCORDING TO JOHN-Chapter 11-Verse 23

Verse 23. *Thy brother shall rise again.* Martha had spoken of the power of Jesus. He said nothing of himself in reply. It was not customary for him to speak of himself, unless it was demanded by necessity. It cannot be doubted that by *rising again*, here, Jesus referred to the act which he was about to perform; but as Martha understood it, referring to the future resurrection, it was full of consolation. The idea that departed friends shall rise to glory is one that fills the mind with joy, and one which we owe only to the religion of Christ.

THE GOSPEL ACCORDING TO JOHN-Chapter 11-Verse 24

Verse 24. *At the last day.* The day of judgment. Of this Martha was fully convinced; but this was not all which she desired. She in this manner delicately hinted what she did not presume expressly to declare— her wish that Jesus might even *now* raise him up.

{m} "in the resurrection" Joh 5:29

THE GOSPEL ACCORDING TO JOHN-Chapter 11-Verse 25

Verse 25. *I am the resurrection.* I am the *author* or the *cause* of the resurrection. It so depends on my power and will, that it may be said that I *am* the resurrection itself. This is a most expressive way of saying that the whole doctrine of the resurrection came from him, and the whole power to effect it was his. In a similar manner he is said to be made of God unto us *"wisdom, and righteousness,* and *sanctifcation, and redemption,"* 1 Co 1:30.

And the life. Joh 1:4. As the resurrection of

all

depends on him, he intimated that it was not indispensable that it should be deferred to the *last day.* He had power to do it now as well as then.

Though he were dead. Faith does not save from *temporal* death; but although the believer, as others, will die a temporal@\ death, yet he will hereafter have life. *Even if he dies, he shall hereafter live.*

Shall he live. Shall be restored to life in the resurrection.

{n} "the resurrection" Joh 5:29 {o} "the life" Isa 38:16; Joh 14:6; 1 Jo 1:2

{p} "though he were dead" Job 19:26; Isa 26:19; Ro 4:17

THE GOSPEL ACCORDING TO JOHN-Chapter 11-Verse 26

Verse 26. *Whosoever liveth.* He had just spoken of the prospects of the pious dead. He now says that the same prospects are before the living who have like faith. Greek, "Every one living and believing on me."

Shall never die. As the dead, though dead, shall yet *live,* so the living shall have the same kind of life. They shall never come into eternal death. See Joh 6:50,51,54,58.

Greek, "shall by no means die forever."

Believest thou this? This question was doubtless asked because it implied that he was then able to raise up Lazarus, and because it was a proper time for her to test her own faith. The time of affliction is a favourable period to try ourselves to ascertain whether we have faith. If we still have confidence in God, if we look to him for comfort in such seasons, it is good evidence that we are his friends. He that loves God when he takes away his comforts, has the best evidence possible of true attachment to him.

{q} "whosoever" Joh 3:15; 4:14

THE GOSPEL ACCORDING TO JOHN-Chapter 11-Verse 27

Verse 27. Yea, Lord. this was a noble confession. It showed her full confidence in him as the Messiah, and her full belief that all that he said was true. See Mt 16:16.

THE GOSPEL ACCORDING TO JOHN-Chapter 11-Verse 28

Verse 28. *She went her way.* Jesus probably directed her to go, though the evangelist has not recorded it, for she said to Mary, *The Master calleth for thee.*

Secretly. Privately. So that the others did not hear her. This was done, perhaps, to avoid confusion, or because it was probably that if they knew Jesus was coming they would have made opposition. Perhaps she doubted whether Jesus desired it to be known that he had come.

The Master is come. This appears to have been the appellation by which he was known to the family. It means literally, *teacher*, and was a title which he claimed for himself, "One is you Master, even Christ," Mt 22:8,10. The Syriac has it, "Our Master."

{r} "called Mary" Joh 21:7 {s} "The Master" Joh 13:13 {t} "calleth for thee" Mr 10:49

THE GOSPEL ACCORDING TO JOHN-Chapter 11-Verse 29

Verse 29. No Barnes text on this verse.

THE GOSPEL ACCORDING TO JOHN-Chapter 11-Verse 30

Verse 30. No Barnes text on this verse.

THE GOSPEL ACCORDING TO JOHN-Chapter 11-Verse 31

Verse 31. *Saying, She goeth, unto the grave.* Syriac, "They *thought* that she went to weep." They had not heard Martha call her. The first days of mourning among the Jews were observed with great solemnity and many ceremonies of grief.

{u} "The Jews" Joh 11:19

THE GOSPEL ACCORDING TO JOHN-Chapter 11-Verse 32

Verse 32. No Barnes text on this verse.

{v} "Lord, if thou"

Joh 4:49; 11:21,37

Verse 33. *He groaned in the spirit.* The word rendered *groaned*, here, commonly denotes to be angry or indignant, or to reprove severely, denoting violent agitation of mind. Here it also evidently denotes violent agitation—not from anger, but from *grief.* He saw the sorrow of others, and he was also moved with sympathy and love. The word *groan* usually, with us, denotes an expression of internal sorrow by a peculiar sound. The word here, however, does not mean that *utterance* was given to the internal emotion, but that it was deep and agitating, though internal.

In the spirit. In the mind. See Ac 19:21: "Paul purposed in the spirit "—that is, in his mind, Mt 5:3.

Was troubled. Was affected with grief. Perhaps this expression denotes that his countenance was troubled, or gave indications of sorrow (Grotius).

{2} "was troubled" or, "he troubled himself"

Verse 34. *Where have ye laid him?* Jesus spoke as a man. In all this transaction he manifested the deep sympathies of a man; and though he who could raise the dead man up could also know where he was, yet he chose to lead them to the grave by inducing them to point the way, and hence he asked this question.

Verse 35. *Jesus wept.* It has been remarked that this is the shortest verse in the Bible; but it is exceedingly important and tender. It shows the Lord Jesus as a friend, a tender friend, and evinces his character as a man. And from this we learn,

1st. That the most tender personal friendship is not inconsistent with the most pure religion. Piety binds stronger the ties of friendship, makes more tender the emotions of love, and seals and sanctifies the affections of friends.

2nd. It is right, it is natural, it is indispensable for the Christian to sympathize with others in their afflictions. Ro 12:15: "Rejoice with them that do rejoice, and weep with them that weep."

3rd. Sorrow at the death of friends is not improper. It is right to weep. It is the expression of nature, and religion does not forbid or condemn it. All that religion does in the case is to *temper* and chasten our grief; to teach us to mourn with submission to God; to weep without murmuring, and to seek to banish tears, not by *hardening the heart* or forgetting the friend, but by bringing the soul, made tender by grief, to receive the sweet influences of religion, and to find calmness and peace in the God of all consolation.

4th. We have here an instance of the tenderness of the character of Jesus. The same Saviour wept over Jerusalem, and felt deeply for poor dying sinners. To the same tender and compassionate Saviour Christians may now come (Heb 4:15); and to him the penitent sinner may also come, knowing that he will not cast him away.

{w} "wept" Isa 63:9; Lu 19:41; Heb 2:16,17

Verse 36. No Barnes text on this verse.

Verse 37. No Barnes text on this verse.

Verse 38. *It was a cave.* This was a common mode of burial. See Barnes "Mt 8:28".

A stone lay upon it. Over the mouth of the cave. See Mt 27:60.

Verse 39. *Four days.* This proves that there could be no deception, for it could not have been a case of suspended animation. All these circumstances are mentioned to show that there was no imposture. Impostors do not mention minute *circumstances* like these. They deal in *generals* only. Every part of this narrative bears the marks of truth.
{y} "Take ye away the stone" Mr 16:3 {z} "by this time he stinketh" Ps 49:7,9; Ac 2:27

Verse 40. *Said I not unto thee.* This was implied in what he had said about the resurrection of her brother, Joh 11:23-25. There would be a manifestation of the glory of God in raising him up which *she* would be permitted, with all others, to behold.

The glory of God. The power and goodness displayed in the resurrection. It is probable that Martha did not really expect that Jesus would raise him up, but supposed that he went there merely to see the corpse. Hence, when he directed them to take away the stone, she suggested that by that time the body was offensive.
{a} "Said I not unto thee" Joh 11:4,23

Verse 41. *Lifted up his eyes.* In an attitude of prayer. See Lu 18:13; Mt 14:19.

I thank thee that thou hast heard me. It is possible that John has recorded only the sum or substance of the prayer on this occasion. The thanks which Jesus renders here are evidently in view of the fact that power had been committed to him to raise up Lazarus. On account of the people, and the signal proof which would be furnished of the truth of his mission, he expressed his thanks to God. In all his doings he recognized his union to the Father, and his dependence on him as Mediator.
{b} "Father" Joh 12:28-30

Verse 42. *And I knew.* "As for me. So far as I am concerned. I had no anxiety, no doubt as to myself, that I should always be heard; but the particular ground of gratitude is the benefit that

ccxiii

will result to those who are witnesses." Jesus never prayed in vain. He never attempted to work a miracle in vain; and in all his miracles the ground of his joy was, not that *he* was to be praised or honoured, but that *others* were to be benefited and God glorified.

{b} "Father" Joh 12:28-30

THE GOSPEL ACCORDING TO JOHN-Chapter 11-Verse 43

Verse 43. *A loud voice.* Greek, "A *great* voice." Syriac, "A *high* voice." This was distinctly asserting *his* power. He uttered a distinct, audible voice, that there might be no suspicion of charm or incantation. The ancient magicians and jugglers performed their wonders by whispering and muttering. See Barnes "Isa 8:19".

Jesus spake openly and audibly, and asserted thus his power. So, also, in the day of judgment he will call the dead with a great sound of a trumpet, Mt 24:31; 1 Th 4:16.

Lazarus, come forth. Here we may remark,

1st. That Jesus did this by his own power.

2nd. The power of raising the dead is the highest of which we can conceive. The ancient heathen declared it to be even beyond the power of God. It implies not merely giving life to the deceased body, but the power of entering the world of spirits, of recalling the departed soul, and of reuniting it with the body. He that could do this must be omniscient as well as omnipotent; and if Jesus did it by his own power, it proves that he was divine.

3rd. This is a striking illustration of the general resurrection. In the same manner Jesus will raise *all* the dead. This miracle shows that it is possible; shows the way in which it will be done—by the voice of the Son of God; and demonstrates the certainty that he will do it. Oh how important it is that we be prepared for that moment when his voice shall be heard in our silent tombs, and he shall call us forth again to life!

THE GOSPEL ACCORDING TO JOHN-Chapter 11-Verse 44

Verse 44. *He that was dead.* The same man, body and soul.

Bound hand and foot. It is not certain whether the whole body and limbs were bound together, or each limb separately. When they embalmed a person, the whole body and limbs were *swathed* or bound together by strips of linen, involved around it to keep together the aromatics with which the body was embalmed. This is the condition of Egyptian mummies. SeeAc 5:6. But it is not certain that this was always the mode. Perhaps the body was simply involved in a winding-sheet. The custom still exists in western Asia. No coffins being used, the body itself is more carefully and elaborately wrapped and swathed than is common or desirable where coffins are used. In this method the body is stretched out and the arms laid straight by the sides, after which the whole body, from head to foot, is wrapped round tightly in many folds of linen or cotton cloth; or, to be more precise, a great length of cloth is taken and rolled around the body until the whole is enveloped, and every part is covered with several folds of the cloth. The ends are then sewed, to keep the whole firm and compact; or else a narrow bandage is wound over the whole, forming, ultimately, the exterior surface. The body, when thus enfolded and swathed, retains the profile of the human form; but, as in the Egyptian mummies, the legs are not folded separately, but together; and the arms also are not distinguished, but confined to the sides in the general envelope. Hence it would be clearly impossible for a person thus treated to move his arms or legs, if restored to existence.

The word rendered "grave-clothes" denotes also the bands or clothes in which new-born infants are involved. He went forth, but his walking was impeded by the bands or clothes in which he was involved.

And his face, &c. This was a common thing when they buried their dead. See Joh 20:7. It is not known whether the whole face was covered in this manner, or only the forehead. In the Egyptian mummies it is only the forehead that is thus bound.

Loose him. Remove the bandages, so that he may walk freely. The effect of this miracle is said to have been that many believed on him. It may be remarked in regard to it that there could not be a more striking proof of the divine mission and power of Jesus. There could be here no possibility of deception.

1st. The friends of Lazarus *believed* him to be dead. In this they could not be deceived. There *could* have been among them no design to deceive.

2nd. He was four days dead. It could not be a case, therefore, of suspended animation.

3rd. Jesus was at a distance at the time of his death. There was, therefore, no *agreement* to attempt to impose on others.

4th. No higher power can be conceived than that of raising the dead.

5th. It was not *possible* to impose on his sisters, and to convince them that he was restored to life, if it was not really so.

6th. There were *many* present who were convinced also. God had so ordered it in his providence that to this miracle there should be many witnesses. There was no concealment, no jugglery, no secrecy. It was done publicly, in open day, and was witnessed by many who followed them to the grave, Joh 11:31.

7th. Others, who saw it, and did not believe that Jesus was the Messiah, went and told it to the Pharisees. But they did not *deny* that Jesus had raised up Lazarus. They could not deny it. The very ground of their alarm—the very *reason* why they went—was that he had *actually done it.*

Nor did the Pharisees dare to call the fact in question. If they *could* have done it, they would. But it was not possible; for,

8th. Lazarus was yet alive (Joh 12:10), and the fact of his resurrection could not be denied. Every circumstance in this account is plain, simple, consistent, bearing all the marks of truth. But if Jesus performed this miracle his religion is true. God would not give such power to an impostor; and unless it can be *proved* that this account is false, the Christian religion*must be* from God.

{c} "he that was dead" 1 Ki 17:22; 2 Ki 4:34,35; Lu 7:14,15; Ac 20:9-12.

{d} "his face" Joh 20:7

Verse 45. No Barnes text on this verse.

{e} "and had seen"

Joh 2:23; 10:41,42; 12:11,18

Verse 46. *Some of them*, &c. We see here the different effect which the word and works of God will have on different individuals. Some are converted and others are hardened; yet the *evidence* of this miracle was as clear to the one as the other. But they *would not* be convinced.

Verse 47. *A council*. A meeting of the Sanhedrim, or great council of the nation. See Barnes "Mt 2:4".

They claimed the right of regulating all the affairs of religion. See Barnes "Joh 1:19".

What do we? What measures are we taking to arrest the progress of his sentiments?

For this man doeth many miracles. If they admitted that he performed *miracles*, it was clear what they ought to do. They should have received him as the Messiah. It may be asked, If they really believed that he worked miracles, why did they not believe on him? To this it may be replied that they did not doubt that impostors might work miracles. See Mt 24:24. To this opinion they were led, probably, by the wonders which the magicians performed in Egypt (Exodus chapters 7 & 8), and by the passage in De 13:1. As they regarded the tendency of the doctrines of Jesus to draw off the people from the worship of God, and from keeping his law (Joh 9:16), they did not suppose themselves bound to follow him, even *if he did* work miracles.

{f} "gathered" Ps 2:2

Verse 48. *All men.* That is, all men among the Jews. The whole nation.

And the Romans shall come. They were then subject to the Romans—tributary and dependent. Whatever privileges they had they held at the will of the Roman emperor. They believed, or feigned to believe, that Jesus was intending to set up a *temporal* kingdom. As he claimed to be the Messiah, so they supposed, of course, that he designed to be a temporal prince, and they professed to believe that this claim was, *in fact*, hostility to the Roman emperor. They supposed that it would involve the nation in war if he was not arrested, and that the effect would be that they would be vanquished and destroyed. It was on this charge that they at last arraigned him before Pilate, Lu 23:2,3.

Will take away. This expression means to *destroy*, to ruin, to overthrow, Lu 8:12; Ac

6:13,14.

Our place. This probably refers to the *temple,* Ac 6:13,14. It was called "the place" by way of eminence, as being the chief or principal place on earth—being the seat of the peculiar worship of God. This place was utterly destroyed by the Romans. See Barnes Mt 24:1, and following.

And nation. The nation or *people* of the Jews.

{h} "all men" Joh 12:19

THE GOSPEL ACCORDING TO JOHN-Chapter 11-Verse 49

Verse 49. *Caiaphas.* See Barnes "Lu 3:2".

Being high-priest that same year. It is probable that the office of high-priest was at first for life, if there was no conduct that rendered the person unworthy the office. In that case the incumbent was removed. Thus Abiathar was removed by Solomon, 1 Ki 2:27. Subsequently the kings, and especially the conquerors of Judea, claimed and exercised the right of removing the high-priest at pleasure, so that, in the time of the Romans, the office was held but a short time. (See the Chronological Table at the end of this volume.) Caiaphas held the office about ten years.

Ye know nothing at all. That is, you know nothing respecting the subject under consideration. You are fools to *hesitate* about so plain a case. It is probable that there was a party, even in the Sanhedrim, that was secretly in favour of Jesus as the Messiah. Of that party Nicodemus was certainly one. See Joh 3:1; 7:50,51; 11:45; 12:42.

"Among the chief rulers, also, many believed on him." &c.

{i} "named Caiaphas" Lu 3:3; Joh 18:14; Ac 1:6

THE GOSPEL ACCORDING TO JOHN-Chapter 11-Verse 50

Verse 50. *It is expedient for us.* It *is better* for us. Literally, "It is *profitable* for us."

That one man should die. Jesus they regarded as promoting sedition, and as exposing the nation, if he was successful, to the vengeance of the Romans, Joh 11:48. If *he* was put to death they supposed the people would be safe. This is all, doubtless, that he meant by his dying for the people. He did not *himself* intend to speak of his dying as an *atonement* or a sacrifice; but his words might also express that, and, though he was unconscious of it, he was expressing a *real truth.* In the sense in which he intended it there was no truth in the observation, nor occasion for it, but in the sense which the words *might convey* there was real and most important truth. It was expedient, it was infinitely desirable, that Jesus should die for that people, and for all others, to save them from perishing.

{k} "it is expedient" Lu 24:46

Verse 51. *Not of himself.* Though he uttered what proved to be a *true prophecy*, yet it was accomplished in a way which he did not intend. He had a wicked design. He was plotting murder and crime. Yet, wicked as he was, and little as he intended it, God so ordered it that he delivered a most precious truth respecting the atonement. Remark,

1st. God may fulfil the words of the wicked in a manner which they do not wish or intend.

2nd. He may make even *their* malice and wicked plots the very means of accomplishing his purposes. What they regard as the fulfillment of *their* plans God may make the fulfillment of *his*, yet so as directly to overthrow their designs, and prostrate them in ruin.

3rd. Sinners should tremble and be afraid when they lay plans against God, or seek to do unjustly to others.

Being high-priest that year. It is not to be supposed that Caiaphas was a *true prophet*, or was conscious of the meaning which John has affixed to his words; but his words *express*the truth about the atonement of Jesus, and John records it *as a remarkable circumstance* that the high-priest of the nation should unwittingly deliver a sentiment which turned out to be the truth about the death of Jesus. Great importance was attached to the opinion of the high-priest by the Jews, because it was by him that the judgment by Urim and Thummim was formerly declared in cases of importance and difficulty, Nu 27:21. It is not certain or probable that the high-priest ever was endowed with the gift of prophecy; but he sustained a high office, the authority of his name was great, and it was thence remarkable that he uttered a declaration which the result showed to be true, though not in the sense that he intended.

He prophesied. He uttered words which proved to be prophetic; or he expressed at that time a sentiment which turned out to be true. It does not mean that he was inspired, or that he deserved to be ranked among the true prophets; but his words were such that they accurately expressed a future event. The word *prophecy* is to be taken here not in the strict sense, but in a sense which is not uncommon in the sacred writers. Ac 21:9: "And the same man had four daughters, virgins, which did prophesy." See Barnes "Re 12:6"

See Barnes "1 Co 14:1, comp. See Barnes "Mt 26:68"; See Barnes "Lu 22:64,

That Jesus should die. Die in the *place* of men, or as an atonement for sinners. This is evidently the meaning which John attaches to the words.

For that nation. For the Jews. As a sacrifice for their sins. In no other sense whatever could it be said that he died for them. His death, so far from *saving* them in the sense in which the high-priest understood it, was the very occasion of their destruction. They invoked the vengeance of God when they said, "His blood be on us and on our children" (Mt 27:25), and all these calamities came upon them because they would not come to him and be saved—that is, because they rejected him and put him to death, Mt 23:37-39

Verse 52. *Should gather together in one.* All his chosen among the Jews and Gentiles. See Joh 10:16.

The children of God. This is spoken not of those who *were then* Christians, but of all whom God should bring to him; all who *would be*, in the mercy of God, called, chosen, sanctified among all nations, Joh 10:16.

{l} "not for that nation only" Isa 49:6; Ro 3:29; 1 Jo 2:2

{m} "scattered abroad" Joh 10:16; Eph 2:14-17

Verse 53. *They took counsel.* The judgment of the high-priest silenced opposition, and they began to devise measures to put him to death without exciting tumult among the people. Comp. Mt 26:5.

{n} "they took counsel" Ps 109:4,5

Verse 54. *No more openly.* No more publicly, in the cities and towns. Jesus never exposed his life unnecessarily to hazard. Although the time of his death was determined in the counsel of God, yet this did not prevent his using proper means to preserve his life.

The wilderness. See Barnes "Mt 3:1".

A city called Ephraim. This was probably a small town in the tribe of Ephraim, about five miles west of Jericho.

{p} "Ephraim" 2 Sa 13:23; 2 Ch 13:19

Verse 55. *Jews' passover.* See Barnes "Mt 26:2, also Mt 26:3-17.

Its being called the *Jews'* Passover shows that John wrote this gospel among people who were not Jews, and to whom it was necessary, therefore to explain their customs.

To purify themselves. This purifying consisted in preparing themselves for the proper observation of the Passover, according to the commands of the law. If any were defiled in any manner by contact with the dead or by any other ceremonial uncleanness, they were required to take the prescribed measures for purification, Le 22:1-6. For want of this, great inconvenience was sometimes experienced. See 2 Ch 30:17,18. Different periods were necessary in order to be cleansed from ceremonial pollution. For example, one who had been polluted by the touch of a dead body, of a sepulchre, or by the bones of the dead, was sprinkled on the third and seventh days, by a clean person, with hyssop dipped in water mixed in the ashes of the red heifer. After washing his body and clothes he was then clean. These persons who went up *before* the Passover were doubtless those who had in some manner been ceremonially polluted.

{q} "the Jews' Passover" Joh 2:13; 5:1; 6:4

Verse 56. *Will not come to the feast?* They doubted whether he would come. On the one hand, it was required by law that all males should come. On the other, his coming was attended with great danger. This was the cause of their doubting. It was in this situation that our Saviour, like many of his followers, was called to act. Danger was on the one hand, and duty on the other. He chose, as all should, to do his duty, and leave the event with God. He preferred to do it, though he knew that death was to be the consequence; and we should not shrink, when we have reason to apprehend danger, persecution, or death, from an honest attempt to observe all the commandments of God.

{r} "Then sought they for Jesus" Joh 5:16,18; Joh 11:8

Verse 57. No Barnes text on this verse.

THE GOSPEL ACCORDING TO JOHN-Chapter 12

Verse 1. *Then Jesus came to Bethany.* This was near to Jerusalem, and it was from this place that he made his triumphant entry into the city. See Barnes "Mt 21:1"
and following.

{a} "Lazarus" Joh 11:1,43

Verses 2-8. See this passage explained See Barnes "Mt 26:3, also Mt 26:4-16.

Verse 2. *A supper.* At the house of Simon the leper, Mt 26:6.

Lazarus was, &c. The names of Martha and Lazarus are mentioned because it was not in their own house, but in that of Simon. Lazarus is particularly mentioned, since it was so remarkable that one who had been once dead should be enjoying again the endearments of friendship. This shows, also, that his resurrection was no illusion—that he was *really* restored to the blessings of life and friendship. Calmet thinks that this was about two months after his resurrection, and it is the last that we hear of him. How long he lived is unknown, nor is it recorded that he made any communication about the world of spirits. It is remarkable that none who have been restored to life from the dead have made any communications respecting that world. See Lu 16:31, and See Barnes "2 Co 12:4".

{b} "Martha served" Lu 10:38-42

Verse 3. No Barnes text on this verse.

Verse 4. *Which should betray him.* Greek, "who was to betray him" that is, who *would* do it.

Verse 5. *Three hundred pence.* About forty dollars, or £8, 10s.

And given to the poor. The *avails* or value of it given to the poor.

Verse 6. *Had the bag.* The word translated *bag* is compounded of two words, meaning "tongue," and "to keep or preserve." It was used to denote the bag in which musicians used to keep the tongues or reeds of their pipes when travelling. Hence it came to mean any bag or purse in which travellers put their money or their most precious articles. The disciples appear to have had such a bag or purse in common, in which they put whatever money they had, and which was designed especially for the poor, Lu 8:3; Mt 27:55; Ac 2:44.

The keeping of this, it seems, was intrusted to Judas; and it is remarkable that the only one among them who appears to have been naturally avaricious should have received this appointment. It shows us that every man is tried according to his native propensity. This is the object of trial—to bring out man's native character; and every man will find *opportunity* to do evil according to his native disposition, if he is inclined to it.

And bare, &c. The word translated *bare* means literally to carry as a burden. Then it means to *carry away*, as in Joh 20:15: "If thou hast borne him hence." Hence it means to carry away *as a thief does*, and this is evidently its meaning here. It has this sense often in classic writers. Judas was a thief, and stole what was put into the bag. The money he desired to be intrusted to him, that he might secretly enrich himself. It is clear, however, that the disciples did not at this time know that this was his character, or they would have remonstrated against him. They learned it afterward. We may learn here,

1st. That it is not a new thing for members of the church to be covetous. Judas was so before them.

2nd. That such members will be those who complain of the *great waste* in spreading the gospel.

3rd. That this deadly, mean, and grovelling passion will work all evil in a church. It brought down the curse of God on the children of Israel in the case of Achan (Jos 7:1), and it betrayed our Lord to death. It has often since brought blighting on the church; and many a time it has *betrayed* the cause of Christ, and drowned men in destruction and perdition, 1 Ti 6:9.

{d} "he was a thief" 2 Ki 5:20-27; Ps 50:18 {e} "had the bag" Joh 13:29

THE GOSPEL ACCORDING TO JOHN-Chapter 12-Verse 7
Verse 7. No Barnes text on this verse.

THE GOSPEL ACCORDING TO JOHN-Chapter 12-Verse 8
Verse 8. No Barnes text on this verse.
{f} "For the poor"
De 15:11; Mt 26:11; Mr 14:7
{g} "me you have not" So 5:6; Joh 8:21; 12:35; 13:33; 16:5-7

THE GOSPEL ACCORDING TO JOHN-Chapter 12-Verse 9
Verse 9. No Barnes text on this verse.

THE GOSPEL ACCORDING TO JOHN-Chapter 12-Verse 10
Verse 10. *That they might put Lazarus also to death.* When men are determined not to believe the gospel, there is no end to the crimes to which they are driven. Lazarus was alive, and the evidence of his resurrection was so clear that they could not resist it. They could neither deny

it, nor prevent its effect on the people. As it was determined to kill Jesus, so they consulted about the propriety of removing Lazarus first, that the number of his followers might be lessened, and that the death of Jesus might make less commotion. Unbelief stops at no crime. Lazarus was innocent; they could bring no charge against him; but they deliberately plotted murder rather than believe on the Lord Jesus Christ.

{h} "put Lazarus to death" Mt 21:8; Mr 11:8; Lu 19:36

Verse 11. No Barnes text on this verse.

{i} "that by reason"

Joh 11:45; 12:18

Verses 12-19. See this passage explained in See Barnes "Mt 21:1, also Mt 21:2-16, also See Barnes "Mr 11:1, Mr 11:2-11, See Barnes "Lu 19:29, also Lu 19:30-44.

{k} "the next day" Mt 21:8; Mr 11:8; Lu 19:36

Verse 13. No Barnes text on this verse.

{l} "Hosanah"

Ps 118:25,26

Verse 14. No Barnes text on this verse.

Verse 15. No Barnes text on this verse.

{m} "Fear not"

Zec 9:9

Verse 16. *Was glorified.* Was raised from the dead, and had ascended to heaven.

{n} "These things" Lu 18:34

Verse 17. *Bare record.* Testified that he had raised him, and, as was natural, spread the report through the city. This excited much attention, and the people came out in multitudes to me one who had power to work such miracles.

Verse 18. No Barnes text on this verse.

{q} "For this cause" Joh 12:11

Verse 19. *Prevail nothing*. All your efforts are ineffectual to stop the progress of his opinions, and to prevent the people from believing on him.

The world. As we should say, "Everybody—all the city has gone out." The fact that he met with such success induced them to hasten their design of putting him to death, Joh 11:53.

{r} "Perceive ye how ye prevail nothing" Joh 11:47,48

Verse 20. *Certain Greeks*. In the original, "some Hellenists"— the name commonly given to the Greeks. The same name was commonly used by the Jews to denote *all* the pagan nations, because most of those whom they knew spoke the Greek language, Joh 7:34; Ro 1:16; 2:9,10; 3:9

"Jews and Greeks." The Syriac translates this place, "Some of the Gentiles." There are three opinions in regard to these persons:

1st. That they were Jews who spoke the Greek language, and dwelt in some of the Greek cities. It is known that Jews were scattered in Asia Minor, Greece, Macedonia, Egypt, &c., in all which places they had synagogues. See Barnes "Joh 7:35".

2nd. That they were *proselytes* from the Greeks.

3rd. That they were still Gentiles and idolaters, who came to bring offerings to Jehovah to be deposited in the temple. Lightfoot has shown that the surrounding pagans were accustomed not only to send presents, sacrifices, and offerings to the temple, but that they also frequently attended the great feasts of the Jews. Hence the outer court of the temple was called the *court of the Gentiles*. Which of these opinions is the correct one cannot be determined.

{s} "certain Greeks" Ac 17:4; Ro 1:16 {t} "them that came up" 1 Ki 8:41,42

Verse 21. *Bethsaida of Galilee*. See Barnes "Joh 1:44".

Would see Jesus. It is probable that the word see, here, implies also a desire to converse with him, or to hear his doctrine about the nature of his kingdom. They had seen or heard of his triumphal entry into Jerusalem, and, either by curiosity or a desire to be instructed, they came and interceded with his disciples that they might be permitted to see him. In this there was nothing wrong. Christ made the *curiosity* of Zaccheus the means of his conversion, Lu 19:1-9. If we wish to find the Saviour, we must seek for him and take the proper means.

{u} "to Philip" Joh 1:44

Verse 22. *Telleth Andrew*. Why he did not at once tell Jesus is not known. Possibly he was doubtful whether Jesus would wish to converse with *Gentiles*, and chose to consult with Andrew about it.

Tell Jesus. Whether the Greeks were with them cannot be determined. From the following discourse it would seem probable that they were, or at least that Jesus admitted them to his presence and delivered the discourse to them.

THE GOSPEL ACCORDING TO JOHN-Chapter 12-Verse 23

Verse 21. *The hour is come.* The *time* is come. The word *hour* commonly means a definite part or a division of a day; but it also is used to denote a brief period, and a *fixed, definite, determined* time. It is used in this sense here. The appointed, fixed time is come—that is, is so near at hand that it may be said *to be come.*

The Son of man. This is the favourite title which Jesus gives to himself, denoting his union with man, and the interest he felt in his welfare. The title is used here rather than "The Son of God," because as a *man* he had been humble, poor, and despised; but the time had come when, as a man, he was to receive the appropriate honours of the Messiah.

Be glorified. Be honoured in an appropriate way—that is, by the testimony which God would give to him at his death, by his resurrection, and by his ascension to glory. See Joh 7:39.

{v} "The hour is come" Joh 13:32; 17:1

THE GOSPEL ACCORDING TO JOHN-Chapter 12-Verse 24

Verse 24. *Verily, verily.* An expression denoting the great importance of what he was about to say. We cannot but admire the wisdom by which he introduces the subject of his death. They had seen his triumph. They supposed that he was about to establish his kingdom. He told them that the time *had* come in which he was to be glorified, but not in the manner in which they expected. It was to be by his death. But as they would not at once see how this could be, as it would appear to dash their hopes, he takes occasion to illustrate it by a beautiful comparison. All the beauty and richness of the *harvest* results from the fact that the grain had *died.* If it had not died it would never have germinated or produced the glory of the yellow harvest. So with him. By this he still keeps before them the truth that he was to be glorified, but he delicately and beautifully introduces the idea still that he *must die.*

A corn. A grain.

Of wheat. Any kind of grain —wheat, barley, &c. The word includes all grain of this kind.

Into the ground. Be buried in the earth, so as to be accessible by the proper moisture.

And die The whole *body* or substance of the grain, except the germ, dies in the earth or is decomposed, and this decomposed substance constitutes the first nourishment of the tender germ—a nutriment wonderfully adapted to it, and fitted to nourish it until it becomes vigorous enough to derive its support entirely from the ground. In this God has shown his wisdom and goodness. No one thing could be more *evidently* fitted for another than this provision made in the grain itself for the future wants of the tender germ.

Abideth alone. Produces no fruit. It remains without producing the rich and beautiful harvest. So Jesus intimates that it was only by his death that he would be glorified in the salvation of men, and in the honours and rewards of heaven, Heb 2:9: "We see Jesus, who was made a little lower than the angels *for the suffering of death*, crowned with glory and honour." Php 2:8,9: "He humbled himself, and became obedient unto death, even the death of the cross; wherefore God also hath highly exalted him." Heb 12:2: "Who, *for the joy* that was set before him, endured the cross, despising the shame, and is set down at the right hand of the throne of God." See also Eph 1:20-23.

THE GOSPEL ACCORDING TO JOHN-Chapter 12-Verse 25

Verse 25. *He that loveth his life*, &c. This was a favorite principle, a sort of *axiom* with the Lord Jesus, which he applied to himself as well as to his followers. See Barnes "Mt 10:39".

See Barnes "Lu 9:24".

{x} "loveth his life" Mt 10:39; 16:25; Mr 8:35; Lu 9:24; 17:33

THE GOSPEL ACCORDING TO JOHN-Chapter 12-Verse 26

Verse 26. *Serve me.* Will be my disciple, or will be a Christian. Perhaps this was said to inform the Greeks (Joh 12:20) of the nature of his religion.

Let him follow me. Let him imitate me; do what I do, bear what I bear, and love what I love. He is discoursing here particularly of his own sufferings and death, and this passage has reference, therefore, to calamity and persecution.

"You see me triumph—you see me enter Jerusalem, and
you supposed that my kingdom was to be set up without
opposition or calamity; but it is not. I am to die;
and if you will serve me, you must follow me even in
these scenes of calamity; be willing to endure trial
and to bear shame, looking for future reward."

Where I am. See Joh 14:3; 17:24. That is, he shall be in heaven, where the Son of God then *was* in his divine nature, and where he would be as the glorified Messiah. See Barnes "Joh 3:13".

The natural and obvious meaning of the expression "I am" implies that he was then in heaven. The design of this verse is to comfort them in the midst of persecution and trial. They were to follow him to any calamity; but, as he was to be glorified as the result of his sufferings, so they also were to look for their reward in the kingdom of heaven, Re 3:21: "To him that overcometh will I grant to sit with me in my throne."

{y} "If any man serve" Lu 6:46; Joh 14:15; 1 Jo 5:3
{z} "Where I am" Joh 14:3; 17:24; 1 Th 4:17
{a} "if any man serve" 1 Sa 2:30; Pr 27:18

Verse 27. *Now is my soul troubled.* The mention of his death brought before him its approaching horrors, its pains, its darkness, its unparalleled woes. Jesus was full of acute sensibility, and his human nature shrunk from the scenes through which he was to pass. See Lu 23:41-44.

What shall I say? This is an expression denoting intense anxiety and perplexity. *As if* it were a subject of debate whether he *could* bear those sufferings; or whether the work of man's redemption should be abandoned, and he should call upon God to save him. Blessed be his name that he was willing to endure these sorrows, and did not forsake man when he was *so near* being redeemed! On the decision of that moment—the fixed and unwavering purpose of the Son of God — depended man's salvation. If Jesus had forsaken his purpose then, all would have been lost.

Father, save me. This ought undoubtedly to have been read as a question—"Shall I say, Father, save me?" Shall I apply to God to rescue me? or shall I go forward to bear these trials? As it is in our translation, it represents him as actually offering the prayer, and then checking himself. The Greek will bear either interpretation. The whole verse is full of deep feeling and anxiety. Comp. Mt 26:38 Lu 12:50.

This hour. These *calamities.* The word hour, here, doubtless has reference to his approaching sufferings—the appointed hour for him to suffer. Shall I ask my Father to save me from this *hour* —that is, from these approaching sufferings? That it *might* have been done, see Mt 26:53.

But for this cause. That is, to suffer and die. As this was the *design* of his coming—as he did it deliberately—as the salvation of the world depended on it, he felt that it would not be proper to pray to be delivered from it. He came to suffer, and he submitted to it. See Lu 23:42.

{c} "but for this reason" Joh 18:37

Verse 28. *Glorify thy name.* The meaning of this expression in this connection is this: "I am willing to bear any trials; I will not shrink from any sufferings. Let thy name be honoured. Let thy character, wisdom, goodness, and plans of mercy be manifested and promoted, whatever sufferings it may cost me." Thus Jesus showed us that *God's glory* is to be the great end of our conduct, and that we are to seek that, whatever sufferings it may cost us.

I have both glorified it. The word *it* is not here in the original, but it is not improperly supplied by the translators. There can be no doubt that when God says here that he had glorified his name, he refers to what had been done by Christ, and that this was to be understood as an *attestation* that he attended him and approved his work. See Joh 12:30. He *had* honoured his name, or had glorified *him*, by the pure instructions which he had given to man through him; by the power displayed in his miracles; by proclaiming his mercy through him; by appointing him to be the Messiah, &c.

Will glorify it *again*. By the death, the resurrection, and ascension of his Son, and by extending the blessings of the gospel among all nations. It was thus that he sustained his Son in view of approaching trials; and we may learn,

1st. That God will minister grace to us in the prospect of suffering.

2nd. That the fact that God will be honoured by our afflictions should make us willing to bear them.

3rd. That whatever was done by Christ tended to honour the name of God. This was what he had in view. He lived and suffered, not for himself, but to glorify God in the salvation of men.

{d} "a voice" Mt 3:17

THE GOSPEL ACCORDING TO JOHN-Chapter 12-Verse 29

Verse 29. *The people.* A part of the people.

It thundered. The unexpected sound of the voice would confound and amaze them; and though there is no reason to doubt that the words were spoken distinctly (Mt 3:17), yet some of the people, either from amazement or envy, would suppose that this was a mere natural phenomenon.

An angel spake. It was the opinion of many of the Jews that God did not speak to men except by the ministry of angels, Heb 2:2: "The word spoken *by angels*;" Ga 3:19: "It was ordained *by angels* in the hand of a mediator."

THE GOSPEL ACCORDING TO JOHN-Chapter 12-Verse 30

Verse 30. *Came not because of me.* Not to strengthen or confirm me; not that I had any doubts about my course, or any apprehension that God would *not* approve me and glorify his name.

For your sakes. To give you a striking and indubitable proof that I am the Messiah; that you may remember it when I am departed, and be *yourselves* comforted, supported, and saved.

{e} "but for your sakes" Joh 11:42

THE GOSPEL ACCORDING TO JOHN-Chapter 12-Verse 31

Verse 31. *Now is the judgment of this world.* Greek, "crisis." This expression, doubtless, has reference to his approaching death, and whatever he means by *judgment* here relates to something that was to be accomplished *by* that death. It cannot mean that then was to be the time in which the world was to be finally judged, for he says that he did not come then to judge the world (Joh 12:47; 8:15), and he has clearly declared that there shall be a *future* day when he will judge all mankind. The meaning of it may be thus expressed:

"Now is approaching the decisive scene, the eventful
period—the crisis—when it shall be determined who

shall rule this world. There has been a long
conflict between the powers of light and darkness—
between God and the devil. Satan has so effectually
ruled that he may be said to be the prince of this
world; but my approaching death will destroy his
kingdom, will break down his power, and will be the
means of setting up the kingdom of God over man."

The death of Christ was to be the most grand and effectual of all means that could be used to establish the authority of the law and the government of God, Ro 8:3,4. This it did by showing the regard which God had for his law; by showing his hatred of sin, and presenting the strongest motives to induce man to leave the service of Satan; by securing the influences of the Holy Spirit, and by his putting forth his own direct power in the cause of virtue and of God. The death of Jesus was the determining cause, the grand crisis, the concentration of all that God had ever done, or ever will do, to break down the kingdom of Satan, and set up his power over man. Thus was fulfilled the prediction (Ge 3:15),

"I will put enmity between thee and the woman, and
between thy seed and her seed; it shall bruise thy
head, and thou shalt bruise his heel."

Now shall the prince of this world. Satan, or the devil, Joh 14:30; 16:11. He is also called the god of this world, 2 Co 4:4; Eph 6:12: "The rulers of the darkness of this world "—that is, the rulers of this dark world—a well-known Hebraism. He is also called "the prince of the power of the air, the spirit that now worketh in the children of disobedience," Eph 2:2. All these names are given him from the influence or power which he has over the men of this world, because the great mass of men have been under his control and subject to his will.

Be cast out. His kingdom shall be destroyed; his empire shall come to an end. It does not mean that his reign over all men would entirely cease then, but that then would be the*crisis*, the grand conflict in which *he* would be vanquished, and from that time his kingdom begin to decline, until it would finally cease, and then be free altogether from his dominion. See Lu 10:18; Col 1:18-20; Ac 26:18; 1 Co 15:25,26; Re 20:14.

{f} "the prince of this world" Lu 10:18; Joh 16:11; Ac 26:18; Eph 2:2

Verse 32. *Be lifted up.* See Joh 3:14; 8:28.
Will draw. Joh 6:44. The same word is used in both places.

All men. I will incline all kinds of men; or will make the way open by the cross, so that all men may come. I will provide a way which shall present a strong motive or inducement—the strongest that *can* be presented—to all men to come to me.

{g} "lifted up" Joh 8:28 {h} "will draw all *men*" Ro 5:18

Verse 33. No Barnes text on this verse.

{i} "signifying what death"

Ro 5:18

Verse 34. *We have heard out of the law.* Out of the Old Testament; or rather we have been so taught by those who have interpreted the law to us.

That Christ. That *the* Messiah.

Abideth for ever. Will *remain* for ever, or will live for ever. The doctrine of many of them certainly was that the Messiah would not die; that he would reign as a prince for ever over the people. This opinion was founded on such passages of Scripture as these: Ps 110:4, "Thou art a priest for ever;" Da 2:44; 8:13,14.

In the interpretation of these passages they had overlooked such places as Isa 53:1-12; nor did they understand how the fact that he would reign for ever could be reconciled with the idea of his death. To us, who understand that his reign does not refer to a *temporal*, an earthly kingdom, it is easy.

How sayest thou, &c. We have understood by the title "the Son of man" the same as the Messiah, and that he is to reign for ever. How can he be put to death?

Who is this Son of man? "The Son of man *we* understand to be the Messiah spoken of by Daniel, who is to reign for ever. To *him*, therefore, you cannot refer when you say that he must be lifted up, or must die. Who is it—what *other Son of man* is referred to but the *Messiah*? Either ignorantly or wilfully, they supposed he referred to some one else than the Messiah.

{k} "We have heard" Ps 89:36,37; 110:4; Isa 9:7

{l} "out of the law" Ro 5:18; Ps 72:17-19

Verse 35. *Yet a little while is the light with you.* Jesus did not reply directly to may their question. He saw that they were offended by the mention of his death, and he endeavoured to arrive at the same thing *indirectly.* He tells them, therefore, that the light would be with them a little while, and that they ought to improve the opportunity while they had it to listen to his instructions, to inquire with candour, and thus to forsake their false notions respecting the Messiah.

The light. Joh 1:4. It is probable that they understood this as denoting the Messiah. See Joh

8:12 "I am the light of the world;" Joh 9:4

Walk, &c. Joh 11:9. Whatever you have to do, do it while you enjoy this light. Make good use of your privileges before they are removed. That is, while the Messiah is with you, avail yourselves of his instructions and learn the way to life.

Lest darkness. Lest God should take away all your mercies, remove all light and instruction from you, and leave you to ignorance, blindness, and woe. This was true that darkness and calamity were to come upon the Jewish people when the Messiah was removed; and it is also true that God leaves a sinner to darkness and misery when he has long rejected the gospel.

For he, &c. See Joh 11:10.

{m} "the light" Joh 8:32 {n} "with you" Jer 13:16

THE GOSPEL ACCORDING TO JOHN-Chapter 12-Verse 36

Verse 36. *While ye have light.* This implied two things:

1st. That *he* was the light, or was the Messiah.

2nd. That he was soon to be taken away by death. In this manner he answered their question—not *directly*, but in a way to convey the truth to their minds, and at the same time to administer to them a useful admonition. Jesus never aroused the prejudices of men unnecessarily, yet he never shrank from declaring to them the truth *in some way*, however unpalatable it might be.

Believe in the light. That is, in the Messiah, who is the light of the world.

That ye may be the children, &c. That ye may be the friends and followers of the Messiah. See Barnes "Mt 1:1".

Comp. Joh 8:12 Eph 5:8: "Now are ye light in the Lord; walk as children of light."

Did hide himself from them. Joh 8:59. He went out to Bethany, where he commonly passed the night, Lu 21:37.

{p} "be the children of light" Eph 5:8

THE GOSPEL ACCORDING TO JOHN-Chapter 12-Verse 37

Verse 37. *So many miracles.* This does not refer to any miracles wrought on this occasion, but to all his miracles wrought in view of the nation, in healing the sick, opening the eyes of the blind, raising the dead, &c. John here gives the *summary* or the result of all his works. Though Jesus had given the most undeniable proof of his being the Messiah, yet the nation did not believe on him.

Before them. Before the Jewish nation. Not in the presence of the people whom he was then addressing, but before the Jewish people.

They believed not. The Jewish nation did not believe *as a nation*, but rejected him.

THE GOSPEL ACCORDING TO JOHN-Chapter 12-Verse 38

Verse 38. *The saying* The *word* of Isaiah, or that which Isaiah predicted. This occurs in Isa

ccxxxi

53:1.

Might be fulfilled. That the same effect should occur which occurred in the time of Isaiah. This does not mean that the Pharisees rejected Christ *in order* that the prophecy of Isaiah should be fulfilled, but that *by* their rejection of him the same thing had occurred which took place in the time of Isaiah. *His* message was despised by the nation, and he himself put to death. And it was also true—by the same causes, by the same nation—that the same gospel message was rejected by the Jews in the time of Christ. The same language of the prophet would express *both* events, and no doubt it was *intended* by the Holy Spirit to mark both events. In this Way it was completely fulfilled. See Barnes on "Is 53:1".

Our report. Literally, by *report* is meant "what is heard." Our speech, our message. That is, few or none have received the message. The form of the question is an emphatic way of saying that it was rejected.

The arm of the Lord. The *arm* is a symbol of power, as it is the instrument by which we execute our purposes. It is put for the power of God, Isa 51:9; 52:10. Thus he is said to have brought out the children of Israel from Egypt with *a high arm*—that is, with great power. It hence means God's power in defending his people, in overcoming his enemies, and in saving the soul. In this place it clearly denotes the power displayed by the miracles of Christ.

Revealed. Made known, seen, understood. Though the power of God was displayed, yet the people did not see and understand it.

{q} "Lord, who hath believed our report" Isa 53:3

THE GOSPEL ACCORDING TO JOHN-Chapter 12-Verse 39

Verse 39. *They could not believe.* See Mr 6:5. "He could there do no mighty works," &c. The words *can* and *could* are often used in the Bible to denote the existence of such obstacles as to make a result certain, or as affirming that while one thing exists another thing cannot follow. Thus, Joh 5:44: "How *can* ye believe which receive honour one of another." That is, while this propensity to seek for honour exists, it will effectually prevent your believing. Thus (Ge 37:4) it is said of the brethren of Joseph that they "*could* not speak peaceably unto him." That is, while their hatred continued so strong, the other result would follow. See also Mt 12:34; Ro 8:7; Joh 6:60; Am 3:3.

In this case it means that there was some obstacle or difficulty that made it certain that while it existed they would not believe. What that was is stated in the next verse; and while that blindness of mind and that hardness of heart existed, it was impossible that they should believe, for the two things were incompatible. But this determines nothing about their power of *removing that blindness,* or of yielding their heart to the gospel. It simply affirms that while one exists the other cannot follow. Chrysostom and Augustine understand this of a *moral inability,* and not of any natural want of power. "They could not, because they would not" (Chrysostom *in loco*). So on Jer 13:23, "Can the Ethiopian change his skin," &c., he says, "he does not say it is impossible for a wicked man to do well, but, BECAUSE *they will not, therefore they cannot.*" Augustine says on this place: "If I be asked why they could not believe, I answer without hesitation, because they *would not*: because God foresaw their *evil will*, and he announced it beforehand by the prophet."

Said again, Isa 6:9,10.

Verse 40. *He hath blinded their eyes.* The expression in Isaiah is, "Go, make the heart of this people fat, and shut their eyes." That is, go and proclaim truth to them—truth that will *result* in blinding their eyes. Go and proclaim the law and the will of God, and the *effect will be*, owing to the hardness of their heart, that their eyes will be blinded and their hearts hardened. As God knew that this would be the result—as it was to be the effect of the message, his commanding Isaiah to go and proclaim it was the same *in effect*, or in the *result*, as if he had commanded him to blind their eyes and harden their hearts. It is this *effect* or *result* to which the evangelist refers in this place. He states that God did it—that is, he did it in the manner mentioned in Isaiah, for we are limited to that in our interpretation of the passage. In that case it is clear that the mode specified is not a *direct* agency on the part of God in blinding the mind—which we cannot reconcile with any just notions of the divine character—but *in suffering the truth to produce a regular effect on sinful minds, without putting forth any positive supernatural influence to prevent it.* The effect of truth on such minds is to irritate, to enrage, and to harden, unless counteracted by the grace of God. See Ro 7:8,9,11; 2 Co 2:15-16.

And as God *knew* this, and, knowing it, still sent the message, and suffered it to produce the *regular* effect, the evangelist says "*he* hath blinded their minds," thus retaining the *substance* of the passage in Isaiah without quoting the precise language; but in proclaiming the truth there was nothing *wrong* on the part of God or of Isaiah, nor is there any indication that God was unwilling that they should believe and be saved.

That they should not see, &c. This does not mean that it was the *design* of God that they should not be converted, but that it was the *effect* of their rejecting the message.

See Barnes "Mt 13:14, See Barnes "Mt 13:15".

{r} "hath blinded" Isa 6:9,10

Verse 41. *When he saw his glory*, Isa 6:1-10. Isaiah saw the LORD (in Hebrew, JEHOVAH) sitting on a throne and surrounded with the seraphim. This is perhaps the only instance in the Bible in which Jehovah is said to have been seen by man, and *for* this the Jews affirm that Isaiah was put to death. God had said (Ex 33:20), "No man shall see me and live;" and as Isaiah affirmed that he had seen Jehovah, the Jews, for that and other reasons, put him to death by sawing him asunder. See Barnes "Is 1:1".

In the prophecy Isaiah is said expressly to have seen JEHOVAH (Isa 6:1); and in Isa 6:5, "Mine eyes have seen the King JEHOVAH of hosts." By his *glory* is meant the manifestation of him—the *shechinah*, or visible cloud that was a representation of God, and that rested over the mercy-seat. This was regarded as equivalent to seeing God, and John here expressly applies this to the Lord Jesus Christ; for he is not affirming that the people did not believe in God, but is assigning the reason why they believed not on Jesus Christ as the Messiah. The whole discourse has respect to the Lord Jesus, and the natural construction of the passage requires us to refer it to him. John affirms that it was the glory *of the Messiah* that Isaiah saw, and yet Isaiah affirms that it was JEHOVAH; and from this the inference is irresistible that John regarded Jesus as the Jehovah whom Isaiah saw. The name Jehovah is never, in the Scriptures, applied to a man, or an angel, or to any creature. It is the peculiar, incommunicable name of God. So great was the reverence of the Jews for that name that they would not even pronounce it. This passage is therefore conclusive proof that Christ is equal with the Father.

Spake of him. Of the Messiah. The connection requires this interpretation.

{s} "Said Esias when he saw his glory" Isa 6:3

THE GOSPEL ACCORDING TO JOHN-Chapter 12-Verse 42

Verse 42. *The chief rulers.* Members of the Sanhedrim — Nicodemus, Joseph, and others like them.

Because of the Pharisees. The Pharisees were a majority of the council.

Put out of the synagogue. Excommunicated. See Barnes "Joh 9:22,23".

{t} "because of the Pharisees" Joh 9:22

THE GOSPEL ACCORDING TO JOHN-Chapter 12-Verse 43

Verse 43. *The praise of men.* The approbation of men. It does not appear that they had a living, active faith, but that they were convinced in their understanding that he was the Messiah. They had that kind of faith which is so common among men—a speculative acknowledgment that religion is true, but an acknowledgment which leads to no self-denial, which shrinks from the active duties of piety, and fears man more than God. True faith is active. It overcomes the fear of man; it prompts to self-denying duties, Heb 11:1. Nevertheless, it was no unimportant proof that Jesus was the Messiah, that *any part* of the great council of the Jews were even speculatively convinced of it: and it shows that the evidence could not have been slight when it overcame their prejudices and pride, and constrained them to admit that the lowly and poor man of Nazareth was the long-expected Messiah of their nation.

Did not confess him. Did not openly avow their belief that he was the Messiah. Two of them, however, did afterward evince their attachment to him. These were Joseph and Nicodemus, Joh 19:38,39. That Joseph was one of them appears from Mr 15:43; Lu 23:50,51.

{u} "For they loved the praise" Joh 5:44; Ro 2:29

THE GOSPEL ACCORDING TO JOHN-Chapter 12-Verse 44

Verse 44. *Jesus cried and said.* John does not say *where* or *when* this was; it is probable, however, that it was a continuation of the discourse recorded in Joh 12:30-36. Jesus saw their unbelief, and proceeded to state the consequence of believing on him, and of rejecting him and his message.

Believeth not on me. That is, not on me *alone*, or his faith does not terminate on *me*. Comp. Mt 10:20; Mr 9:37. It *involves*, also, belief in him that sent me. Jesus uniformly represents the union between himself and God as so intimate that there could not be faith in *him* unless there was also faith in God. *He* did the same works (Joh 5:17-20,36; 10:25,37), and taught the very doctrine which God had commissioned him to do, Joh 8:38; 5:30,20-23.

{v} "He that believeth" Joh 1:5; 3:19

THE GOSPEL ACCORDING TO JOHN-Chapter 12-Verse 45

Verse 45. *Seeth me.* This verse is a strong confirmation of his equality with god. In no other way can it be true that he who saw Jesus saw him that sent him, unless he were the same in essence. Of no *man* could it be affirmed that he who saw him saw God. To say this of Paul or Isaiah would have been blasphemy. And yet Jesus uses this language familiarly and constantly. It shows that he had a consciousness that he was divine and that it was the *natural* and proper way of speaking when speaking of himself.

Comp. Joh 5:17

THE GOSPEL ACCORDING TO JOHN-Chapter 12-Verse 46

Verse 46. *A light unto the world.* Joh 13:12; 1:9; 3:19.

Walk in darkness. In gross and dangerous errors. Darkness is put for error as well as for sin Joh 3:19; 1 Jo 1:5. It is also used to denote the state when the *comforts* of religion are withdrawn from the soul Isa 8:22; Joe 2:2; Is 59:9; Joh 8:12.

{w} "I am come a light" Joh 1:5; 3:19

THE GOSPEL ACCORDING TO JOHN-Chapter 12-Verse 47

Verse 47. *I judge him not,* &c. Joh 8:15. It was not his *present* purpose to condemn men. He would come to *condemn* the guilty at a future time. At present he came to save them. hence he did not now even pronounce decisively on the condition of those who rejected him, but still gave them an opportunity to be saved.

{x} "for I came not to judge the world" Joh 3:17

Verse 48. *He that rejecteth me.* Lu 10:16. The word *reject* means to *despise*, or to refuse to receive him.

Hath one. That is, he needs not my voice to condemn him. He will carry his own condemnation with him, even should I be silent. His own conscience will condemn him. The words which I have spoken will be remembered and will condemn him, if there were nothing farther. From this we learn,

1st. That a guilty conscience needs no accuser.

2nd. That the words of Christ, and the messages of mercy which the sinner has rejected, will be remembered by him.

3rd. That this will be the source of his condemnation. This will make him miserable, and there will be no possibility of his being happy.

4th. That the conscience of the sinner will *concur* with the sentence of Christ in the great day, and that he will go to eternity *self-condemned*. It is this which will make the pains of hell so intolerable to the sinner.

5th. The word that Christ has spoken, the doctrines of his gospel, and the messages of mercy, will be that by which the sinner will be judged in the last day. Every man will be judged by that message, and the sinner will be punished according to the frequency and clearness with which the rejected message has been presented to his mind, Mt 12:41.

Verse 49. *Of myself.* Joh 7:16-18

Verse 50. *Is life everlasting.* Is the *cause* or *source* of everlasting life. He that *obeys* the commandment of God shall obtain everlasting life; and this is his commandment, that we believe in the name of his only-begotten Son, 1 Jo 3:22. We see here the reason of the earnestness and fidelity of the Lord Jesus. It was because he saw that *eternal life* depended on the faithful preaching of the message of God. He therefore proclaimed it in the face of all opposition, contempt, and persecution. And we see also,

1st. That every minister of religion should have a deep and abiding conviction that he delivers a message that is to be connected with the eternal welfare of his hearers. And,

2nd. Under the influence of this belief, he should fearlessly deliver his message in the face of bonds, poverty, contempt, persecution, and death.

It may not be improper to remark here that this is the close of the public preaching of Christ. The rest of his ministry was employed in the private instruction of his apostles, and in preparing them for his approaching death. It is such a close as all his ministers should desire to make—a solemn, deliberate, firm exhibition of the truth of God, under a belief that on it was depending the eternal salvation of his hearers, and uttering without fear the solemn message of the Most

High to a lost world.
    {z} "his commandments" 1 Jo 3:22

THE GOSPEL ACCORDING TO JOHN- Chapter 13

Verse 1. *The feast of the passover.* See Barnes "Mt 26:2, See Barnes "Mt 26:17".

His hour was come. The hour appointed in the purpose of God for him to die, Joh 12:27. *Having loved his own.* Having given to them decisive and constant proofs of his love. This was done by his calling them to follow him; by patiently teaching them; by bearing with their errors and weaknesses; and by making them the heralds of his truth and the heirs of eternal life.

He loved them unto the end. That is, he *continued* the proofs of his love until he was taken away from them by death. Instances of that love John proceeds immediately to record in his washing their feet and in the institution of the Supper. We may remark that Jesus is the same yesterday, today, and for ever. He does not change; he always loves the same traits of character; nor does he *withdraw* his love from the soul. If his people walk in darkness and wander from him, the fault is theirs, not his. His is the character of a friend that never leaves or forsakes us; a friend that sticketh closer than a brother. Ps 37:28: "The Lord forsaketh not his saints." Isa 49:14-17; Pr 18:24.

{a} "Now before the feast" Mt 26:2 {b} "his hour was come" Joh 17:1,11 {c} "having loved his own" Jer 31:3; Eph 5:2; 1 Jo 4:12; Re 1:5

Verse 2. *Supper being ended.* This translation expresses too much. The original means *while they were at supper*; and that this is the meaning is clear from the fact that we find them still eating after this. The Arabic and Persic translations give it this meaning. The Latin Vulgate renders it like the English.

The devil. The leader or prince of evil spirits.

Having now put it into the heart. Literally, having *cast* it into the heart. Comp. Eph 6:16: "The fiery darts of the wicked." See Ac 5:3; Lu 22:3. The meaning of this passage is that Satan inclined the mind of Judas to do this, or he tempted him to betray his Master. We know not precisely how this was done, but we know that it was by means of his *avarice*. Satan*could* tempt no one unless there was some inclination of the mind, some natural or depraved propensity that he could make use of. He presents objects in alluring forms fitted to that propensity, and under the influence of a strong or a corrupt inclination the soul yields to sin. In the case of Judas it was the love of money; and it was necessary to present to him only the possibility of obtaining money, and it found him ready for any crime.

{d} "the devil" Lu 22:3,53; Joh 6:70

Verse 3. *Jesus knowing*, &c. With the full understanding of his dignity and elevation of character, he yet condescended to wash their feet. The evangelist introduces his washing their feet by saying that he was fully conscious of his elevation above them, as being intrusted with all things, and this made his humiliation the more striking and remarkable. Had he been a mere human teacher or a prophet, it would have been remarkable; but when we remember the dignity of his nature, it shows how low he would stoop to teach and save his people.

Had given all things, &c. See Barnes "Mt 28:18".

Was come from God. See Barnes "Joh 8:42".

Went to God. Was about to return to heaven. See Joh 6:61,62.
{e} "knowing that the Father" Mt 28:18; He 2:8 {f} "he was come from God" Joh 17:11

Verse 4. *He riseth from supper*. Evidently while they were eating. See Joh 13:2.
Laid aside his garments. His outer garment. See Barnes "Mt 5:40".

This was his *mantle* or robe, which is said to have been without seam. It was customary to lay this aside when they worked or ran, or in the heat of summer.

Took a towel and girded himself. This was the manner of a servant or slave. See Barnes "Lu 17:8"

Verse 5. *Began to wash*, &c. It was uniformly the office of a servant to wash the feet of guests, 1 Sa 25:41. It became a matter of necessity where they travelled without shoes, and where they reclined on couches at meals. It should be remembered here that the disciples were not *sitting* at the table, as we do, but were lying with their feet extended from the table, so that Jesus could easily have access to them. See Barnes "Mt 23:6".

Verse 6. *Dost thou wash my feet?* Every word here is emphatic. Dost *thou*— the Son of God, the Messiah—perform the humble *office of a servant*—toward me, a sinner? This was an expression of Peter's humility, of his reverence for Jesus, and also a refusal to allow him to do it. It is *possible*, though not certain from the text, that he came to Simon Peter first.

{1} "Peter", or "he" {g} "dost thou wash my feet" Mt 3:14

Verse 7. *Thou knowest not now*. Though he saw the action of Jesus, yet he did not fully understand the *design* of it. It was a symbolical action, inculcating a lesson of humility, and intended to teach it to them in such a manner that it would be impossible for them ever to forget it. Had he simply *commanded* them to be humble, it would have been far less forcible and impressive than when they saw him actually performing the office of a servant.

Shalt know hereafter. Jesus at that time partially explained it (Joh 13:14,15); but he was teaching them by this expressive act a lesson which they would continue to learn all their lives. Every day they would see more and more the necessity of humility and of kindness to each other, and would see that *they* were the servants of Christ and of the church, and ought not to aspire to honours and offices, but to be willing to perform the humblest service to benefit the world. And we may remark here that God often does things which we do not fully understand now, but which we may hereafter. He often afflicts us; he disappoints us; he frustrates our plans. Why it is we do not know now, but we yet shall learn that it was for our good, and designed to teach us some important lesson of humility and piety. So he will, in heaven, scatter all doubts, remove all difficulties, and show us the reason of the whole of his mysterious dealings in his leading us in the way to our future rest. We ought also, in view of this, to submit ourselves to him; to hush every murmur, and to believe that he does all things well. It is one evidence of piety when we are willing to receive affliction at the hand of God, the *reason* of which we cannot see, content with the belief that we *may* see it hereafter; or, even if we never do, still having so much confidence in God as to believe that WHAT HE DOES IS RIGHT.

THE GOSPEL ACCORDING TO JOHN-Chapter 13-Verse 8

Verse 8. *Thou shalt never wash my feet.* This was a decided and firm expression of his reverence for his Mater, and yet it was improper. Jesus had just declared that it had a meaning, and that he ought to submit to it. We should yield to all the plain and positive requirements of God, even if we cannot now see how obedience would promote his glory.

If I wash thee not. This had *immediate* reference to the act of washing his feet; and it denotes that if Peter had not so much confidence in him as to believe that an act which he performed was proper, though he could not see its propriety—if he was not willing to submit *his* will to that of Christ and implicitly obey him, he had no evidence of piety. As Christ, however, was accustomed to pass from temporal and sensible objects to those which were spiritual, and to draw instruction from whatever was before him, some have supposed that he here took occasion to state to Peter that if his soul was not made pure by him he could not be his follower. Washing is often thus put as an emblem of moral purification, 1 Co 6:11; Tit 3:5, 6.

This is the meaning, also, of baptism. If this was the sense in which Jesus used these words, it denotes that unless Christ should purify Peter, he could have no evidence that he was his disciple. "Unless by my doctrine and spirit I shall purify you, and remove your *pride* (Mt 26:33), your want of constant watchfulness (Mt 26:40), your anger (Mt 26:51), your timidity and fear (Mt 26:70,74), you can have no part in me" (Grotius).

Hast no part with me. Nothing *in common* with me. No evidence of possessing my spirit, of being interested in my work, and no participation in my glory:

{h} "If I wash thee not" 1 Co 6:11; Eph 5:26; Tit 3:5

Verse 9. *Not my feet only*, &c. Peter, with characteristic readiness and ardour, saw now that everything depended on this. His whole salvation, the entire question of his attachment to his Master, was involved. If to refuse to have his feet washed was to be regarded as evidence that he had no part with Jesus, he was not only *willing*, but *desirous* that it should be done; not only anxious that his feet should be cleansed, but his hands and his head—that is, that he should be cleansed *entirely, thoroughly*. Perhaps he saw the spiritual meaning of the Saviour, and expressed his ardent wish that his whole soul might be made pure by the work of Christ. A true Christian is desirous of being cleansed from all sin. He has no reserve. He wishes not merely that *one* evil propensity should be removed, but all; *that every thought should be brought into captivity to the obedience of Christ* (2 Co 10:5); and that his whole body, soul, and spirit

should be sanctified wholly and be preserved blameless unto the coming of the Lord Jesus Christ, 1 Th 5:23. His intellect, his will, his affections, his fancy, memory, judgment, he desires should be all brought under the influence of the gospel, and every power of the body and mind be consecrated unto God.

Verse 10. *He that is washed*. This is a difficult passage, and interpreters have been divided about its meaning. Some have supposed that it was customary to *bathe* before eating the paschal supper, and that the apostles did it; Jesus having said, "he that hath bathed his body is clean except in regard to his *feet*—to the dirt contracted in returning from the bath, and that there was need only that the feet should be washed in order to prepare them properly to receive the supper." They suppose, also, that the lesson which Jesus meant to teach was that they were really pure (Joh 15:3); that they were qualified to partake of the ordinances of religion, and needed only to be purified from *occasional* blemishes and impurities (Grotius). Others say that there is not evidence that the Jews *bathed* before partaking of the paschal supper, but that reference is made to the custom of washing their *hands* and their *face*. It is known that this was practised. See Barnes "Mt 15:2".

See Barnes "Mr 7:3".

See Barnes "Mr 7:4".

Peter had requested him to wash his hands and his head. Jesus told him that as that had been done, it was unnecessary to repeat it; but to wash the feet was an act of hospitality, the office of a servant, and that all that was needed now was for him to show this condescension and humility. Probably reference is had here to *internal purity*, as Jesus was fond of drawing illustrations from every quarter to teach them spiritual doctrine; as if he had said, "You are clean by my word and ministry Joh 15:3; you are my followers, and are prepared for the scene before you. But one thing remains. And as, when we come to this rite, having washed, there remains no need of washing except to wash the feet, so there is now nothing remaining but for *me* to show you an example that you will always remember, and that shall *complete* my public instructions to you."

Is clean. This word may apply to the body or the soul.

Every whit. Altogether, wholly.

Ye are clean. Here the word has doubtless reference to the mind and heart.

But not all. You are not all my true followers, and fitted for the ordinance before us.

{i} "For he knew" Joh 6:64

THE GOSPEL ACCORDING TO JOHN-Chapter 13-Verse 11

Verse 11. *Who should betray him.* Greek, "He knew him who was about to betray him."

{i} "For, he knew" Joh 6:64

THE GOSPEL ACCORDING TO JOHN-Chapter 13-Verse 12

Verse 12. *Know ye what,* &c. Do you know the *meaning* or *design* of what I have done unto you?

THE GOSPEL ACCORDING TO JOHN-Chapter 13-Verse 13

Verse 13. *Ye call me Master.* Teacher.

And Lord. This word is applied to one who *rules*, and is often given to God as being the *Proprietor* and *Ruler* of all things. It is given to Christ many hundred times in the New Testament,

Ye say well, &c. Mt 23:8,10.

So *I am.* That is, he was their *Teacher* and Instructor, and he was their Sovereign and King.

{k} "call me Master and Lord" Mt 23:8-10; Php 2:11.

THE GOSPEL ACCORDING TO JOHN-Chapter 13-Verse 14

Verses 14,15. *Ye also ought to wash,* &c. Some have understood this *literally as instituting a religious rite* which we ought to observe; but this was evidently not the design; for,

1st. There is not evidence that Jesus intended it as a *religious* observance, like the Lord's Supper or the ordinance of baptism.

2nd. It was not observed by the apostles or the primitive Christians as a religious rite.

3rd. It was a rite of hospitality among the Jews, a common, well-know thing, and performed by servants.

4th. it is the manifest design of humility; to teach them by his example that they ought to condescend to the most humble offices for the benefit of others. They ought not to be proud, and vain, but to regard themselves as the servants of each other in every way. And especially as they were to be founders of the church, and to be greatly honoured, he took this occasion of warning them against the dangers of ambitions, and of teaching them, by an example that they *could not forget*, the duty of humility.

Verse 15. No Barnes text on this verse.

{l} "For I have given you" 1 Pe 2:21

Verses 16,17. *The servant is not.* This was universally true, and this they were to remember always, that *they* were to manifest the same spirit that he did, and that they were to expect the same treatment from the world. See Barnes "Mt 10:24"; See Barnes "Mt 10:25".

Verse 17. No Barnes text on this verse.

{m} "If ye know these things" Jas 1:25

Verse 18. *I speak not of you all.* That is, in addressing you as *clean*, I do not mean to say that you *all* possess this character.

I know whom I have chosen. He here means evidently to say that he had not chosen them all, implying that Judas had not been chosen. As, however, this word is applied to Judas in one place (Joh 6:70), "Have not I *chosen* you twelve, and one of you is a devil?" it must have a different meaning here from that which it has there. *There* it evidently refers to the *apostleship.* Jesus *had* chosen him to be an *apostle*, and had treated him as such. *Here* is refers to purity *of heart*, and Jesus implies that, though Judas had been chosen to the office of apostleship, yet he had not been chosen to purity of heart and life. The remaining eleven had been, and would be saved. It was not, however, the fault of Jesus that Judas was not saved, for he was admitted to the same teaching, the same familiarity, and the same office; but his execrable love of gold gained the ascendency, and rendered vain all the means used for his conversion.

But that the scripture, &c. These things have occurred in order that the prophecies may receive their completion. It does not mean that Judas was *compelled* to this course in order that the Scripture might be fulfilled, but that this was foretold, and that by this the prophecy did receive a completion.

The scripture. This is written in Ps 41:9. It is commonly understood of Ahithophel, and of the enemies of David who had been admitted to his friendship, and who had now proved ungrateful to him.

May be fulfilled. See Barnes "Mt 1:22".

It is difficult to tell whether this prophecy had a primary reference to Judas, or whether it be meant that it received a more complete fulfillment in his case than in the time of David. The cases were similar; the same words would describe both events, for there was an exhibition of similar ingratitude and baseness in both cases, so that the same words would fitly describe both events.

He that eateth bread with me. To eat with one was a proof of friendship. See 2 Sa 9:11; Mt

9:11; Ge 43:32.

This means that Judas had been admitted to all the privileges of friendship, and had partaken of the usual evidences of affection. It was this which greatly aggravated his offence. It was base ingratitude as well as murder.

Hath lifted up his heel. Suidas says that this figure is taken from those who are running in a race, when one attempts to trip the other up and make him fall. It was a base and ungrateful return for kindness to which the Lord Jesus referred, and it means that he who had been admitted to the intimacies of friendship had ungratefully and maliciously injured him. Some suppose the expression means to lay *snares* for one; others, to kick or injure a man after he is cast down (Calvin on Ps 41:9). It is clear that it denotes great injury, and injury aggravated by the fact of professed friendship. It was not merely the common people, the open enemies, the Jewish nation that did it, but one who had received all the usual proofs of kindness. It was this which greatly aggravated our Saviour's sufferings.

{n} "He that eateth bread" Ps 41:9

THE GOSPEL ACCORDING TO JOHN-Chapter 13-Verse 19

Verse 19. *Now I tell you before it come*, &c. They would see by that that he had a knowledge of the heart and the power of foretelling future events, and must therefore have been sent by God. This does not imply that they had no faith before this, but that their faith would be increased and strengthened by it.

{2} "Now", or "From henceforth" {o} "I tell you" Joh 14:29; 16:4

THE GOSPEL ACCORDING TO JOHN-Chapter 13-Verse 20

Verse 20. *He that receiveth*, &c. This sentiment is found in the instructions which Jesus gave to his disciples in Mt 10:40. Why he repeats it at this time cannot now be known. It is certain that it is not closely connected with the subject of his conversation. Perhaps, however, it was to show how intimately united he, his Father, his apostles, and all who received them were. They who received *them* received *him*, and they who received *him* received *God*. So he who betrayed *him*, betrayed, for the same reason, *God*. Hence Judas, who was about to betray *him*, was also about to betray the cause of religion in the world, and to betray God and his cause. Everything pertaining to religion is connected together. A man cannot do dishonour to one of the institutions of religion without injuring *all*; he cannot dishonour its ministers or the Saviour without dishonouring God. And this shows that one prominent ground of the Saviour's solicitude was that his Father might be honoured, and one source of his deep grief at the treason of Judas was that it would bring injury upon the whole cause of religion in the world.

{p} "He that receiveth" Mt 10:40

THE GOSPEL ACCORDING TO JOHN-Chapter 13-Verse 21

Verse 21. *Trouble in spirit.* See Joh 12:27. The reason of his trouble here was that Judas, a professed friend, was about to betray him. He doubtless foresaw the deep and dreadful sorrows of his approaching death, and was also deeply affected with the ingratitude and wickedness of a professed friend. Jesus was *man* as well as *God*, and he felt like other men. His human nature shrank from suffering, and his tender sensibilities were affected not less deeply than would be those of other men by baseness and treason.

Testified. He bore witness to the truth; openly declared what he had before intimated — that one of them would betray him.

{q} "When Jesus had thus said" Mt 26:21; Mr 14:18; Lu 22:21

THE GOSPEL ACCORDING TO JOHN-Chapter 13-Verse 22

Verse 22. *Doubting of whom*, &c. The word translated *doubting* denotes that kind of anxiety which a man feels when he is in perplexity, and knows not what to say or do. We should say they were at a loss. See Barnes "Mt 26:22".

THE GOSPEL ACCORDING TO JOHN-Chapter 13-Verse 23

Verse 23. *Leaning on Jesus' bosom.* This does not mean that he was at that time *actually* lying on his bosom, but that he occupied a situation *next* to him at the table, so that his head naturally fell back on his bosom when he spoke to him. See Barnes "Mt 23:6".

Whom Jesus loved. This was doubtless John himself. The evangelists are not accustomed to mention their own *names* when any mark of favour or any good deed is recorded. They did not seek publicity or notoriety. In this case the appellation is more tender and honourable than any mere *name*. John was admitted to peculiar friendship, perhaps, because the natural disposition of our Saviour was more nearly *like* the amiableness and mildness of John than any of the other disciples (Robert Hall). The highest honour that can be conferred on any man is to say that Jesus *loved him.* Yet this is an honour which *all may* possess, but which none *can* inherit without his spirit and without loving him. It is an honour which cannot be won by wealth or learning, by beauty or accomplishments, by rank or earthly honours, but only by the possession of a meek and quiet spirit, which is in the sight of God of great price, 1 Pe 3:4; comp. Re 8:9.

{r} "one of his disciples" Joh 20:2; 21:7,20

THE GOSPEL ACCORDING TO JOHN-Chapter 13-Verse 24

Verse 24. No Barnes text on this verse.

THE GOSPEL ACCORDING TO JOHN-Chapter 13-Verse 25

Verse 25. *He then lying on Jesus' breast.* This a different word from the one rendered Joh 13:23 *leaning.* It means *falling back* or *laid his head back* on the bosom of Jesus, so that he could speak to him privately without being heard by the others.

THE GOSPEL ACCORDING TO JOHN-Chapter 13-Verse 26

Verse 26. *Jesus answered.* That is, he answered *John.* It does not appear that either Judas or the other apostles heard him.

Shall give a sop. The word translated *sop* means a *morsel*, a piece of bread, or anything else eaten—as much as we are accustomed to take at a mouthful. Jesus was about to dip it in the sauce which was used at the Passover. The word *dip*, in the original, is that from which is derived the word *baptize*. It means here that Jesus would dip it into the sauce as we do a piece of bread. It is probable that it was not an unusual thing for the master of a feast to help others in this way, as it does not appear to have attracted the attention of the others as at all remarkable. It was an indication to *John* who the betrayer was, and a hint which *Judas* also probably understood.

{3} "sop" or, "morsel"

THE GOSPEL ACCORDING TO JOHN-Chapter 13-Verse 27

Verse 27. *After the sop.* After he had taken and probably eaten it. By this Judas saw that Jesus knew his design, and that he could not conceal his plan. He saw, also, that the other disciples would be acquainted with it; and, aroused by sudden anger, or with the apprehension that he should lose his reward, or that Jesus might escape, he resolved on executing his plan at once.

Satan entered into him. The devil had *before* this put it into his heart to betray Jesus (Joh 13:2), but he now excited him to a more decided purpose. See Lu 22:3; Ac 5:3. "Why hath Satan filled thine heart," &c.

What thou doest, do quickly. This showed to Judas that Jesus was acquainted with his design. He did not *command* him to betray him, but he left him to his own purpose. He had used means enough to reclaim him and lead him to a holy life, and now he brought him to a decision. He gave him to understand that he was acquainted with his plan, and submitted it to the *conscience* of Judas to do quickly what he would do. If he relented, he called on him to do it at once. If he could still pursue his wicked plan, could go forward when he was conscious that the Saviour knew his design, he was to do it at once. God adopts all means to bring men to a decision. He calls upon them to act decisively, firmly, immediately. He does not allow them the privilege to *deliberate* about wicked deeds, but calls on them to act at once, and to show whether they will obey or disobey him; whether they will serve him, or whether they will betray his cause. He knows *all* their plans, as Jesus did that of Judas, and he calls on men to act under the full conviction that *he* knows all their soul. Sin thus is a vast evil. When men can sin knowing that God sees it all, it shows that the heart is *fully* set in them to do evil, and that there is nothing that *will* restrain them.

THE GOSPEL ACCORDING TO JOHN-Chapter 13-Verse 28

Verses 28,29. *No man at the table knew.* This shows that Jesus had signified to *John* only who it was that should betray him.

The bag. The travelling-bag in which they put their common property. See Barnes "Joh 12:6".

Have need of against the feast. The feast continued seven days, and they supposed that Jesus had directed him to make preparation for their wants on those days.

THE GOSPEL ACCORDING TO JOHN-Chapter 13-Verse 29

Verse 29. No Barnes text on this verse.

{t} "Judas" Joh 12:6

THE GOSPEL ACCORDING TO JOHN-Chapter 13-Verse 30

Verse 30. *If was night.* It was in the evening, or early part of the night. What is recorded in the following chapters took place in the same night.

THE GOSPEL ACCORDING TO JOHN-Chapter 13-Verse 31

Verse 31. *Now is the Son of man glorified.* The last deed is done that was necessary to secure the death of the Son of man, the glory that shall result to him from that death, the wonderful success of the gospel, the exaltation of the Messiah, and the public and striking attestation of God to him in the view of the universe. See Barnes "Joh 12:32".

{u} "Now is the Son" Joh 12:23; 17:1-6 {v} "God is glorified in him" Joh 14:13; 1 Pe 4:11

THE GOSPEL ACCORDING TO JOHN-Chapter 13-Verse 32

Verse 32. *If God be glorified in him.* If God be honoured by him. If the life and death of the Messiah be such as to lead to the honour of God, such as shall manifest its perfections, and show his goodness, truth, and justice, then he will *show* that he thus approves his work.

God shall also glorify him. He will honour the Messiah. He will not suffer him to go without a proper attestation of his acceptance, and of the honour that God puts on him. Jesus here confidently anticipated that the Father *would* show that he was pleased with what he had done. He did it in the miracles that attended his death, in his resurrection, ascension, exaltation, and in the success of the gospel. We may remark that God *will always*, in the proper time and way, *manifest* his approbation of those who live so as to promote the honour of his name.

In himself Or *by* himself; by a direct and public expression of his approbation. Not by the ministry of *angels* or by any other *subordinate* attestation, but by an expression that shall be *direct* from him. This was done by his direct interposition in his resurrection and ascension to heaven.

Shall straightway. Immediately, or without delay. This refers to the fact that the time when God would put this honour on him was at hand. His death, resurrection, and ascension were near.

THE GOSPEL ACCORDING TO JOHN-Chapter 13-Verse 33

Verse 33. *Little children.* An expression of great tenderness, denoting his deep interest in their welfare. As he was about to leave them, he endeavours to mitigate their grief by the most tender expressions of attachment, showing that he felt for them the deep interest in their welfare which a parent feels for his children. The word *children* is often given to Christians as implying—

1st. That God is their Father, and that they sustain toward him that endearing relation, Ro 8:14,15.

2nd. As denoting their need of teaching and guidance, as children need the aid and counsel of a father. See the corresponding term *babes* used in 1 Co 3:1; 1 Pe 2:2

3rd. It is used, as it is here, as an expression of tenderness and affection. See Ga 4:19; 1 Jo 2:1,12,28; 3:7,18; 4:4; 5:21.

Yet a little while I am with you. He did not conceal the fact that he was soon to leave them. There is something exceedingly tender in this address. It shows that he loved them to the end; that as their friend and guide, *as a man*, he felt deeply at the thoughts of parting from them, and leaving them to a cold and unfeeling world. A parting scene at death is always one of tenderness; and it is well when, like this, there is the presence of the Saviour to break the agony of the parting pang, and to console us with the words of his grace.

As I said unto the Jews. See Joh 7:34.

So now I say to you. That is, they could not follow him *then*, Joh 13:36; 14:2. He was about to die and return to God, and for a time they must be willing to be separated from him. But he consoled them (Joh 13:36) with the assurance that the separation would be only temporary, and that they should afterward follow him.

{w} "as I said unto the Jews" Joh 7:34; 8:21

THE GOSPEL ACCORDING TO JOHN-Chapter 13-Verse 34

Verse 34. *A new commandment.* This command he gave them as he was about to leave them, to be a *badge* of discipleship, by which they might be known as his friends and followers, and by which they might be *distinguished* from all others. It is called *new*, not because there was no command before which required men to love their fellow-men, for one great precept of the law was that they should love their neighbour as themselves (Le 19:18); but it was *new* because it had never before been made that by which any class or body of men had been *known and distinguished*. The *Jew* was known by his external rites, by his peculiarity of dress, &c.; the philosopher by some other mark of distinction; the military man by another, &c. In none of these cases had love *for each other* been the distinguishing and peculiar badge by which they were known. But in the case of Christians they were not to be known by distinctions of wealth, or learning, or fame; they were not to aspire to earthly honours; they were not to adopt any peculiar style of dress or *badge*, but they were to be distinguished by tender and constant attachment to each other. This was to surmount all distinction of country, of colour, of rank, of office, of sect. Here they were to feel that they were on a level, that they had common wants, were redeemed by the same sacred blood, and were going to the same heaven. They were to befriend each other in trials; be careful of each other's feelings and reputation; deny themselves to promote each other's welfare. See 1 Jo 3:23; 1 Th 4:9; 1 Pe 1:22; 2 Th 1:3; Ga 6:2; 2 Pe 1:7. In all these places the command of Jesus is repeated or referred to, and it shows that the first disciples considered this indeed as the peculiar law of Christ. This command or law was, moreover, *new* in regard to the *extent* to which this love was to be carried; for he immediately adds, "*As I have loved you, that ye also love one another.*" His love for them was strong, continued, unremitting, and he was now about to show his love for them in death. Joh 15:13, "Greater love hath no man than this, that a man lay down his life for his friends." So in 1 Jo 3:16 it is said that "we ought also to lay down our lives for the brethren." This was a *new* expression of love; and it showed the strength of attachment which we ought to have for Christians, and how ready we should be to endure hardships, to encounter dangers, and to practise self-denial, to benefit those for whom the Son of God laid down his life.

{x} "new commandment" Le 19:18; Joh 15:12,17; Eph 5:2; 1 Th 4:9
Jas 2:8; 1 Pe 1:22; 1 Jo 2:7,8; 3:11,23; 4:20,21

THE GOSPEL ACCORDING TO JOHN-Chapter 13-Verse 35

Verse 35. *By this shall all men*, &c. That is, your love for each other shall be so decisive evidence that you are like the Saviour, that all men shall see and know it. It shall be the thing by which you shall be known among all men. You shall not be known by peculiar rites or habits; not by a peculiar form of dress or manner of speech; not by peculiar austerities and unusual customs, like the Pharisees, the Essenes, or the scribes, but by deep, genuine, and tender affection. And it is well known it was this which eminently distinguished the first Christians, and was the subject of remark by the surrounding pagans. "See," said the heathen, "see how they love one another! They are ready to lay down their lives for each other." Alas! how changed is the spirit of the Christian world since then! Perhaps, of all the commands of Jesus, the observance of this is that which is least apparent to a surrounding world. It is not so much that they are divided into different sects, for this *may* be consistent with love for each other; but it is the want of deep-felt, genuine love toward Christians even of our own denomination; the absence of genuine self-denial; the pride of rank and wealth; and the fact that professed Christians are often known by anything else rather than by true attachment to those who bear the same Christian name and image. The true Christian loves religion wherever it is found—equally in a prince or in a slave, in the mansion of wealth or in the cottage of poverty, on the throne or in the hut of want. He overlooks the distinction of sect, of colour, and of nations; and wherever he finds a man who bears the Christian *name* and *manifests the Christian spirit*, he loves him. And this, more and more as the millennium draws near, will be the peculiar badge of the professed children of God. Christians will love their own denominations *less* than they love the spirit and temper of *the Christian*, wherever it may be found.

THE GOSPEL ACCORDING TO JOHN-Chapter 13-Verse 36
Verse 36. No Barnes text on this verse.
{y} "but thou shalt follow me" Joh 21:18; 2 Pe 1:14

THE GOSPEL ACCORDING TO JOHN-Chapter 13-Verse 37
Verse 37. No Barnes text on this verse.
{z} "I will lay down my life"
Mt 26:33; Mr 14:29; Lu 22:33

THE GOSPEL ACCORDING TO JOHN-Chapter 13-Verse 38
Verse 38. No Barnes text on this verse.

THE GOSPEL ACCORDING TO JOHN-Chapter 14

Verse 1. *Let not your heart be troubled.* The disciples had been greatly distressed at what Jesus had said about leaving them. Comp. Joh 16:6,22. Perhaps they had indicated their distress to him in some manner by their countenance or their expressions, and he proceeds now to administer to them such consolations as their circumstances made proper. The discourse in this chapter was delivered, doubtless, while they were sitting at the table partaking of the Supper (Joh 16:33); that in the two following chapters, and the prayer in the 17th chapter, were while they were on their way to the Mount of Olives. There is nowhere to be found a discourse so beautiful, so tender, so full of weighty thoughts, and so adapted to produce comfort, as that which occurs in these three chapters of John. It is the consolatory part of our religion, where Christ brings to bear on the mind full of anxiety, and perplexity, and care, the tender and inimitably beautiful truths of his gospel—truths fitted to allay every fear, silence every murmur, and give every needed consolation to the soul. In the case of the disciples there *was* much to *trouble* them. They were about to part with their beloved, tender friend. They were to be left alone to meet persecutions and trials. They were without wealth, without friends, without honours. And it is not improbable that they felt that *his death* would demolish all their schemes, for they had not yet fully learned the doctrine that the Messiah must suffer and die, Lu 24:21.

Ye believe in God. This may be read either in the indicative mood or the imperative. Probably it should be read in the imperative—"Believe on God, and believe on me." If there were no other reason for it, this is sufficient, that there was no more evidence that they *did* believe in God than that they believed in Jesus. All the ancient versions except the Latin read it thus. The Saviour told them that their consolation was to be found at this time in confidence in God and in him; and he intimated what he had so often told them and the Jews, that there was an *indissoluble union* between him and the Father. This union he takes occasion to explain to them more fully, Joh 13:7-12.

Believe in. Put confidence in, rely on for support and consolation.

{a} "Let not" Isa 43:1,2; 14:27; 2 Th 2:2

{b} "believe also" Isa 12:2,3; Eph 1:12,13; 1 Pe 1:21

Verses 2,3. *In my Father's house.* Most interpreters understand this of heaven, as the peculiar dwelling-place or *palace* of God; but it *may* include the *universe*, as the abode of the omnipresent God.

Are many mansions. The word rendered *mansions* means either the *act* of dwelling in any

ccli

place (Joh 14:23), "we will make our abode with him"), or it means *the place* where one dwells. It is taken from the verb *to remain*, and signifies the place where one dwells or remains. It is applied by the Greek writers to the *tents* or temporary habitations which soldiers pitch in their marches. It denotes a dwelling of less *permanency* than the word *house*. It is commonly understood as affirming that in heaven there is *ample room* to receive all who will come; that therefore the disciples might be sure that they would not be excluded. Some have understood it as affirming that there will be different *grades* in the joys of heaven; that some of the mansions of the saints will be nearer to God than others, agreeably to 1 Co 15:40,41. But perhaps this passage may have a meaning which has not occurred to interpreters. Jesus was consoling his disciples, who were affected with grief at the idea of his separation. To comfort them he addresses them in this language:

> "The universe is the dwelling-place of my Father. All
> is his *house*. Whether on earth or in heaven, we
> are still in his habitation. In that vast abode of
> God there are many mansions. The earth is one of them,
> heaven is another. Whether here or there, we are still
> in the house, in one of the mansions of our Father, in
> one of the *apartments* of his vast abode. This we
> ought continually to feel, and to rejoice that we are
> permitted to occupy *any part* of his dwelling-place.
> Nor does it differ much whether we are in *this* mansion
> or another. It should not be a matter of grief when we
> are called to pass from one part of this vast habitation
> of God to another. I am indeed about to leave you, but I
> am going only to another part of the vast dwelling-place
> of God. I shall still be in the same universal habitation
> with you; still in the house of the same God; and am going
> for an important purpose—to fit up another abode for
> your eternal dwelling."

If this be the meaning, then there is in the discourse true consolation. We see that the *death* of a Christian is not to be dreaded, nor is it an event over which we should immoderately weep. It is but removing from *one apartment* of God's universal dwelling-place to another—one where we shall still be in his house, and still feel the same interest in all that pertains to his kingdom. And especially the removal of the Saviour from the earth was an event over which Christians should rejoice, for he is still in the house of God, and still preparing mansions of rest for his people.

If it were *not* so, &c.
"I have concealed from you no truth. You have been
cherishing this hope of a future abode with God.
Had it been ill founded I would have told you plainly,
as I have told you other things. Had any of you been
deceived, as Judas was, I would have made it known to
you, as I did to him."

I go to prepare a place for you. By his *going* is meant his death and ascent to heaven. The figure here is taken from one who is on a journey, who goes before his companions to provide a place to lodge in, and to make the necessary preparations for their entertainment. It evidently means that he, by the work he was yet to perform in heaven, would secure their admission there, and obtain for them the blessings of eternal life. That work would consist mainly in his *intercession,* Heb 10:12-13,19-22; 7:25-27; 4:14-16.

That where I am. This language could be used by no one who was not then in the place of which he was speaking, and it is just such language as one would naturally use who was both God and man —in reference to his human nature, speaking of his *going* to his Father; and in reference to his divine nature, speaking as if he was *then* with God.

Ye may be also. This was language eminently fitted to comfort them. Though about to leave them, yet he would not *always* be absent. He would come again at the day of judgment and gather all his friends to himself, and they should be ever with him, He 9:28. So shall *all* Christians be with him. And so, when we part with a beloved Christian friend by death, we may feel assured that the separation will not be *eternal*. We shall meet again, and dwell in a place where there shall be no more separation and no more tears.

{c} "I go" He 6:20; 9:8,24; Re 21:2

{d} "prepare a place for you" He 9:28 {e} "where I am" Joh 12:26; 17:24; 1 Th 4:17

THE GOSPEL ACCORDING TO JOHN-Chapter 14-Verse 3
Verse 3. No Barnes text on this verse.

THE GOSPEL ACCORDING TO JOHN-Chapter 14-Verse 4
Verse 4. *Whither I go ye know.* He had so often told them that he was to die, and rise, and ascend to heaven, that they could not but understand it, Mt 16:21; Lu 9:22; 18:31,32.

The way ye know. That is, the way that leads to the dwelling-place to which he was going. The way which they were to tread was to obey his precepts, imitate his example, and follow him, Joh 14:6.

Verse 5. *We know not whither thou goest.* Though Jesus had so often told them of his approaching death and resurrection, yet it seems they did not understand him, nor did they fully comprehend him until after his resurrection. See Lu 24:21. They entertained the common notions of a *temporal kingdom*; they supposed still that he was to be an earthly prince and leader, and they did not comprehend the reason why he should die. Thomas confessed his ignorance, and the Saviour again patiently explained his meaning. All this shows the difficulty of believing when the mind is full of prejudice and of contrary opinions. Had Thomas *laid aside* his previous opinions—had he been willing to receive the truth as Jesus plainly spoke it, there would have been no difficulty. Faith would have been an easy and natural exercise of the mind. And so with the sinner. If he were *willing* to receive the plain and unequivocal doctrines of the Bible, there would be no difficulty; but his mind is full of opposite opinions and plans, occupied with errors and vanities, and these are the reasons, and the only reasons, why he is not a Christian. Yet who would say that, after the plain instructions of Jesus, Thomas *might* not have understood him? And who will dare to say that any sinner*may not* lay aside his prejudices and improper views, and receive the plain and simple teaching of the Bible?

Verse 6. *I am the way.* See Isa 35:8. By this is meant, doubtless, that they and all others were to have access to God only by obeying the instructions, imitating the example, and depending on the merits of the Lord Jesus Christ. He was the *leader* in the road, the guide to the wandering, the teacher of the ignorant, and the example to all. See Joh 6:68: "Thou hast the words of eternal life;" 1 Pe 2:21. "Christ—suffered for us, leaving us an example that ye should follow his steps;" Heb 9:8,9.

The truth. The source of truth, or he who originates and communicates truth for the salvation of men. Truth is a representation of things as they are. The life, the purity, and the teaching of Jesus Christ was the most complete and perfect representation of the things of the eternal world that has been or can be presented to man. The ceremonies of the Jews were shadows; the life of Jesus was the truth. The opinions of men are fancy, but the doctrines of Jesus were nothing more than a representation of *facts* as they exist in the government of God. It is implied in this, also, that Jesus was the fountain of all truth; that by his inspiration the prophets spoke, and that by him all truth is communicated to men. See Barnes "Joh 1:17".

The life. See Joh 11:25, See Barnes "Joh 1:4".

No man cometh to the Father but by me. To come to the Father is to obtain his favour, to have access to his throne by prayer, and finally to enter his kingdom. No man can obtain any of these things except by the merits of the Lord Jesus Christ. By coming *by him* is meant coming in his name and depending on his merits. We are ignorant, and he alone can guide us. We are sinful, and it is only by his merits that we can be pardoned. We are blind, and he only can enlighten us. God has appointed him as the Mediator, and has ordained that all blessings shall descend to this world through him. Hence he has put the world under his control; has given the affairs of men into his hand, and has appointed him to dispense whatever may be necessary for our peace, pardon, and salvation, Ac 4:22; 5:31.

{f} "the way" Isa 35:8,9; Joh 10:9; Heb 10:19,20

{g} "the truth" Joh 1:17; 15:1 {h} "the life" Joh 1:4; 11:25 {i} "no man" Ac 4:12

THE GOSPEL ACCORDING TO JOHN-Chapter 14-Verse 7

Verse 7. *If ye had known me*. By this Jesus does not intend to say that they were not truly his disciples, but that they had not a *full* and *accurate* knowledge of his character and designs. They still retained, to a large extent, the Jewish notions respecting a temporal Messiah, and did not fully understand that he was to die and be raised from the dead.

Ye should have known my Father also. You would have known the counsels and designs of my Father respecting my death and resurrection. If you had been divested of your Jewish prejudices about the Messiah, if you had understood that it was proper for me to die, you would also have understood the purposes and plans of God in my death; and, *knowing that*, you would have seen that it was wise and best. We see here that a correct knowledge of the character and work of Christ is the same as a correct knowledge of the counsels and plans of God; and we see, also, that the reasons why we have not such a knowledge are our previous prejudices and erroneous views.

From henceforth. From this time. From my death and resurrection you shall understand the plans and counsels of God.

Ye know him. You shall have just views of his plans and designs.

Have seen him. That is, they had seen Jesus Christ, his image, and the brightness of his glory (Heb 1:3), which was the same as having seen the Father, Joh 14:9.

THE GOSPEL ACCORDING TO JOHN-Chapter 14-Verse 8

Verse 8. *Lord, show us the Father*. Philip here referred to some outward and visible manifestation of God. God had manifested himself in various ways to the prophets and saints of old, and Philip affirmed that if some such manifestation should be made to them they would be satisfied. It was right to desire evidence that Jesus was the Messiah, but such evidence had been afforded abundantly in the miracles and teaching of Jesus, and that should have sufficed them.

THE GOSPEL ACCORDING TO JOHN-Chapter 14-Verse 9

Verse 9. *So long time*. For more than three years Jesus had been with them. He had raised the dead, cast out devils, healed the sick, done those things which no one could have done who had not come from God. In that time they had had full opportunity to learn his character and his mission from God. Nor was it needful, after so many proofs of his divine mission, that God should *visibly manifest* himself to them in order that they might be convinced that he came from him.

He that hath seen me. He that has seen my works, heard my doctrines, and understood my character. He that has given *proper attention* to the proofs that I have afforded that I came from God.

Hath seen the Father. The word *Father* in these passages seems to be used with reference to the divine nature, or to God represented *as a Father*, and not particularly to the distinction in the Trinity of Father and Son. The idea is that God, as God, or *as a Father*, had been manifested in the incarnation, the works, and the teachings of Christ, so that they who had seen and heard him might be said to have had a real view of God. When Jesus says, "hath *seen* the Father," this cannot refer to the *essence* or *substance* of God, for he is invisible, and in that respect no man has seen God at any time. All that is meant when it is said that *God is seen*, is that some manifestation of him has been made, or some such *exhibition* as that we may learn his *character*, his *will*, and his *plans*. In this case it cannot mean that he that had seen Jesus with the bodily eyes had *in the same sense* seen God; but he that had been a witness of his miracles and of his transfiguration—that had heard his doctrines and studied his character —had had full evidence of his divine mission, and of *the will and purpose* of the Father in sending him. The knowledge of the Son was itself, of course, the knowledge of the Father. There was such an intimate *union* in their nature and design that he who understood the one understood also the other. See Barnes "Mt 11:27"

See Barnes "Lu 10:22"; See Barnes "Joh 1:18".

{k} "he that hath seen me" Col 1:15

THE GOSPEL ACCORDING TO JOHN-Chapter 14-Verse 10

Verse 10. *I am in the Father.* See Barnes "Joh 10:38".

The words that I speak, &c. See Barnes "Joh 7:16"
See Barnes "Joh 7:17".

The Father that dwelleth in me. Literally, "The Father *remaining* in me." This denotes most *intimate union*, so that the works which Jesus did might be said to be done by the Father. It implies a more intimate union than can subsist between a mere man and God. Had Jesus been a mere man, like the prophets, he would have said, "The Father who *sent* or *commissioned* me doeth the works;" but here there is reference, doubtless, to that mysterious and peculiar union which subsists between the Father and the Son.

He doeth the works. The miracles which had been wrought by Jesus. The Father could be said to do them on account of the intimate union between him and the Son. See Joh 5:17,19,36; 10:30.

THE GOSPEL ACCORDING TO JOHN-Chapter 14-Verse 11

Verse 11. *Believe me*, &c. Believe my declarations that I am in the Father, &c. There were two grounds on which they might believe; one was his *own testimony*, the other was *his works*.

Or else. If credit is not given to my *words*, let there be to my miracles.

For the very works' sake. On account of the works; or, be convinced by the miracles themselves. Either his own testimony was sufficient to convince them, or the many miracles which he had wrought in healing the sick, raising the dead, &c.

THE GOSPEL ACCORDING TO JOHN-Chapter 14-Verse 12

Verse 12. *He that believeth on me.* This promise had doubtless peculiar reference to the apostles themselves. They were full of grief at his departure, and Jesus, in order to console them directed them to the great honour which was to be conferred on them, and to the assurance that God would not leave them, but would attend them in their ministry with the demonstrations of his mighty power. It cannot be understood of *all* his followers, for the circumstances of the promise do not require us to understand it thus, and it has not been a matter of fact that *all* Christians have possessed power to do greater works than the Lord Jesus. It is a general promise that greater works than he performed should be done by his followers, without specifying that *all* his followers would be instrumental in doing them.

The works that I do. The miracles of healing the sick, raising the dead, &c. This was done by the apostles in many instances. See Ac 5:15; 19:12; 13:11; 5:1-10.

Greater works than these shall he do. Interpreters have been at a loss in what way to understand this. The most probable meaning of the passage is the following: The word "greater" cannot refer to the miracles themselves, for the works of the apostles did not exceed those of Jesus in *power*. No higher exertion of power was put forth, or could be, than raising the dead. But, though not greater *in themselves considered*, yet they were greater *in their effects*. They made a deeper impression on mankind. They were attended with more extensive results. They were the means of the conversion of more sinners. The works of Jesus were confined to Judea. They were seen by few. The works of the apostles were witnessed by many nations, and the effect of their miracles and preaching was that thousands from among the Jews and Gentiles were converted to the Christian faith. The word *greater* here is used, therefore, not to denote the *absolute exertion* of power, but the effect which the miracles would have on mankind. The word "works" here probably denotes not merely miracles, but *all things that the apostles did* that made an impression on mankind, including their travels, their labours, their doctrine, &c.

Because I go unto my Father. He would there intercede for them, and especially by his going to the Father the Holy Spirit would be sent down to attend them in their ministry, Joh

14:26,28; 16:7-14.

See Mt 28:18. By his going to the Father is particularly denoted his exaltation to heaven, and his being placed as head over all things to his church, Eph 1:20-23; Php 2:9-11. By his being exalted there the Holy Spirit was given (Joh 16:7), and by his power thus put forth the Gentiles were brought to hear and obey the gospel.

{l} "He that believeth on me" Mt 21:21

THE GOSPEL ACCORDING TO JOHN-Chapter 14-Verse 13

Verse 13. *Whatsoever ye shall ask.* This promise referred particularly to the apostles in their work of spreading the gospel; it is, however, true of all Christians, if what they ask is in *faith,* and according to the will of God, Jas 1:6; 1 Jo 5:14.

In my name. This is equivalent to saying *on my account,* or for my sake. If a man who has money in a bank authorizes us to draw it, we are said to do it in his name. If a son authorizes us to apply to his father for aid because we are his friends, we do it in the name of the son, and the favour will be bestowed on us from the regard which the parent has to his son, and through him to all his friends. So we are permitted to apply to God in the name of his Son Jesus Christ, because God is in him well pleased (Mt 3:17), and because we are the friends of his Son he answers our requests. Though we are undeserving, yet he loves us on account of his Son, and because he sees in us his image. No privilege is greater than that of approaching God in the name of his Son; no blessings of salvation can be conferred on any who do not come in his name.

That will I do. Being exalted, he will be possessed of all power in heaven and earth (Mt 28:18), and he therefore could fulfil all their desires.

That the Father may be glorified in the Son.

See Barnes "Mt 13:31"

{m} "And whatsoever" 1 Jo 5:14

THE GOSPEL ACCORDING TO JOHN-Chapter 14-Verse 14

Verse 14. No Barnes text on this verse.

THE GOSPEL ACCORDING TO JOHN-Chapter 14-Verse 15

Verse 15. *If ye love me.* Do not show your love by grief at my departure merely, or by profession, but by obedience.

Keep my commandments. This is the only proper evidence of love to Jesus, for mere profession is no proof of love; but that love for him which leads us to do all his will, to love each other, to deny ourselves, to take up our cross, and to follow him through evil report and through good report, is true attachment. The evidence which we have that a child loves its parents is when that child is willing, without hesitation, gainsaying, or murmuring, to do *all* that the parent requires him to do. So the disciples of Christ are required to show that they are attached to him supremely by yielding to all his requirements, and by patiently doing his will in the face of ridicule and opposition, 1 Jo 5:2,3.

{n} "If ye love me" Joh 15:10,14; 14:21,23; 1 Jo 5:3

THE GOSPEL ACCORDING TO JOHN-Chapter 14-Verse 16

Verse 16. *I will pray the Father.* This refers to his intercession after his death and ascension to heaven, for this prayer was to be connected with their keeping his commandments. In what *way* he makes *intercession* in heaven for his people we do not know. The *fact*, however, is clearly made known, Ro 8:34; Heb 4:14,15; 7:25.

It is as the result of his intercession in heaven that we obtain all our blessings, and it is through him that our prayers are to be presented and made efficacious before God.

Another Comforter. Jesus had been to them a counsellor, a guide, a friend, while he was with them. He had instructed them, had borne with their prejudices and ignorance, and had administered consolation to them in the times of despondency. But he was about to leave them now to go alone into an unfriendly world. The *other* Comforter was to be given as a compensation for his absence, or to perform the offices toward them which he would have done if he had remained personally with them. And from this we may learn, in part, what is the office of the Spirit. *It is to furnish to all Christians the instruction and consolation which would be given by the personal presence of Jesus*, Joh 16:14. To the apostles it was particularly to inspire them with the knowledge of all truth, Joh 14:26; 15:26. Besides this, he came to convince men of sin. See Barnes "Joh 16:8-11".

It was proper that such an agent should be sent into the world—

1st. Because it was a part of the plan that Jesus should ascend to heaven after his death.

2nd. Unless some heavenly agent should be sent to carry forward the work of salvation, man would reject it and perish.

3rd. Jesus could not be personally and bodily present in all places with the vast multitudes who should believe on him. The Holy Spirit is omnipresent, and can reach them all. See Barnes "Joh 16:7".

4th. It was manifestly a part of the plan of redemption that each of the persons of the Trinity should perform his appropriate work—the Father in sending his Son, the Son in making atonement and interceding, and the Spirit in applying the work to the hearts of men.

The word translated *Comforter* is used in the New Testament five times. In four instances it is applied to the Holy Spirit— Joh 14:16,26; 15:26; 16:7.

In the other instance it is applied to the Lord Jesus—1 Jo 2:1: "We have an *advocate* (Paraclete — Comforter) with the Father, Jesus Christ the righteous."

It is used, therefore, only by John. The verb from which it is taken has many significations. Its proper meaning is to *call one* to us (Ac 27:20); then to call one *to aid us*, as an advocate in a court; then to exhort or entreat, to pray or implore, as an advocate does, and to comfort or console, by suggesting *reasons* or *arguments* for consolation. The word "comforter" is frequently used by Greek writers to denote *an advocate* in a court; one who intercedes; a monitor, a teacher, an assistant, a helper. It is somewhat difficult, therefore, to fix the precise meaning of the word. It may be translated either advocate, monitor, teacher, or helper. What the office of the Holy Spirit in this respect is, is to be learned from what we are elsewhere told he does. We learn particularly from the accounts that our Saviour gives of his work that that office was,

1st. To comfort the disciples; to be with them in his absence and to supply his place; and this is properly expressed by the word *Comforter.*

2nd. To *teach them,* or remind them of truth; and this might be expressed by the word *monitor* or *teacher,* Joh 14:26 Joh 15:26, 27.

3rd. To aid them in their work; to advocate their cause, or to assist them in advocating the cause of religion in the world, and in bringing sinners to repentance; and this may be expressed by the word *advocate,* Joh 16:7-13. It was also by the Spirit that they were enabled to stand before kings and magistrates, and boldly to speak in the name of Jesus, Mt 10:20. These seem to comprise all the meanings of the word in the New Testament, but no *single* word in our language expresses fully the sense of the original.

That he may abide with you for ever. Not that he should remain with you for a few years, as I have done, and then leave you, but be with you in all places to the close of your life. He shall be your constant guide and attendant.

{o} "another Comforter" Joh 15:26

THE GOSPEL ACCORDING TO JOHN-Chapter 14-Verse 17

Verse 17. *The Spirit of truth.* He is thus called here because he would teach them the truth, or would guide them into all truth, Joh 16:13. He would keep them from all error, and teach them the truth, which, either by writing or preaching, they were to communicate to others.

The world. The term world is often used to denote all who are entirely under the influence of the things of this world —pride, ambition, and pleasure; all who are not Christians, and especially all who are addicted to gross vices and pursuits, 1 Co 1:21; 11:32; Joh 12:31; 2 Co 4:4.

Cannot receive. Cannot admit as a teacher or comforter, or cannot receive in his offices of enlightening and purifying. The reason why they could not do this is immediately added.

Because it seeth him not. The men of the world are under the influence of the senses. They walk by sight, and not by faith. Hence what they cannot perceive by their senses, what does not gratify their sight, or taste, or feeling, makes no impression on them. As they cannot *see* the operations of the Spirit (Joh 3:8), they judge that all that is said of his influence is delusive, and hence they cannot receive him. They have an erroneous mode of judging of what is for the welfare of man.

Neither knoweth him. To *know*, in the Scriptures, often means more than the act of the mind in simply *understanding a* thing. It denotes *every* act or *emotion* of the mind that is requisite in receiving the proper *impression* of a truth. Hence it often includes the idea of *approbation*, of *love*, of *cordial feeling*, Ps 1:6; Ps 37:18; 138:6; Na 1:7; 2 Ti 2:19.

In this place it means the approbation of the heart; and as the people of the world do not *approve* of or *desire* the aid of the Spirit, so it is said they cannot receive him. They have no love for him, and they reject him. Men often consider his work in the conversion of sinners and in revivals as delusion. They love the world so much that they cannot understand his work or embrace him.

He dwelleth in you. The Spirit dwells in Christians by his sacred influences. There is no personal union, no physical indwelling, for God is essentially present in one place as much as in another; but he works in us repentance, peace, joy, meekness, &c. He teaches us, guides us, and comforts us. See Barnes "Ga 5:22-24".

Thus he is said to *dwell in us* when we are made pure, peaceable, holy, humble; when we become *like him*, and cherish his sacred influences. The word "dwelleth" means to *remain* with them. Jesus was to be taken away, but the Spirit would remain. It is also implied that they would know his presence, and have assurance that they were under his guidance. This was true of the apostles as *inspired men*, and it is true of all Christians that by ascertaining that they have the *graces of the Spirits*—joy, peace, long-suffering, &c.—they *know* that they are the children of God, 1 Jo 3:24; 5:10.

{q} "and shall be in you" Ro 8:9; 1 Jo 2:27

THE GOSPEL ACCORDING TO JOHN-Chapter 14-Verse 18

Verse 18. *Comfortless.* Greek, *orphans.* Jesus here addresses them as children, Joh 13:33. He says that he would show them the kindness of a *parent*, and, though he was going away, he would provide for their future welfare. And even while *he* was absent, yet they would sustain to him *still* the relation of children. Though he was to die, yet he would live again; though absent in body, yet he would be present with them by his Spirit; though he was to go away to heaven, yet he would return again to them. See Joh 14:3.

{1} "comfortless" or, "orphans" {r} "I will come to you" Joh 14:3,28.

THE GOSPEL ACCORDING TO JOHN-Chapter 14-Verse 19

Verse 19. *A little while.* This was the day before his death.

Seeth me no more. No more until the day of judgment. The men of the world would not see him visibly, and they had not the eye of faith to discern him.

But ye see me. Ye shall continue to see me by faith, even when the world cannot. You will continue to see me by the eye of faith as still your gracious Saviour and Friend.

Because I live. Though the Saviour was about to die, yet was he also about to be raised from the dead. He was to *continue* to live, and though absent from them, yet he would feel the same interest in their welfare as when he was with them on earth. This expression does not refer *particularly* to his *resurrection*, but his *continuing to live*. He had a nature which could not die. As Mediator also he would be raised and continue to live; and he would have both power and inclination to give them also life, to defend them, and bring them with him.

Ye shall live also. This doubtless refers to their future life. And we learn from this,

1st. That the life of the Christian depends on that of Christ, They are united; and if they were separated, the Christian could neither enjoy spiritual life here nor eternal joy hereafter.

2nd. The fact that Jesus lives is a pledge that all who believe in him shall be saved. He has power over all our spiritual foes, and he can deliver us from the hands of our enemies, and from all temptations and trials.

{s} "because I live" Heb 7:25

THE GOSPEL ACCORDING TO JOHN-Chapter 14-Verse 20

Verse 20. *At that day.* In the time when my life shall be fully manifested to you, and you shall receive the assurance that I live. This refers to the time *after* his resurrection, and to the manifestations which in various ways he would make that he was alive.

That I am in my Father, &c. That we are most intimately and indissolubly united. See Barnes "Joh 10:38".

Ye in me. That there is a union between us which can never be severed. See Barnes "Joh 15:1, also Joh 15:2-7.

THE GOSPEL ACCORDING TO JOHN-Chapter 14-Verse 21

Verse 21. *He that hath*, &c. This intimate union is farther manifested by these facts:

1st. That true love to Jesus will produce obedience. See Joh 14:15.

2nd. That those who love *him* will be loved of the *Father*, showing that there is a union between the Father and the Son.

3rd. That Jesus also will love them, evincing still the same union. Religion is love. The love of one holy being or object is the love of all. The kingdom of God is one. His people, though called by different names, are one. They are united to each other and to God, and the bond which unites the whole kingdom in one is love.

Will manifest myself to him. To *manifest* is to show, to make appear, to place before the eyes so that an object may be seen. This means that Jesus would so *show* himself to his followers that they should *see* and *know* that he was their Saviour. In what way this is done, see Joh 14:23.

{t} "He that hath" Joh 14:15,23

THE GOSPEL ACCORDING TO JOHN-Chapter 14-Verse 22

Verse 22. *Judas saith unto him.* This was the same as Lebbeus or Thaddeus. See Mt 10:3.

He was the brother of James, and the author of the Epistle of Jude.

How is it, &c. Probably Judas thought that he spake only of his resurrection, and he did not readily see how it could be that he could show himself to them, and not be seen also by others.

{u} Lu 6:16

Verse 23. *Will keep my words.* See Joh 14:15.

We will come to him. We will come to him with the manifestation of pardon, peace of conscience, and joy in the Holy Ghost. It means that God will manifest himself to the soul as a Father and Friend; that Jesus will manifest himself as a Saviour; that is, that there will be shed abroad in the heart just views and proper feelings toward God and Christ. The Christian will rejoice in the perfections of God and of Christ, and will delight to contemplate the glories of a present Saviour. The condition of a sinner is represented as one who has gone astray from God, and from whom God has withdrawn, Ps 58:3; Pr 27:10 Eze 14:11. He is *alienated* from God, Eph 2:12; Is 1:4; Eph 4:18

Col 1:21. Religion is represented as God returning to the soul, and manifesting himself as reconciled through Jesus Christ, 2 Co 5:18; Col 1:21.

Make our abode. This is a figurative expression implying that God and Christ would *manifest* themselves in no temporary way, but that it would be the privilege of Christians to enjoy their presence continually. They would take up their residence in the heart as their dwelling-place, as a temple fit for their abode. See 1 Co 3:16: "Ye are the temple of God;" Joh 14:19: "Your body is the temple of the Holy Ghost;" 2 Co 6:16: "Ye are the temple of the living God." This does not mean that there is any personal union between Christians and God—that there is any peculiar indwelling of the *essence* of God in us— for God is essentially present in all places in the same way; but it is a figurative mode of speaking, denoting that the Christian is under the influence of God; that he rejoices in his presence, and that he has the views, the feelings, the joys which God produces in a redeemed soul, and with which he is pleased.

{v} "and we will come into him" 1 Jo 2:24; Re 3:20

Verse 24. *The word which you hear is not mine.* See Barnes on "Joh 5:19, See Barnes on "Joh 7:16".

Verse 25. *Have I spoken.* For your consolation and guidance. But, though he had said so many things to console them, yet the Spirit would be given also as their Comforter and Guide.

Verse 26. *Will send in my name.* On my account. To perfect my work. To execute it as I would in applying it to the hearts of men. See Joh 14:13.

Shall teach you all things. All things which it was needful for them to understand in the apostolic office, and particularly those things which they were not prepared then to hear or could not then understand. See Joh 16:12. Comp. See Barnes "Mt 10:19, See Barnes "Mt 10:20".

This was a full promise that they would be inspired, and that in organizing the church, and in recording the truths necessary for its edification, they would be under the infallible guidance of the Holy Ghost.

Bring all things to your remembrance. This probably refers to two things:

1st. He would seasonably remind them of the sayings of Jesus, which they might otherwise have forgotten. In the organization of the church, and in composing the sacred history, he would preside over their *memories,* and recall such truths and doctrines as were necessary either for their comfort or the edification of his people. Amid the multitude of things which Jesus spake during a ministry of more than three years, it was to be expected that many things which he had uttered, that would be important for the edification of the church, would be forgotten. We see, hence, the nature of their inspiration. The Holy Spirit made use of their *memories,* and doubtless of all their natural faculties. He so presided over their memories as to recall what they had forgotten, and *then* it was recorded as a thing which they distinctly remembered, in the same way as we remember a thing which would have been forgotten had not some friend recalled it to our recollection.

2nd. The Holy Spirit would teach them the *meaning* of those things which the Saviour had spoken. Thus they did not understand that he ought to be put to death till after his resurrection, though he had repeatedly told them of it, Lu 24:21,25,26.

So they did not till then understand that the gospel was to be preached to the Gentiles, though this was also declared before. Comp. Mt 4:15,16; Mt 12:21, with Ac 10:44-48.

{w} "but the Comforter" Joh 16:23; 1 Jo 2:20,27

THE GOSPEL ACCORDING TO JOHN-Chapter 14-Verse 27

Verse 27. *Peace I leave with you.* This was a common form of benediction among the Jews. See Barnes "Mt 10:13".

It is the invocation of the blessings of peace and happiness. In this place it was, however, much more than a mere form or an empty wish. It came from Him who had power to make peace and to confer it on all, Eph 2:15. It refers here particularly to the consolations which he gave to his disciples in view of his approaching death. He had exhorted them not to be troubled (Joh 14:1), and he had stated *reasons* why they should not be. He explained to them why he was about to leave them; he promised them that he would return; he assured them that the Holy Ghost would come to comfort, teach, and guide them. By all these truths and promises he provided for their peace in the time of his approaching departure. But the expression refers also, doubtless, to the *peace* which is given to all who love the Saviour. They are by nature enmity against God, Ro 7:7. Their minds are like the troubled sea, which cannot rest, whose waters cast up mire and dirt,

Isa 57:20. They were at war with conscience, with the law and perfections of God, and with all the truths of religion. Their state after conversion is described as a state *of peace*. They are *reconciled to God*; they acquiesce in all his claims; and they have a joy which the world knows not in the word, the promises, the law, and the perfections of God, in the plan of salvation, and in the hopes of eternal life. See Ro 1:7; 5:1; 8:6; 14:7; Ga 5:22; Eph 2:17; 6:15; Php 4:7; Col 3:15.

My peace. Such as I only can impart. The peculiar peace which my religion is fitted to impart.

Not as the world.

1st. Not as the objects which men commonly pursue— pleasure, fame, wealth. They leave care, anxiety, remorse. They do not meet the desires of the immortal mind, and they are incapable of affording that peace which the soul needs.

2nd. Not as the men of the world give. They salute you with empty and flattering words, but their professed friendship is often feigned and has no sincerity. You cannot be sure that they are sincere, but I am.

3rd. Not as systems of philosophy and false religion give. They profess to give peace, but it is not real. It does not still the voice of conscience; it does not take away sin; it does not reconcile the soul to God.

4th. My peace is such as meets all the wants of the soul, silences the alarms of conscience, is fixed and sure amid all external changes, and will abide in the hour of death and for ever. How desirable, in a world of anxiety and care, to possess this peace! and how should all who have it not, seek that which the world can neither give nor take away!

Neither let it be afraid. Of any pain, persecutions, or trials. You have a Friend who will never leave you; a peace that shall always attend you. See Joh 14:1.

{y} "Peace" Eph 2:14-17; Php 4:7

THE GOSPEL ACCORDING TO JOHN-Chapter 14-Verse 28

Verse 28. *Ye have heard*, &c. Joh 14:2,3.

If ye loved me. The expression is not to be construed as if they had then no love to him, for they evidently had; but they had also low views of him as the Messiah; they had many Jewish prejudices, and they were slow to believe his plain and positive declarations. This is the slight and tender reproof of a friend, meaning manifestly if you had *proper* love for me; if you had the *highest* views of my character and work; if you would lay aside your Jewish prejudices, and put *entire*, *implicit* confidence in what I say.

Ye would rejoice. Instead of grieving, you would rejoice in the completion of the plan which requires me to return to heaven, that greater blessings may descend on you by the influences of the Holy Spirit.

Unto the Father. To heaven; to the immediate presence of God, from whom all the blessings of redemption are to descend.

For my Father is greater than I. The object of Jesus here is not to compare his *nature* with that of the Father, but his *condition.* Ye would rejoice that I am to leave this state of suffering and humiliation, and resume that glory which I had with the Father before the world was. You ought to rejoice at my exaltation to bliss and glory with the Father (Professor Stuart). The object of this expression is to *console* the disciples in view of his absence. This he does by saying that *if* he goes away, the Holy Spirit will descend, and great success will attend the preaching of the gospel, Joh 16:7-10. In the plan of salvation the Father is represented as giving the Son, the Holy Spirit, and the various blessings of the gospel. As the *Appointer,* the *Giver,* the *Originator,* he may be represented as in office superior to the Son and the Holy Spirit. The discourse has no reference, manifestly, to the *nature* of Christ, and cannot therefore be adduced to prove that he is not divine. Its whole connection demands that we interpret it as relating solely to the imparting of the blessings connected with redemption, in which the Son is represented all along as having been *sent* or *given,* and in this respect as sustaining a relation subordinate to the Father.

{z} "I go to the Father" Joh 14:12 {a} "for my Father is greater" 1 Co 15:27,28

THE GOSPEL ACCORDING TO JOHN-Chapter 14-Verse 29

Verse 29. *Before it come to pass.* Before my death, resurrection, and ascension.

Ye might believe. Ye might be confirmed or strengthened in faith by the evidence which I gave that I came from God—the power of foretelling future events.

THE GOSPEL ACCORDING TO JOHN-Chapter 14-Verse 30

Verse 30. *Will not talk much.* The time of my death draws nigh. It occurred the next day.

The prince of this world. See Barnes "Joh 12:31".

Cometh. Satan is represented as approaching him to try him in his sufferings, and it is commonly supposed that no small part of the pain endured in the garden of Gethsemane was from some dreadful conflict with the great enemy of man. See Lu 22:53: "This is your hour *and the power of darkness."* Comp. Lu 4:13.

Hath nothing in me. There is in me no principle or feeling that accords with his, and nothing, therefore, by which he can prevail. Temptation has only power because there are some principles in us which accord with the designs of the tempter, and which may be *excited* by presenting corresponding objects till our virtue be overcome. Where there is no such propensity, temptation has no power. As the principles of Jesus were wholly on the side of virtue, the meaning here may be that, though he had the natural appetites of man, his virtue was so supreme that Satan "had nothing in him" which could constitute any danger that he would be led into sin, and that there was no fear of the result of the conflict before him.

{b} "prince of this world" Joh 16:11; Eph 2:2 {c} "hath nothing in me" 2 Co 5:21; He 4:15; 1 Jo 3:5

Verse 31. *That the world may know that I love the Father.* That it might not be alleged that his virtue had not been subjected to *trial*. It *was* subjected. He was tempted in all points like as we are, yet without sin, Heb 4:15. He passed through the severest forms of temptation, that it might be seen and known that his holiness was proof to *all* trial, and that human nature *might be* so pure as to resist all forms of temptation. This *will* be the case with all the saints in heaven, and it was the case with Jesus on earth.

Even so I do. In all things he obeyed; and he showed that, in the face of calamities, persecutions, and temptations, he was still disposed to obey his Father. This he did that the world might know that he loved the Father. So should we bear trials and resist temptation; and so, through persecution and calamity, should we show that we are actuated by the love of God.

Arise, let us go hence. It has been commonly supposed that Jesus and the apostles now rose from the paschal supper and went to the Mount of Olives, and that the remainder of the discourse in chapters 15-16, together with the prayer in chapter 17, was delivered while on the way to the garden of Gethsemane; but some have supposed that they merely rose from the table, and that the discourse was finished before they left the room. The former is the more correct opinion. It was now probably toward midnight, and the moon was at the full, and the scene was one, therefore, of great interest and tenderness. Jesus, with a little band, was himself about to die, and he went forth in the stillness of the night, counselling his little company in regard to their duties and dangers, and invoking the protection and blessing of God his Father to attend, to sanctify, and guide them in the arduous labours, the toils, and the persecutions they were yet to endure, chapter 17.

{d} "as the Father gave me commandment" Ps 40:8; Php 2:8

THE GOSPEL ACCORDING TO JOHN-
Chapter 15

Verse 1. *I am the true vine.* Some have supposed that this discourse was delivered in the room where the Lord's Supper was instituted, and that, as they had made use of *wine*, Jesus took occasion from that to say that he was the true vine, and to intimate that his blood was the real wine that was to give strength to the soul. Others have supposed that it was delivered in the temple, the entrance to which was adorned with a golden vine (Josephus), and that Jesus took occasion thence to say that he was the *true* vine; but it is most probable that it was spoken while they were going from the paschal supper to the Mount of Olives. Whether it was suggested by the sight of *vines* by the way, or by the wine of which they had just partaken, cannot now be determined. The comparison was frequent among Jews, for Palestine abounded in vineyards, and the illustration was very striking. Thus the Jewish people are compared to a vine which God had planted, Isa 5:1-7; Ps 80:8-16; Joe 1:7; Jer 2:21; Eze 19:10.

When Jesus says he was the true vine, perhaps allusion is had to Jer 2:21. The word *true,* here, is used in the sense of *real, genuine*. He really and truly gives what is emblematically represented by a vine. The point of the comparison or the meaning of the figure is this: A *vine* yields proper juice and nourishment to all the branches, whether these are large or small. All the nourishment of each branch and tendril passes through the main stalk, or the vine, that springs from the earth. So Jesus is the source of all real strength and grace to his disciples. He is their leader and teacher, and imparts to them, as they need, grace and strength to bear the fruits of holiness.

And my Father is the husbandman. The word *vine-dresser* more properly expresses the sense of the original word than husbandman. It means one who has the care of a vineyard; whose office it is to nurture, trim, and defend the vine, and who of course feels a deep interest in its growth and welfare. See Barnes "Mt 21:33".

The figure means that God gave, or appointed his Son *to be*, the source of blessings to man; that all grace descends *through* him; and that God takes care of all the branches of this vine— that is, of all who are by faith united to the Lord Jesus Christ. In Jesus and all his church he feels the deepest interest, and it is an object of great solicitude that his church *should*receive these blessings and bear much fruit.

{a} "true vine" Isa 4:2 {b} "husbandman" So 8:12

Verse 2. *Every branch in me.* Every one that is a true follower of me, that is united to me by faith, and that truly derives grace and strength from me, as the branch does from the vine. The word *branch* includes all the boughs, and the smallest tendrils that shoot out from the parent stalk. Jesus here says that he sustains the same relation to his disciples that a parent stalk does to the branches; but this does not denote any *physical* or incomprehensible union. It is a union formed by *believing* on him; resulting from our feeling our dependence on him and our need of him; from embracing him as our Saviour, Redeemer, and Friend. We become united to him in all our interests, and have common feelings, common desires, and a common destiny with him. We seek the same objects, are willing to encounter the same trials, contempt, persecution, and want, and are desirous that his God shall be ours, and his eternal abode ours. It is a union of friendship, of love, and of dependence; a union of weakness with strength; of imperfection with perfection; of a dying nature with a living Saviour; of a lost sinner with an unchanging Friend and Redeemer. It is the most tender and interesting of all relations, but not more mysterious or more *physical* than the union of parent and child, of husband and wife (Eph 5:23), or friend and friend.

That beareth not fruit. As the vinedresser will remove all branches that are dead or that bear no fruit, so will God take from his church all professed Christians who give no evidence by their lives that they are truly united to the Lord Jesus. He here refers to such cases as that of Judas, the apostatizing disciples, and all false and merely *nominal Christians* (Dr. Adam Clarke).

He taketh away. The vine-dresser cuts it off. God removes such in various ways:

1st. By the discipline of the church.

2nd. By suffering them to fall into temptation.

3rd. By persecution and tribulation, by the deceitfulness of riches, and by the cares of the world (Mt 13:21,22); by suffering the man to be placed in such circumstances as Judas, Achan, and Ananias were—such as to show what *they were*, to bring their characters *fairly out*, and to let it be seen that they had no true love to God.

4th. By death, for God has power thus at any moment to remove unprofitable branches from the church.

Every branch *that beareth fruit.* That is, all true Christians, for all such bear fruit. To *bear fruit* is to show by our lives that we are under the influence of the religion of Christ, and that that religion produces in us its appropriate effects, Ga 5:22,23. See Barnes "Mt 7:16-20".

It is also to live so as to be useful to others. As a vineyard is worthless unless it bears fruit that may promote the happiness or subsistence of man, so the Christian principle would be worthless unless Christians should live so that others may be made holy and happy by their example and labours, and so that the *world* may be brought to the cross of the Saviour.

He purgeth it. Or rather he *prunes* it, or cleanses it by pruning. There is a use of words here —a paronomasia-in the original which cannot be retained in the translation. It may be imperfectly seen by retaining the Greek words—"Every branch in me that beareth not fruit he *taketh away (airei)*; every branch that beareth fruit, he purgeth it (*kathairei*); now ye *are clean (katharoi)*," &c. The same Greek word in different forms is still retained. God purifies all true Christians so that they may be more useful. He takes away that which hindered their usefulness;

teaches them; quickens them; revives them; makes them more pure in motive and in life. This he does by the regular influences of his Spirit in sanctifying them, purifying their motives, teaching them the beauty of holiness, and inducing them to devote themselves more to him. He does it by taking away what opposes their usefulness, however much they may be attached to it, or however painful to part with it; as a vine-dresser will often feel himself compelled to lop off a branch that is large, apparently thrifty, and handsome, but which bears no fruit, and which *shades* or injures those which do. So God often takes away the *property* of his people, their children, or other idols. He removes the objects which bind their affections, and which render them inactive. He takes away the things around man, as he did the valued gourds of Jonah (Joh 4:5-11), so that he may feel his dependence, and live more to the honour of God, and bring forth more proof of humble and active piety.

{c} "Every branch" Mt 15:13 {d} "that beareth" Heb 12:15; Re 3:19

THE GOSPEL ACCORDING TO JOHN-Chapter 15-Verse 3

Verse 3. *Now ye are clean.* Still keeping up the figure (*katharoi*). It does not mean that they were *perfect*, but that they had been under a process of purifying by his instructions all the time he had been with them. He had removed their erroneous notions of the Messiah; he had gradually reclaimed them from their fond and foolish views respecting earthly honours; he had taught them to be willing to forsake all things; and he had so trained and disciplined them that immediately after his death they would be ready to go and bear fruit among all nations to the honour of his name. In addition to this, Judas had been removed from their number, and they were now all true followers of the Saviour. See Barnes "Joh 13:10".

Through the word. By means of the *teachings* of Jesus while he had been with them.

{e} "Now, you are clean" Joh 17:17; Eph 5:26; 1 Pe 1:22

THE GOSPEL ACCORDING TO JOHN-Chapter 15-Verse 4

Verse 4. *Abide in me.* Remain united to me by a living faith. Live a life of dependence on me, and obey my doctrines, imitate my example, and constantly exercise faith in me.

And I in you. That is, if you remain attached to me, I will remain with you, and will teach, guide, and comfort you. This he proceeds to illustrate by a reference to the vine. If the branch should be cut off an instant, it would die and be fruitless. As long as it is in the vine, from the nature of the case, the parent stock imparts its juices, and furnishes a constant circulation of sap adapted to the growth and fruitfulness of the branch. So our piety, if we should be separate from Christ, or if we cease to feel our union to him and dependence on him, withers and droops. While we are united to him by a living faith, *from the nature of the case*, strength flows from him to us, and we receive help as we need. Piety then, manifested in good works, in love, and self-denial, is as natural, as easy, as unconstrained, and as lovely as the vine covered with fruitful branches is at once useful and enticing.

{f} "abide in me" Joh 2:6 {g} "As the branch" Hos 14:8; Ga 2:20; Php 1:11

THE GOSPEL ACCORDING TO JOHN-Chapter 15-Verse 5

Verse 5. *I am the vine*, Joh 15:1

Without me ye can do nothing. The expression "without me" denotes the same as *separate from me*. As the branches, if separated from the parent stock, could produce no fruit, but would immediately wither and die, so Christians, if separate from Christ, could do nothing. The expression is one, therefore, strongly implying dependence. The Son of God was the original source of life, Joh 1:4. He also, by his work as Mediator, gives life to the world (Joh 6:33), and it is by the same grace and agency that it is continued in the Christian. We see hence,

1st. That to him is due all the praise for all the good works the Christian performs.

2nd. That they will perform good works just in proportion as they feel their dependence on him and look to him. And

3rd. That the reason why others fail of being holy is because they are unwilling to look to him, and seek grace and strength from him who alone is able to give it.

{1} "without me", or "severed from me"

THE GOSPEL ACCORDING TO JOHN-Chapter 15-Verse 6

Verse 6. *If a man abide not in me.* See Joh 15:4. If a man is not truly united to him by faith, and does not live with a continual sense of his dependence on him. This doubtless refers to those who are professors of religion, but who have never known anything of true and real connection with him.

Is cast forth. See Barnes "Joh 15:2".

See Barnes "Mt 8:12, Also See Barnes "Mt 22:13".

Is withered. Is dried up. A branch cut off withers. So of a soul unconnected with Christ, however fair it may have appeared, and however flourishing when a profession of religion was first made, yet when it is tried, and it is seen that there was no true grace, everything withers and dies. The zeal languishes, the professed love is gone, prayer is neglected, the sanctuary is forsaken, and the soul becomes like a withered branch reserved for the fire of the last great day. See a beautiful illustration of this in Eze 15:1-8.

Men gather them. The word men is not in the original, and should not have been in the translation. The Greek is "they gather them," a form of expression denoting simply they are gathered, without specifying by whom it is done. From Mt 13:40-42, it seems that it will be done by the angels. The expression means, as the withered and useless branches of trees are gathered for fuel, so shall it be with all hypocrites and false professors of religion.

Are burned. See Mt 13:42.

{h} "If a man abide" Mt 3:10; 7:19

Verse 15. *My words.* My doctrine; my commandments.

Abide in you. Not only are *remembered*, but are suffered to remain in you as a living principle, to regulate your affections and life.

Ye shall ask, &c. See Joh 14:13. This promise had particular reference to the apostles. It is applicable to other Christians only so far as they are in circumstances similar to the apostles, and only so far as they possess their spirit. We learn from it that it is only when we keep the commandments of Christ—only when we live by faith in him, and his words are suffered to control our conduct and affections, that our prayers will be heard. Were we *perfect* in all things, he would always hear us, and we should be kept from making an improper petition; but just so far as men regard iniquity in their heart, the Lord will not hear them, Ps 66:18.

{i} "Ye shall ask" Joh 16:23

Verse 8. *Herein.* In this—to wit, in your bearing much fruit.

Glorified. Honoured.

Bear much fruit. Are fruitful in good works; are faithful, zealous, humble, devoted, always abounding in the work of the Lord. This honours God,

1st. Because it shows the excellence of his law which requires it.

2nd. Because it shows the power of his gospel, and of that grace which can overcome the evil propensities of the heart and *produce* it.

3rd. Because the Christian is restored to the divine image, and it shows how excellent is the character after which they are formed. They imitate God, and the world sees that the whole tendency of the divine administration and character is to make man holy; to produce in us that which is lovely, and true, and honest, and of good report. Comp. Mt 7:20; Php 4:8.

So. That is, in doing this.

Shall ye be my disciples. This is a true test of character. It is not by profession, but it is by a holy life, that the character is tried. This is a test which it is easy to apply, and one which decides the case. It is worthy of remark that the Saviour says that those who bear MUCH *fruit* are they who are his disciples. The design and tendency of his religion is to excite men to do much good, and to call forth *all* their strength, and time, and talents in the work for which the Saviour laid down his life. Nor should anyone take comfort in the belief that he is a Christian who does not aim to do *much* good, and who does not devote to God all that he has in an honest effort to glorify his name, and to benefit a dying world. The apostles obeyed this command of the Saviour, and went forth preaching the gospel everywhere, and aiming to bring all men to the knowledge of the truth; and it is this spirit only, manifested in a proper manner, which can constitute any certain evidence of piety.

Verse 9. *As the Father hath loved me.* The love of the Father toward his only-begotten Son is the highest affection of which we can conceive. Comp. Mt 3:17; 17:5. It is the love of God toward his coequal Son, who is like him in all things, who always pleased him, and who was willing to endure the greatest sacrifices and toils to accomplish his purpose of mercy. Yet this love is adduced to illustrate the tender affection which the Lord Jesus has for all his friends.

So have I loved you. Not to the same degree, for this was impossible, but with the same kind of love—deep, tender, unchanging; love prompting to self-denials, toils, and sacrifices to secure their welfare.

Continue ye. The reason which he gives for their doing this is the *strength* of the love which he had shown for them. His love was so great for them that he was about to lay down his life. This constitutes a strong reason why we should continue in his love.

1st. Because the love which he shows for us is unchanging.

2nd. It is the love of our best friend—love whose strength was expressed by toils, and groans, and blood.

3rd. As he is unchanging in the character and strength of his affection, so should we be. Thus only can we properly express our gratitude; thus only show that we are his true friends.

4th. Our happiness here and for ever depends altogether on our *continuing* in the love of Christ. We have no source of permanent joy but in that love.

In my love. In love to me. Thus it is expressed in the Greek in the next verse. The connection also demands that we understand it of our love to him, and not of his love to us. The latter cannot be the subject of a command; the former may. See also Lu 11:42; 1 Jo 2:5 Jude 1:21

Verse 10. See Joh 14:23,24

{k} "If ye keep my commandments" Joh 14:21,23

Verse 11. *These things.* The discourse in this and the previous chapter. This discourse was designed to comfort them by the promise of the Holy Spirit and of eternal life, and to direct them in the discharge of their duty.

My joy. This expression probably denotes the happiness which Jesus had, and would continue to have, by their obedience, love, and fidelity. Their obedience was to him a source of joy. It was that which he sought and for which he had laboured. He now clearly taught them the path of duty, and encouraged them to persevere, notwithstanding he was about to leave them. If they obeyed him, it would continue to him to be a source of joy. Christ rejoices in the obedience of all his friends; and, though his happiness is not dependent on them, yet their fidelity is an object which he desires and in which he finds delight. The same sentiment is expressed in Joh 17:13.

Your joy might be full. That you might be delivered from your despondency and grief at my departure; that you might see the reason why I leave you, be comforted by the Holy Spirit, and be sustained in the arduous trials of your ministry. See 1 Jo 1:4; 2 Jo 1:12. This promise of the Saviour was abundantly fulfilled. The apostles with great frequency speak of the fulness of their joy—joy produced in just the manner promised by the Saviour— by the presence of the Holy Spirit. And it showed his great love, that he promised such joy; his infinite knowledge, that, in the midst of their many trials and persecutions, he knew that they would possess it; and the glorious power and loveliness of his gospel, that it could impart such joy amid so many tribulations. See instances of this joy in Ac 13:52; Re 14:17; 2 Co 2:3; Ga 5:22; 1 Th 1:6; 2:19, 20; 3:9; 1 Pe 1:8; Ro 5:11

2 Co 7:4.

{l} "that your joy" Joh 16:24; 17:13

THE GOSPEL ACCORDING TO JOHN-Chapter 15-Verse 12

Verse 12. *This is my commandment.* The peculiar law of Christianity, called hence the *new* commandment. See Barnes "Joh 13:34".

As I have loved you. That is, with the same tender affection, willing to endure trials, to practise self-denials, and, if need be, to lay down your lives for each other, 1 Jo 3:16.

{m} "This is my commandment" Joh 13:24

THE GOSPEL ACCORDING TO JOHN-Chapter 15-Verse 13

Verse 13. *Greater love hath,* &c. No higher expression of love could be given. Life is the most valuable object we possess; and when a man is willing to lay that down for his friends or his country, it shows the utmost extent of love. Even this love for friends has been rarely witnessed. A *very few cases*—like that of Damon and Pythias—have occurred where a man was willing to save the life of his friend by giving his own. It greatly enhances the love of Christ, that while the instances of those who have been willing to die for *friends* have been so rare, he was willing to die for *enemies*—bitter foes, who rejected his reign, persecuted him, reviled him, scorned him, and sought his life, 1 Jo 4:10; Re 5:6,10.

It also shows us the extent of his love that he gave himself up, not to common sufferings, but to the most bitter, painful, and protracted sorrows, not for himself, not for friends, but for a thoughtless and unbelieving world.

"O Lamb of God, was ever *pain,*
Was ever LOVE like thine!"

{n} "greater love" Ro 5:7,8

Verse 14. No Barnes text on this verse.
{n} "Greater love"
Joh 15:10

Verse 15. *I call you not servants.* This had been the *common* title by which he addressed them (Mt 10:24,25; Joh 12:26; 13:13); but he had also before this, on one occasion, called them *friends* (Lu 12:4), and on one occasion after this he called them servants, Joh 15:20. He here means that the *ordinary* title by which he would henceforth address them would be that of friends.

The servant knoweth not, &c. He receives the command of his master without knowing the reason why this or that thing is ordered. It is one of the conditions of slavery not to be let into the counsels and plans of the master. It is the privilege of friendship to be made acquainted with the plans, wishes, and wants of the friend. This instance of friendship Jesus had given them by making them acquainted with the reasons why he was about to leave them, and with his secret wishes in regard to them. As he had given them this *proof* of friendship, it was proper that he should not withhold from them the title of friends.

His lord. His master.

I have called you friends. I have given you the name of friends. He does not mean that the usual appellation which he had given them had been than of friends, but that such was the title which he had now given them.

For all things, &c. The reason why he called them friends was that he had now treated them as friends. He had opened to them his mind; made known his plans; acquainted them with the design of his coming, his death, his resurrection, and ascension; and, having thus given them the clearest *proof* of friendship, it was proper that he should give them the *name.*

That I have heard, &c. Jesus frequently represents himself as commissioned or sent by God to accomplish an important work, and as being instructed by him in regard to the nature of that work. See Barnes "Joh 5:30".

By what he had *heard of the Father,* he doubtless refers to the *design* of God in his coming and his death. This he had made known to them.

{p} "friends" Jas 2:23

Verse 16. *Ye have not chosen me.* The word here translated *chosen* is that from which is derived the word *elect,* and means the same thing. It is frequently thus translated, Mr 13:20; Mt 24:22,24,31; Col 3:12. It refers here, doubtless, to his choosing or electing them to be apostles. He says that it was not because *they* had chosen *him* to be their teacher and guide, but because *he* had designated them to be his apostles. See Barnes "Joh 6:70"; See Barnes "Mt 4:18, also Mt

4:19-22. He thus shows them that his love for them was pure and disinterested; that it commenced when they had no affection for him; that it was not a matter of obligation on his part, and that therefore it placed them under more tender and sacred obligations to be entirely devoted to his service. The same may be said of all who are endowed with talents of any kind, or raised to any office in the church or the state. It is not that they have originated these talents, or laid God under obligation. What they have they owe to his sovereign goodness, and they are bound to devote all to his service. Equally true is this of all Christians. It was not that by nature they were more *inclined* than others to seek God, or that they had any native goodness to recommend them to him, but it was because he graciously inclined them by his Holy Spirit to seek him; because, in the language of-the Episcopal and Methodist articles of religion, "The grace of Christ PREVENTED them;" that is, *went before them, commenced* the work of their personal salvation, and thus God in sovereign mercy chose them as his own. Whatever Christians, then, possess, they owe to God, and by the most tender and sacred ties they are bound to be his followers.

I have chosen you. To be apostles. Yet all whom he now addressed were true disciples. Judas had left them; and when Jesus says he had chosen them to *bear fruit,* it may mean, also, that he had "chosen them to salvation, through sanctification of the Spirit and belief of the truth," 2 Th 2:13.

Ordained you. Literally, I have *placed you,* appointed you, set you apart. It does not mean that he had done this by any formal public act of the imposition of hands, as we now use the word, but that he had *designated* or appointed them to this work, Lu 6:13-16; Mt 10:2-5.

Bring forth fruit. That you should be rich in good works; faithful and successful in spreading my gospel. This was the great business to which they were set apart, and this they faithfully accomplished. It may be added that this is the great end for which Christians are chosen. It is not to be idle, or useless, or simply to seek enjoyment. It is to do good, and to spread as far as possible the rich temporal and spiritual blessings which the gospel is fitted to confer on mankind.

Your fruit should remain This probably means,

1st. That the effect of their labours would be *permanent* on mankind. Their efforts were not to be like those of false teachers, the result of whose labours soon vanish away (Ac 5:38,39), but their gospel was to spread—was to take a deep and permanent hold on men, and was ultimately to fill the world, Mt 16:18. The Saviour knew this, and never was a prediction more cheering for man or more certain in its fulfillment.

2nd. There is included, also, in this declaration the idea that their labours were to be *unremitted.* They were sent forth to be diligent in their work, and untiring in their efforts to spread the gospel, until the day of their death. Thus their fruit, the continued *product* or *growth* of religion in their souls, was to remain, or to be continually produced, until God should call them from their work. The Christian, and especially the Christian minister, is devoted to the Saviour for life. He is to toil without intermission, and without being weary of his work, till God shall call him home. The Saviour never called a disciple to serve him merely for a part of his life, nor to feel himself at liberty to relax his endeavours, nor to suppose himself to be a Christian when his religion produced no fruit. He that enlists under the banners of the Son of God does it for life. He that *expects* or *desires* to grow weary and cease to serve him, has never yet put on the Christian armour, or known anything of the grace of God. See Lu 9:62.

That whosoever, &c. See Joh 15:7.

{q} "Ye have not chosen me" 1 Jo 4:10,19 {r} "ordained you" Eph 2:10 {s} "whatsoever you shall ask" Joh 15:7; 14:13

THE GOSPEL ACCORDING TO JOHN-Chapter 15-Verse 17

Verse 17. No Barnes text on this verse.

{r} "These things"

Joh 15:12

THE GOSPEL ACCORDING TO JOHN-Chapter 15-Verse 18

Verse 18. *If the world hate you.* The friendship of the world they were not to expect, but they were not to be deterred from their work by its hatred. They had seen the example of Jesus. No opposition of the proud, the wealthy, the learned, or the men of power, no persecution or gibes, had deterred him from his work. Remembering this, and having his example steadily in the eye, they were to labour not less because wicked men should oppose and deride them. It is enough for the disciple to be as his Master, and the servant as his Lord, Mt 10:25.

{u} "If the world hate you" 1 Jo 3:13

THE GOSPEL ACCORDING TO JOHN-Chapter 15-Verse 19

Verse 19. *If ye were of the world.* If you were actuated by the principles of the world. If, like them, you were vain, earthly, sensual, given to pleasure, wealth, ambition, they would not oppose you.

Because ye are not of the world. Because you are influenced by different principles from men of the world. You are actuated by the love of God and holiness; they by the love of sin.

I have chosen you out of the world. I have, by choosing you to be my followers, separated you from their society, and placed you under the government of my holy laws.

Therefore, &c. A Christian may esteem it as one evidence of his piety that he is hated by wicked men. Often most decided evidence is given that a man is the friend of God by the opposition excited against him by the profane, by Sabbath-breakers, and by the dissolute, 1 Jo 3:13; Joh 7:7.

{v} "therefore the world hateth you" Joh 17:14

THE GOSPEL ACCORDING TO JOHN-Chapter 15-Verse 20

Verse 20. *Remember the word that I said*, &c. At their first appointment to the apostolic office. See Mt 10:24,25.

{w} "Remember" Mt 10:24; Lu 6:40; Joh 13:16

{x} "if they have kept" Eze 3:7

Verse 21. *My name's sake.* On my account. Because you are my followers and possess my spirit. See Barnes "Joh 14:13".

Because they know not him that sent me. They will not believe that God has sent me. They do not so understand his character, his justice, or his law, as to see that it was fit that he should send his Son to die. They are so opposed to it, so filled with pride and opposition to a plan of salvation that is so humbling to men, as to be resolved not to believe it, and thus they persecute me, and will also you.

{y} "But all these things" Mt 10:22; 24:9

Verse 22. *And spoken unto them.* Declared unto them the will of God, and made known his requirements. Jesus had not less certainly shown by his own *arguments* that he was the Messiah than by his miracles. By *both* these kinds of proof their guilt was to be measured. See Joh 16:26. No small part of the gospel of John consists of arguments used by the Saviour to convince the Jews that he came from God. He here says if he had not used these arguments, and proved to them his divine mission, they had not had sin.

Had not had sin. This is evidently to be understood of the particular sin of persecuting and rejecting him. Of this he was speaking; and though, if he had not come, they would have been guilty of many other sins, yet of this, their great crowning sin, they would not have been guilty. We may understand this, then, as teaching,

1st. That they would not have been guilty of this *kind of sin.* They would not have been chargeable with rejecting the signal grace of God if Jesus had not come and made an offer of mercy to them.

2nd. They would not have been guilty of the same *degree of sin.* The rejection of the Messiah was the crowning act of rebellion which brought down the vengeance of God, and led on their peculiar national calamities. By way of eminence, therefore, this might be called *the sin*—the peculiar sin of their age and nation. Comp. Mt 23:34-39; 27:25. And this shows us, what is so often taught in the Scriptures, that our guilt will be in proportion to the light that we possess and the mercies that we reject, Mt 11:20-24; Lu 12:47,48.

If it was such a crime to reject the Saviour then, it is a crime now; and if the rejection of the Son of God brought such calamities on the Jewish nation, the same rejection will involve the sinner now in woe, and vengeance, and despair.

No cloak. No covering, no excuse. The proof has been so clear that they cannot plead ignorance; it has been so often presented that they cannot allege that they had no opportunity of knowing it. It is still so with all sinners.

{z} "If I had not come" Joh 9:41 {a} "but now " Jas 4:17 {2} "cloak" or, "excuse"

Verse 23. *He that hateth me,* &c. To show them that this was no slight crime, he reminds them that a rejection of himself is also a rejection of God. Such is the *union* between them, that no one can hate the one without also hating the other. See Joh 5:19,20 Joh 14:7,9.

Verse 24. *The works which none other man did.* The miracles of Jesus surpassed those of Moses and the prophets—

1st. In their number. He healed great multitudes, and no small part of his life was occupied in doing good by miraculous power.

2nd. In their nature. They involved a greater exertion of power. He healed *all* forms of disease. He showed that his power was superior to all kinds of pain. He raised Lazarus after he had been four days dead. He probably refers also to the fact that he had performed miracles of a different *kind* from all the prophets.

3rd. He did all this by his *own power*; Moses and the prophets by the invoked power of God. Jesus spake and it was done, showing that he had power of himself to do more than all the ancient prophets had done. It may be added that his miracles were done in a short time. They were constant, rapid, continued, in all places. Wherever he was, he showed that he had this power, and in the short space of three years and a half it is probable that he wrought *more* miracles than are recorded of Moses and Elijah, and all the prophets put together.

{b} "the works" Joh 7:31

Verse 25. *In their law,* Ps 35:19. All the Old Testament was sometimes called the law. The meaning here is that the same thing happened to him which did to the psalmist. The same words which David used respecting his enemies would express, also, the conduct of the Jews and their treatment of the Messiah. In both cases it was without cause. Jesus had broken no law, he had done no injury to his country or to any individual. It is still true that sinners hate him in the same way. He injures no one, but, amid all their hatred, he seeks their welfare; and, while they reject him in a manner for which they *can give no reason in the day of judgment,* he still follows them with mercies and entreats them to return to him. Who has ever had any reason to *hate* the Lord Jesus? What injury has he ever done to any one of the human race? What evil has he ever said or thought of any one of them? What cause or reason had the Jews for putting him to death? What reason has the sinner for hating him now? What reason for neglecting him? No one can give a reason for it that will satisfy his own conscience, none that has the least show of plausibility. Yet no being on earth has ever been more hated, despised, or neglected, and in every instance it has been "without a cause." Reader, do *you* hate him? If so, I ask you WHY? Wherein has he injured you? or why should you think or speak reproachfully of the benevolent and pure Redeemer?

{c} "They hated me without cause" Ps 35:19; 69:4

Verse 26. No Barnes text on this verse.

{d} "Comforter is come"

Joh 14:17

{e} "he shall testify of me" 1 Jo 5:6

Verse 27. *Ye also shall bear witness.* You shall be witnesses to the world to urge on them the evidences that the Lord Jesus is the Messiah.

Have been with me. They had for more than three years seen his works, and were therefore qualified to bear witness of his character and doctrines.

From the beginning. From his entrance on the public work of the ministry, Mt 4:17-22. Comp. Ac 1:21,22.

{f} "And ye also shall bear witness" Lu 24:48; Ac 2:32; 4:20,33

2 Pe 1:16

{g} "ye have been with me from the beginning" 1 Jo 1:2.

THE GOSPEL ACCORDING TO JOHN- Chapter 16

Verse 1. *These things*. The things spoken in the two previous chapters, promising them divine aid and directing them in the path of duty.

Be offended. For the meaning of the word *offend*, See Barnes "Mt 5:29".

It means here the same as to *stumble* or *fall* —that is to apostatize. He proceeds immediately to tell them, what he had often apprised them of, that they would be subject to great persecutions and trials. He was also himself about to be removed by death. They were to go into an unfriendly world. All these things were in themselves greatly fitted to shake their faith, and to expose them to the danger of apostasy. Comp. Lu 24:21. If they had not been apprise of this, if they had not known *why* Jesus was about to die, and if they had not been encouraged with the promised aid of the Holy Ghost, they would have sunk under these trials, and forsaken him and his cause. And we may learn hence,

1st. That if Christians were left to themselves they would fall away and perish.

2nd. That God affords means and helps *beforehand* to keep them in the path of duty.

3rd. That the instructions of the Bible and the help of the Holy Spirit are all granted to keep them from apostasy.

4th. That Jesus beforehand *secured* the fidelity and made certain the continuance in faith of his apostles, seeing all their danger and knowing all their enemies. And, in like manner, we should be persuaded that "he is able to keep that which we commit to him against that day," 2 Ti 1:2,12.

Verse 2. *Out of the synagogues*. See Barnes "Joh 9:22".

They would *excommunicate* them from their religious assemblies. This was often done. Comp. Ac 6:13,14; 9:23,24; 17:5; 21:27-31.

Whosoever killeth you. This refers principally to the Jews. It is also true of the Gentiles, that in their persecution of Christians they supposed they were rendering acceptable service to their gods.

God service. The Jews who persecuted the apostles regarded them as blasphemers, and as seeking to overthrow the temple service, and the system of religion which God had established. Thus they supposed they were rendering service to God in putting them to death, Ac 6:13,14; Ac 21:28-31. Sinners, especially hypocrites, often cloak enormous crimes under the pretence of great zeal for religion. Men often suppose, or profess to suppose, that they are rendering God service when they persecute others; and, under the pretence of great zeal for truth and purity, evince all possible bigotry, pride, malice, and uncharitableness. The people of God have suffered most from those who have been *conscientious persecutors* and some of the most malignant foes which true Christians have ever had have been *in* the church, and have been professed ministers of the gospel, persecuting them under pretence of great zeal for the cause of purity and religion. It is no evidence of piety that a man is full of zeal against those whom he supposes to be heretics; and it is one of the best proofs that a man knows nothing of the religion of Jesus when he is eminent for self-conceit in his own views of orthodoxy, and firmly fixed in the opinion that all who differ from him and his sect must of course be wrong.

{a} "whosoever killeth you" Ac 26:9-11.

Verse 3. See Joh 15:21

{b} "And these things" Joh 15:21 {c} "they have not known" 1 Co 2:8; 1 Ti 1:13

Verse 4. These things which are about to happen, Joh 16:1,2. He had foretold then that they would take place.

Ye may remember, &c. By calling to mind that he had foretold these things they would perceive that he was omniscient, and would remember, also, the consolations which he had afforded them and the instructions which he had given them. Had these calamities come upon them without their having been foretold, their faith might have failed; they might have been tempted to suppose that Jesus was not aware of them, and of course that he was not the Messiah. God does not suffer his people to fall into trials without giving them sufficient warning, and without giving all the grace that is needful to bear them.

At the beginning. In the early part of the ministry of Jesus. The expression *these things* here refers, probably, to *all* the topics contained in these chapters. He had, in the early part of his ministry, forewarned them of calamities and persecutions (Mt 10:16; 5:10-12; Mt 9:15), but he had not so fully acquainted them with the nature, and design, and sources of their trials; he had not so fully apprised them of the fact, the circumstances, and the object of his death and of his ascension to heaven; he had not revealed to them so clearly that the Holy Spirit would descend, and sanctify, and guide them; and especially he had not, in one continued discourse, *grouped* all these things together, and placed their sorrows and consolations so fully before their minds. All these are included, it is supposed, in the expression "these things."

Because I was with you. This is the reason which he gives why he had not at *first* made known to them clearly the certainty of their calamities and their joys; and it implies,

1st. That it was not needful to do it at once, as he was to be with them for more than three years, and could have abundant opportunity *gradually* to teach these things, and to prepare them for the more full announcement when he was about to leave them.

2nd. That while he was with them he would go before them, and the weight of calamities would fall on *him*, and consequently they did not so much then need the presence and aid of the Holy Spirit as they would when he was gone.

3rd. That his presence was to them what the presence of the Holy Spirit would be after his death, Joh 16:7.

He could teach them all needful truth. He could console and guide them. Now that he was to leave them, he fully apprised them of what was before them, and of the descent of the Holy Spirit to do for them what he had done when with them.

THE GOSPEL ACCORDING TO JOHN-Chapter 16-Verse 5

Verses 5,6. *Now I go my way.* Now I am about to die and leave you, and it is proper to announce all these things to you.

None of you asketh me, &c. They gave themselves up to grief instead of inquiring why he was about to leave them. Had they made the inquiry, he was ready to answer them and to comfort them. When we are afflicted we should not yield ourselves to excessive grief. We should inquire why it is that God thus tries us; and we should never doubt that if we come to him, and spread out our sorrows before him, he will give us consolation.

THE GOSPEL ACCORDING TO JOHN-Chapter 16-Verse 6

Verse 6. No Barnes text on this verse.

{d} "sorrow hath filled" Joh 16:21

THE GOSPEL ACCORDING TO JOHN-Chapter 16-Verse 7

Verse 7. *It is expedient for you,* &c. The reason why it was expedient for them that he should go away, he states to be, that in this way only would the Comforter be granted to them. Still, it may be asked why the presence of the Holy Spirit was more valuable to them than that of the Saviour himself? To this it may be answered,

1st. That by his departure, his death, and ascension—by having these great *facts* before their eyes—they would be led by the Holy Spirit to see more fully the design of his coming than they would by his presence. While he was with them, notwithstanding the plainest teaching, their minds were filled with prejudice and error. They still adhered to the expectation of a temporal kingdom, and were unwilling to believe that he was to die. When he should have actually left them they could no longer doubt on this subject, and would be *prepared* to understand why he came. And this was done. See the Acts of the Apostles everywhere. It is often needful that God should visit us with severe affliction before our pride will be humbled and we are willing to understand the plainest truths.

2nd. While on the earth the Lord Jesus could be bodily present but in one place at one time. Yet, in order to secure the great design of saving men, it was needful that there should be some agent who could be in all places, who could attend all ministers, and who could, at the same time, apply the work of Christ to men in all parts of the earth.

3rd. It was an evident arrangement in the great plan of redemption that each of the persons of the Trinity should perform a part. As it was not the work of the Spirit to make an atonement, so it was not the work of the Saviour to apply it. And until the Lord Jesus had performed this great work, the way was not open for the Holy Spirit to descend to perform his part of the great plan yet, when the Saviour had completed *his* portion of the work and had left the earth, the Spirit would carry forward the same plan and apply it to men.

4th. It was to be expected that far more signal success would attend the preaching of the gospel when the atonement was actually made than before. It was the office of the Spirit to carry forward the work only when the Saviour had died and ascended; and this was actually the case. See Acts chapter 2. Hence it was expedient that the Lord Jesus should go away, that the Spirit might descend and apply the work to sinners. The departure of the Lord Jesus was to the apostles a source of deep affliction, but had they seen *the whole case* they would not have been thus afflicted. So God often takes away from us one blessing that he may bestow a greater. All affliction, if received in a proper manner, is of this description; and could the afflicted people of God always *see the whole case* as God sees it, they would think and feel, as he does, that it was best for them to be thus afflicted.

It is expedient. It is *better* for you.

The Comforter. See Barnes "Joh 14:16".

THE GOSPEL ACCORDING TO JOHN-Chapter 16-Verse 8

Verse 8. *He will reprove.* The word translated *reprove* means commonly to demonstrate by argument, to prove, to persuade anyone to do a thing by presenting reasons, It hence means also to *convince* of anything, and particularly to *convince of crime*. This is its meaning here. He will *convince* or *convict* the world of sin. That is, he will so apply the truths of God to men's own minds as to *convince* them by fair and sufficient arguments that they are sinners, and cause them to *feel* this. This is the nature of conviction always.

The world. Sinners. The men of the world. All men are by nature sinners, and the term *the world* may be applied to them all, Joh 1:10; 12:31; 1 Jo 5:19.

{1} "reprove" or, "convince" Ac 2:37

THE GOSPEL ACCORDING TO JOHN-Chapter 16-Verse 9

Verse 9. *Of sin.* The first thing specified of which the world would be convinced is sin. Sin, in general, is any violation of a law of God, but the particular sin of which men are here said to be convinced is that of rejecting the Lord Jesus. This is placed *first*, and is deemed the sin of chief magnitude, as it is the principal one of which men are guilty. This was particularly true of the Jews who had rejected him and crucified him; and it was the great crime which, when brought home to their consciences by the preaching of the apostles, overwhelmed them with confusion, and filled their hearts with remorse. It was their rejection of the Son of God that was made the great truth that was instrumental of their conversion, Ac 2:22,23,37; 3:13-15; 4:10,26-28; comp. Joh 16:31-33. It is also true of other sinners. Sinners, when awakened, often feel that it has been the great crowning sin of their lives that they have rejected the tender mercy of God, and trampled on the blood of his Son; and that they have for months and years refused to submit to him, saying that they would not have him to reign over them. Thus is fulfilled what is spoken by Zechariah, Zec 3:10: "And they shall look upon me whom they have pierced, and mourn." Throughout the New Testament this is regarded as the sin that is pre-eminently offensive to God, and which, if unrepented of, will certainly lead to perdition, Mr 16:16; Joh 3:36. Hence it is placed *first* in those sins of which the Spirit will convince men; and hence, if we have not yet been brought to see *our* guilt in rejecting God's tender mercy through his Son, we are yet in the gall of bitterness and under the bond of iniquity.

{e} "of sin" Ro 3:20; 7:9

THE GOSPEL ACCORDING TO JOHN-Chapter 16-Verse 10

Verse 10. *Of righteousness.* This seems clearly to refer to the righteousness or innocence of Jesus himself. He was now persecuted. He was soon to be arraigned on heavy charges, and condemned by the highest authority of the nation as guilty. Yet, though condemned, he says that the Holy Spirit would descend and *convince* the world that he was innocent.

Because I go to my Father. That is, the amazing miracle of his resurrection and ascension to God would be a demonstration of his innocence that would satisfy the Jews and Gentiles. God would not raise up an impostor. If he had been truly *guilty*, as the Jews who condemned him pretended, God would not have set his seal to the imposture by raising him from the dead; but when he did raise him up and exalt him to his own right hand, he gave his attestation to his *innocence*; he showed that he approved his work, and gave evidence conclusive that Jesus was sent from God. To this proof of the *innocence* of Jesus the apostles often refer, Ac 2:22-24; 17:31; Ro 1:4; 1 Co 15:14; 1 Ti 3:16.

This same proof of the innocence or righteousness of the Saviour is as satisfactory now as it was then. One of the deepest feelings which an awakened sinner has, is his conviction of the righteousness of Jesus Christ. He sees that he is holy; that his own opposition to him has been unprovoked, unjust, and base; and it is this which so often overwhelms his soul with the conviction of his own unworthiness, and with earnest desires to obtain a better righteousness than his own.

And ye see me no more. That is, he was to be taken away from them, and they would not see him till his return to judgment; yet this source of grief to them would be the means of establishing his religion and greatly blessing others.

{f} "righteousness" Isa 42:21; Re 1:17

Verse 11. *Of judgment*. That God is just, and will execute judgment. This is proved by what he immediately states.

The prince of this world. Satan. See Barnes "Joh 12:31".

The death of Christ was a judgment or a condemnation of Satan. In this struggle Jesus gained the victory and subdued the great enemy of man. This proves that God will execute judgment or justice on all his foes. If he vanquished his great enemy who had so long triumphed in this world, he will subdue all others in due time. All sinners in like manner may expect to be condemned. Of this great truth Jesus says the Holy Spirit will convince men. God showed himself to be *just* in subduing his great enemy. He showed that he was resolved to vanquish his foes, and that *all* his enemies in like manner must be subdued. This is deeply felt by the convicted sinner. He knows that he is guilty. He learns that God is just. He fears that he will condemn him, and trembles in the apprehension of approaching condemnation. From this state of alarm there is no refuge but to flee to Him who subdued the great enemy of man, and who is able to deliver him from the vengeance due to his sins. Convinced, then, of the righteousness of Jesus Christ, and of his ability and willingness to save him, he flees to his cross, and seeks in him a refuge from the coming storm of wrath.

In these verses we have a condensed and most striking view of the work of the Holy Spirit. These three things comprise the whole of his agency in the conversion of sinful men; and in the accomplishment of this work he still awakens, convinces, and renews. He attends the preaching of the gospel, and blesses the means of grace, and manifests his power in revivals of religion. He thus imparts to man the blessings purchased by the death of Jesus, carries forward and extends the same plan of mercy, and will yet apply it to all the kingdoms and tribes of men. Have *we* ever felt his power, and been brought by his influence to mourn over our sins, and seek the mercy of a dying Saviour?

{g} "judgment" Ac 17:31; Ro 2:2; Re 20:12,13

{h} "the prince of this world is judged" Joh 12:31

Verse 12. *I have yet many things to say*, &c. There were many things pertaining to the work of the Spirit and the establishment of religion which might be said. Jesus had given them the outline; he had presented to them the great doctrines of the system, but he had not gone into details. These were things which they could not then bear. They were still full of Jewish prejudices, and were not prepared for a full development of his plans. Probably he refers here to the great *changes* which were to take place in the Jewish system—the abolition of sacrifices and the priest-hood, the change of the Sabbath, the rejection of the Jewish nation, &c. For these doctrines they were not prepared, but they would in due time be taught them by the Holy Spirit.

{i} "ye cannot bear them now" Heb 5:12

Verse 13. *The Spirit of truth.* So called because he would teach them all needful truth.

Will guide you into all truth. That is, truth which pertained to the establishment of the Christian system, which they were not then prepared to hear. We may here remark that this is a full promise that they would be inspired and guided in founding the new church; and we may observe that the plan of the Saviour was replete with wisdom. Though they had been long with him, yet they were not prepared *then* to hear of the changes that were to occur; but his death would open their eyes, and the Holy Spirit, making use of the striking and impressive scenes of his death and ascension, would carry forward with vast rapidity their views of the nature of the Christian scheme. Perhaps in the few days that elapsed, of which we have a record in the first and second chapters of the Acts of the Apostles, they learned more of the true nature of the Christian plan than they would have done in months or years even under the teaching of Jesus himself. The more we study the plan of Christ, the more shall we admire the profound wisdom of the Christian scheme, and see that it was eminently fitted to the great design of its Founder —to introduce it in such a manner as to make on man the deepest impression of its wisdom and its truth.

Not speak of himself. Not as *prompted* by himself. He shall declare what is communicated to him. See Barnes "Joh 7:18".

Whatsoever he shall hear. What he shall receive of the Father and the Son; represented by hearing, because in this way instruction is commonly received. See Barnes "Joh 5:30".

Things to come. Probably this means *the meaning of things* which were to take place *after* the time when he was speaking to them —to wit, the design of his death, and the nature of the changes which were to take place in the Jewish nation. It is also true that the apostles were inspired by the Holy Spirit to predict future events which would take place in the church and the world. See Ac 11:28; Ac 20:29; 21:11; 1 Ti 4:1-3; 2 Ti 3:1; 2 Pe 1:14; and the whole book of Revelation.

{k} "guide you into all truth" Joh 14:26 {l} "he will show you things to come" Re 1:1,19

Verse 14. *Shall glorify me.* Shall honour me. The nature of his influence shall be such as to exalt my character and work in view of the mind.

Shall receive of mine. Literally, "shall take of or from me." He shall receive his commission and instructions as an ambassador from me, to do my will and complete my work.

Shall show it. Shall announce or communicate it to you. This is always the work of the Spirit. All serious impressions produced by him lead to the Lord Jesus (1 Co 12:3), and by this we may easily test our feelings. If we have been truly convicted of sin and renewed by the Holy

Ghost, the tendency of all his influences has been to lead us to the Saviour; to show us our need of him; to reveal to us the loveliness of his character, and the fitness of his work to our wants; and to incline us to cast our eternal interests on his almighty arm, and commit all to his hands.

THE GOSPEL ACCORDING TO JOHN-Chapter 16-Verse 15

Verse 15. *All things*, &c. See Mt 28:18; 11:27. No one could have said this who was not equal with the Father. The union was so intimate, though mysterious, that it might with propriety be said that whatever was done in relation to the Son, was also done in regard to the Father. See Joh 14:9.

THE GOSPEL ACCORDING TO JOHN-Chapter 16-Verse 16

Verse 16. *A little while* His death would occur in a short time. It took place the next day. See Joh 16:19.

Ye shall not see me. That is, he would be concealed from their view in the tomb.

And again a little while. After three days he would rise again and appear to their view.

Because I go, &c. Because it is a part of the plan that I should ascend to God, it is necessary that I should rise from the grave, and then you will see me, and have evidence that I am still your Friend. Comp. Joh 7:33. Here are three important events foretold for the consolation of the disciples, yet they were stated in such a manner that, in their circumstances and with their prejudices, it appeared difficult to understand him.

THE GOSPEL ACCORDING TO JOHN-Chapter 16-Verse 17

Verse 17. No Barnes text on this verse.

THE GOSPEL ACCORDING TO JOHN-Chapter 16-Verse 18

Verse 18. No Barnes text on this verse.

THE GOSPEL ACCORDING TO JOHN-Chapter 16-Verse 19

Verse 19. No Barnes text on this verse.

{m} "Now Jesus"

Joh 2:24,25

{n} "A little while" Joh 16:16; 7:33; 13:33; 14:19

THE GOSPEL ACCORDING TO JOHN-Chapter 16-Verse 20

Verse 20. *Ye shall weep*, &c. At my crucifixion, sufferings, and death. Comp. Lu 23:27.

The world. Wicked men. The term *world* is frequently used in this sense. See Joh 16:8. It refers particularly, here, to the Jews who sought his death, and who would rejoice that their object was obtained. ¶

Shall be turned into joy. You will not only rejoice at my resurrection, but even my death, now the object of so much grief to you, will be to you a source of unspeakable joy. It will procure for you peace and pardon in this life, and eternal joy in the world to come. Thus their greatest apparent calamity would be to them, finally, the source of their highest comfort; and though *then* they could not see *how* it could be, yet if they had known *the whole case* they would have seen that they might rejoice. As it was, they were to be consoled by the assurance of the Saviour that it would be for their good. And thus, in our afflictions, if we could see the whole case, we should rejoice. As it is, when they appear dark and mysterious, we may trust in the promise of God that they will be for our welfare. We may also remark here that the apparent triumphs of the wicked, though they may produce grief at present in the minds of Christians, will be yet overruled for good. *Their* joy shall be turned into mourning, and the mourning of Christians into joy; and wicked men may be doing the very thing—as they were in the crucifixion of the Lord Jesus—that shall yet be made the means of promoting the glory of God and the good of his people, Ps 76:10.

{o} "ye shall weep and lament" Lu 24:17,21

THE GOSPEL ACCORDING TO JOHN-Chapter 16-Verse 21

Verse 21. No Barnes text on this verse.

{p} "A woman when she has travail"

Isa 26:17

THE GOSPEL ACCORDING TO JOHN-Chapter 16-Verse 22

Verse 22. *I will see you again.* After my resurrection.

Your joy no man taketh from you. You shall be so firmly persuaded that I have risen and that I am the Messiah, that neither the threats nor persecutions of men shall ever be able to shake your faith and produce doubt or unbelief, and thus take away your joy. This prediction was remarkably fulfilled. It is evident that after his ascension not one of the apostles ever doubted for a moment that he had risen from the dead. No persecution or trial was able to shake their faith; and thus, amid all their afflictions, they had an unshaken source of joy.

{q} "you now therefore have sorrow" Joh 16:6 {r} "But I shall see you again" Lu 24:41,52; Joh 20:20

{s} "and your joy" 1 Pe 1:8

THE GOSPEL ACCORDING TO JOHN-Chapter 16-Verse 23

Verse 23. *In that day.* After my resurrection and ascension.

Ye shall ask me nothing. The word rendered *ask* here may have two significations, one to ask by way of inquiry, the other to ask for assistance. Perhaps there is reference here to both these senses. While he was with them they had been accustomed to depend on him for the supply of their wants, and in a great degree to propose their trials to him, expecting his aid. See Mt 8:25; Joh 11:3. They were also dependent on his personal instructions to explain to them the mysteries of his religion, and to remove their perplexities on the subject of his doctrines. They had not sought to God through him *as the Mediator*, but they had directly applied to the Saviour himself.

He now tells them that henceforward their requests were to be made to God in his name, and that he, by the influences of his Spirit, would make known to them what Jesus would himself do if bodily present. The emphasis in this verse is to be placed on the word "*me*." Their requests were not to be made to him, but to the Father.

Whatsoever ye shall ask, &c. See Joh 14:13.

Verse 24. *Hitherto*. During his ministry, and while he was with them.

Have ye asked, &c. From the evangelists, as well as from this declaration, it seems that they had presented their requests for instruction and aid to Jesus himself. If they had prayed to God, it is probable that they had not done it in his name. This great truth—that we must approach God in the name of the Mediator—was reserved for the last that the Saviour was to communicate to them. It was to be presented at the close of his ministry. Then they were prepared in some degree to understand it; and then, amid trials, and wants, and a sense of their weakness and unworthiness, they would see its preciousness, and rejoice in the privilege of being thus permitted to draw near to God. Though he would be bodily absent, yet their blessings would still be given through the same unchanging Friend.

Ask, &c. Now they had the assurance that they might approach God in his name; and, amid all their trials, they, as well as all Christians since, might draw near to God, knowing that he would hear and answer their prayers.

That your joy, See Joh 15:11.

{t} "ask, and you shall receive" Mt 7:7,8; Jas 4:2,3

{u} "that your joy may be full" Joh 15:11

Verse 25. *In proverbs*. In a manner that appears obscure, enigmatical, and difficult to be understood. It is worthy of remark, that though his declarations in these chapters about his death and resurrection appear to us to be plain, yet to the apostles, filled with Jewish prejudices, and unwilling to believe that he was about to die, they would appear exceedingly obscure and perplexed. The plainest declarations to them on the subject would appear to be involved in mystery.

The time cometh. This refers, doubtless, to the time *after* his ascension to heaven, when he would send the Holy Spirit to teach them the great truths of religion. It does not appear that he himself, after his resurrection, gave them any more clear or full instruction than he had done before.

I shall show you plainly. As Jesus said that he would send the Holy Spirit (Joh 16:7) and as he came to carry forward the work of Christ, so it may be said that the teachings of the Holy Spirit were the teachings of Christ himself.

Of the Father. Concerning the will and plan of the Father; particularly his plan in the establishment and spread of the Christian religion, and in organizing the church. See Ac 10:26.

{2} "proverbs" or, parables

THE GOSPEL ACCORDING TO JOHN-Chapter 16-Verse 26

Verse 26. *I say not unto you that I will pray,* &c. In Joh 14:16, Jesus says that he would pray the Father, and that he would send the Comforter. In chapter 17, he offered a memorable prayer for them. In Heb 7:25, it is said that Jesus ever liveth to make intercession for us; and it is constantly represented in the New Testament that it is by his intercession in heaven now that we obtain the blessings of pardon, peace, strength, and salvation. Comp. Heb 9:24. This declaration of Jesus, then, does not mean that he *would not* intercede for them, but that there was no need then of his mentioning it to them again. They knew that; and, in *addition* to that, he told them that God was ready and willing to confer on them all needful blessings.

{v} "At that day" Joh 16:23

THE GOSPEL ACCORDING TO JOHN-Chapter 16-Verse 27

Verse 27. See Joh 14:21,23

{w} "For the Father himself loveth" Joh 14:21,23 {x} "I came out from God" Joh 16:30; 17:8

THE GOSPEL ACCORDING TO JOHN-Chapter 16-Verse 28

Verse 28. *I came forth from the Father.* I came sent by the Father.
And am come into the world. See Joh 3:19; 6:14,62; 9:39.

THE GOSPEL ACCORDING TO JOHN-Chapter 16-Verse 29

Verse 29. *Now speakest thou plainly.* What he had said that perplexed them was that which is contained in Joh 16:16. Comp. Joh 16:17-19: "A little while and ye shall not see me," &c. This he had now explained by saying (Joh 16:28), "Again, *I leave the world,* and go to the Father." In this there was no ambiguity, and they expressed themselves satisfied with this explanation.

{3} "proverb" or, parable

THE GOSPEL ACCORDING TO JOHN-Chapter 16-Verse 30

Verse 30. *Now are we sure that thou knowest,* &c. Their difficulty had been to understand what was the meaning of his declaration in Joh 16:16. About this they conversed among themselves, Joh 16:17-19. It is evident that they had not mentioned their difficulty to him, and that he had not even heard their conversation among themselves, Joh 16:19. When, therefore, by his answers to them (Joh 16:20-28), he showed that he clearly understood their doubts; and when he gave them an answer so satisfactory without their having *inquired* of him, it satisfied them that he knew the heart, and that he assuredly came from God. They were convinced that there was *no need that any man should ask him,* or propose his difficulties to him, since he knew them all and could answer them.

Verse 31. *Do ye now believe?* Do you truly and really believe? This question was evidently asked to put them on a full examination of their hearts. Though they supposed that they had unshaken faith—faith that would endure every trial, yet he told them that they were about to go through scenes that would test them, and where they would need all their confidence in God. When we feel strong in the faith we should examine ourselves. It may be that we are deceived; and it may be that God may even then be preparing trials for us that will shake our faith to its foundation. The Syriac and Arabic read this in the indicative as an affirmation—"Ye do now believe." The sense is not affected by this reading.

Verse 32. *The hour cometh.* To wit, on the next day, when he was crucified.

Ye shall be scattered. See Mt 26:31.

Every man to his own. That is, as in the margin, to his own home. You shall see me die, and suppose that my work is defeated, and return to your own dwellings. It is probable that the two disciples going to Emmaus were on their way to their dwellings, Luke, chapter 24. After his death all the disciples retired into Galilee, and were engaged in their common employment of fishing, Joh 21:1-14; Mt 28:7.

Leave me alone. Leave me to die without human sympathy or compassion. See Barnes "Mt 26:31, See Barnes "Mt 26:56".

Because the Father is with me. His Father was his friend. He had all along trusted in God. In the prospect of his sufferings he could still look to him for support. And though in his dying moments he suffered so much as to use the language, "Why hast thou forsaken me?" yet it was language addressed to him still as *his* God—"*My* God, *my* God." Even then he had confidence in God—confidence so strong and unwavering that he could say, "Into *thy* hands I commend my spirit," Lu 23:46. In all these sufferings he had the assurance that God was his friend, that he was doing his will, that he was promoting his glory, and that he looked on him with approbation. It matters little who else forsakes us if God be with us in the hour of pain and of death; and though poor, forsaken, or despised, yet, if we have the consciousness of his presence and his favour, then we may fear no evil. His rod and his staff, they will comfort us. Without his favour then, death will be full of horrors, though we be surrounded by weeping relatives, and by all the honour, and splendour, and wealth which the world can bestow. The Christian can die saying, I am not alone, because the Father is with me. The sinner dies without a friend that can alleviate his sufferings —without one source of real joy.

{a} "in me ye might have peace" Joh 14:27; Ro 5:1; Eph 2:14

{b} "In the world" Joh 15:19-21; 2 Ti 3:12

Verse 33. *In me.* In my presence, and in the aid which I shall render you by the Holy Spirit.

In the world. Among the men to whom you are going. You must expect to be persecuted, afflicted, tormented.

I have overcome the world. He overcame the prince of this world by his death, Joh 12:31. He vanquished the great foe of man, and triumphed over all that would work our ruin. He brought down aid and strength from above by his death; and by procuring for us the friendship of God and the influence of the Spirit; by his own instructions and example; by revealing to us the glories of heaven, and opening our eyes to see the excellence of heavenly things, he has furnished us with the means of overcoming all our enemies, and of triumphing in all our temptations. See Barnes "Joh 14:19"; See Barnes "Ro 8:34, also Ro 8:35-37, See Barnes "1 Jo 4:4, See Barnes "1 Jo 5:4, See Barnes "Re 12:11".

Luther said of this verse "that it was worthy to be carried from Rome to Jerusalem upon one's knees." The world is a vanquished enemy; Satan is a humbled foe; and all that believers have to do is to put their trust in the Captain of their salvation, putting on the whole armour of God, assured that the victory is theirs, and that the church shall yet shine forth fair as the moon, clear as the sun, and terrible as an army with banners, So 6:10.

{a} "in me you might have peace" Joh 14:27; Ro 5:1; Eph 2:14

{b} "In the world" Joh 15:19-21; 2 Ti 3:12

THE GOSPEL ACCORDING TO JOHN-
Chapter 17

Verse 1. *These words*. The words addressed to them in the preceding chapters. They were proceeding to the garden of Gethsemane. It adds much to the interest of this prayer that it was offered in the stillness of the night, in the open air, and in the peculiarly tender circumstances in which Jesus and his apostles were. It is the *longest* prayer recorded in the New Testament. It was offered on the most tender and solemn occasion that has ever occurred in our world, and it is perhaps the most sublime composition to be found anywhere. Jesus was about to die. Having expressed his love to his disciples, and made known to them his last desires, he now commends them to the protection and blessing of the God of grace. This prayer is moreover a specimen of the manner of his *intercession*, and evinces the interest which he felt in behalf of all who should become his followers in all ages of the world.

Lifted up his eyes. This was the common attitude of prayer. Comp. Lu 18:13.

The hour is come. That is, the appointed time for his sufferings and death. Comp. See Barnes "Lu 12:27".

Glorify thy Son. Honour thy Son. See Joh 11:4. Give to the world demonstration that I am thy Son. So sustain me, and so manifest thy power in my death, resurrection, and ascension, as to afford indubitable evidence that I am the Son of God.

That thy Son also may glorify thee. This refers clearly to the manifestation of the honour of God which would be made by the spread of the gospel among men, Joh 17:2. Jesus prayed that God would so honour him in his death that striking proof might be furnished that he was the Messiah, and men thus be brought to honour God. By his death the law, the truth, and the mercy of God were honoured. By the spread of his gospel and the conversion of sinners; by all that Christ will do, now that he is glorified, to spread his gospel, God will be honoured. The conversion of a single sinner honours God; a revival of religion is an eminent means of promoting his honour; and the spread of the gospel among all nations shall yet do more than all other things to promote the honour of God among men. Whatever honours the Saviour honours God. Just as he is exalted in view of the mind, so will God be honoured and obeyed.

{a} "the hour is come" Joh 12:28; 13:32

Verse 2. *As thou hast given him power*. It was on the ground of this power given to Christ that the apostles were commanded to go and teach all nations. See Barnes "Mt 28:18,19".

All flesh. All men, Mt 24:22; Lu 3:6.

That he should give eternal life. See Barnes "Joh 5:24".

To as many as thou hast given him. See Barnes "Joh 10:16; 6:37".

To all on whom the Father has purposed to bestow the blessings of redemption through his Son. God has a plan in all he does, extending to men as well as to other objects. One part of his plan was that the atonement of Christ should not be in vain. Hence he promised him that he should see of the travail of his soul and should be satisfied (Isa 53:11); and hence the Saviour had the assurance that the Father had given him a portion of the human family, and would apply this great work to them. It is to be observed here that the Saviour in this prayer makes an important distinction between "all flesh" and those who were "given him." He has power over all. He can control, direct, restrain them. Wicked men are so far under his universal dominion, and so far restrained by his power, that they will not be *able* to prevent his bestowing redemption on those were given him—that is, all who will believe on him. Long ago, if they had been able, they would have banished religion from the world; but they are under the power of Christ, and it is his purpose that there shall be "a seed to serve him," and that "the gates of hell shall not prevail" against his church. Men who oppose the gospel should therefore feel that they *cannot* prevent the salvation of Christians, and should be alarmed lest they be found "fighting against God."

{b} "that he should give" Joh 5:27; 16:24

Verse 3. *This is life eternal*. This is the source of eternal life; or it is in this manner that it is to be obtained. The knowledge of God and of his Son Jesus Christ is itself a source of unspeakable and eternal joy. Comp. Joh 11:25; 6:63; 12:50.

Might know thee. The word *know* here, as in other places, expresses more than a mere speculative acquaintance with the character and perfections of God. *It includes all the impressions on the mind and life which a just view of God and of the Saviour is fitted to produce.* It includes, of course, love, reverence, obedience, honour, gratitude, supreme affection. To *know* God as he is to know and regard him as a lawgiver, a sovereign, a parent, a friend. It is to yield the whole soul to him, and strive to obey his law.

The only true God. The only God, in opposition to all false gods. What is said here is in opposition to idols, not to Jesus himself, who, in 1 Jo 5:20, is called "the true God and eternal life."

And Jesus Christ. To know Jesus Christ is to have a practical impression of him *as he is* that is, to suffer his character and work to make their due impression on the heart and life. Simply to have *heard* that there is a Saviour is not to *know it*. To have been taught in childhood and trained up in the belief of it is not to know it. To know him is to have a just, practical view of him in all his perfections—as God and man; as a mediator; as a prophet, a priest, and a king. It is to feel our need of such a Saviour, to see that we are sinners, and to yield the whole soul to him, *knowing* that he is a Saviour fitted to our wants, and that in his hands our souls are safe. Comp. Eph 3:19; Tit 1:16; Php 3:10; 1 Jo 5:20.

In this verse is contained the sum and essence of the Christian religion, as it is distinguished from all the schemes of idolatry and philosophy, and all the false plans on which men have sought to obtain eternal life. The Gentiles worshipped many gods; the Christian worships one — the living and the true God; the Jew, the Deist, the Mohammedan, the Socinian, profess to acknowledge one God, without any atoning sacrifice and Mediator; the true Christian approaches him through the great Mediator, equal with the Father, who for us became incarnate, and died that he might reconcile us to God.

{c} "this is life eternal" 1 Jo 5:11 {d} "know thee" Jer 9:23,24 {e} "the only true God" 1 Th 1:9

THE GOSPEL ACCORDING TO JOHN-Chapter 17-Verse 4

Verse 4. *Have glorified thee.* In my instructions and life. See his discourses everywhere, the whole tendency of which is to put honour on God.

I have finished the work. Comp. Joh 19:30. When he says "I *have* finished," he probably means to include also his death. All the *preparations* for that death were made. He had preached to the Jews; he had given them full proof that he was the Messiah; he had collected his disciples; he had taught them the nature of his religion; he had given them his parting counsel, and there was nothing remaining to be done but to return to God. We see here that Jesus was careful that his great and important work should be done *before* his dying hour. He did not postpone it to be performed just as he was leaving the world. So completely had he done his work, that even *before* his death he could say, "*I have finished* the work." How happy would it be if men would imitate his example, and not leave their great work of life to be done on a dying bed! Christians should have their work accomplished, and when that hour approaches, have nothing to do but to die, and return to their Father in heaven.

{g} "I have glorified" Joh 14:13 {h} "I have finished" Joh 19:30; 2 Ti 4:7

THE GOSPEL ACCORDING TO JOHN-Chapter 17-Verse 5

Verse 5. *With thine own self.* In heaven, granting me a participation of the same honour which the Father has. He had just said that he *had* glorified God *on the earth*; he now prays that God would glorify him *in heaven*.

With the glory. With the honour. This word also includes the notion of happiness, or everything which could render the condition blessed.

Before the world was. There could not be a more distinct and clear declaration of the pre-existence of Christ than this. It means before the creation of the world; before there was any world. Of course, the speaker here must have existed then, and this is equivalent to saying that he existed from eternity. See Joh 1:1,2; 6:62; 3:13

Joh 16:28. The glory which he had then was that which was proper to the Son of God, represented by the expression *being in the bosom of the Father* (Joh 1:18), denoting intimacy, friendship, united felicity. The Son of God, by becoming incarnate, is represented as *humbling himself* (Greek, he "emptied himself"), Php 2:8. He laid aside for a time the external aspect of honour, and consented to become despised, and to assume the form of a servant. He now prays that God would raise him up to the dignity and honour which he had before his incarnation. This is the state to which he is now exalted, with the *additional* honour of having made atonement for sin, and having opened the way to save a race of rebels from eternal death. The lowest condition on earth is frequently connected with the highest honours of heaven. Man looks on the outward appearance. God looks to him that is humble and of a contrite spirit.

{i} "with the glory" Joh 1:1,2; Php 2:6; He 1:3,10

THE GOSPEL ACCORDING TO JOHN-Chapter 17-Verse 6

Verse 6. *Have manifested thy name.* The word *name* here includes the attributes or character of God. Jesus had made known his character, his law, his will, his plan of mercy—or, in other words, he had revealed GOD to them. The word *name* is often used to designate the person, Joh 15:21; Mt 10:22; Ro 2:24; 1 Ti 6:1.

Which thou gavest me. God gave them to him in his purpose. He gave them by his providence. He so ordered affairs that they heard him preach and saw his miracles; and he gave them by disposing them to follow him when he called them.

Thine they were. All men are God's by creation and by preservation, and he has a right to do with them as seemeth good in his sight. These men he chose to designate to be the apostles of the Saviour; and he committed them to him to be taught, and then commissioned them to carry his gospel, though amid persecutions, to the ends of the world. God has a right to the services of all; and he has a right to appoint us to any labour, however humble, or hazardous, or wearisome, where we may promote his glory and honour his name.

{k} "manifested" Ps 22:22; Joh 17:26 {l} "the men which thou gavest" Ro 8:30; Joh 17:2,9,11

{m} "they have kept thy word" Heb 3:6

THE GOSPEL ACCORDING TO JOHN-Chapter 17-Verse 7

Verse 7. *They have known.* They have been *taught* that and have believed it.

Hast given me. This refers, doubtless, to the doctrine of Christ, Joh 17:8. They are assured that all my instructions are of God.

Verse 8. *The words*. The doctrines. Christ often represented himself as *instructed* and sent to teach certain great truths to men. Those he taught, and no others. See Barnes "Joh 5:30".

{n} "the words thou givest me" Joh 6:68; 14:10

Verses 9,10. *I pray for them*. In view of their dangers and trials, he sought the protection and blessing of God on them. His prayer was always answered.

Not for the world. The term *world* here, as elsewhere, refers to wicked, rebellious, vicious men. The meaning of this expression here seems to be this: Jesus is praying for his disciples. As a *reason* why God should bless them, he says that they were not of the world; that they had been taken out of the world; that they belonged unto God. The petition was not offered for wicked, perverse, rebellious men, but for those who were the friends of God and were disposed to receive his favours. This passage, then, settles nothing about the question whether Christ prayed for sinners. He *then* prayed for his disciples, who were not those who hated him and disregarded his favours. He *afterward* extended the prayer for all who should become Christians, Joh 17:20. When on the cross he prayed for his crucifiers and murderers, Lu 23:34.

For they are thine. This is urged as a reason why God should protect and guide them. His honour was concerned in keeping them; and we may always *fill our mouths with* such *arguments* when we come before God, and plead that his honour will be advanced by keeping *us* from evil, and granting us all needful grace.

I am glorified in them. I am honoured by their preaching and lives. The sense of this passage is, "Those who are my disciples are thine. That which promotes my honour will also promote thine. I pray, therefore, that they may have needful grace to honour my gospel, and to proclaim it among men."

{o} "I pray not for the world" 1 Jo 5:19

Verse 10. No Barnes text on this verse.

{p} "all mine are thine"

Joh 16:15

{q} "I am glorified in them" Ga 1:24; 1 Pe 2:9

Verse 11. *I am no more in the world*. I have finished my work among men, and am about to leave the world. See Joh 17:4.

These are in the world. They will be among wicked men and malignant foes. They will be subject to trials and persecutions. They will *need* the same protection which I could give them if I were with them.

Keep. Preserve, defend, sustain them in trials, and save them from apostasy.

Through thine own name. Our translators seem to have understood this expression as meaning "keep by thy power," but this probably is not its meaning. It is literally "keep *in* thy name." And if the term *name* be taken to denote God himself and his perfections (See Barnes "Joh 17:6"), it means "keep in the knowledge of thyself. Preserve them in obedience to thee and to thy cause. Suffer them not to fall away from thee and to become apostates."

That they may be one. That they may be united.

As we are. This refers not to a union of *nature*, but of feeling, plan, purpose. Any other union between Christians is impossible; but a union *of affection* is what the Saviour sought, and this he desired might be so strong as to be an illustration of the unchanging love between the Father and the Son. See Joh 17:21-23.

{r} "keep through" 1 Pe 1:5; Jude 1:24 {s} "thine own name" Pr 18:10

THE GOSPEL ACCORDING TO JOHN-Chapter 17-Verse 12

Verse 12. *While I was with them in the world.* While I was engaged with them among other men—surrounded by the people and the temptations of the world. Jesus had now finished his work among the men of the world, and was performing his last offices with his disciples.

I kept them. By my example, instructions, and miracles. I preserved them from apostasy.

In thy name. In the knowledge and worship of thee. Joh 17:6-11.

Those that thou gavest me, &c. The word "gavest" is evidently used by the Saviour to denote not only to give to him to be his real followers, but also as apostles, It is here used, probably, in the sense of giving as apostles. God had so ordered it by his providence that they had been given to him to be his apostles and followers; but the terms "thou gavest me" do not of necessity prove that they were true believers. Of Judas Jesus knew that he was a deceiver and a devil, Joh 6:70: "Have not I chosen you twelve, and one of you is a devil?" Judas is there represented as having been *chosen* by the Saviour to the apostleship, and this is equivalent to saying that he was given to him for this work; yet at the same time he knew his character, and understood that he had never been renewed. *None of them.* None of those chosen to the apostolic office.

But the son of perdition. See Barnes "Mt 1:1".

The term *son* was given by the Hebrews to those who possessed the character described by the word or name following. Thus, sons of Belial-those who possessed his character; children of wisdom-those who were wise, Mt 11:19. Thus Judas is called a son of perdition because he had the character of a *destroyer.* He was a traitor and a murderer. And this shows that he who knew the heart regarded his character as that of a wicked man—one whose appropriate name was that of a son of perdition.

That the scripture, &c. See Barnes "Joh 13:18".

Comp. Ps 41:9.

{t} "that the scripture might be fulfilled" Ps 109:8; Ac 1:20

Verse 13. *My joy fulfilled*, &c. See Barnes "Joh 15:11".

The expression "my joy" here probably refers to the joy of the apostles respecting the Saviour—the joy which would result from his resurrection, ascension, and intercession in heaven.

Verse 14. *I have given them* &c. See Joh 17:18.

The world hath hated them. Joh 15:18-21.

Verse 15. *That thou shouldest take them out of the world.* Though they were going into trials and persecutions, yet Jesus did not pray that they might be removed soon from them. It was better that they should endure them, and thus spread abroad the knowledge of his name. It would be easy for God to remove his people at once to heaven, but it is better for them to remain, and show the power of religion in supporting the soul in the midst of trial, and to spread his gospel among men.

Shouldest keep them, from the evil. This may mean either from the evil one—that is, the devil, or from evil in general—that is, from apostasy, from sinking in temptation. Preserve them from that evil, or give them such grace that they may endure all trials and be sustained amid them. See Barnes "Mt 16:13".

It matters little how long we are in this world if we are kept in this manner.

{v} "that thou shouldest" Ga 1:4

Verse 16. See Joh 15:19

Verse 17. *Sanctify them.* This word means to render pure, or to cleanse from sins, 1 Th 5:20; 1 Co 6:11. Sanctification in the heart of a Christian is progressive. It consists in his becoming more like God and less attached to the world; in his getting the ascendancy over evil thoughts, and passions, and impure desires; and in his becoming more and more weaned from earthly objects, and attached to those things which are unseen and eternal. The word also means to *consecrate*, to set apart to a holy office or purpose. See Joh 17:19; also See Barnes "Joh 10:36".

When Jesus prayed here that God would sanctify them, he probably included both these ideas, that they might be made personally more holy, and might be truly consecrated to God as the ministers of his religion. Ministers of the gospel will be *really* devoted to the service of God just in proportion as they are personally pure.

Through thy truth. Truth is a representation of things as they are. The Saviour prayed that through those just views of God and of themselves they might be made holy. To see things as they are is to see God to be infinitely lovely and pure; his commands to be reasonable and just; heaven to be holy and desirable; his service to be easy, and religion pleasant, and sin odious; to see that life is short, that death is near; that the pride, pomp, pleasures, wealth, and honours of this world are of little value, and that it is of infinite importance to be prepared to enter on the eternal state of being. He that sees all this, or *that looks on things as they are*, will desire to be holy. He will make it his great object to live near to God and to glorify his name. In the sanctification of the soul God makes use of *all truth*, or of everything fitted to make a representation of things as they are to the mind. His Word states that and no more; his Spirit and his providence do it. The earth and the heavens, the seasons, the sunshine and the rain, are all fitted to teach us his goodness and power, and lead us to him. His daily mercies tend to the same end, and afflictions have the same design. Our own sickness teaches us that we are soon to die. The death of a friend teaches us the instability of all earthly comforts, and the necessity of seeking better joys. All these things are fitted to make *just representations* to the mind, and thus to sanctify the soul. As the Christian is constantly amid these objects, so he should be constantly growing in grace, and daily and hourly gaining new and deeper impressions of the great truths of religion.

Thy word is truth. All that thou hast spoken—that is, all that is contained in the Bible. All the commands and promises of God; his representations of his own character and that of man; his account of the mission and death of his Son; of the grave, the resurrection, judgment, and eternity, all tend to *represent things as they are*, and are thus fitted to sanctify the soul. We have here also the testimony of the Saviour that the revelation which God has given is true. *All* that God has spoken is true, and the Christian should rejoice and the sinner should tremble. See Ps 19:7-14.

{w} "Sanctify" Ac 15:9; Eph 5:26; 2 Th 2:13
{x} "thy word is truth" Ps 119:151

THE GOSPEL ACCORDING TO JOHN-Chapter 17-Verse 18
Verse 18. No Barnes text on this verse.

THE GOSPEL ACCORDING TO JOHN-Chapter 17-Verse 19
Verse 19. *I sanctify myself.* I consecrate myself exclusively to the service of God. The word *sanctify* does not refer here to personal sanctification, for he had no sin, but to setting himself apart entirely to the work of redemption.

That they also, &c.

1st. That they might have an *example* of the proper manner of labouring in the ministry, and might learn of me how to discharge its duties. Ministers will understand their work best when they most faithfully study the example of their great model, the Son of God.

2nd. That they might be made pure by the *effect* of my sanctifying myself—that is, that they might be made pure by the shedding *of that blood which cleanses from all sin.* By this only can men be made holy; and it was because the Saviour so sanctified himself, or set himself to this work so unreservedly as to shed his own blood, that any soul can be made pure and fit for the kingdom of God.

{y} "And for their sakes" 1 Co 1:2,30 {1} "sanctified", or "truly sanctified"

Verses 20,21. *Neither pray I for these alone,* &c. Not for the apostles only, but for all who shall be converted under the preaching of the gospel. They will all need similar grace and be exposed to similar trials. It is a matter of unspeakable joy that *each* Christian, however humble or unknown to men—however poor, unlearned, or despised, can reflect that he was remembered in prayer by *him whom God heareth always.* We value the prayers of pious friends. How much more should we value this petition of the Son of God! To that single prayer we who are Christians owe infinitely more real benefits than the world can ever bestow; and in the midst of any trials we may remember that the Son of God *prayed for us,* and that the prayer was assuredly heard, and will be answered in reference to all who truly believe.

All may be one. May be united as brethren. Christians are all redeemed by the same blood, and are going to the same heaven. They have the same wants, the same enemies, the same joys. Though they are divided into different denominations, yet they will meet at last in the same abodes of glory. Hence they *should* feel that they belong to the same family, and are children of the same God and Father. There are no ties so tender as those which bind us in the gospel. There is no friendship so pure and enduring as that which results from having the same attachment to the Lord Jesus. Hence Christians, in the New Testament, are represented as being indissolubly united—parts of the same body, and members of the same family.Ac 4:32-35. 1 Co 12:4-31; Eph 2:20-22; Ro 12:5.

On the ground of this union they are exhorted to love one another, to bear one another's burdens, and to study the things that make for peace, and things wherewith one may edify another, Eph 4:3; Ro 12:5-16.

As thou, Father, art in me. See Joh 14:10 This does not affirm that the union between Christians should be *in all respects* like that between the Father and the Son, but only in the points in which they are capable of being compared. It is not the union of *nature* which is referred to, but the union of plan, of counsel, of purpose—seeking the same objects, and manifesting attachment to the same things, and a desire to promote the same ends.

That they also may be one in us. To be *in* God and *in* Christ is to be *united to* God and Christ. The expression is common in the New Testament. The phrase here used *denotes a union among all Christians founded on and resulting from a union to the same God and Saviour.*

That the world may believe, &c. That the world, so full of animosities and fightings, may see the power of Christian principle in overcoming the sources of contention and producing love, and may thus see that a religion that could produce this *must* be from heaven. See Barnes "Joh 13:34".

This was done. Such was the attachment of the early Christians to each other, that a heathen was constrained to say, "See how these Christians love one another!"

Verse 21. No notes from Barnes on this verse.

{z} "That they all may be one" Ro 12:5

Verse 22. *And the glory,* &c. The *honour* which thou hast conferred on *me* by admitting me to *union* with thee, the same honour I have conferred on them by admitting them to *like union* with me.

May be one, even as we are one. Not in *nature*, or in the mode of existence-for this was not the subject of discourse, and would be impossible—but in feeling, in principle, in purpose. Evincing, as the Father and the Son had always done, the same great aim and plan; not pursuing different interests, or counteracting each other's purposes, or forming parties, but seeking the same ends by the same means. This is the union between the Father and the Son. Always, in the creation, preservation, and redemption of the world, the Father and the Son have sought the same object, and this is to be the model on which Christians should act.

{a} "And the glory which thou gavest" 2 Co 3:15

Verse 23. *May be made perfect in one.* That their union may be complete. That there may be no jars, discords, or contentions. A machine is perfect or complete when it has all its parts and is in good order—when there is no portion of it wanting. So the union of Christians, for which the Saviour prayed, would be complete or perfect if there were no controversies, no envyings, no contentions, and no heart-burnings and jealousies. It is worthy of remark here how entirely *the union of his people* occupied the mind of Jesus as he drew near to death. He saw the danger of strifes and contentions in the church. He knew the imperfections of even the best of men. He saw how prone they would be to passion and ambition; how ready to mistake love of sect or party for zeal for pure religion; how selfish and worldly men in the church might divide his followers, and produce unholy feeling and contention; and he saw, also, how much this would do to dishonour religion. Hence he took occasion, when he was about to die, to impress the importance of union on his disciples. By solemn admonition, and by most tender and affecting appeals to God in supplication, he showed his sense of the value of this union. He used the most sublime and impressive illustration; he adverted to the eternal union between the Father and himself; he reminded them of his love, and of the effect that their union would have on the world, to fix it more deeply in their hearts. The effect has shown the infinite wisdom of the Saviour. The contentions and strifes of Christians have shown his knowledge in foreseeing it. The effect of all this on religion has shown that *he*understood the value of union. Christians have contended long enough. It is time that they should hear the parting admonitions of their Redeemer, and go unitedly against their common foe. The world still lies in wickedness; and the friends of Jesus, bound by the cords of eternal love, should advance together against the common enemy, and spread the triumphs of the gospel around the globe. All that is needful now, under the blessing of God, to convince the world that *God sent the Lord Jesus, is that very union among all Christians for which heprayed*; and when that union of feeling, and purpose, and action shall take place, the task of sending the gospel to all nations will be soon accomplished, and the morning of the millennial glory will dawn upon the world.

THE GOSPEL ACCORDING TO JOHN-Chapter 17-Verse 24

Verse 24. *I will*. This expression, though it commonly denotes *command*, is here only expressive of *desire*. It is used in *prayer*, and it was not the custom of the Saviour to use language of *command* when addressing God. It is often used to express *strong* and *earnest* desire, or a pressing and importunate *wish*, such as we are exceedingly anxious should not be denied, Mr 6:25; 10:35; Mt 12:38; 15:28.

Where I am. In heaven. The Son of God was still in the bosom of the Father, Joh 1:18. See Barnes "Joh 7:34".

Probably the expression here means where *I shall be*.

My glory. My honour and dignity when exalted to the right hand of God. The word "behold" implies more than simply seeing; it means also to participate, to enjoy. See Barnes "Joh 3:3, See Barnes "Mt 5:8".

Thou lovedst me, &c. This is another of the numerous passages which prove that the Lord Jesus existed before the creation of the world. It is not possible to explain it on any other supposition.

{b} "be with me where I am" 1 Th 4:17

THE GOSPEL ACCORDING TO JOHN-Chapter 17-Verse 25

Verse 25. *Hath not known thee*. See Barnes "Joh 17:3".

THE GOSPEL ACCORDING TO JOHN-Chapter 17-Verse 26

Verse 26. *Thy name*. See Barnes "Joh 17:6".

And will declare it. After my resurrection, and by the influence of the Holy Spirit, Lu 24:45; Ac 1:3.

I in them. By my doctrines and the influences of my Spirit. That my religion may show its power, and produce its proper fruits in their minds, Ga 4:19. The discourse in the fourteenth, fifteenth, and sixteenth chapters is the most tender and sublime that was ever pronounced in our world. No composition can be found anywhere so fitted to sustain the soul in trial or to support it in death. This sublime and beautiful discourse is appropriately closed by a solemn and most affecting prayer—a prayer at once expressive of the profoundest reverence for God and the tenderest love for men—simple, grave, tender, sublime, and full of consolation. It is the model for our prayers, and with like reverence, faith, and love we should come before God. This prayer for the church will yet be fully answered; and he who loves the church and the world cannot but cast his eyes onward to that time when all believers shall be one; when contentions, bigotry, strife, and anger shall cease; and when, in perpetual union and love, Christians shall show forth the power and purity of that holy gospel with which the Saviour came to bless mankind. Soon may that happy day arise!

THE GOSPEL ACCORDING TO JOHN- Chapter 18

Verse 1. *The brook Cedron.* This was a small stream that flowed to the east of Jerusalem, through the valley of Jehoshaphat, and divided the city from the Mount of Olives. It was also called *Kidron* and *Kedron.* In summer it is almost dry. The word used here by the evangelist—*ceimarrou* denotes properly a water-stream (from *ceima shower* or *water*, and *rew, rodv,* to*flow, flowing*), and the idea is that of a stream that was swollen by rain or by the melting of the snow (Passow, Lex.). This small rivulet runs along on the east of Jerusalem till it is joined by the water of the pool of Siloam, and the water that flows down on the west side of the city through the valley of Jehoshaphat, and then goes off in a south-east direction to the Dead Sea. (See the Map of the Environs of Jerusalem in vol. i.) Over this brook David passed when he fled from Absalom, 2 Sa 15:23. It is often mentioned in the Old Testament, 1 Ki 15:13;2 Ch 15:16; 2 Ch 30:14; 2 Ki 23:6,12.

Where was a garden. On the west side of the Mount of Olives. This was called *Gethsemane.* See Barnes "Mt 26:36".

It is probable that this was the property of some wealthy man in Jerusalem—perhaps some friend of the Saviour. It was customary for the rich in great cities to have country-seats in the vicinity. This, it seems, was so accessible that Jesus was accustomed to visit it, and yet so retired as to be a suitable place for devotion.

{a} "Cedron" 2 Sa 15:23

Verse 2. *Jesus ofttimes resorted thither.* For what purpose he went there is not declared, but it is probable that it was for retirement and prayer. He had no home in the city, and he sought this place, away from the bustle and confusion of the capital, for private communion with God. Every Christian should have some place—be it a grove, a room, or a garden—where he may be alone and offer his devotions to God. We are not told much of the private habits of Jesus, but we are permitted to know so much of him as to be assured that he was accustomed to seek for a place of retirement, and during the great feasts of the Jews the Mount of Olives was the place which he chose, Lu 21:37; Mt 21:17; Joh 8:1.

Verse 3. *A band.* See Barnes "Mt 26:47"

See Barnes "Mt 27:27"; John passes over the agony of Jesus in the garden, probably because it was so fully described by the other evangelists.

    Lanterns, &c. This was the time of the full moon, but it might have been cloudy, and their taking lights with them shows their determination to find him.

    {b} "Judas, then" Mt 26:47; Mr 14:43; Lu 22:47

THE GOSPEL ACCORDING TO JOHN-Chapter 18-Verse 4

    Verse 4. No Barnes text on this verse.

    {c} "knowing all things that should"

    Joh 10:17,18; Ac 2:28

THE GOSPEL ACCORDING TO JOHN-Chapter 18-Verse 5

    Verse 5. No Barnes text on this verse.

    {d} "Jesus of Nazareth"

    Mt 2:23; Joh 19:19

THE GOSPEL ACCORDING TO JOHN-Chapter 18-Verse 6

    Verse 6. *They went backward*, &c. The *cause* of their retiring in this manner is not mentioned. Various things might have produced it. The frank, open, and fearless *manner* in which Jesus addressed them may have convinced them of his innocence, and deterred them from prosecuting their wicked attempt. His disclosure of himself was sudden and unexpected; and while they perhaps anticipated that he would make an effort to escape, they were amazed at his open and bold profession. Their consciences reproved them for their crimes, and probably the firm, decided, and yet mild manner in which Jesus addressed them, the expression of his unequalled power in knowing how to find the way to the consciences of men, made them feel that they were in the presence of more than mortal man. There is no proof that there was here any miraculous power, any mere physical force, and to suppose that there was greatly detracts from the moral sublimity of the scene.

    {e} "they went backward"

THE GOSPEL ACCORDING TO JOHN-Chapter 18-Verse 7

    Verse 7. No Barnes text on this verse.

THE GOSPEL ACCORDING TO JOHN-Chapter 18-Verse 8

    Verse 8. *Let these go their way.* These apostles. This shows his care and love even in the hour of danger. He expected to die. *They were* to carry the news of his death to the ends of the earth. Hence he, the faithful Captain of salvation, went foremost into trials; he, the Good Shepherd, secured the safety of the flock, and went before them into danger. By the *question* which he asked those who came out against him, he had secured the safety of his apostles. He was answered that they sought for *him.* He demanded that, agreeably to their declaration, they should take him only, and leave his followers at liberty. The wisdom, caution, and prudence of Jesus forsook him in no peril, however sudden, and in no circumstances, however difficult or trying.

{f} "I am he" Isa 53:6; Eph 5:25

Verse 9. *The saying.* Joh 17:12. As he had kept them for more than three years, so he still sought their welfare, even when his death was near.

{g} "Of them which thou gavest" Joh 17:12

Verses 10,11. See Barnes "Mt 26:51, See Barnes "Mt 26:52".

The servant's name was Malchus. His name is mentioned by neither of the other evangelists, nor is it said by the other evangelists who was the disciple that gave the blow. It is probable that both Peter and the servant were alive when the other gospels were written.

{h} "Then Simon Peter" Mt 26:51; Mr 14:47; Lu 22:49,50

Verse 11. No Barnes text on this verse.

{i} "the cup which my Father"

Mt 20:22; 26:39,42

Verse 12. See Mt 26:50.

Verse 13. *To Annas first.* Probably his house was nearest to them, and he had great authority and influence in the Jewish nation. He had been himself a long time high-priest; he had had five sons who had successively enjoyed the office of high-priest, and that office was now filled by his son-in-law. It was of importance, therefore, to obtain his sanction and counsel in their work of evil.

That same year. Joh 11:14.

{k} "Annas" Lu 3:2 {1} "that same year" "And Annas send Christ bound unto Caiphas,
the high priest," Joh 18:24

Verse 14. *Which gave counsel,* &c. Joh 11:49,50. This is referred to her, probably, to show how little prospect there was that Jesus would have *justice* done him in the hands of a man who had already pronounced on the case.

{1} "gave counsel to the Jews. Joh 11:49,50

Verses 15-18. See Barnes "Mt 26:57, See Barnes "Mt 26:58".

Another disciple. Not improbably John. Some critics, however, have supposed that this disciple was one who dwelt at Jerusalem, and who, not being a Galilean, could enter the palace without suspicion. John, however, mentions the circumstance of his being *known* to them, to show why it was that he was not questioned as Peter was. It is not probable that any danger resulted from its being known that he was a follower of Jesus, or that any harm was meditated on *them* for this. The questions asked *Peter* were not asked by those in authority, and his apprehensions which led to his denial were groundless.

THE GOSPEL ACCORDING TO JOHN-Chapter 18-Verse 16
Verse 16. No Barnes text on this verse.

THE GOSPEL ACCORDING TO JOHN-Chapter 18-Verse 17
Verse 17. No Barnes text on this verse.

THE GOSPEL ACCORDING TO JOHN-Chapter 18-Verse 18
Verse 18. No Barnes text on this verse.

THE GOSPEL ACCORDING TO JOHN-Chapter 18-Verse 19
Verse 19. *The high-priest then asked Jesus of his disciples.* To ascertain their number and power. The charge on which they wished to arraign him was that of sedition, or of rebellion against Caesar. To make that plausible, it was necessary to show that he had made *so many* disciples as to form a strong and dangerous faction; but, as they had no direct proof of that, the high-priest insidiously and improperly attempted to draw the Saviour into a confession. Of this he was aware, and referred him to the proper source of evidence—his open, undisguised conduct before the world.

His doctrine. His teaching. The sentiments that he inculcated. The object was doubtless to convict him of teaching sentiments that tended to subvert the Mosaic institutions, or that were treasonable against the Roman government. Either would have answered the design of the Jews, and they doubtless expected that he—an unarmed and despised Galilean, now completely in their power—would easily be drawn into confessions which art and malice could use to procure his condemnation.

THE GOSPEL ACCORDING TO JOHN-Chapter 18-Verse 20
Verse 20. *Openly to the world.* If his doctrine had tended to excite sedition and tumult, if he had aimed to overthrow the government, he would have trained his friends in secret; he would have retired from public view, and would have laid his plans in private. This is the case with all who attempt to subvert existing establishments. Instead of that, he had proclaimed his views to all. He had done it in every place of public concourse—in the synagogue and in the temple. He here speaks the language of one conscious of innocence and determined to insist on his rights.

Always resort. Constantly assemble. They were required to assemble there three times in a year, and great multitudes were there constantly.

In secret, &c. He had taught no private or concealed doctrine. He had taught nothing to his disciples which he had not himself taught in public and commanded them to do, Mt 10:27; Lu 12:3.

{n} "I spoke openly to the world" Lu 4:15; Joh 7:14,26,28; 8:2

{o} "in secret have I said nothing" Ac 26:26

THE GOSPEL ACCORDING TO JOHN-Chapter 18-Verse 21

Verse 21. *Why askest thou me?* Ask them, &c. Jesus here insisted on his rights, and reproves the high-priest for his unjust and illegal manner of extorting a confession from him. If he had done wrong, or taught erroneous and seditious doctrines, it was easy to prove it, and the course which he had a right to demand was that they should establish the charge by fair and incontrovertible evidence. We may here learn,

1st. That, though Jesus was willing to be reviled and persecuted, yet he also insisted that *justice* should be done him.

2nd. He was conscious of innocence, and he had been so open in his conduct that he could appeal to the vast multitudes which had heard him as witnesses in his favour.

3rd. It is proper for us, when persecuted and reviled, meekly but firmly to insist on our rights, and to demand that justice shall be done us. Laws are made to *protect* the innocent as well as to condemn the guilty.

4th. Christians, like their Saviour, should so live that they may confidently appeal to all who have known them as witnesses of the sincerity, purity, and rectitude of their lives, 1 Pe 4:13-16.

THE GOSPEL ACCORDING TO JOHN-Chapter 18-Verse 22

Verse 22. *One of the officers.* One of the *inferior* officers, or those who attended on the court.

With the palm of his hand. This may mean, wave him a blow either with the open hand or with a rod"—the Greek does not determine which. In whatever way it was done, it was a violation of all law and justice. Jesus had showed no disrespect for the office of the high-priest, and if he had, *this* was not the proper way to punish it. The Syriac reads thus: "Smote the *cheek* of Jesus." The Vulgate and Arabic: "Gave him a blow."

{2} "with the palm of his hand" or, "with a rod"

THE GOSPEL ACCORDING TO JOHN-Chapter 18-Verse 23

Verse 23. *Spoken evil.* In my answer to the high-priest. If there was any disrespect to the office, and want of regard for the law which appointed him, then testify to the fact, and let punishment be inflicted according to the law; comp. Ex 22:28.

But if well, an accused person is on trial he is under the protection of the court, and has a right to *demand* that all *legal* measures shall be taken to secure his rights. On this right Jesus insisted, and thus showed that, though he had no disposition to take revenge, yet he claimed that, when arraigned, strict justice should be done. This shows that his precept that *when we are smitten on one cheek we should turn the other* (Mt 5:39), is consistent with a firm demand that justice should be done us. That precept refers, besides, rather to *private* matters than to judicial proceedings. It does not demand that, when we are unjustly arraigned or assaulted, and when the law is in our favour, we should sacrifice our rights to the malignant accuser. Such a surrender would be injustice to the law and to the community, and be giving *legal* triumph to the wicked, and destroying the very *end* of all law. In private matters this effect would not follow, and we should there bear injuries without reviling or seeking for vengeance.

{q} "but if well" 1 Pe 2:19-23

THE GOSPEL ACCORDING TO JOHN-Chapter 18-Verse 24
Verse 24. Comp. Joh 18:13 with Mt 26:57.
{3} "Now Annas" Joh 18:13

THE GOSPEL ACCORDING TO JOHN-Chapter 18-Verse 25
Verses 25,26. See Barnes "Mt 27:1,2".
See Barnes "Mt 26:72, also Mt 26:73-74.

THE GOSPEL ACCORDING TO JOHN-Chapter 18-Verse 26
Verse 26. No Barnes text on this verse.

THE GOSPEL ACCORDING TO JOHN-Chapter 18-Verse 27
Verse 27. No Barnes text on this verse.

THE GOSPEL ACCORDING TO JOHN-Chapter 18-Verse 28
Verse 28. See
Mt 27:1,2.

Hall of judgment. The *praetorium*—the same word that in Mt 27:27, is translated common hall. See Barnes "Mt 27:27".

It was the place where the Roman *praetor*, or governor, heard and decided cases brought before him. Jesus had been condemned by the Sanhedrim, and pronounced guilty of death (Mt 26:66); but they had not power to carry their sentence into execution (Joh 18:31), and they therefore sought that he might be condemned and executed by Pilate.

Lest they should be defiled. They considered the touch of a Gentile to be a defilement, and on this occasion, at least, seemed to regard it as a pollution to enter the *house* of a Gentile. They took care, therefore, to guard themselves against what they considered ceremonial pollution, while they were wholly unconcerned at the enormous crime of putting the innocent Saviour to death, and imbruing their hands in their Messiah's blood. Probably there is not anywhere to be found among men another such instance of petty regard to the mere ceremonies of the law and attempting to keep from pollution, at the same time that their hearts were filled with malice, and they were meditating the most enormous of all crimes. But it shows us how much more concerned men will be at the violation of the mere *forms* and *ceremonies* of religion than at real crime, and how they endeavour to keep their consciences at ease amid their deeds of wickedness by the observance of some of the outward ceremonies of religion—by mere sanctimoniousness.

That they might eat the passover. See Barnes "Mt 26:2, See Barnes "Mt 26:17".

This defilement, produced by contact with a Gentile, they considered as equivalent to that of the contact of a dead body (Le 22:4-6; Nu 5:2), and as disqualifying them to partake of the passover in a proper manner. The word translated *passover* means properly the paschal lamb which was slain and eaten on the observance of this feast. This rite Jesus had observed with his disciples the day before this. It has been supposed by many that he *anticipated* the usual time of observing it one day, and was crucified on the day on which the Jews observed it; but this opinion is improbable. The *very day* of keeping the ordinance was specified in the law of Moses, and it is not probable that the Saviour departed from the commandment. All the circumstances, also, lead us to suppose that he observed it at the usual time and manner, Mt 26:17,19. The only passage which has led to a contrary opinion is this in John; but here the word *passover* does not, of necessity, mean the *paschal* lamb. It probably refers to the feast which followed the sacrifice of the lamb, and which continued seven days. Comp. Nu 28:16,17. *The whole feast* was called the Passover, and they were unwilling to defile themselves, even though the paschal lamb had been killed, because it would disqualify them for participating in the remainder of the ceremonies (Lightfoot).

{s} "Then led they Jesus" Mt 27:2; Mr 15:1; Lu 23:1

{4} "the hall of judgment" or, "Pilate's house" {t} "lest they should be defiled" Ac 10:28

THE GOSPEL ACCORDING TO JOHN-Chapter 18-Verse 29

Verse 29. No Barnes text on this verse.

THE GOSPEL ACCORDING TO JOHN-Chapter 18-Verse 30

Verse 30. *If he were not a malefactor.* A violator of the law. If we had not *determined* that he was such, and was worthy of death, Mt 26:66. From this it appears that they did not deliver him up to be *tried,* but hoped that Pilate would *at once* give sentence that he should be executed according to their request. It is probable that in ordinary cases the Roman governor was not accustomed to make very strict inquiry into the justice of the sentence. The Jewish Sanhedrim tried causes and pronounced sentence, and the sentence was usually approved by the governor; but in this case Pilate, evidently contrary to their expectations, proceeded *himself* to rehear and retry the cause. He had doubtless heard of the miracles of Jesus. He seems to have been strongly prepossessed with the belief of his innocence. He knew that they had delivered him from mere envy (Mt 27:18), and hence he inquired of them the nature of the case, and the kind of charge which they expected to substantiate against him.

Verse 31. *Judge him,* &c. The Jews had not directly *informed* him that they *had* judged him and pronounced him worthy of death. Pilate therefore tells them to inquire into the case; to ascertain the proof of his guilt, and to decide on what the law of Moses pronounced. It has been doubted whether this gave them the power of putting him to death, or whether it was not rather a direction to them to inquire into the case, and inflict on him, if they judged him guilty, the mild punishment which they were yet at liberty to inflict on criminals. Probably the former is intended. As they had already determined that in their view this case demanded the punishment of death, so in their answer to Pilate they *implied* that they *had* pronounced on it, and that he ought to die. They *still,* therefore, *pressed* it on his attention, and refused to obey his injunction to judge him.

It is not lawful, &c. The Jews were accustomed to put persons to death still in a popular tumult (Ac 7:59,60), but they had not the power to do it in any case in a regular way of justice. When they first laid the plan of arresting the Saviour, they did it *to kill him* (Mt 26:4); but whether they intended to do this secretly, or in a tumult, or by the concurrence of the Roman governor, is uncertain. The Jews themselves say that the power of inflicting capital punishment was taken away about forty years before the destruction of the temple; but still it is probable that in the time of Christ they had the power of determining on capital cases in instances that pertained to religion (Josephus, Antiq., b. xiv. ch. 10, 2; comp. *Jewish Wars,* b. vt. ch. 2, § 4). In this case, however, it is supposed that their sentence was to be *confirmed* by the Roman governor. But it is admitted on all hands that they had *not* this power in the case of seditions, tumults, or treason against the Roman government. If they had this power in the case of blasphemy and irreligion, they did not dare to exert it here, because they were afraid of tumult among the people (Mt 26:5); hence they sought to bring in the authority of Pilate. To do this, they endeavoured to make it appear that it was a case of *sedition* and *treason,* and one which therefore *demanded* the interference of the Roman governor. Hence it was on *this charge* that they arraigned him, Lu 23:2. Thus a tumult might be avoided, and the *odium* of putting him to death they expected would fall, not on themselves, but on Pilate.

{u} "It is not lawful" Ge 49:10; Eze 21:27

Verse 32. *That the saying of Jesus,* &c. To wit, that he would be delivered into the hands of the *Gentiles* and be *crucified,* Mt 20:19. Neither of these things would have happened if he had been put to death in the way that the Jews first contemplated, Mt 26:4. Though it should be admitted that they had the power, in *religious cases,* to do this, yet in such a case it would not have been done, as Jesus predicted, by the Gentiles; and even if it should be admitted that they had the right to take life, yet they had not the right to do it by *crucifixion.* This was particularly a Roman punishment. And thus it was ordered, in the providence of God, that the prediction of

Jesus in both these respects was fulfilled.

{v} "That the saying of Jesus" Mt 20:19; Lu 18:32,33

THE GOSPEL ACCORDING TO JOHN-Chapter 18-Verse 33

Verse 33. *Art thou the King of the Jews?* This was *after* they had accused him of perverting the nation, and forbidding to give tribute to Caesar, Lu 23:2,3.

THE GOSPEL ACCORDING TO JOHN-Chapter 18-Verse 34

Verse 34. *Of thyself.* From any conviction of your own mind, or any apprehension of danger. During all the time in which you have been praetor, have you seen anything in me that has led you to apprehend sedition or danger to the Roman power? This evidently was intended to remind Pilate that nothing was proved against him, and to caution him against being influenced by the malicious accusations of others. Jesus demanded a just trial, and claimed that Pilate should not be influenced by any *reports* that he might have heard of him.

THE GOSPEL ACCORDING TO JOHN-Chapter 18-Verse 35

Verse 35. *Am I a Jew?* Am I likely to be influenced by Jewish prejudices and partialities? Am not I, being a Roman, likely to judge impartially, and to decide on the accusations without being biassed by the malignant charges of the accusers?

Thine own nation &c. In this Pilate denies that it was from anything thing that *he* had observed that Jesus was arraigned. He admits that it was from the accusation of others; but then he tells the Saviour that the charge was one of moment, and worthy of the deepest attention. It had come from the *very nation* of Jesus, from his own countrymen, and from the highest authority among the people. As such it demanded consideration, and Pilate besought him to tell him *what he had done*—that is, what there had been in his conduct that had given occasion for this charge.

{w} "own nation" Joh 19:11; Ac 3:13

THE GOSPEL ACCORDING TO JOHN-Chapter 18-Verse 36

Verse 36. *My kingdom,* &c. The charge on which Jesus was arraigned was that of laying claim to the office of a king. He here substantially admits that he *did* claim to be a king, but not in the sense in which the Jews understood it. *They* charged him with attempting to set up an *earthly* kingdom, and of exciting sedition against Caesar. In reply to this, Jesus says that *his kingdom is not of this world*—that is, it is not of the same nature as earthly kingdoms. It was not originated for the same purpose, or conducted on the same plan. He immediately adds a circumstance in which they differ. The kingdoms of the world are defended by arms; they maintain armies and engage in wars. If the kingdom of Jesus had been of this *kind*, he would have excited the multitudes that followed him to prepare for battle. He would have armed the hosts that attended him to Jerusalem. He would not have been alone and unarmed in the garden of Gethsemane. But though he *was* a king, yet his dominion was over the heart, subduing evil passions and corrupt desires, and bringing the soul to the love of peace and unity.

Not from hence. That is, not from this world.

{x} "answered" 1 Ti 6:13 {y} "My kingdom" Ps 45:3,6; Isa 9:6,7; Da 2:44; 7:14; Zec 9:9; Lu 12:14

Joh 6:15; Ro 14:17; Col 1:13

Verse 37. *Art thou a king then?* Dost thou *admit* the charge in any sense, or dost thou lay claim to a kingdom of any kind?

Thou sayest, &c. This is a form of expression denoting *affirmation.* It is equivalent to *yes.*

That I am a king. This does not mean simply that Pilate *affirmed* that he was a king; it does not appear that he had done this; but it means, "Thou affirmest the truth; thou declarest what is correct, for I am, a king." I *am* a king in a certain sense, and do not deny it.

To this end, &c. Comp. Joh 3:11,12, &c. Jesus does not here affirm that he was born to *reign,* or that this was the design of his coming; but it was to bear witness to and to exhibit the truth. By this he showed what was the *nature* of his kingdom. It was not to assert power; not to collect armies; not to subdue nations in battle. It was simply to present *truth* to men, and to exercise dominion only *by* the truth. Hence the only power put forth in restraining the wicked, in convincing the sinner, in converting the heart, in guiding and leading his people, and in sanctifying them, is that which is produced by applying truth to the mind. Men are not *forced* or *compelled* to be Christians. They are made to *see* that they are sinners, that God is merciful, that they need a Redeemer, and that the Lord Jesus is fitted to their case, and yield themselves then wholly to his reign. This is all the power ever used in the kingdom of Christ, and no men in his church have a right to use any other. Alas! how little have persecutors remembered this! And how often, under the pretence of great regard for the kingdom of Jesus, have bigots attempted by force and flames to make all men think as *they* do! We see here the importance which Jesus attached to *truth.* It was his sole business in coming into the world, He had no other end than to establish it. *We* therefore should value it, and seek for it as for hid treasures, Pr 23:23.

Every one, &c. See Joh 8:47.

{z} "I should bear witness" Isa 55:4; Re 1:5; 3:14

{a} "Every one that is of the truth" Joh 8:47; 1 Jo 4:6

Verse 38. *What is truth?* This question was probably asked in *contempt,* and hence Jesus did not answer it. Had the question been sincere, and had Pilate *really* sought it as Nicodemus had done (Joh 3:1), Jesus would not have hesitated to explain to him the nature of his kingdom. They were now alone in the judgment-hall (Joh 18:33), and as soon as Pilate had asked the question, without waiting for an answer, he went out. It is evident that he was satisfied, from the answer of

Jesus (Joh 18:36,37), that he was not a king in the sense in which the Jews accused him; that he would not endanger the Roman government, and consequently that he was *innocent* of the charge alleged against him. He regarded him, clearly, as a fanatic—poor, ignorant, and deluded, but innocent and not dangerous. Hence he sought to release him; and hence, in *contempt*, he asked him this question, and immediately went out, not expecting an answer. This question had long agitated the world. It was the great subject of inquiry in all the schools of the Greeks. Different sects of philosophers had held different opinions, and Pilate now, in derision, asked him, whom *he* esteemed an ignorant fanatic, whether he could solve this long-agitated question. He *might* have had an answer. Had he patiently waited in sincerity, Jesus would have told him what it was. Thousands ask the question in the same way. They have a fixed contempt for the Bible; they deride the instructions of religion; they are unwilling to *investigate* and to wait at the gates of wisdom; and hence, like Pilate, they remain ignorant of the great Source of truth, and die in darkness and in error. *All might* find truth if they would seek it; none ever *will* find it if they do not apply for it to the great source of light—the God of truth, and seek it patiently in the way in which he has chosen to communicate it to mankind. How highly should we prize the Bible! And how patiently and prayerfully should we *search* the Scriptures, that we may not err and die for ever! See Barnes "Joh 14:6".

I find in him no fault. See Lu 23:4.

THE GOSPEL ACCORDING TO JOHN-Chapter 18-Verse 39
Verses 39-40. See Barnes "Mt 27:15"; also Mt 27:16-21.

THE GOSPEL ACCORDING TO JOHN-Chapter 18-Verse 40
Verse 40. No Barnes text on this verse.

THE GOSPEL ACCORDING TO JOHN-
Chapter 19

Verses 1-3.

See Barnes "Mt 27:26, also Mt 27:27-30.

{a} "Then Pilate" Mt 27:26; Mr 15:15 {b} "scourged him" Isa 53:5

Verse 2. No Barnes text on this verse.

Verse 3. No Barnes text on this verse.

Verse 4. *Behold, I bring him forth,* &c. Pilate, after examining Jesus, had gone forth and *declared* to the Jews that he found no fault in him, Joh 18:38. At that time Jesus remained in the judgment-hall. The Jews were not satisfied with that, but demanded still that he should be put to death, Joh 18:39,40. Pilate, disposed to gratify the Jews, returned to Jesus and ordered him to be scourged, as if preparatory to death, Joh 19:1. The patience and meekness with which Jesus bore this seem to have convinced him still more that he was innocent, and he *again* went forth to *declare* his conviction of this; and, to do it more effectually, he said, "Behold, I bring him forth to you, that ye may know," &c.—that they might themselves *see,* and be satisfied, as he had been, of his innocence. All this shows his anxiety to release him, and also shows that the meekness, purity, and sincerity of Jesus had power to convince a Roman governor that he was not guilty. Thus the highest evidence was given that the charges were false, even when he was condemned to die.

Verse 5. *Behold the man.* It is probable that Pilate *pointed* to the Saviour, and his object evidently was to move them to compassion, and to convince them, by a sight of the Saviour himself, that he was innocent. Hence he brought him forth with the crown of thorns, and the purple robe, and with the marks of scourging. Amid all this Jesus was meek, patient, and calm, giving evident proofs of innocence. The conduct of Pilate was as if he had said, \-

"See! The man whom you accuse is arrayed in a gorgeous
robe, as if a king. He has been scourged and mocked.
All this he has borne with patience. See! How calm
and peaceful! Behold his countenance! How mild! His

body scourged, his heard pierced with thorns! Yet in
all this he is meek and patient. This is the man that
you accuse; and he is now brought forth, that you
may see that he is not guilty."

Verse 6. *They cried out, saying, Crucify* him, &c. The view of the Saviour's meekness only exasperated them the more. They had *resolved* on his death; and as they saw Pilate disposed to acquit him, they redoubled their cries, and endeavoured to gain by tumult, and clamour, and terror, what they saw they could not obtain by justice. When men are*determined* on evil, they cannot be reasoned with. Every *argument* tends to defeat their plans, and they press on in iniquity with the more earnestness in proportion as sound reasons are urged to stay their course. Thus sinners go in the way of wickedness down to death. They make up in firmness of purpose what they lack in reason. They are more fixed in their plans in proportion as God faithfully warns them and their friends admonish them.

Take ye him, &c. These are evidently the words of a man *weary* with their importunity and with the subject, and yet resolved not to sanction their conduct. It was not the act of a*judge* delivering him up according to the forms of the law, for they did not understand it so. It was equivalent to this:

"I am satisfied of his innocence, and shall not
pronounce the sentence of death. If *you* are bent
on his ruin—if you are determined to put to death an
innocent man—if *my* judgment does not satisfy you—take
him and put him to death *on your own responsibility,*
and take the consequences. It cannot be done with
my consent, nor in the due form of law; and if done,
it must be by you, without authority, and in the face
of justice."

See Mt 27:24.

Verse 7. *We have a law.* The law respecting blasphemy, Le 24:16; De 13:1-5. They had arraigned Jesus on that charge before the Sanhedrim, and condemned him for it, Mt 26:63-65. But *this* was not the charge on which they had arraigned him before Pilate. They had accused him of *sedition,* Lu 23:2. On *this charge* they were now convinced that they could not get Pilate to condemn him. He declared him innocent. Still bent on his ruin, and resolved to gain their purpose, they now, contrary to their first intention, adduced the *original* accusation on which they had already pronounced him guilty. If they could not obtain his condemnation as *a rebel,* they now sought it as a *blasphemer*, and they appealed to Pilate to sanction what they believed was required in their law. Thus to Pilate himself it became more manifest that he was innocent, that they had attempted to *deceive* HIM, and that the charge on which they had arraigned him was a mere pretence to obtain *his* sanction to their wicked design.

Made himself. Declared himself, or claimed to be.

The Son of God. The law did not forbid this, but it forbade *blasphemy*, and they considered the assumption of this title as the same as blasphemy (Joh 10:30,33,36), and therefore condemned him.

{d} "We have a law" Le 24:16 {e} "because he made himself" Joh 5:18; 10:33

THE GOSPEL ACCORDING TO JOHN-Chapter 19-Verse 8

Verse 8. *When Pilate therefore heard that saying.* That they had accused him of blasphemy. As this was not the charge on which they had arraigned him before his bar, he had not before heard it, and it now convinced him more of their malignity and wickedness.

He was the more afraid. What was the ground of his fear is not declared by the evangelist. It was probably, however, the alarm of his *conscience*, and the fear of vengeance if he suffered such an act of injustice to be done as to put an innocent man to death. He was convinced of his innocence. He saw more and more clearly the design of the Jews; and it is not improbable that a *heathen*, who believed that the gods often manifested themselves to men, dreaded their *vengeance* if he suffered one who claimed to be divine, and who *might* be, to be put to death. It is clear that Pilate was convinced that Jesus was innocent; and in this state of agitation between the convictions of his own conscience, and the clamours of the Jews, and the fear of vengeance, and the certainty that he would do wrong if he gave him up, he was thrown into this state of alarm, and resolved again to question Jesus, that he might obtain satisfaction on the subjects that agitated his mind.

THE GOSPEL ACCORDING TO JOHN-Chapter 19-Verse 9

Verse 9. *Whence art thou?* See Barnes "Joh 7:27".

Pilate knew that he was a Galilean, but this question was asked to ascertain whether he claimed to be the Son of God—whether a mere man, or whether divine.

Jesus gave him no answer. Probably for the following reasons:

1st. He had already told him his design, and the nature of his kingdom, Joh 18:36,37.

2nd. He had said enough to satisfy him of his innocence. Of that Pilate was convinced. His duty was clear, and if he had had firmness to do it, he would not have asked this. Jesus, by his silence, there-fore *rebuked* him for his want of firmness, and his unwillingness to do what his conscience told him was right.

3rd. It is not probable that Pilate would have understood him if he had declared to him the truth about his origin, and about his being the Son of God.

4th. After what had been done —after he had satisfied Pilate of his innocence, and then had been beaten and mocked by his permission—he had no reason to expect justice at his hands, and therefore properly declined to make any farther defence. By this the prophecy Isa 53:7 was remarkably fulfilled.

{f} "Jesus gave him no" Ps 33:13; Isa 53:7; Mt 27:12,14; Php 1:28

THE GOSPEL ACCORDING TO JOHN-Chapter 19-Verse 10

Verse 10. *Speakest thou not*, &c. This is the expression of a man of pride. He was not accustomed to be met with silence like this. He endeavoured, therefore, to address the *fears* of Jesus, and to appall him with the declaration that his life was at his disposal, and that his safety depended on his favour. This arrogance called forth the reply of the Saviour, and he told him that he had *no* power except what was given him from above. Jesus was not, therefore, to be intimidated by any claim of *power* in Pilate. His life was not in his hands, and he could not stoop to ask the *favour* of a *man*.

{g} "I have power to crucify" Da 3:14,15

THE GOSPEL ACCORDING TO JOHN-Chapter 19-Verse 11

Verse 11. *No power*. No such power as you claim. You have not *originated* the power which you have. You have just as much as is *given*, and your ability ex tends no farther.

Except it were given thee. It has been conceded or granted to you. God has ordered your life, your circumstances, and the extent of your dominion. This was a reproof of a proud man in office, who was forgetful of the great Source of his authority, and who supposed that by his own talents or fortune he had risen to his present place. Alas! how many men *in office* forget that God gives them their rank, and vainly think that it is owing to their own talents or merits that they have risen to such an elevation. Men of office and talent, as well as others, should remember that *God* gives them what they have, and that they have no influence except as it is conceded to them from on high.

From above. From God, or by his direction, and by the arrangements of his providence. Ro 13:1: "There is no power but of God; the powers that be are ordained of God." The words "from above" often refer to *God* or to *heaven*, Jas 1:17; Jas 3:15,17; Joh 3:3

(in the Greek). The providence of God was remarkable in so ordering affairs that a man, flexible and yielding like Pilate, should be intrusted with power in Judea. Had it been a man firm and unyielding in his duty—one who could not be terrified or awed by the multitude— Jesus would *not* have been delivered to be crucified, Ac 2:23. God thus brings about his wise ends; and while Pilate was *free*, and *acted out his nature* without compulsion, yet the purposes of God, long before predicted, were fulfilled, and Jesus made an atonement for the sins of the world. Thus God overrules the wickedness and folly of men. He so orders affairs that the *true character* of men shall be *brought out*, and makes use of that character to advance his own great purposes.

Therefore. On this account.

"You are a magistrate. Your power, as such, is given

you by God. You are not, indeed, guilty for *accusing* me, or malignantly arraigning me; but you have power *intrusted* to you over my life; and the Jews, who knew this, and who knew that the power of a magistrate was given to him by God, have the *greater sin* for seeking my condemnation before a tribunal appointed by God, and for endeavouring to obtain so solemn a sanction to their own malignant and wicked purposes. They have endeavoured to avail themselves of the civil power, the sacred appointment of God, and *on this account* their sin is greater."

This does not mean that their sin was greater than that of Pilate, though that was true; but their sin was greater *on account* of the fact that they perseveringly and malignantly endeavoured to obtain the sanction of the magistrate to their wicked proceedings. Nor does it mean, because God had *purposed* his death (Ac 2:23), and given power to Pilate, that *therefore* their sin was greater, for *God's purpose* in the case made it neither more nor less. It did not change the nature of their free acts. This passage teaches no such doctrine, but that their sin was *aggravated* by malignantly endeavouring to obtain the sanction of a magistrate who was invested with authority *by God*, and who wielded the power that *God* gave him. By this Pilate *ought* to have been convinced, and *was* convinced, of their wickedness, and hence he sought more and more to release him.

He that delivered me. The singular here is put for the plural, including Judas, the high-priests, and the Sanhedrim.

{h} "thou couldest have no power" Lu 22:53; Joh 7:30 {i} "except" Ps 39:9 {k} "he that delivered me" Mr 14:44; Joh 18:3 {l} "the greater sin" He 6:4-8; Jas 4:17

Verse 12. *Sought to release him.* He was more and more convinced of his innocence, and more unwilling to yield him to mere malice and envy in the face of justice.

But the Jews cried out, &c. This moved Pilate to deliver Jesus into their hands. He feared that he would be accused of unfaithfulness to the interests of the Roman emperor if he did not condemn a man whom *his own nation* had accused of sedition. The Roman emperor then on the throne was exceedingly jealous and tyrannical, and the *fear* of losing his favour induced Pilate to deliver Jesus into their hands.

Caesar's friend. The friend of the Roman emperor. The name of the reigning emperor was Tiberius. After the time of Julius Caesar all the emperors were called *Caesar*, as all the kings of Egypt were called *Pharaoh*. This emperor was, during the latter part of his reign, the most cruel, jealous, and wicked that ever sat on the Roman throne.

{m} "whosoever maketh himself" Lu 23:2; Ac 17:7

Verse 13. *Judgment-seat.* The tribunal or place of pronouncing sentence. He came here to deliver him, in due form of law, into the hands of the Jews.

Pavement. This was an area or room of the judgment-hall whose floor was made of small square stones of various colours. This was common in palaces and houses of wealth and splendour. See Barnes "Mt 9:2".

Gabbatha. This word is not elsewhere used. It comes from a word signifying to be elevated. The name given to the place by the Hebrews was conferred from its being the place of the tribunal, as an elevated place.

{n} "When Pilate therefore heard" Pr 29:25; Ac 4:19

Verse 14. *The preparation of the passover.* See Barnes "Mr 15:42".

The sixth hour. Twelve o'clock. Mark says (Mr 15:25) that it was the third hour. See the difficulty explained in the Notes on that place. See Barnes "Mr 15:42".

{o} "it was the preparation" Mt 27:62

Verse 15. No Barnes text on this verse.

{p} "We have no king"

Ge 49:10

Verses 16-22. See Barnes "Mt 27:32"; also Mt 27:33-37.

{q} "delivered him" Mt 27:26; Mr 15:15; Lu 23:24

Verse 17. No Barnes text on this verse.

{r} "went forth"

Nu 15:36; He 13:12

Verse 18. No Barnes text on this verse.

Verse 19. No Barnes text on this verse.

    Mt 27:37; Mr 15:26; Lu 23:38

THE GOSPEL ACCORDING TO JOHN-Chapter 19-Verse 20
    Verse 20. No Barnes text on this verse.

THE GOSPEL ACCORDING TO JOHN-Chapter 19-Verse 21
    Verse 21. No Barnes text on this verse.

THE GOSPEL ACCORDING TO JOHN-Chapter 19-Verse 22
    Verse 22. *What I have written,* &c. This declaration implied that he would make no change. He was impatient, and weary of their solicitations. He had yielded to them contrary to the convictions of his own conscience, and he now declared his purpose to yield no farther.

THE GOSPEL ACCORDING TO JOHN-Chapter 19-Verse 23
    Verse 23. *His garments.* The plural here is used to denote the *outer garment.* It was made, commonly, so as to be easily thrown on or off, and when they laboured or walked it was girded about the loins. See Barnes "Mt 5:40".

    Four parts. It seems, from this, that there were four soldiers employed as his executioners.
    His coat. His under garment, called the *tunic.*
    Was without seam. Josephus (Antiq., b. iii. ch. 8, 4) says of the garment or coat of the high-priest that

    "this vesture was not composed of two pieces, nor was
    it sewed together upon the shoulders and the sides;
    but it was one long vestment, so woven as to have
    an aperture for the neck. It was also parted where
    the hands were to come out."

    It seems that the Lord Jesus, the great High-priest of his people, had also a coat made in a similar manner. Comp. Ex 39:22.
    {1} "woven" or, "wrought" {t} "from the top throughout" Ex 39:22

THE GOSPEL ACCORDING TO JOHN-Chapter 19-Verse 24
    Verse 24. *Let us not rend it.* It would then have been useless. The *outer* garment, being composed of several parts—fringes, borders. &c. De 12:12 could be easily divided.
    That the scripture Ps 22:18.
    {u} "They parted my raiment" Ps 22:18

THE GOSPEL ACCORDING TO JOHN-Chapter 19-Verse 25
    Verse 25. No Barnes text on this verse.

{2} "Cleophas" or, "Clopas" {v} "and Mary Magdalene"
Lu 24:18

Verse 26. *The disciple—whom he loved.* See Joh 13:23.

Woman. This appellation certainly implied no disrespect. See Barnes "Joh 2:4".

Behold thy son! This refers to *John*, not to Jesus himself. Behold, my beloved disciple shall be to you *a son*, and provide for you, and discharge toward you the duties of an affectionate child. Mary was poor. It would even seem that now she had no home. Jesus, in his dying moments, filled with tender regard for his mother, secured for her an adopted son, obtained for her a home, and consoled her grief by the prospect of attention from him who was the most beloved of all the apostles. What an example of filial attention! What a model to all children! And how lovely appears the dying Saviour, thus remembering his afflicted mother, and making her welfare one of his last cares on the cross, and even when making atonement for the sins of the world!

{x} "Woman" Joh 13:23

Verse 27. *Behold thy mother!* One who is to be to thee as a mother. The fact that she was the mother of Jesus would secure the kindness of John, and the fact that she was now intrusted to him demanded of him affectionate regard and tender care.

From that hour, &c. John seems to have been in better circumstances than the other apostles. See Joh 18:16. Tradition says that she continued to live with him in Judea till the time of her death, which occurred about fifteen years after the death of Christ.

{y} "thy mother" 1 Ti 5:2

Verses 28-30. See Barnes "Mt 27:46, also Mt 27:47-50.

That the scripture might be fulfilled, saith, I thirst. See Ps 69:21. Thirst was one of the most distressing circumstances attending the crucifixion. The wounds were highly inflamed, and a raging fever was caused, usually, by the sufferings on the cross, and this was accompanied by insupportable thirst. See Barnes "Mt 27:35".

A Mameluke, or Turkish officer, was crucified, it is said in an Arabic manuscript recently translated, on the banks of the river Barads, under the castle of Damascus. He was nailed to the cross on Friday, and remained till Sunday noon, when he died. After giving an account of the crucifixion, the narrator proceeds:

"I have heard this from one who witnessed it; and he

thus remained till he died, patient and silent,
without wailing, but looking around him to the
right and the left, upon the people. But he begged
for water, and none was given him; and the hearts of
the people were melted with compassion for him,
and with pity on one of God's creatures, who, yet a
boy, was suffering under so grievous a trial. In the
meantime the water was flowing around him, and he
gazed upon it, and longed for one drop of it; and he
complained of thirst all the first day, after which
he was silent, for God gave him strength."

—Wiseman's Lectures, p. 164, 165, ed. Andover.
{a} "scripture might be fulfilled" Ps 69:21

THE GOSPEL ACCORDING TO JOHN-Chapter 19-Verse 29
Verse 29. No Barnes text on this verse.

THE GOSPEL ACCORDING TO JOHN-Chapter 19-Verse 30
Verse 30. *It is finished.* The sufferings and agonies in redeeming man are over. The work long contemplated, long promised, long expected by prophets and saints, is done. The toils in the ministry, the persecutions and mockeries, and the pangs of the garden and the cross, are ended, and man is redeemed. What a wonderful declaration was this! How full of consolation to man! And how should this dying declaration of the Saviour reach every heart and affect every soul!
{b} "It is finished" Joh 17:4 {c} "gave up the ghost" Isa 53:10,12; Heb 2:14,15

THE GOSPEL ACCORDING TO JOHN-Chapter 19-Verse 31
Verse 31. *The preparation.* See Joh 19:4. The law required that the bodies of those who were hung should not remain suspended during the night. See De 21:22,23. That law was made when the punishment by crucifixion was unknown, and when those who were suspended would almost immediately expire. In the punishment by crucifixion, life was lengthened out for four, five, or eight days. The Jews therefore requested that their death might be hastened, and that the land might not be polluted by their bodies remaining suspended on the Sabbath-day.
Was an high day. It was,
1st. The Sabbath.
2nd. It was the day on which the paschal feast properly commenced. It was called a *high day* because that year the feast of the Passover commenced on the Sabbath. Greek, "Great day."
Their legs might be broken. To hasten their death. The effect of this, while they were suspended on the cross, would be to increase their pain by the act of breaking them, and to

deprive their body of the support which it received from the feet, and to throw the whole weight on the hands. By this increased torment their lives were soon ended. Lactantius says that this was commonly done by the Romans to persons who were crucified. The common period to which persons crucified would live was several days. To *compensate* for those *lingering*agonies, so that the full amount of suffering might be endure, they *increased* their sufferings by breaking their limbs, and thus hastening their death.

THE GOSPEL ACCORDING TO JOHN-Chapter 19-Verse 32
Verse 32. No Barnes text on this verse.

THE GOSPEL ACCORDING TO JOHN-Chapter 19-Verse 33
Verse 33. *Saw that he was dead.* Saw by the indications of death on his person, and perhaps by the testimony of the centurion, Mt 27:54. The death of Jesus was doubtless hastened by the intense agony of the garden, and the peculiar sufferings endured as an atonement for sin on the cross. Comp. Mt 27:46.

THE GOSPEL ACCORDING TO JOHN-Chapter 19-Verse 34
Verse 34. *One of the soldiers.* One of those appointed to watch the bodies till they were dead. This man appears to have doubted whether he was dead, and, in order to see whether he was not yet sensible, he pierced him with his spear. The Jews designed that his legs should be broken, but this was prevented by the providence of God; yet in another way more satisfactory proof was obtained of his death than would have been by the breaking of his legs. This was so ordered, no doubt, that there might be the *fullest proof* that he was truly dead; that it could not be pretended that he had swooned away and revived, and so, therefore, that there could not be the least doubt of his resurrection to life.

With a spear. The common spear which soldiers used in war. There can be no doubt that such a stroke from the strong arm of a Roman soldier would have caused death, if he had not been already dead; and it was, doubtless, to furnish this conclusive proof that he was *actually dead*, and that an atonement had thus been made for mankind, that John mentions so particularly this fact. Let the following circumstances be remembered, showing that death *must* have ensued from such a wound:

1st. The Saviour was elevated but a little from the ground, so as to be easily reached by the spear of a soldier.

2nd. The wound must have been *transversely upward*, so as to have penetrated into the body, as he could not have stood directly under him.

3rd. It was probably made with a strong arm and with violence.

4th. The spear of the Roman soldier was a lance which tapered very gently to a point, and would penetrate easily.

5th. The wound was comparatively a *large* wound. It was so large *as to admit the hand* (Joh

20:27); but for a lance thus tapering to have made a wound so wide as to admit the hand, it must have been *at least* four or five inches in depth, and must have been such as to have made death certain. If it be remembered that this blow was *probably* in the left side, the conclusion is inevitable that death would have been the consequence of such a blow. To make out this fact was of special importance, probably, in the time of John, as the reality of the death of Jesus was denied by the Gnostics, many of whom maintained that he died *in appearance only*.

Pierced his side. Which side is not mentioned, nor can it be certainly known. The common opinion is that it was the left side. Car. Frid. Gruner (*Commentatio Anti-guavia Medica de Jesu Christi Morte, p. 30-36*) has attempted to show that it must have been the left side. See Wiseman's *Lectures*, p. 161,162, and Kuinoel on Joh 19:34, where the arguments of Gruner are fully stated. It is clear that the spear pierced to the region of the heart.

And forthwith came, &c. This was evidently a natural effect of thus piercing the side. Such a flowing of blood and water makes it probable that the spear reached the heart, and if Jesus had not before been dead, this would have closed his life. The heart is surrounded by a membrane called the *pericardium*. This membrane contains a serous matter or liquor resembling water, which prevents the surface of the heart from becoming dry by its continual motion (Webster). It was this which was pierced and from which the water flowed. The point of the spear also reached one of the ventricles of the heart, and the blood, yet warm, rushed forth, either mingled with or followed by the water of the pericardium, so as to *appear* to John to be blood and water flowing together. This was a natural effect, and would follow in any other case. Commentators have almost uniformly supposed that this was significant; as, for example, that the blood was an emblem of the eucharist, and the water of baptism, or that the blood denoted justification, and the water sanctification; but that this was the design there is not the slightest evidence. It was strictly a natural result, adduced by John to establish *one* fact on which the whole of Christianity turns —*that he was truly dead.* On this depends the doctrine of the atonement, of his resurrection, and all the prominent doctrines of religion. This fact it was of importance to prove, that it might not be pretended that he had only suffered a *syncope*, or had fainted. This John establishes. He shows that those who were sent to hasten his death *believed* that he had expired; that then a soldier inflicted a wound which *would* have terminated life if he had not been already dead; and that the infliction of this wound was followed by the fullest proof that he had truly expired. On this *fact* he dwells with the interest which became a subject of so much importance to the world, and thus laid the foundation for undoubted assurance that the Lord Jesus *died* for the sins of men.

{g} "blood" Heb 9:22,23; 1 Jo 5:6,8

{h} "water" 1 Pe 3:21.

THE GOSPEL ACCORDING TO JOHN-Chapter 19-Verse 35

Verse 35. *He that saw it.* John himself. He is accustomed to speak of himself in the third person.

His record is true. His testimony is true. Such was the *known* character of this writer, such his sacred regard for truth, that he could appeal to that with full assurance that all would put confidence in him. He often appeals thus to the fact that his testimony was *known* to be true. It would be well if *all* Christians had such a character that their *word* would be assuredly believed.

{i} "And he that saw" Joh 1:1-3

Verse 36. *That the scripture should be fulfilled.* See Ex 12:46. John here regards the paschal lamb as an emblem of Christ; and as in the law it was commanded that a bone of that lamb should not be broken, so, in the providence of God, it was ordered that a bone of the Saviour should not be broken. The Scripture thus received a complete fulfillment respecting both the type and the antitype. Some have supposed, however, that John referred to Ps 34:20.

Verse 37. *Another scripture*, Zec 12:10. We must here be struck with the wonderful providence of God, that so *many* scriptures were fulfilled in his death. All these things happened without any such *design* on the part of the men engaged in these scenes; but whatever was done by Jew or Gentile tended to the fulfillment of prophecies long on record, and with which the Jews themselves ought to have been familiar. Little did they suppose, when delivering him to Pilate—when he was mocked—when they parted his garments—when they pierced him—that they were fulfilling ancient predictions, But in this way God had so ordered it that the firmest foundation should be laid for the belief that he was the true Messiah, and that the designs of wicked men should all be overruled to the fulfillment of the great plans which God had in sending his Son.

{l} "another scripture" Ps 22:16; Zec 12:10; Re 1:7

Verses 38-42. See Barnes "Mt 27:57, also Mt 27:58-61.

{m} "for fear of the Jews" Joh 9:22

Verse 39. No notes from Barnes on this verse.

{n} "Nicodemus"

Joh 3:1,2; 7:50

{o} "brought a mixture" 2 Ch 16:14

Verse 40. No notes from Barnes on this verse.

{p} "wound it in linen"

Ac 5:6

Verse 41. No notes from Barnes on this verse.

Verse 42. No notes from Barnes on this verse.
{q} "laid they Jesus"
Isa 53:9; 1 Co 15:4
{r} "because of the Jew's" Joh 19:31

THE GOSPEL ACCORDING TO JOHN- Chapter 20

Verses 1-12. For an account of the resurrection of Christ, See Barnes Notes on Matthew 27.

{a} "first day of week"

Mt 28:1; Mr 16:1; Lu 24:1

Verse 2. No notes from Barnes on this verse.

{b} "other disciple"

Joh 13:23; 19:26; 21:7,24

Verse 3. No notes from Barnes on this verse.

{c} "Peter"

Lu 24:12

Verse 4. No notes from Barnes on this verse.

{d} "did outrun"

Lu 13:30

Verse 5. No notes from Barnes on this verse.

{e} "the linen clothes"

Joh 19:40

Verse 6. No notes from Barnes on this verse.

Verse 7. No notes from Barnes on this verse.

{f} "napkin"

Joh 11:44

Verse 8. No notes from Barnes on this verse.

Verse 9. *The scripture.* See Lu 24:26,46. The sense or meaning of the various predictions that foretold his death, as, for example, Ps 2:7, compare Ac 13:33; Ps 16:9,10, compare Ac 2:25-32; Ps 110:1 compare Ac 2:34,35.

{g} "the scripture" Ps 16:10; Ac 2:25-31; 13:34,35

THE GOSPEL ACCORDING TO JOHN-Chapter 20-Verse 10
Verse 10. No notes from Barnes on this verse.

THE GOSPEL ACCORDING TO JOHN-Chapter 20-Verse 11
Verse 11. No notes from Barnes on this verse.
{h} "and looked"
Mr 16:5

THE GOSPEL ACCORDING TO JOHN-Chapter 20-Verse 12
Verse 12. No notes from Barnes on this verse.

THE GOSPEL ACCORDING TO JOHN-Chapter 20-Verse 13
Verse 13. *They have taken away*. That is, the disciples or friends of Jesus who had laid him there. Perhaps it was understood that the body was deposited there only to remain over the Sabbath, with an intention then of removing it to some other place of burial. Hence they hastened *early* in the morning to make preparation, and Mary supposed they had arrived before her and had taken him away.

THE GOSPEL ACCORDING TO JOHN-Chapter 20-Verse 14
Verse 14. *Knew not that it was Jesus*. She was not expecting to see him. It was yet also twilight, and she could not see distinctly.

{i} "saw Jesus standing" Mt 28:9; Mr 16:9 {k} "knew not that" Lu 24:16,31; Joh 21:4

THE GOSPEL ACCORDING TO JOHN-Chapter 20-Verse 15
Verse 15. No notes from Barnes on this verse.
{l} "and I will take him away"
So 3:2

THE GOSPEL ACCORDING TO JOHN-Chapter 20-Verse 16
Verse 16. *Jesus saith unto her, Mary*. This was spoken, doubtless, in a tone of voice that at once recalled him to her recollection.

Rabboni. This is a Hebrew word denoting, literally,*my great master*. It was one of the titles given to Jewish teachers. This title was given under three forms: (a) *Rab*, or master—the lowest degree of honour. (b) *Rabbi*, my master—a title of higher dignity. (c) *Rabboni*, my great master —the most honourable of all. This title, among the Jews, was only given to seven persons, all persons of great eminence. As given by Mary to the Saviour, it was at once an expression of her joy, and an acknowledgment of him as her Lord and Master. It is not improbable that she, filled with joy, was about to cast herself at his feet.

{m} "Mary" Is 43:1; Joh 10:3

Verse 17. *Touch me not*, &c. This passage has given rise to a variety of interpretations. Jesus required Thomas to touch him (Joh 20:27), and it has been difficult to ascertain why he forbade this now to Mary. The reason why he directed Thomas to do this was, that he doubted whether he had been restored to life. Mary did not doubt that. The reason why he forbade her to touch him now is to be sought in the circumstances of the case. Mary, filled with joy and gratitude, was about to prostrate herself at his feet, disposed to *remain* with him, and offer him there her homage as her risen Lord. This is probably included in the word *touch* in this place; and the language of Jesus may mean this: "Do not approach me *now* for this purpose. Do not *delay* here. Other opportunities will yet be afforded to see me. I have not yet ascended— that is, I am not *about* to ascend *immediately*, but shall remain yet on earth to afford opportunity to my disciples to enjoy my presence." From Mt 28:9, it appears that the women, when they met Jesus, *held him by the feet and worshipped him.* This species of adoration it was probably the intention of Mary to offer, and this, *at that time*, Jesus forbade, and directed her to go at once and give his disciples notice that he had risen.

My brethren. See Joh 15:15.

My Father and your Father, &c. Nothing was better fitted to afford them consolation than this assurance that *his* God was *theirs*, and that, though he had been slain, they were still indissolubly united in attachment to the same Father and God.

{o} "my brethren" Ps 22:22; Ro 8:29; Heb 2:11

{p} "I ascend" Joh 16:28 {q} "your Father" Ro 8:14,15; 2 Co 6:18; Ga 3:26; 4:6,7

{r} "my God" Eph 1:17 {s} "your God" Ge 17:7,8; Ps 43:4,5; 48:14; Isa 41:10; Jer 31:33

Eze 36:28; Zec 13:9; Heb 11:16; Re 21:3

Verse 18. No notes from Barnes on this verse.

{t} "Mary Magdalene"

Mt 28:10

Verse 19. *The same day at evening.* On the first day of the week, the day of the resurrection of Christ.

When the doors were shut. This does not mean that the doors were *fastened*, though that might have been the case, but only that they were closed. Jesus had been taken from them, and it was natural that they should apprehend that the Jews would next attempt to wreak their vengeance on his followers. Hence they met in the evening, and with closed doors, lest the Jews should bring against them the same charge of sedition that they had against the Lord Jesus. It is not certainly said what was the *object* of their assembling, but it is not unreasonable to suppose that it was to talk over the events which had just occurred, to deliberate about their condition, and to engage in acts of worship. Their minds were doubtless much agitated. They had seen their Master taken away and put to death; but a part of their number also had affirmed that they had seen him alive. In this state of things they naturally came together in a time and place of safety. It was not uncommon for the early Christians to hold their meetings for worship in the *night*. In times of persecution they were forbidden to assemble during the day, and hence they were compelled to meet in the night. Pliny the younger, writing to Trajan, the Roman emperor, and giving an account of Christians, says that "they were wont to meet together on a stated day before it was light, and sing among themselves alternately a hymn to Christ as God." True Christians will love to meet together for worship. Nothing will prevent this; and one of the evidences of piety is a desire to assemble to hear the Word of God, and to offer to him prayer and praise. It is worthy of remark that this is the first assembly that was convened for worship on the Lord's day, and in that assembly Jesus was present. Since that time, the day has been observed in the church as the Christian Sabbath, particularly to commemorate the resurrection of Christ.

Came Jesus, &c. There is no evidence that he came into their assembly in any *miraculous* manner. For anything that appears to the contrary, Jesus entered in the usual way and manner, though *his* sudden appearance alarmed them.

Peace be unto you. The *sudden* manner of his appearance, and the fact that most of them had not before seen him since his resurrection, tended to alarm them. Hence he addressed them in the usual form of salutation to allay their fears, and to assure them that it was their own Saviour and Friend.

{u} "The same day at evening" Mr 16:14; Lu 24:36; 1 Co 15:5

THE GOSPEL ACCORDING TO JOHN-Chapter 20-Verse 20

Verse 20. *He showed unto them his hands*, &c. In this manner he gave them indubitable proofs of his identity. He showed them that he was the *same* Being who had suffered; that he had truly risen from the dead, and had come forth with the same body. That body had not yet put on its glorified form. It was necessary *first* to establish the proof of his resurrection, and that could be done *only* by his appearing as he was when he died.

{v} "Then were his disciples" Joh 16:22

THE GOSPEL ACCORDING TO JOHN-Chapter 20-Verse 21

Verse 21. *As my Father hath sent me.* As God sent me to preach, to be persecuted, and to suffer; to make known his will, and to offer pardon to men, so I send you. This is the design and the extent of the commission of the ministers of the Lord Jesus. He is their model; and they will be successful only as they *study HIS character* and imitate his example. This commission he proceeds to confirm by endowing them all with the gift of the Holy Ghost.

{w} "Peace be unto you" Joh 14:27 {x} "so send I you" Mt 28:19; Joh 17:18; 2 Ti 2:2; Heb 3:1

Verse 22. *He breathed on* them. It was customary for the prophets to use some significant act to *represent* the nature of their message. See Jeremiah chapters 13 and 18, etc. In this case the act of *breathing* was used to represent the nature of the influence that would come upon them, and the *source* of that influence. When man was created, God *breathed* into him the breath of life, Ge 2:7. The word rendered *spirit* in the Scriptures denotes *wind, air, breath,* as well as Spirit. Hence the operations of the Holy Spirit are compared to the wind,Joh 3:8; Ac 2:2.

Receive ye the Holy Ghost. His breathing on them was a certain sign or pledge that they would be endowed with the influences of the Holy Spirit. Comp. Ac 1:4, John chapter 2.

{y} "Receive ye" Ac 2:4,33

Verse 23. *Whose soever sins,* &c. See Barnes "Mt 16:19"

See Barnes "Mt 18:18".

It is worthy of remark here that Jesus confers the same power on *all* the apostles. He gives to no one of them any peculiar authority. If *Peter,* as the Papists pretend, had been appointed to any peculiar authority, it is wonderful that the Saviour did not here hint at any such pre-eminence. This passage conclusively proves that they were invested with equal power in organizing and governing the church. The authority which he had given Peter to preach the gospel *first* to the Jews and the Gentiles, does not militate against this. See Barnes "Mt 16:18, See Barnes "Mt 16:19".

This authority given them was full proof that they were inspired. The meaning of the passage is not that *man* can forgive sins—that belongs only to God (Isa 43:23), but that they should be *inspired*; that in founding the church, and in declaring the will of God, they should be taught by the Holy Ghost to *declare on what terms, to what characters, and to what temper of mind* God would extend forgiveness of sins. It was not authority to *forgive individuals,* but to establish in all the churches the *terms* and *conditions* on which men might be pardoned, with a promise that God would *confirm* all that they taught; that all might have assurance of forgiveness who would comply with those terms; and that those who did not comply should not be forgiven, but that their sins should be retained. This commission is *as far as possible* from the authority which the Roman Catholic claims of remitting sin and of pronouncing pardon.

{z} "Whose soever" Mt 16:19; 18:18

Verse 24. No Barnes text on this verse.

{a} "Thomas"

Joh 11:16

Verse 25. *Except I shall see*, &c. It is not known what was the ground of the incredulity of Thomas. It is probable, however, that it was, in part, at least, the effect of deep grief, and of that despondency which fills the mind when a long-cherished hope is taken away. In such a case it requires proof of uncommon clearness and strength to over-come the despondency, and to convince us that we *may* obtain the object of our desires. Thomas has been much blamed by expositors, but he asked only for proof that would be satisfactory in his circumstances. The testimony of *ten* disciples *should* have been indeed sufficient, but an opportunity was thus given to the Saviour to convince the last of them of the truth of his resurrection. This incident shows, what all the conduct of the apostles proves, that they had not *conspired* together to impose on the world. Even they were slow to believe, and one of them refused to rely even on the testimony of *ten* of his brethren. How unlike this to the conduct of men who *agree* to impose a story on mankind! Many are like Thomas. Many *now* are unwilling to believe because they do not *see* the Lord Jesus, and with just as little reason as Thomas had. The *testimony* of those eleven men— including Thomas— who saw him alive after he was crucified; who were willing to lay down their lives to attest that they had seen him alive; who had nothing to gain by imposture, and whose conduct was removed as far as possible from the appearance of imposture, should be regarded as ample proof of the fact that he rose from the dead.

{b} "But he said unto them" Ps 78:11,32

Verse 26. *And after eight days again.* That is, on the return of the first day of the week. From this it appears that they thus early set apart this day for assembling together, and Jesus countenanced it by appearing twice with them. It was *natural* that the apostles should observe this day, but not probable that they would do it without the sanction of the Lord Jesus. His repeated presence gave such a sanction, and the historical fact is indisputable that from this time this day was observed as the Christian Sabbath. See Ac 20:7; 1 Co 16:2; Re 1:10.

{c} "Peace be unto you" Isa 26:12

Verse 27. No Barnes text on this verse.

{d} "hand"

1 Jo 1:1

{e} "be not faithless" 1 Ti 1:14

Verse 28. *My Lord and my God.* In this passage the name *God* is expressly given to Christ, in his own presence and by one of his own apostles. This declaration has been considered as a clear proof of the divinity of Christ, for the following reasons:

1st. There is no evidence that this was a mere expression, as some have supposed, of surprise or astonishment.

2nd. The language was addressed to Jesus himself— "*Thomas*— said *UNTO HIM.*"

3rd. The Saviour did not *reprove* him or *check* him as using any improper language. If he had not been divine, it is impossible to reconcile it with his *honesty* that he did not rebuke the disciple. No *pious man* would have allowed such language to be ad dressed to him. Comp. Ac 14:13-15; Re 22:8,9.

4th. The Saviour proceeds immediately to *commend* Thomas for believing; but what was the *evidence* of his believing? It was this declaration, and this only. If this was a mere exclamation of *surprise*, what proof was it that Thomas believed? Before this he doubted. Now he believed, and gave utterance to his belief, *that Jesus was his Lord and his God.*

5th. If this was not the meaning of Thomas, then his exclamation was a mere act of profaneness, and the Saviour would not have commended him for taking the name of the Lord his God in vain. The passage proves, therefore, that it is proper to apply to Christ the name *Lord* and GOD, and thus accords with what John affirmed in Joh 1:1, and which is established throughout this gospel.

{f} "My Lord and my God." Ps 118:28; Joh 5:23; 1 Ti 3:16

THE GOSPEL ACCORDING TO JOHN-Chapter 20-Verse 29

Verse 29. *Because thou hast seen me.* Because you have looked upon my body, and seen the proofs that I am the same Saviour that was crucified. Jesus here *approves* the faith of Thomas, but more highly commends the faith of those who should believe without having seen.

Blessed. Happy, or worthy of the divine approbation. The word has here the force of the comparative degree, signifying that they would be in some respects *more* blessed than Thomas. They would evince higher faith.

That have not seen, &c. Those who should be convinced by the testimony of the apostles, and by the influences of the Spirit. They would evince *stronger faith. All faith* is of things not seen; and God blesses those most who most implicitly rely on his word.

{g} "blessed are they" 1 Pe 1:8

THE GOSPEL ACCORDING TO JOHN-Chapter 20-Verse 30

Verse 30. *Other signs.* Other miracles. Many were recorded by the other evangelists, and many which he performed were never recorded. Joh 21:25,

{h} "And many other signs" Joh 21:25

Verse 31. *These are written.* Those recorded in this *gospel.*

That ye might believe, &c. This is a clue to the design which John had in view in writing this *gospel.* The whole *scope* or *end* of the book is to accomplish two objects:

1st. To prove that Jesus was the Messiah; and,

2nd. That they who looked at the proof might be convinced and have eternal life. This design is kept in view throughout the book. The miracles, facts, arguments, instructions, and conversations of our Lord all tend to this. This point had not been kept in view so directly by either of the other evangelists, and it was reserved for the last of the apostles to collect those arguments, and make out a connected demonstration *that Jesus was the Messiah.* If this design of John is kept steadily in view, it will throw much light on the book, and the argument is unanswerable, framed after the strictest rules of reasoning, infinitely beyond the skill of man, and having throughout the clearest evidence of demonstration.

{i} "But these are written" Lu 1:4

THE GOSPEL ACCORDING TO JOHN-Chapter 21

Verse 1. *The sea of Tiberias.* Called also the Sea of Galilee, being situated in Galilee. See Barnes "Mt 4:18".

In this place Jesus had promised to meet them, Mr 14:28; 16:7; Mt 26:32; 28:10.

This interview of Jesus is but just mentioned by Matthew (Mt 28:16), and is omitted by both Mark and Luke. This is the reason why John relates so particularly what occurred there. Galilee was a retired place where they would be free from danger, and was therefore a safe and convenient situation for Jesus to meet them, in order to give them his last instructions.

On this wise. Thus. In this manner.

Verse 2. *There were together.* Probably residing in the same place. While they were waiting for the promise of the Holy Spirit, they still found it proper to be usefully employed. Their Master had been taken away by death, and the promised Spirit had not descended on them. In the interval—before the promised Spirit was poured upon them— they chose not to be idle, and therefore returned to their former employment. It is to be remarked, also, that they had no other means of support. While with Jesus, they were commonly supplied by the kindness of the people; but now, when the Saviour had died, they were cut off from this means of support, and returned to the honest labour of their early lives. Moreover, they had been directed by the Saviour to repair to a mountain in Galilee, where he would meet them, Mt 28:10. This was probably not far from the Sea of Galilee, so that, until he came to them, they would naturally be engaged in their old employment. Ministers of the gospel should be willing to labour, if necessary, for their own support, and should not esteem such labour dishonourable. God has made *employment* indispensable to man, and if the field of labour is not open in one way, they should seek it in another. If at any time the people withhold the supply of their wants, they should be able and willing to seek support in some other honest occupation.

{a} "Nathanael of Cana" Joh 1:45 {b} "the *sons* of Zebedee" Mt 4:21

Verse 3. *That night they caught nothing.* This was so ordered in the providence of God that the miracle which was wrought might appear more remarkable.

Verse 4. *Knew not that it was Jesus.* Probably it was yet twilight, and in the distance they could not distinctly recognize him.

{c} "knew not that it was Jesus" Joh 20:14

Verse 5. *Children.* A term of affection and friendship, 1 Jo 2:18.

Any meat. This word (Greek) means anything eaten with bread. It was used by the Greeks especially to denote *fish* (Schleusner)

{d} "Jesus saith unto them" Lu 24:41 {1} "Children" or, "Sirs"

Verse 6. *On the right side.* Why the *right* side is mentioned is not known. Grotius supposes that it was the side nearest the shore, where there was *less* probability of taking fish. It does not appear that they yet recognized the Lord Jesus but from some cause they had sufficient confidence in him to make another trial. Perhaps they judged that he was one skilled in that employment, and knew where there was the greatest probability of success.

{e} "Cast the net on the right" Lu 5:4-7

Verse 7. *Therefore that disciple whom Jesus loved.* Joh 13:23.

It is the Lord. He was convinced, perhaps, by the apparent miracle, and by looking more attentively on the person of one who had been the means of such unexpected and remarkable success.

His fisher's coat. His upper or outer garment or tunic, in distinction from the inner garment or tunic which was worn next the skin. In the case of Peter it may have been made of coarse materials such as fishermen commonly wore, or such as Peter usually wore when he was engaged in this employment. Such garments are common with men of this occupation. This outer garment he probably had laid aside.

He was naked. He was *undressed,* with nothing on but the under garment or tunic. The word does not require us to suppose a greater degree of nakedness than this. See Barnes "Mr 14:51, See Barnes "1 Sa 19:24".

Did cast himself into the sea. With characteristic ardour, desirous of meeting again his Lord, and showing his affection for him.

Verse 8. *Two hundred cubits.* About 350 feet, or a little more than 20 rods.

Verse 9. *They saw a fire,* &c. We have no knowledge whence this was produced— whether it was, as Grotius supposes, by a miracle, or whether it was a place occupied by other fishermen, where *they* also might cook the fish which they had caught. As no miracle is mentioned, however, there is no reason for supposing that any existed in the case.

Verse 10. No Barnes text on this verse.

Verse 11. *An hundred and fifty and three.* The number is mentioned because it seems to have been a very unusual draught, and it was particularly gratifying and striking to them after they had spent the whole night and had caught *nothing.* This convinced them that it was no other than the same Saviour who had so often worked wonders before them that was now with them.

Verse 12. *Come and dine.* The word in the original means the meal which is taken in the *morning,* or breakfast.

Verse 13. *Jesus then cometh*, and taketh bread, &c. It is not said that Jesus himself *ate* with them, but he gave them food. The design of this interview seems to have been to convince them that he had truly risen from the dead. Hence he performed a miracle *before* they suspected that it was he, that there might be no room to say that they had ascribed to him the power of the miracle through friendship and collusion with him. The miracle was such as to satisfy them of its truth, and was, in accordance with all his works, not for mere display, but for utility. He remained with them, was with them at their meal, conversed with them, and thus convinced them that he was the same Friend who had died.

{f} "Jesus then cometh" Ac 10:41

Verse 14. *The third time.* See the "Harmony of the Accounts of the Resurrection of Jesus" at the end of Matthew.

{g} "This is now the third time" Joh 20:19,26

Verse 15. *Lovest thou me more than these*? There is a slight ambiguity here in the original, as there is in our translation. The word *these* may be in the neuter gender, and refer to these *things*—his boat, his fishing utensils, and his employments; or it may be in the masculine, and refer to the apostles. In the former sense it would mean, "Lovest thou me more than thou lovest these objects? Art thou now willing, from love to me, to forsake all these, and go and preach my gospel to the nations of the earth?" In the other sense, which is probably the true sense, it would mean, "Lovest thou me more than these other apostles love me?" In this question Jesus refers to the profession of superior attachment to him which Peter had made before his death (Mt 26:33): "Though all men shall be offended because of thee, yet will I never be offended." Comp. Joh 13:37. Jesus here slightly reproves him for that confident assertion, reminds him of his sad and painful denial, and now puts this direct and pointed question to him to know what was the *present* state of his feelings. After all that Peter had had to humble him, the Saviour inquired of him what had been the *effect* on his mind, and whether it had tended to prepare him for the arduous toils in which he was about to engage. This question we should all put to ourselves. It is a matter of much importance that we should ourselves know what is the effect of the dealings of divine Providence on our hearts, and what is our *present* state of feeling toward the Lord Jesus Christ.

Thou knowest that I love thee. Peter now made no pretensions to love superior to his brethren. His sad denial had convinced him of the folly of that claim; but still he could appeal to the Searcher of the heart, and say that he *knew* that he loved him. Here is the expression of a humbled soul—a soul made sensible of its weakness and need of strength, yet with evidence of true attachment to the Saviour. It is not the most confident pretensions that constitute the highest proof of love to Christ; and the happiest and best state of feeling is when we can with humility, yet with confidence, look to the Lord Jesus and say, "Thou *knowest* that I love thee."

Feed my lambs. The word *here* rendered *feed* means the care afforded by furnishing *nutriment* for the flock. In the next verse there is a change in the Greek, and the word rendered *feed* denotes rather the *care, guidance, and protection* which a shepherd extends to his flock. By the use of both these words, it is supposed that our Saviour intended that a shepherd was both to offer the proper food for his flock and to govern it; or, as we express it, to exercise the office of a pastor. The expression is taken from the office of a *shepherd*, with which the office of a minister of the gospel is frequently compared. It means, as a good shepherd provides for the wants of his flock, so the pastor in the church is to furnish food for the soul, or so to exhibit truth that the faith of believers may be strengthened and their hope confirmed.

My lambs. The church is often compared to a flock. See Joh 10:1-16. Here the expression *my lambs* undoubtedly refers to the *tender* and the *young* in the Christian church; to those who are young in years and in Christian experience. The Lord Jesus saw, what has been confirmed in the experience of the church, that the success of the gospel among men depended on the care which the ministry would extend to those in early life. It is in obedience to this command that Sunday-schools have been established, and no means of fulfilling this command of the Saviour have been found so effectual as to extend patronage to those schools. It is not merely, therefore, the *privilege*, it is the solemn *duty* of ministers of the gospel to countenance and patronize those schools.

{h} "more than these" Mt 26:33,35 {i} "Feed my lambs" Isa 40:11; Jer 3:15; Eze 34:2-10; Ac 20:28

1 Pe 5:2,4

THE GOSPEL ACCORDING TO JOHN-Chapter 21-Verse 16

Verse 16. *Feed my sheep.* The word here rendered *feed*, as has been remarked, is different from the word in the previous verse. It has the sense of *governing, caring for, guiding, protecting* —the kind of faithful vigilance which a shepherd uses to guide his flock, and to make provision against their wants and dangers. It *may* be implied here that the care needed for the young in the church is to *instruct* them, and for those in advanced years both to instruct and govern them.

My sheep. This term commonly denotes the church in general, without respect to age, John, chapter 10.

{k} "Feed my sheep" Heb 13:20; 1 Pe 2:25

Verse 17. *The third time.* It is probable that Jesus proposed this question three times because Peter had thrice denied him. Thus he tenderly admonished him of his fault and reminded him of his sin, while he solemnly charged him to be faithful and vigilant in the discharge of the duties of the pastoral office. The reason why the Saviour addressed Peter in this manner was doubtless because he had just denied him—had given a most melancholy instance of the instability and weakness of his faith, and of his liability to fall. As he had thus been prominent in forsaking him, he took this occasion to give to him a *special* charge, and to *secure* his future obedience. Hence he so administered the charge as to remind him of his fault; and he made him so prominent as to show the solicitude of the Saviour that henceforward he might not be left to dishonour his high calling. This same charge, in substance, he had on other occasions given to the apostles (Mt 18:18), and there is not the slightest evidence here that Christ intended, as the Papists pretend, to give Peter any *peculiar* primacy or eminence in the church. The charge to Peter arose, manifestly, from his prominent and melancholy act in denying him, and was the kind and tender means used by a faithful Saviour to keep him from similar acts in the future dangers and trials of life. It is worthy of remark that the admonition was effectual. Henceforward Peter was one of the most firm and unwavering of all the apostles, and thus fully justified the appellation of a *rock*, which the Saviour by anticipation had given him. See Barnes "Joh 1:42".

{m} "thou knowest all things" Joh 16:30

Verse 18. *When thou wast young.* When in early life thou didst gird *thyself* &c. The Jews, in walking or running, girded their outer garments around them, that they might not be impeded. See Barnes "Mt 5:38-41".

Thou girdedst. The expression here denotes *freedom.* He did as he pleased—he girded himself or not—he went or remained, as he chose. Perhaps the expression refers rather *to that time* than to the previous period of Peter's life. "Thou being young or in the rigour of life, hast just girded thyself and come freely to the shore." In either case the Saviour intimates that at the end of his life he would not be thus free.

When thou shalt be old. Ancient writers say that Peter was put to death about thirty-four years after this. His precise age at that time is not known.

Thou shalt stretch forth thy hands. When Peter was put to death, we are told that he requested that he might be crucified with his head downward, saying that he who had denied his Lord as he had done was not *worthy* to die as he did. This expression of Christ may intimate the *readiness* of Peter thus to die. Though he was not at liberty as when he was young, though bound by others, yet he *freely* stretched out his hands on the cross, and was ready to give up his life.

Another shall gird thee. Another shall *bind* thee. The limbs of persons crucified were often *bound* instead of being *nailed*, and even the *body* was sometimes girded to the cross. See Barnes "Mt 27:35".

Carry thee, &c. Shall *bear* thee, or shall *compel* thee to go to prison and to death. This is not said to intimate that Peter would be unwilling to suffer martyrdom, but it stands opposed to the freedom of his early life. Though willing when compelled to do it, yet he would not *seek it*; and though he would not needlessly expose himself to it, yet he would not shrink from it when it was the will of God.

{n} "When thou was young" Joh 13:36; Ac 12:3,4
{o} "shall gird thee" Ac 21:11

THE GOSPEL ACCORDING TO JOHN-Chapter 21-Verse 19

Verse 19. *By what death*, &c. In these words two things are implied:

1st. That Peter would die a violent death; and,

2nd. That his death would be such as to honour God.

The ancients say that Peter was crucified at Rome, about thirty-four years after this, with his head downward. Clemens says that he was led to the crucifixion with his wife, and sustained her in her sufferings by exhorting her to remember the example of her Lord. He also adds that he died, not as the philosophers did, but with a firm hope of heaven, and patiently endured the pangs of the cross (*Strom.* vii.). This declaration of the Saviour was doubtless continually before the mind of Peter, and to the hour of his death he maintained the utmost constancy and fidelity in his cause, thus justifying the appellation which the Lord Jesus gave him——a rock.

{p} "what death" 2 Pe 1:14 {q} "Follow me" Nu 14:24; 1 Sa 12:20; Mt 19:28; Joh 12:26

THE GOSPEL ACCORDING TO JOHN-Chapter 21-Verse 20

Verse 20. *Which also leaned*, &c. See Joh 13:24,25

THE GOSPEL ACCORDING TO JOHN-Chapter 21-Verse 21

Verse 21. *What shall this man do*? This question probably means, "What death shall he die?" But it is impossible to ascertain certainly why Peter asked this question. John was a favourite disciple, and *perhaps* Peter suspected that he would have a happier lot, and not be put to death in this manner. Peter was *grieved* at the question of Jesus; he was probably deeply affected with the account of his own approaching sufferings; and, with *perhaps* a mixture of grief and *envy*, he asked what would be his lot. But it is *possible*, also, that it was from *kindness* to John—a deep solicitude about him, and a wish that he might not die in the same manner as one who had denied his Lord. Whatever the motive was, it was a curiosity which the Lord Jesus did not choose to gratify.

Verse 22. *That he tarry*. That he *live*. The same word is used to express life in Php 1:24,25; 1 Co 15:6.

Till I come. Some have supposed this to refer to the destruction of Jerusalem; others to the day of judgment; others to signify that he would not die a violent death; but the plain meaning is, "If I will that he should not *die at all*, it is nothing to thee." In this way the apostles evidently understood it, and hence raised a report that he would *not* die. It is remarkable that John was the last of the apostles; that he lived to nearly the close of the first century, and then died a peaceful death at Ephesus, being the only one, as is supposed, of the apostles who did not suffer martyrdom. The testimony of antiquity is clear on this point; and though there have been many idle *conjectures* about this passage and about the fate of John, yet no fact of history is better attested than that John died and was buried at Ephesus.

What is that to thee? From this passage we learn,

1st. That our main business is to follow the Lord Jesus Christ.

2nd. That there are many subjects of religion on which a vain and impertinent curiosity is exercised. All such curiosity Jesus here reproves.

3rd. That Jesus will take care of all his true disciples, and that we should not be unduly solicitous about them.

4th. That we should go forward to whatever he calls us—to persecution or death—not envying the lot of any other man, and anxious only to do the will of God.

{r} "till I come" Mt 25:31; Re 1:7; 22:20

{s} "Follow thou me" Joh 21:19

Verse 23. *Then went this saying*, &c. This mistake arose very naturally—

1st. From the *words* of Jesus, which might be easily misunderstood to mean that he should not die; and,

2nd. It was probably confirmed when it was seen that John survived *all* the other apostles, had escaped all the dangers of persecution, and was leading a peaceful life at Ephesus. This mistake John deemed it proper to correct before he died, and has thus left on record what Jesus *said* and what he *meant*.

Verse 24. *This is the disciple,* &c. This proves that the beloved disciple was John.

We know. That is, *it is known*; it is universally admitted. It was so decidedly his character that he always declared the truth, that it had become known, and was unquestioned, so that *he himself* might appeal to the universal testimony in his behalf. In this case, therefore, we have the testimony of a man whose character for nearly a *century* was that of a man of truth—-so much so that it had become, in a manner, proverbial, and was put beyond a doubt. It is impossible to believe that such a man would sit down deliberately to impose on mankind, or to write a book which was false; and if not, then this book is true, and that is the same as saying that Christianity is a religion from heaven.

{t} "and we know" Joh 19:35; 3 Jo 1:12

Verse 25. *Many other things.* Many miracles, Joh 20:30. Many discourses delivered, &c.

I suppose, &c. This is evidently the figure of speech called a *hyperbole.* It is a mode of speech where the *words* express more or less than is *literally* true. It is common among all writers; and as the sacred writers, in recording a revelation to men, used human language, it was proper that they should express themselves as men ordinarily do if they wished to be understood. This figure of speech is commonly the effect of *surprise,* or having the mind *full* of some object, and not having words to express the ideas: at the same time, the words convey no *falsehood.* The statement is to be taken as it would be understood among the persons to whom it is addressed; and as no one *supposes* that the author means to be understood *literally,* so there is no deception in the case, and consequently no impeachment of his veracity or inspiration. Thus, when Longinus said of a man that "he was the owner of a piece of ground not larger than a Lacedaemonian letter," no one understood him literally. He meant, evidently, a *very small* piece of land, and no one would be deceived. So Virgil says of a man, "he was so tall as to reach the stars," and means only that he was *very tall.* So when John says that the world could not contain the books that would be written if *all* the deeds and sayings of Jesus were recorded, he clearly intends nothing more than that a *great many books would be required,* or that it would be extremely difficult to record them all; intimating that his life was active, that his discourses were numerous, and that he had not *pretended* to give them all, but only such as would go to establish the main point for which he wrote—that he was the Messiah, Joh 20:30,31. The figure which John uses here is not uncommon in the Scriptures, Ge 11:4; 15:5; Nu 13:33; Da 4:20.

This gospel contains in itself the clearest proof of inspiration. It is the work of a fisherman of Galilee, without any proof that he had any unusual advantages. It is a connected, clear, and satisfactory argument to establish the great truth that Jesus was the Messiah. It was written many years after the ascension of Jesus. It contains the record of the Saviour's profoundest discourses, of his most convincing arguments with the Jews, and of his declarations respecting himself and God. It contains the purest and most elevated views of God to be found anywhere, as far exceeding all the speculations of philosophers as the sun does the blaze of a taper. It is in the highest degree absurd to suppose that an unlettered fisherman could have *originated* this book. Anyone may be convinced of this by comparing it with what would be the production of a man in that rank of life now. But if John has preserved the record of what has occurred so many years before, then it shows that he was under the divine guidance, and is himself a proof, a full and standing proof, of the fulfillment of the promise which he has recorded— that the Holy Spirit would guide the apostles into all truth, Joh 14:26. Of this book we may, in conclusion, apply the words spoken by John respecting his vision of the future events of the church: "Blessed is he that readeth and they that hear the words of this book, and keep those things which are written therein, for the time is at hand," Re 1:3.

{u} "And there are also" Joh 20:30 {v} "the world could not contain" Am 7:10

27230784R00190

Printed in Great Britain
by Amazon